A Selective Bibliography of Shakespeare

A Selective Bibliography of
Shakespeare
Editions, Textual Studies, Commentary

James G. McManaway and Jeanne Addison Roberts

The Folger Shakespeare Library

Library of Congress Cataloging in Publication Data

McManaway, James Gilmer, 1899-
A selective bibliography of Shakespeare.

1. Shakespeare, William, 1564-1616—Bibliography.
I. Roberts, Jeanne Addison, joint author. II. Title.
Z8811.M23 016.8223'3 74-6285 ISBN 0-918016-03-7

Printed in the United States of America

Preface

"Small have continual plodders ever won," Biron gives warning, "save base authority by others' books." Even the most assiduous of plodders would more quickly find despair than base authority should he attempt to read each year all that is published about Shakespeare. In many lands and in many tongues the books and essays proliferate until even the most highly specialized research libraries run short of funds to purchase, and book stacks to shelve, the output. Captain William Jaggard could hope in 1911 to list all editions and record all the important publications; by 1931, Ebisch and Schücking were constrained to be selective. Their *Bibliography* (**120**) and *Supplement* (**120**) were dwarfed by Gordon Ross Smith's *Bibliography* (**146**) for the years 1936-58.

The purpose of the present *Bibliography* is more modest. Assuming that *William Shakespeare: A Study of Facts and Problems* (**437**) by E. K. Chambers is in most areas (textual studies being the major exception) the Great Divide between the old and the new, it attempts to draw attention to the best and most important publications since 1930. A scattering of representative works of earlier date is given to serve as background. Publications in languages other than English, however meritorious, are rarely included, partly because many of them are not widely accessible and partly because they would swell the *Bibliography* beyond reasonable compass. This is much to be regretted, for the reading, enjoyment, and theatrical production of Shakespeare is now worldwide. The volume of Shakespeareana is too great, however, to be recorded systematically and comprehensively until a center for Shakespeare studies can be established where all contemporary, and eventually all previously published, editions, translations, books, essays, notes, and theatrical and operatic notices and reviews—including the cinema and television—will be stored in a computerized data bank. Recourse to such a reservoir of information will stimulate and facilitate research and original criticism immeasurably, while at the same time reducing to a minimum the duplication of research and also repetitive publication. Until that not far off (we hope) terrene event, consideration is requested for the unavoidable limitations of this intended aid to Shakespeare studies.

The method of organization is to be found in the Table of Contents. The early sections of the *Bibliography* list general works that are desirable in modest college, school, and municipal libraries. Such books as Chambers's *William Shakespeare* (**437**) or *The London Stage* (**70**) or *A New Companion to Shakespeare Studies* (**2800**) find logical inclusion in several categories. To reduce duplicating entries to a minimum, cross-references are given to many titles that fit into more than one category. Problem Plays, for example, in which classification various scholars have included comedies, tragedies, and Roman plays, are given only a section heading followed by cross-references to works listed in other sections. So with The Roman Plays and The Romances. But it is assumed that anyone interested in *Measure for Measure* or *Troilus and Cressida* or *Antony and Cleopatra* or *1 Henry 4*, for example, after turning to the sections on each of these plays, will then scan the entries listed under Comedies, History Plays, Tragedies, Sources, and so on. In the interest of brevity, articles and notes dealing with specific short passages of text or allusions have been omitted unless they bear on such matters as authorship or date of composition. Most of the editions of a single play or poem have required similar treatment.

Except for a few items of major importance such as the *Catalog of the Shakespeare Collection in the Folger Shakespeare Library* (**124**), Muir and Schoenbaum's *A New Companion to Shakespeare Studies* (**2800**), Philip Gaskell's *A New Introduction to Bibliography* (**30**), and T. H. Howard-Hill's bibliography of *Shakespearian Bibliography and Textual Criticism* (**296**), the cutoff date is December 31, 1970.

The Index lists the names of authors, editors, and translators of the numbered entries and gives the numbers of the entries in which the names appear. There are no subject entries.

The abbreviations of the titles of Shakespeare's plays and poems are identical with those used in the "Annotated World Bibliography" in the Summer numbers of *Shakespeare Quarterly* (**398**), in the Hinman facsimile of *The First Folio* (**724**), in "The Oxford Old-Spelling Shakespeare Concordances" (**170**), and in forthcoming volumes of The New Variorum Shakespeare (**627**). Titles of learned journals, serials, and the like are abbreviated as in the *PMLA International Bibliography* (**139**), with a few exceptions such as *SAB* which is used here for *Shakespeare Association Bulletin* (**393**).

Because scholarly books often go quickly out of print, many reprints are listed. The references to paperbacks will be found, enclosed in square brackets, following the other publication information. Abbreviations are taken from *Paperbound Books in Print.*

The roughly 4,500 entries in this *Bibliography* constitute "the abstract and brief chronicles" of Shakespeare studies of the past four decades, supplemented by references to significant representative works of earlier date. The general reader may quickly find guidance to the play or poem of immediate interest or to the reference works in the principal fields of study. For the teacher or specialist, but equally for the graduate and undergraduate student, the *Bibliography* offers between the covers of one book references to a selection of helpful interpretations and criticism. Some students will need to go on from this *Bibliography* to Jaggard, Ebisch and Schücking, Smith, and the several annual bibliographies of Shakespeare; but it is the hope of the compilers that for a wide variety of readers this work will suffice.

The bibliography has greatly benefited from tireless checking and cross-checking by Megan Lloyd of the Folger Shakespeare Library. A large debt to her is gratefully acknowledged. Thanks are also given to O. B. Hardison, Jr., Director of the Folger, who perceived the need for such an aid to Shakespeareans and first initiated the project.

James G. McManaway, Jr.
University of Maryland

Jeanne Addison Roberts
The American University

Contents

Abbreviations of
Journal and Yearbook Titles

AI	*American Imago*
AnM	*Annuale Mediaevale* (Duquesne U.)
Archiv	*Archiv für das Studium der Neueren Sprachen und Literaturen*
ASch	*American Scholar*
BC	*Book Collector*
BFLS	*Bulletin de la Faculté des Lettres de Strasbourg*
BJRL	*Bulletin of the John Rylands Library*
BNYPL	*Bulletin of the New York Public Library*
BSUF	*Ball State U. Forum*
BuR	*Bucknell Review*
BUSE	*Boston U. Studies in English*
CamJ	*Cambridge Journal*
CE	*College English*
CentR	*The Centennial Review* (Michigan State U.)
CJ	*Classical Journal*
CL	*Comparative Literature*
CLAJ	*College Language Association Journal* (Morgan State College, Baltimore)
CLS	*Comparative Literature Studies* (U. of Illinois)
ColQ	*Colorado Quarterly*
CompD	*Comparative Drama*
CQ	*The Cambridge Quarterly*
CQR	*Church Quarterly Review*
CritQ	*Critical Quarterly*
CSHVB	*Computer Studies in the Humanities and Verbal Behavior*
CUF	*Columbia U. Forum*
DownR	*Downside Review*
DR	*Dalhousie Review*
DramS	*Drama Survey* (Minneapolis)
DUJ	*Durham U. Journal*
EA	*Études Anglaises*
E&S	*Essays and Studies by Members of the English Association*
EDH	*Essays by Divers Hands*
EdL	*Études de Lettres* (U. de Lausanne)

EIC	*Essays in Criticism*
EIE	*English Institute Essays*
EJ	*English Journal*
ELH	*Journal of English Literary History*
ELN	*English Language Notes*
EM	*English Miscellany*
English	*English* (London)
ES	*English Studies*
EStn	*Englische Studien*
EUQ	*Emory U. Quarterly*
HAB	*Humanities Association Bulletin* (Canada)
HLB	*Harvard Library Bulletin*
HLQ	*Huntington Library Quarterly*
HudR	*Hudson Review*
JEGP	*Journal of English and Germanic Philology*
JGE	*Journal of General Education*
JHI	*Journal of the History of Ideas*
JNMD	*Journal of Nervous and Mental Diseases*
KR	*Kenyon Review*
L&P	*Literature and Psychology* (U. of Hartford)
LC	*Library Chronicle* (U. of Pennsylvania)
Library	*The Library*
MLN	*Modern Language Notes*
MLQ	*Modern Language Quarterly*
MLR	*Modern Language Review*
MP	*Modern Philology*
MQR	*Michigan Quarterly Review*
MuK	*Maske und Kothurn* (Gras-Wien)
N&Q	*Notes and Queries*
Neophil	*Neophilologus* (Groningen)
NHQ	*New Hungarian Quarterly*
NS	*Die Neueren Sprachen*
OUR	*Ohio U. Review* (Athens)
PAPS	*Proceedings of the American Philosophical Society*
PBA	*Proceedings of the British Academy*
PBSA	*Papers of the Bibliographical Society of America*
PELL	*Papers on English Language and Literature*
Person	*The Personalist*
PLL	*Papers on Language and Literature*
PLPLS-LHS	*Proceedings of the Leeds Philosophical and Literary Society, Literary and Historical Section*
PMASAL	*Papers of the Michigan Academy of Science, Arts, and Letters*
PMLA	*Publications of the Modern Language Association of America*

PQ	*Philological Quarterly*
PR	*Partisan Review*
PsyR	*Psychoanalytic Review*
QJS	*Quarterly Journal of Speech*
QQ	*Queen's Quarterly*
QR	*Quarterly Review*
REL	*Review of English Literature*
RenD	*Renaissance Drama* (Northwestern U.)
RenP	*Renaissance Papers*
RenQ	*Renaissance Quarterly*
RES	*Review of English Studies*
RN	*Renaissance News*
RS	*Research Studies* (Washington State U.)
SAB	*Shakespeare Association Bulletin*
SAQ	*South Atlantic Quarterly*
SB	*Studies in Bibliography*
SEL	*Studies in English Literature, 1500-1900*
SFQ	*Southern Folklore Quarterly*
ShakS	*Shakespeare Studies* (U. of Cincinnati, Vanderbilt, U. of South Carolina)
ShN	*Shakespeare Newsletter*
ShS	*Shakespeare Survey*
SJ	*Shakespeare-Jahrbuch* (Up to 1964. For later entries, see next two items.)
SJ (East)	*Shakespeare-Jahrbuch* (Weimar)
SJ (West)	*Shakespeare-Jahrbuch* (Heidelberg)
SoAB	*South Atlantic Bulletin*
SocR	*Social Research*
SoR	*Southern Review*
SP	*Studies in Philology*
SQ	*Shakespeare Quarterly*
SR	*Sewanee Review*
SRen	*Studies in the Renaissance*
SRO	*Shakespearean Research Opportunities: The Report of the MLA Conference*
TDR	*The Drama Review* (formerly *Tulane Drama Review*)
ThR	*Theatre Research*
ThS	*Theatre Survey*
TLS	*Times Literary Supplement*
TN	*Theatre Notebook*
TSE	*Tulane Studies in English*
TSL	*Tennessee Studies in Literature*
TSLL	*Texas Studies in Literature and Language*

TxSE	*Texas Studies in English*
UCSLL	*U. of Colorado Studies in Language and Literature*
UKCR	*U. of Kansas City Review*
Univ	*Universitas* (Stuttgart)
UR	*University Review* (Kansas City, Mo.; formerly *UKCR*)
UTQ	*U. of Toronto Quarterly*
VQR	*Virginia Quarterly Review*
YR	*Yale Review*
ZAA	*Zeitschrift für Anglistik und Amerikanistik* (East Berlin)

Abbreviations of Titles of Works

Ado	*Much Ado About Nothing*
Ant	*Antony and Cleopatra*
AWW	*All's Well that Ends Well*
AYL	*As You Like It*
Cardenio	*Cardenio*
Cor	*Coriolanus*
Cym	*Cymbeline*
Edw3	*Edward III*
Err	*The Comedy of Errors*
Ham	*Hamlet*
1H4	*Henry IV, Part I*
2H4	*Henry IV, Part II*
H5	*Henry V*
1H6	*Henry VI, Part I*
2H6	*Henry VI, Part II*
3H6	*Henry VI, Part III*
H8	*Henry VIII*
JC	*Julius Caesar*
Jn	*King John*
LC	*A Lover's Complaint*
LLL	*Love's Labour's Lost*
Lr	*King Lear*
Luc	*The Rape of Lucrece*
Mac	*Macbeth*
MM	*Measure for Measure*
MND	*A Midsummer Night's Dream*
More	*Sir Thomas More*
MV	*The Merchant of Venice*
Oth	*Othello*
Per	*Pericles, Prince of Troy*
PhT	*The Phoenix and the Turtle*
PP	*The Passionate Pilgrim*
R2	*Richard II*
R3	*Richard III*

Rom	*Romeo and Juliet*
Shr	*The Taming of the Shrew*
Son	*Sonnets*
TGV	*Two Gentlemen of Verona*
Tim	*Timon of Athens*
Tit	*Titus Andronicus*
Tmp	*The Tempest*
TN	*Twelfth Night*
TNK	*Two Noble Kinsmen*
Tro	*Troilus and Cressida*
Wiv	*The Merry Wives of Windsor*
WT	*The Winter's Tale*
Ven	*Venus and Adonis*

A Selective Bibliography of Shakespeare

General Reference Works

Some of the items listed here could as readily be placed elsewhere. Cross-references to them are intended to make them readily available.

1   ABBOTT, Edwin A. *A Shakespearian Grammar.* London: Macmillan, 1869. Rev. and enl. 1871. [Dover AL5-3755.]

2   ADAMS, Joseph Q. "Another Fragment from Henslowe's Diary." *Library,* 20 (1939-40): 154-58.

3   ——. "The Author Plot of an Early Seventeenth-Century Play." *Library,* 26 (1945-46): 17-27.

4   ——. *The Dramatic Records of Sir Henry Herbert, Master of the Revels, 1623-1673.* Yale U.P., 1917.

5   ——. "Elizabethan Playhouse Manuscripts and Their Significance for the Text of Shakespeare." *The Johns Hopkins Alumni Magazine,* 21 (1932): 21-52.

6   ——. "Hill's List of Early Plays in Manuscript." *Library,* 20 (1939-40): 71-99.

7   ——. "The Office-Book, 1622-1642, of Sir Henry Herbert, Master of the Revels." In *To Doctor R.* Ed. Percy Lawlor, John F. Fleming, and Edwin Wolf 2nd. Philadelphia: n.p., 1946.

8   ALBRIGHT, Evelyn M. *Dramatic Publication in England, 1580-1640.* MLA Monograph Series. New York: Heath, 1927.

9   ARBER, Edward, ed. *The Term Catalogues, 1682-1709.* 3 vols. London: Arber, 1903-6.

10 ——, ed. *A Transcript of the Registers of the Company of Stationers of London, 1554-1640.* 5 vols. London, 1875-77; Birmingham, 1894. Repr. New York: Peter Smith. For 1640-1708, see **28.**

11 BATE, John. *How to Find Out about Shakespeare.* Oxford: Pergamon, 1968.

12 BENNETT, H. Stanley. *English Books and Readers, 1585-1603, Being a Study in the History of the Book Trade in the Reign of Elizabeth I.* Cambridge U.P., 1969.

13 BENTLEY, Gerald E. *The Jacobean and Caroline Stage.* 7 vols. Oxford U.P., 1941-68.

14 BISHOP, William W. *A Checklist of American Copies of Short-Title Catalogue Books.* 2nd ed. U. of Michigan P., 1950. For British copies, see **86**.

15 BOADEN, James. *A Letter to George Steevens, Esq., Containing a Critical Examination of the Papers of Shakespeare, Published by Mr. Samuel Ireland, . . . Extracts from Vortigern.* London: Martin & Bain, 1776. Repr. New York: AMS.

16 BOWERS, Fredson T. *Principles of Bibliographical Description.* Princeton U.P., 1949. Repr. New York: Russell & Russell.

17 BRIQUET, Charles M. *Les Filigranes.* 4 vols. Paris: A. Picard & fils, 1907. Repr. in facs. with additions, Amsterdam: Paper Publications Society, 1968 (ed. Allan H. Stevenson).

18 BUSH, Douglas. *English Literature in the Earlier Seventeenth Century, 1600-1660.* 2nd ed. Oxford U.P., 1962.

18a *Cambridge History of English Literature.* Ed. A. W. Ward and Alfred R. Waller. 15 vols. Cambridge U.P., 1907-16. Repr. 1961-63. [Esp. vol. 5, *The Drama to 1642, Part One.*]

19 CHALMERS, George. *An Apology for the Believers in the Shakspeare-papers.* London: T. Egerton, 1797. [See also Chalmers, *A Supplemental Apology for the Believers* (London: Egerton, 1799), on the Ireland forgeries.]

20 CHAMBERS, Edmund K. *The Elizabethan Stage.* 4 vols. Oxford U.P., 1923. For Index, see **100**.

21 CHILD, Harold H. "Revivals of English Dramatic Works, 1919-1925." *RES,* 2 (1926): 177-88. [See also Child, "Revivals . . . , 1901-1918, 1926." *RES,* 3 (1927): 169-85.]

22 *Collections.* Oxford U.P. for the Malone Society, 1907–. [Theatrical documents and records; various editors.]

23 COLLIER, John P. *Notes and Emendations to the Text of Shakespeare's Plays, from Early MS Corrections . . . Forming a Supplemental Volume to the Works of Shakespeare.* London: Whittaker, 1853. Repr. New York: Franklin.

24 CUNNINGHAM, Peter, ed. *Extracts from the Accounts of the Revels at Court, in the Reigns of Queen Elizabeth and King James I, from the Original Office Books.* London: Shakespeare Society, 1842. Repr. New York: AMS.

25 DAWSON, Giles E., ed. *Records of Plays and Players in Kent, 1450-1642.* Malone Society *Collections,* 7. Oxford U.P., 1965.

26 DICKEY, Franklin M. "The Old Man at Work: Forgeries in the Stationers' Registers." *SQ,* 11 (1960): 39-47. [J. P. Collier.]

27 DOWNES, John. *Roscius Anglicanus; or, An Historical Review of the Stage . . . with the Names of the Most Taking Plays . . . from 1660 to 1706.* London: Playford, 1708. Repr. London: Fortune, 1928 (ed. Montague Summers); Los Angeles: William Andrews Clark Library, 1969 (ed. John Loftis).

28 EYRE, G. E. Briscoe, ed. *A Transcript of the Registers of the Worshipful Company of Stationers from 1640-1708.* 3 vols. London: Privately printed, 1913-14. See also **10** and **9**.

29 FEUILLERAT, Albert, ed. *Documents Relating to the Office of the Revels in the Time of Queen Elizabeth.* Materialien zur Kunde des älteren Englischen Dramas, 21. Louvain: Uystpruyst, 1908. Repr. Vaduz: Kraus.

30 GASKELL, Philip. *A New Introduction to Bibliography.* Oxford U.P., 1972.

31 GENEST, John. *Some Account of the English Stage from the Restoration in 1660 to 1830.* 10 vols. Bath: Carrington, 1832.

32 GILDERSLEEVE, Virginia C. *Government Regulation of the Elizabethan Drama.* Columbia U.P.; Oxford U.P., 1908. Repr. New York: Franklin.

33 GREBANIER, Bernard D. *The Great Shakespeare Forgery.* New York: Norton, 1965. [Ireland.]

34 GREEN, A. Wigfall. *The Inns of Court and Early English Drama.* Oxford U.P., 1931.

35 GREG, Walter W. "The Bakings of Betsy." *Library*, 2 (1911): 225-59. [The supposed destruction of play MSS, including some attributed to Shakespeare. See also John Freehafer, "John Warburton's Lost Plays." *SB*, 23 (1970): 154-64.]

36 ——. "Bibliography—A Retrospect." In *The Bibliographical Society, 1892-1942: Studies in Retrospect.* Ed. Frank C. Francis. Oxford U.P. for the Bibliographical Society, 1945. Rev. ed., Oxford U.P., 1970 (ed. Helen Gardner).

37 ——. *A Bibliography of the English Printed Drama to the Restoration.* 4 vols. Oxford U.P. for the Bibliographical Society, 1939-59.

38 ——. "The Decrees and Ordinances of the Stationers' Company, 1576-1602." *Library*, 8 (1927-28): 395-425.

39 ——. *Dramatic Documents from the Elizabethan Playhouses, Stage Plots, Actors' Parts, Prompt Books.* 2 vols. Oxford U.P., 1931. See also **3**.

40 ——. *Licensers for the Press, &c. to 1640.* London: Bibliographical Society, 1962.

41 ——. *Some Aspects and Problems of London Publishing between 1550 and 1650.* Oxford U.P., 1956.

42 ——. "Some Notes on the Stationers' Registers." *Library*, 7 (1926-27): 376-86. [Signatures of publishers; entries of plays by Sh.]

43 ——, and Eleanore Boswell, eds. *Records of the Court of the Stationers' Company, 1576 to 1602, from Register B.* London: Bibliographical Society, 1930. See also **59**.

44   HAMILTON, Nicholas E. S. A. *An Inquiry into the Genuineness of the Manuscript Corrections in Mr. J. Payne Collier's Annotated Shaksperc Folio, 1632, and of Certain Shaksperian Documents.* London: R. Bentley, 1860. Repr. New York: AMS.

45   HARBAGE, Alfred. *Annals of English Drama, 975-1700.* U. Pennsylvania P.; Oxford U.P., 1940. Rev. ed., London: Methuen, 1964 (ed. S. Schoenbaum). [Occasional supplements.]

46   ——. *William Shakespeare: A Reader's Guide.* New York: Farrar, Straus, 1963.

47   *Henslowe Papers, Being Documents Supplementary to Henslowe's Diary.* Ed. Walter W. Greg. London: Bullen, 1907.

48   *Henslowe's Diary.* Ed. Walter W. Greg. 2 vols. London: Bullen, 1904-8. [See also Greg, ed., "A Fragment from Henslowe's Diary." *Library*, 19 (1938-39): 180-84; see also **2**.]

49   *Henslowe's Diary.* Ed. Reginald A. Foakes and R. T. Rickert. Cambridge U.P., 1961.

HERBERT, Henry. See **4**.

50   HILLEBRAND, Harold N. *The Child Actors: A Chapter in Elizabethan Stage History.* U. of Illinois P., 1926.

51   HOGAN, Charles B. *Shakespeare in the Theatre, 1701-1800: A Record of Performances in London.* 2 vols. Oxford U.P., 1952-57.

52   HUGHES, Cecil E., ed. *The Praise of Shakespeare: An English Anthology (1596-1902).* London: Methuen, 1904. Repr. New York: AMS.

53   INGLEBY, Clement M. *A Complete View of the Shakspere Controversy, concerning the Authenticity and Genuineness of Manuscript Matter Affecting the Works and Biography of Shakspere, Published by Mr. J. Payne Collier as the Fruits of His Researches.* London: Nattali & Bond, 1861. Repr. New York: AMS.

54   ——. *The Shakspeare Fabrications: or, The MS. Notes of the Perkins Folio Shown to Be of Recent Origin, with an Appendix of the Authorship of the Ireland Forgeries.* London: J. R. Smith, 1859. Repr. New York: AMS.

55   IRELAND, Samuel. *Miscellaneous Papers and Legal Instruments under the Hand and Seal of W. Shakespeare, Including the Tragedy of King Lear.* London: Egerton, 1796.

56   IRELAND, William H. *An Authentic Account of the Shaksperian Manuscripts.* London: J. Debrett, 1796.

57   ——. *The Confessions of... Containing the Particulars of His Fabrication of the Shakspeare Manuscripts.* London: T. Goddard, 1805. Repr. New York ed. of 1874, New York: Franklin.

58   ISAAC, Frank. "Elizabethan Roman and Italic Types." *Library*, 14 (1933-34): 85-100, 212-28.

59 JACKSON, William A. *Records of the Court of the Stationers' Company, 1576 to 1640.* 2 vols. London: Bibliographical Society, 1930-57. See also **43**. [Court-Book C.]

60 ——. "Variant Entry Fees of the Stationers' Company." *PBSA*, 51 (1957): 103-10.

61 KIRSCHBAUM, Leo. "Author's Copyright in England before 1640." *PBSA*, 40 (1946): 43-80. [See p. 159 for a dissent.]

62 ——. "The Copyright of Elizabethan Plays." *Library*, 14 (1959): 231-50.

63 ——. "The Elizabethan Licenser of 'Copy' and His Fee." *RES*, 13 (1937): 453-55. [Instances of payment for license to print.]

64 KLEIN, David. "The Case of Forman's *Bocke of Plaies.*" *PQ*, 11 (1932): 385-95.

65 LANGBAINE, Gerard. *An Account of the English Dramatick Poets.* Oxford: G. West & H. Clements, 1691. Repr. New York: Franklin.

66 ——. *The Lives and Characters of the English Dramatick Poets.* Rev. Charles Gildon. London: N. Cox & W. Turner, 1699. Repr. New York: AMS.

67 ——. *A New Catalogue of English Plays.* London: N. Cox, 1688. [Originally issued as *Momus Triumphans,* this work begins the study of sources and of plagiarism. See Greg, *Bibliography*, **37**, 3:1320.] Repr. of *Momus,* New York: AMS.

68 LAW, Ernest. *Some Supposed Shakespeare Forgeries.* London: G. Bell, 1911. [See also Law, *More about Shakespeare "Forgeries"* (London: Bell, 1931).]

69 LEWIS, Charles S. *English Literature in the Sixteenth Century Excluding Drama.* Oxford U.P., 1954.

70 *The London Stage, 1660-1800: A Calendar of Plays, Entertainments, and Afterpieces, Together with Casts, Box-Receipts, and Contemporary Comment Compiled from the Playbills, Newspapers, and Theatrical Diaries of the Period.* Comp. William Van Lennep, Emmett L. Avery, Arthur H. Scouten, George W. Stone, and Charles B. Hogan. 5 parts in 11 vols. Southern Illinois U.P., 1965-68. [Introds. only, Southern Ill., 1968, 5 vols. Paper.]

71 McKERROW, Ronald B. *A Dictionary of the Printers and Booksellers Who Were at Work in England, Scotland, and Ireland and of Foreign Printers of English Books, 1557-1640.* London: Bibliographical Society, 1910. For 1641-1667, see **82**.

72 ——. *Introduction to Bibliography for Literary Students.* Oxford U.P., 1925. Repr. 2nd, corr. ed. of 1927, 1968. See also **30**.

73 ——. *Printers' and Publishers' Devices in England and Scotland, 1485-1640.* Oxford U.P., 1913.

74 MacMILLAN, Dougald, ed. *Drury Lane Calendar, 1747-1776, Compiled from the Playbills.* Oxford U.P., 1938.

75   MAIR, John. *The Fourth Forger: William Ireland and the Shakespeare Papers.* London: Cobden-Sanderson, 1938; New York: Macmillan, 1939.

Malone Society. See **22**.

76   MARCHAM, Frank, ed. *The King's Office of the Revels, 1610-1622: Fragments of Documents in the Department of Manuscripts, British Museum.* London: Marcham, 1925.

77   MOXON, Joseph. *Mechanick Exercises on the Whole Art of Printing.* Ed. Herbert Davis and Harry Carter. Oxford U.P., 1958.   2nd ed., 1962.

78   MURRAY, John T. *English Dramatic Companies, 1558-1642.* 2 vols. Boston: Houghton Mifflin, 1910. Repr. New York: Russell & Russell.

79   NICOLL, Allardyce. *A History of English Drama, 1660-1900.* 6 vols. Cambridge U.P., 1952-55.

80   —. *Masques, Mimes, and Miracles.* London: Harrap, 1931.

81   NUNGEZER, Edwin. *A Dictionary of Actors and Other Persons Associated with the Public Representation of Plays in England before 1642.* Yale U.P.; Oxford U.P., 1929. Repr. New York: AMS.

82   PLOMER, Henry R. *A Dictionary of the Booksellers and Printers Who Were at Work in England, Scotland, and Ireland from 1641-1667.* London: Bibliographical Society, 1907. For 1557-1640, see **71**.

83   —, et al. *A Dictionary of the Printers and Booksellers Who Were at Work in England, Scotland, and Ireland from 1668-1725.* London: Bibliographical Society, 1922.

84   POLLARD, Alfred W. "The Stationers' Company's Records." *Library*, 6 (1925-26): 348-57. [A detailed catalogue of contents.]

85   —, and Gilbert R. Redgrave. *A Short-Title Catalogue of Books Printed in England, Scotland, and Ireland, and of English Books Printed Abroad, 1475-1640.* 2 vols. London: Bibliographical Society, 1926. Repr. in reduced size, 1948. [See also Paul G. Morrison, *Index of Printers, Publishers, and Booksellers in . . . A Short-Title Catalogue, 1475-1640* (Charlottesville: Bibliographical Society of the U. of Virginia, 1950).]

86   RAMAGE, David. *A Finding-List of English Books to 1640 in Libraries in the British Isles (Excluding the National Libraries and the Libraries of Oxford and Cambridge).* Council of the Durham Colleges, 1958. For American copies, see **14**.

87   RIEWALD, J. G. "Some Later Elizabethan and Early Stuart Actors and Musicians." *ES*, 40 (1959): 33-41.

88   SAINTSBURY, George E. B. *History of English Prosody.* 3 vols. London: Macmillan, 1906-10. Repr. 1923.

89   SCHWARTZ, Elias. "Sir George Buc's Authority as Licenser for the Press." *SQ*, 12 (1961): 467-68.

90 SISSON, Charles J. "The Laws of Elizabethan Copyright: The Stationers' View." *Library*, 15 (1960): 8-20.

91 ——. *Lost Plays of Shakespeare's Age.* Cambridge U.P., 1936.

92 SMITH, G. Gregory, ed. *Elizabethan Critical Essays.* 2 vols. Oxford U.P., 1904.

93 SPENCER, Hazelton. "The Forger at Work: A New Case against Collier." *PQ*, 6 (1927): 32-38.

94 SPINGARN, Joel E., ed. *Critical Essays of the Seventeenth Century.* 3 vols. Oxford U.P., 1908-9.

95 STAMP, Alfred E. *The Disputed Revels Accounts Reproduced in Collotype Facsimile.* Oxford U.P., 1930.

96 STOPES, Charlotte (Carmichael). *The Seventeenth-Century Accounts of the Masters of the Revels.* Oxford U.P., 1922.

97 TANNENBAUM, Samuel A. "The Forman Notes on Shakspere." In *Shaksperian Scraps and Other Elizabethan Fragments.* Columbia U.P., 1933.

98 ——. *Shakspere Forgeries in the Revels Accounts.* Columbia U.P., 1928. [See also Tannenbaum, *More about the Forged Revels Accounts* (New York: Tenny, 1932).]

99 WELLS, Henry W. *A Chronological List of Extant Plays Produced in or about London, 1581-1642.* Columbia U.P., 1940.

100 WHITE, Beatrice, comp. *An Index . . . to* The Elizabethan Stage *and* William Shakespeare *by Sir Edmund Chambers.* Oxford U.P., 1934. Repr. New York: Blom. See **20** and **437**.

101 WICKHAM, Glynne. *Early English Stages, 1300-1660.* 2 vols in 3. London: Routledge & Kegan Paul, 1959-71.

102 ——. "The Privy Council Order of 1597 for the Destruction of All London's Theatres." In *Elizabethan Theatre*, **4009**.

103 WILLOUGHBY, Edwin E. *A Printer of Shakespeare: The Books and Times of William Jaggard.* London: P. Allen, 1934.

103a WILSON, Frank P. *The English Drama, 1485-1585.* Oxford History of English Literature. Oxford U.P., 1969. [Bibliog. by George K. Hunter.]

104 WILSON, J. Dover, and R. W. Hunt. "The Authenticity of Simon Forman's *Bocke of Plaies.*" *RES*, 23 (1947): 193-200.

105 WING, Donald. *A Gallery of Ghosts: Books Published between 1641-1700 Not Found in the* Short-Title Catalogue. New York: Modern Language Association of America, 1967.

106 ——. *Short-Title Catalogue of Books Printed in England, Scotland, Ireland, Wales, and British America and of English Books Printed in Other Countries, 1641-1700.* 3 vols. Columbia U.P. for the Index Society, 1945-51. [See also Paul G. Morrison, *Index of Printers, Publishers, and Booksellers in . . . Wing's* Short-Title Catalogue. (U. of Virginia P. for the Bibliographical Society, 1955).]

107   WOODWARD, Gertrude L., and James G. McManaway, eds. *A Check List of English Plays, 1641-1700.* Chicago: Newberry Library, 1945. [See also Fredson T. Bowers, *Supplement* (Charlottesville: Bibliographical Society of the U. of Virginia, 1949).]

Bibliographies—Enumerative

For lists of editions of Shakespeare's works, see Collected Editions (**613-53**) and individual plays and poems under title. See also such general bibliographies as **37**, **45**, **106**, **107**, and **341**. For another Shakespeare publication that includes bibliography, see **402**. Eighteenth-century adaptations of tragedies are listed in **739**. See also **3074**.

108 *Abstracts of English Studies*, ed. Lewis Sawin et al. Vol. 1, nos. 1-8, Boulder, Colo.: 1958; Vol. 1, nos. 9–, Boulder, Colo.: National Council of Teachers of English, 1958–.

109 *Annual Bibliography of English Language and Literature* [title varies]. Cambridge: Bowes & Bowes, 1921–. Repr. vols. 1-33, New York: AMS. [Also lists important reviews.]

110 ARNOTT, James F., and J. W. Robinson. *English Theatrical Literature, 1559-1900: A Bibliography Incorporating Robert W. Lowe's A Bibliographical Account of English Theatrical Literature.* London: Society for Theatre Research, 1970.

111 Association of Research Libraries. *A Catalog of Books Represented by Library of Congress Printed Cards Issued to July 31, 1942.* Ann Arbor, Mich.: Edwards, 1942-46. [For Sh, see vols. 135-36.] *Supplement... August 1, 1942-December 31, 1947.* Ann Arbor, Mich.: Edwards, 1948. [For Sh, see 34:11-23.]

112 BARTLETT, Henrietta C. *Mr. William Shakespeare: Original and Early Editions of His Quartos and Folios, His Source Books, and Those Containing Contemporary Notices.* Yale U.P., 1922. Repr. New York: AMS.

113 —, and Alfred W. Pollard. *A Census of Shakespeare's Plays in Quarto, 1594-1709.* Yale U.P., 1916. Rev. ed., Yale U.P. and Oxford U.P., 1939; repr. New York: AMS.

114 BERMAN, Ronald S. *A Reader's Guide to Shakespeare's Plays.* Chicago: Scott, Foresman, 1965. [About 3,000 items.]

115 Bibliothèque Nationale. *Catalogue des ouvrages de William Shakespeare conservés au Département des Imprimés et dans les Bibliothèques de l'Arsenal, Mazarine, Saint-Geneviève, de l'Institut et de l'Université de Paris.* Paris: Imprimerie Nationale, 1948.

116   British Museum. *Shakespeare: An Excerpt from the General Catalogue of Printed Books in the British Museum.* London: Trustees of the British Museum, 1964.

117   BROWN, John R. *Select Bibliographies: Shakespeare.* London: Longmans, Green, 1962. Repr. in *Shakespeare: The Writer and His Work,* **2774**. [Incl. recordings.]

118   *The Cambridge Bibliography of English Literature.* Ed. Frederick W. Bateson. 4 vols. Cambridge U.P.; New York: Macmillan, 1941. [Sh section, 1:539-608.] [See also *Supplement*, ed. Frederick W. Bateson (Cambridge U.P., 1937), Sh section, pp. 257-93.]

119   DENT, Robert W. "Reflections of a Shakespeare Bibliographer." In *Pacific Coast Studies in Shakespeare,* **2796**.

120   EBISCH, F. Walther, and Levin L. Schücking, eds. *A Shakespeare Bibliography.* Oxford U.P., 1931. [*Supplement 1930-1935* (Oxford U.P., 1937).]

121   ELLIS-FERMOR, Una. "English and American Shakespeare Studies, 1937-1952." *Anglia*, 71 (1952): 1-49.

122   Folger Shakespeare Library. *Catalog of Manuscripts.* 3 vols. Boston: G. K. Hall, 1971.

123   ——. *Catalog of Printed Books.* 28 vols. Boston: G. K. Hall, 1970. [See vols. 23, 24 for Sh.]

124   ——. *Catalog of the Shakespeare Collection.* 2 vols. Boston: G. K. Hall, 1972.

125   FORD, Herbert L. *Shakespeare, 1700-1740: A Collation of Editions and Separate Plays.* Oxford U.P., 1935. Repr. New York: Blom.

126   FREDERICK, Waveney R. N. (Payne), ed. *A Shakespeare Bibliography: The Catalogue of the Birmingham Shakespeare Library, Birmingham Public Libraries.* 7 vols. London: Mansell, 1971.

127   FUCILLA, Joseph G. "Shakespeare in Italian Criticism." *PQ*, 20 (1941): 559-72. [Supplement to Ebisch and Schücking, **120**.]

128   GUTTMAN, Selma. *The Foreign Sources of Shakespeare's Works: An Annotated Bibliography of the Commentary on This Subject between 1904 and 1940, Together with Lists of Certain Translations Available to Shakespeare.* New York: King's Crown, 1947.

129   HALLIWELL-PHILLIPPS, James O. *A Calendar of the Shakespearean Rarities, Drawings, and Engravings Formerly Preserved at Hollingbury Copse.* 1887. 2nd ed., London: Longmans, Green, 1891.

130   HOWARD-HILL, Trevor H. *Bibliography of British Literary Bibliographies.* Oxford U.P., 1969–. [See esp. vol. 2, which includes *Shakespearian Bibliography and Textual Criticism.*]

131   JAGGARD, William. *Shakespeare Bibliography: A Dictionary of Every Known Issue of the Writings of Our National Poet and of Recorded Opinion Thereon in the English Language.* Stratford-on-Avon: Shakespeare Head P., 1911. Repr. New York: F. Ungar.

132 Library of Congress. *Author Catalog: A Cumulative List of Works Represented by Library of Congress Printed Cards, 1948-1952.* Ann Arbor, Mich.: Edwards, 1953. [For Sh, see 19:88-93.]

133 ——. *The National Union Catalog 1952-1955 Imprints: An Author List Representing Library of Congress Printed Cards and Titles Represented by Other American Libraries.* Ann Arbor, Mich.: Edwards, 1961. *1953-57,* Ann Arbor: Edwards, 1958; *1958-62,* New York: Rowman & Littlefield, 1963; *1963-67,* Ann Arbor: Edwards, 1969. [For Sh, see 24:485-99; 21:462-67; 41:65-82; 49:201-26.]

134 LUDEKE, Hans. "Shakespeare-Bibliographie für die Kriegsjähre 1939-1946." *Archiv,* 188 (1950): 8-40.

135 McNAMEE, Lawrence F. "William Shakespeare." In *Dissertations in English and American Literature: Theses Accepted by American, British, and German Universities, 1865-1964.* New York: Bowker, 1968. [See also *Supplement One, 1964-1968* (New York: Bowker, 1969).]

136 MARDER, Louis. "A Bibliography of Shakespearean Bibliographies." *ShN,* 12 (1962): 24-25.

137 ——. "Shakespearean Biography, a Bibliography." *ShN,* 11 (1961): 20-21.

138 MUMMENDEY, Richard. *Language and Literature of the Anglo-Saxon Nations As Presented in German Doctoral Dissertations, 1885-1950.* Charlottesville: Bibliographical Society of the U. of Virginia, 1954. [200-300 Sh items.]

139 *PMLA.* New York: Modern Language Association of America, 1884–. Repr. of "Bibliography," years 1921-66 (1922-67), New York: AMS. ["American Bibliography" in vols. 37-71 (1922-57); thereafter, "Annual Bibliography" with world coverage.]

140 Canceled.

141 *The Shakespeare Association Bulletin.* See **393.** [Bibliog. in each vol.]

142 *Shakespeare Jahrbuch.* Deutsche Shakespeare-Gesellschaft. Berlin: Georg Reimer, 1865–. See **394, 395.** [Annual bibliog. in each vol.]

143 *Shakespeare Jahrbuch.* Deutsche Shakespeare-Gesellschaft West. Berlin: Quelle & Meyer, 1965–. See **396.** [Annual bibliog. in each vol.]

144 *Shakespeare Quarterly.* See **398.** [Bibliog. in each vol.]

145 *Shakespeare Survey.* See **401.** [Each vol. contains "The Year's Contributions to Shakespearian Study: Critical Studies; Sh's Life and Times; Textual Studies."]

146 SMITH, Gordon R. *A Classified Shakespeare Bibliography, 1936-1958.* Pennsylvania State U.P., 1963.

147 STRATMAN, Carl J. *Bibliography of English Printed Tragedy, 1565 1900.* Southern Illinois U.P., 1966.

148 STUBBINGS, Hilda U. *Renaissance Spain in Its Literary Relations with England and France: A Critical Bibliography.* Vanderbilt U.P., 1969.

149 *Studies in Philology.* U. of North Carolina, 1917–. [In each vol. from 1916 to 1970, "Recent Literature of the English Renaissance" with a section on Sh.]

150 SUMMERS, Montague. *A Bibliography of Restoration Drama.* London: Fortune, 1934.

151 TANNENBAUM, Samuel A., ed. *A Concise Bibliography.* New York: for the ed., 1940-50. [Separate vols. for *Lr, Mac, MV, More, Oth, Rom, Son, Tro.*]

152 THIMM, Franz. *Shakespeariana from 1564 to 1864: An Account of the Shakspearian Literature of England, Germany, France, and Other European Countries during Three Centuries, with Bibliographical Introductions.* London: Franz Thimm, 1865. Rev. ed., 1872.

153 VELZ, John W. *Shakespeare and the Classical Tradition: A Critical Guide to Commentary, 1660-1960.* U. of Minnesota P., 1968.

154 WELLS, Stanley. *Shakespeare: A Reading Guide.* Oxford U.P., 1969.

155 WHEELER, F. A. *A Catalogue of Shakespeareana, with a Prefatory Essay by Sidney Lee.* London: Chiswick Press, 1899. [Over 900 items.]

156 WILEY, Margaret L. "A Supplement to the Bibliography of 'Shakespeare Idolatry.' " *SB*, 4 (1951-52): 164-66.

157 WOOD, Frederick T. "The Attack on the Stage in the XVIII Century." *N&Q*, 173 (1937): 218-22. [A bibliog.]

158 *Year's Work in English Studies.* Ed. Sidney Lee et al. Oxford U.P. for the English Association, 1921–. Repr. vols. 1-32 (1921-53), New York: AMS. [Each annual vol. has a chap. on Sh.]

Dictionaries and Concordances

See also **81**, **82**, and **83**.

159 BAKER, Arthur E. *A Shakespeare Commentary.* 15 pts. Taunton, Mass.: Mountor, 19–. Repr. New York: Ungar. [Pts. 1-13 have title, *A Shakespeare Dictionary.*]

160 BARTLETT, John. *A New and Complete Concordance to Shakespeare.* 2 vols. London: Macmillan, 1894. Repr. London: Macmillan, 1953; New York: St. Martin's.

161 BURTON, Dolores M. "Some Uses of a Grammatical Concordance." *Computers and the Humanities,* 2 (1968): 145-54. [Definite and indefinite articles in *Ant* and *R2.*]

162 CAMPBELL, Oscar J., and Edward G. Quinn, eds. *The Reader's Encyclopedia of Shakespeare.* New York: Crowell, 1966.

163 DONOW, Herbert S. *A Concordance to the Sonnet Sequences of Daniel, Drayton, Shakespeare, Sidney, and Spenser.* Southern Illinois U.P., 1969.

164 FALCONER, Alexander F. *A Glossary of Shakespeare's Sea and Naval Terms Including Gunnery.* London: Constable, 1964; New York: Ungar, 1965.

165 FOGEL, Ephim G. "Electronic Computers and Elizabethan Texts." *SB,* 15 (1962): 15-31.

166 FURNESS, Helen R. (Mrs. Horace H.). *A Concordance to Shakespeare's Poems.* Philadelphia: Lippincott, 1874.

167 HALLIDAY, Frank E. *A Shakespeare Companion, 1550-1950.* London: Duckworth, 1952. [R27 Penguin.]

168 HARBEN, Henry A. *A Dictionary of London.* London: H. Jenkins, 1918.

169 HARTNOLL, Phyllis. *The Oxford Companion to the Theatre.* 3rd ed. Oxford U.P., 1967.

170 HOWARD-HILL, Trevor H. "The Oxford Old-Spelling Shakespeare Concordances." *SB,* 22 (1969): 143-64.

171 ——. *Oxford Shakespeare Concordances.* Oxford U.P., 1969–. [Computerized. Separate vol. for each title.]

172 KÖKERITZ, Helge. *Shakespeare's Names: A Pronouncing Dictionary.* Yale U.P., 1966.

173   NARES, Robert. *A Glossary; or, Collection of Words, Phrases, Names, and Allusions to Customs, Proverbs, . . . [in] Shakespeare and His Contemporaries.* 1822. Rev. ed., 2 vols., London: J. R. Smith, 1859 (ed. J. O. Halliwell-Phillipps and Thomas Wright); repr. Detroit: Gale Research, 1966.

174   ONIONS, Charles T. *A Shakespeare Glossary.* Oxford U.P., 1911.

175   *Oxford Dictionary of English Proverbs.* Ed. William G. Smith. Oxford U.P., 1935. 2nd rev. ed., 1948; 3rd ed., 1970 (rev. Frank P. Wilson).

176   PARRISH, S. M. "Problems in the Making of Computer Concordances." *SB*, 15 (1962): 1-14.

177   SCHMIDT, Alexander. *Shakespeare-Lexicon.* 1874. 3rd ed., 2 vols., Berlin: G. Reimer, 1902 (rev. Gregor I. Sarrazin); repr. Berlin: Walter de Gruyter, 1962; New York: Blom.

178   SKEAT, Walter W. *A Glossary of Tudor and Stuart Words, Especially from the Dramatists.* Ed., with additions, by Anthony L. Mayhew. Oxford U.P., 1914.

179   SPEVACK, Marvin. *A Complete and Systematic Concordance to the Works of Shakespeare.* 6 vols. Hildesheim: G. Olms, 1968-70. [Computerized.]

180   STOKES, Francis G. *A Dictionary of the Characters and Proper Names in Shakespeare.* London: Harrap, 1924.

181   SUGDEN, Edward H. *A Topographical Dictionary to the Works of Shakespeare and His Fellow Dramatists.* U. of Manchester P., 1925.

182   THOMSON, Wilfrid H. *Shakespeare's Characters: A Historical Dictionary.* Altrincham: J. Sherratt; New York: British Book Center, 1951.

183   TILLEY, Morris P. *A Dictionary of the Proverbs in England in the Sixteenth and Seventeenth Centuries.* U. of Michigan P., 1950. [Index to some 4,000 proverbs in Sh.]

Textual Studies
and Critical Bibliography

Several books and studies of major importance are listed elsewhere, such as **16, 17, 36,** and **72.** For others, relating to forgeries, real or supposed, see **15, 23, 24, 44, 53, 55, 64, 75, 76, 93, 95, 97, 98,** and **104.** See also Editions, Editors: Commentary **(654-80)** and Folios: Commentary **(681-717).**

184 ADAMS, Joseph Q. "Elizabethan Playhouse Manuscripts and Their Significance for the Text of Shakespeare." *Johns Hopkins Alumni Magazine*; see **5.**

185 ALEXANDER, Peter. "Restoring Shakespeare: The Modern Editor's Task." *ShS 5* (1952), pp. 1-9.

186 ——. *Shakespeare's Punctuation.* Oxford U.P., 1945. [*PBA 1945*, 31 (1946): 61-84.]

187 ——— "Shakespeare's Punctuation." *RES*, 23 (1947): 263-66.

188 Canceled.

189 BAENDER, Paul. "The Meaning of Copy-Text." *SB*, 22 (1969): 311-18.

190 BAKER, George P. "Some Bibliographical Puzzles in Elizabethan Quartos." *PBSA*, 4 (1909): 9-20. [See comments by G. W. Cole, pp. 20-23.]

191 BALD, R. Cecil. "'Assembled' Texts." *Library*, 12 (1931-32): 243-48. [*TGV, Wiv, WT,* et al.]

192 ——. "Editorial Problems—A Preliminary Survey." *SB*, 3 (1950-51): 3-17.

193 ——. "Evidence and Inference in Bibliography." *EIE 1941* (1942), pp. 159-84.

194 [BARKER, Nicolas?]. "Bibliography and the Printing House." *BC*, 18 (1965): 295-306.

195 BATESON, Frederick W. "Shakespeare's Laundry Bills: The Rationale of External Evidence." *SJ*, 98 (1962): 51-63.

196 BATTLE, Guy A. "A Bibliographical Note from the Beaumont and Fletcher First Folio." *SB*, 1(1948-49): 187-88. [Boxlines a clue to the order in which formes were printed.]

197 BENTLEY, Gerald E. "Authenticity and Attribution in the Jacobean and Caroline Drama." *EIE 1942* (1943), pp. 101-18.

198   BLACK, Matthew W. "Problems in the Editing of Shakespeare: Interpretation." *EIE 1947* (1948), pp. 117-36.

199   BOLTON, Joseph S. G. "Worn Pages in Shakespearian Manuscripts." *SQ,* 7 (1956): 177-82.

200   BOND, William H. "Casting Off Copy by Elizabethan Printers: A Theory." *PBSA*, 42 (1948): 281-91.

201   ——. "Imposition by Half-Sheets." *Library,* 22 (1941-42): 163-67.

202   BOWERS, Fredson T. "Bibliographical Evidence from the Printer's Measure." *SB*, 2 (1949-50): 153-67. [See also W. Craig Ferguson, "A Note on Printer's Measures." *SB*, 15 (1962): 242-43.]

203   ——. *The Bibliographical Way.* U. of Kansas Libraries, 1959.

204   ——. *Bibliography and Textual Criticism.* Oxford U.P., 1964.

205   ——. "Bibliography, Pure Bibliography, and Literary Studies." *PBSA*, 46 (1952): 186-208.

206   ——. "Certain Basic Problems in Descriptive Bibliography." *PBSA*, 42 (1948): 211-28. [See also Paul S. Dunkin, pp. 239-53, and reply by Bowers, p. 341.]

207   ——. "Current Theories of Copy-Text, with an Illustration from Dryden." *MP*, 48 (1950-51): 12-20.

208   ——. "Elizabethan Proofing." In *Adams Memorial Studies,* **2794**.

209   ——. "Established Texts and Definitive Editions." In *Studies . . . Presented to Baldwin Maxwell,* **2824**.

210   ——. "Notes on Running-Titles as Bibliographical Evidence." *Library,* 19 (1938-39): 315-38.

211   ——. "Old-Spelling Editions of Dramatic Texts." In *Studies in Honor of T. W. Baldwin,* **2760**.

212   ——. *On Editing Shakespeare and the Elizabethan Dramatists.* U. of Pennsylvania Library, 1955. Repr. with additions, U.P. of Virginia, 1966.

213   ——. "Purposes of Descriptive Bibliography, with Some Remarks on Methods." *Library*, 8 (1953): 1-22.

214   ——. "Running-Title Evidence for Determining Half-Sheet Imposition." *SB*, 1 (1948-49): 199-202.

215   ——. "Shakespeare's Text and the Bibliographical Method." *SB*, 6 (1954): 71-91.

216   ——. "Some Relations of Bibliography to Editorial Problems." *SB*, 3 (1950-51): 37-62.

217   ——. *Textual and Literary Criticism.* Cambridge U.P., 1959.

218   ——. "Textual Criticism." In *The Aims and Methods of Scholarship in Modern Languages.* Ed. James Thorpe. New York: Modern Language Association of America, 1963.

219   —. "Today's Shakespeare Texts, and Tomorrow's." *SB*, 19 (1966): 39-65. Repr. in *On Editing Shakespeare*, **212**.

220   —. "What Shakespeare Wrote." *SJ*, 98 (1962): 24-50. Repr. in *On Editing Shakespeare*, **212**.

221   BROOKE, C. F. Tucker. "Elizabethan Proof Corrections in a Copy of *The First Part of the Contention*, 1600." *Huntington Library Bulletin*, 2 (1931): 87-89, 8 plates.

222   BROWN, Arthur. "Editorial Problems in Shakespeare: Semi-popular Editions." *SB*, 8 (1956): 15-26.

223   —. "The Printing of Books." In *ShS 17*, **3918**.

224   BROWN, John R. "The Compositors of *Ham* Q2 and *MV*." *SB*, 7 (1955): 17-40.

225   —. "The Printing of John Webster's Plays. Pt. 1." *SB*, 6 (1954): 117-40; "Pt. 2." *SB*, 8 (1956): 113-27.

226   —. "A Proof-Sheet from Nicholas Okes' Printing-Shop." *SB*, 11 (1958): 228-31.

227   —. "The Rationale of Old-Spelling Editions of the Plays of Shakespeare and His Contemporaries." *SB*, 13 (1960): 49-67. [See also Arthur Brown, "A Rejoinder," pp. 69-76.]

228   BYRNE, M. St. Clare. "Anthony Munday's Spelling as a Literary Clue." *Library*, 4 (1923-24): 9-23.

229   —. "Bibliographical Clues in Collaborate Plays." *Library*, 13 (1932-33): 21-48.

230   CAIRNCROSS, Andrew S. "Pembroke's Men and Some Shakespearian Piracies." *SQ*, 11 (1960): 335-49.

231   CAPELL, Edward. *Notes and Various Readings to Shakespeare.* London: E. & C. Dilly, [1775]. Repr. New York: Franklin; AMS. [Withdrawn and then issued as vol. 1 of *Notes and Various Readings*, 3 vols. (London: H. Hughes for the author, [1779-83]). Vol. 3, *The School of Shakespeare.*]

232   CARTER, Albert H. "On the Use of Details of Spelling, Punctuation, and Typography to Determine the Dependence of Editions." *SP*, 44 (1947): 497-503.

233   CHAMBERS, Edmund K. *The Disintegration of Shakespeare.* Oxford U.P., 1924. [*PBA 1924-25*, 11 (1926): 89-108.] Repr. in *Aspects of Shakespeare*, **2761**, and *Shakespearean Gleanings*, **2913**.

234   CRAIG, Hardin. *A New Look at Shakespeare's Quartos.* Stanford U.P., 1961. Repr. New York: AMS.

235   —. "Revised Elizabethan Quartos: An Attempt to Form a Class." In *Studies in . . . Memory of Karl Julius Holzknecht*, **2762**.

236   CRAVEN, Alan E. "The Compositors of the Shakespeare Quartos Printed by Peter Short." *PBSA*, 65 (1971): 393-97.

237   CROW, John. "Editing and Emending." *E&S*, 8 (1955): 1-20.

238 DANIEL, Peter A. *Notes and Conjectural Emendations of Certain Doubtful Passages in Shakespeare's Plays.* London: R. Hardwicke, 1870. Repr. New York: AMS.

239 DAWSON, Giles E. "Authenticity and Attribution of Written Matter." *EIE 1942* (1943), pp. 77-100.

240 —. "Copyright of Plays in the Early Seventeenth Century." *EIE 1947* (1948), pp. 169-92.

241 —. "The Copyright of Shakespeare's Dramatic Works." In *Studies in Honor of A. H. R. Fairchild,* **2804.**

242 —. *Four Centuries of Shakespeare Publication.* U. of Kansas Libraries, 1964.

243 —. "Three Shakespearean Piracies in the Eighteenth Century." *SB*, 1 (1948-49): 47-58.

244 DEARING, Vinton A. "Abaco-Textual Criticism." *PBSA*, 62 (1968): 547-78.

245 —. "Computer Aids to Editing the Text of Dryden." In *Art and Error: Modern Textual Editing.* Ed. Ronald Gottesman and Scott B. Bennett. Indiana U.P., 1970.

246 —. *Methods of Textual Editing.* Los Angeles: William Andrews Clark Memorial Library, 1962. [Role of the computer.]

247 —. "The Poor Man's Mark IV or Ersatz Hinman Collator." *PBSA*, 60 (1966): 149-58.

248 DORAN, Madeleine. "An Evaluation of Evidence in Shakespearean Textual Criticism." *EIE 1941* (1942), pp. 95-114.

249 DUNKIN, Paul S. "The Ghost of the Turned Sheet." *PBSA*, 45 (1951): 246-50.

250 DYCE, Alexander. *A Few Notes on Shakespeare, with Occasional Remarks on the Emendations of the Manuscript Corrector in Mr. Collier's Copy of the Folio 1632.* London: Smith, 1853. Repr. New York: AMS.

251 EDWARDS, Thomas. *The Canons of Criticism, and Glossary.* London: C. Bathurst, 1765. Repr. New York: AMS. [First published as *A Supplement to Mr. Warburton's Edition* (1748).]

252 EVANS, G. Blakemore. "The Douai Manuscript—Six Shakespearean Transcripts (1694-95)." *PQ*, 41 (1962): 158-72.

253 —. "Shakespeare's Text: Approaches and Problems." In *A New Companion to Shakespeare Studies,* **2800.**

254 FERGUSON, W. Craig. "The Compositors of *2H4, Ado, The Shoemaker's Holiday,* and *The First Part of the Contention.*" *SB*, 13 (1960): 19-29.

255 FEUILLERAT, Albert. *The Composition of Shakespeare's Plays: Authorship, Chronology.* Yale U.P., 1953.

256 FLATTER, Richard. "The True Originall Copies." *PLPLS-LHS*, 7 (1952): 31-43.

257 FÖRSTER, Max. "Shakespeare and Shorthand." *PQ*, 16 (1937): 1-29.

258 GASKELL, Philip. "The Lay of the Case." *SB*, 22 (1969): 125-42.

259 GAW, Allison. "Actors' Names in Basic Shakespearean Texts. " *PMLA*, 40 (1925): 530-50. [Esp. *Rom* and *Ado*.]

260 GRAVES, Thornton S. "Ralph Crane and the King's Players." *SP*, 21 (1924): 362-66.

261 GREG, Walter W. "Bibliography—An Apologia." *Library*, 13 (1932-33):113-43. Repr. in *Collected Papers*, **262**.

262 ——. *Collected Papers*. Ed. James C. Maxwell. Oxford U.P.,1966.

263 ——. "Copyright in Unauthorized Texts." In *Elizabethan and Jacobean Studies Presented to F. P. Wilson*, **2772**.

264 ——. *The Editorial Problem in Shakespeare: A Survey of the Foundations of the Text*. Oxford U.P., 1943. Rev. ed., 1951.

265 ——. "An Elizabethan Printer and His Copy." *Library*, 4 (1923-24): 102-18. Repr. in *Collected Papers*, **262**.

266 ——. "Entrance, License, and Publication." *Library*, 25 (1944-45): 1-22.

267 ——. "From Manuscript to Print." *RES*, 13 (1937): 190-205. [Rev. of Simpson, *Proof-reading in the Sixteenth, Seventeenth, and Eighteenth Centuries*, **359**.]

268 ——. "The Function of Bibliography in Literary Criticism Illustrated in a Study of the Text of *Lr.*" *Neophil*, 18 (1933): 241-62. Repr. in *Collected Papers*, **262**.

269 ——. "On Certain False Dates in Shakespearian Quartos." *Library*, 9 (1908): 113-31, 381-409.

270 ——. "The Present Position of Bibliography." *Library*, 11 (1930-31): 241-62. Repr. in *Collected Papers*, **262**.

271 ——. *Principles of Emendation in Shakespeare*. Oxford U.P., 1928. [*PBA 1928*, 14 (1929): 147-216.] Repr. in *Aspects of Shakespeare*, **2761**, and *Shakespeare Criticism, 1919-35*, **2807**.

272 ——. "A Question of Plus or Minus." *RES*, 6 (1930): 300-304. Repr. in *Collected Papers*, **262**. [Repetition of lines.]

273 ——. "The Rationale of Copy-Text." *SB*, 3 (1950-51): 19-36. Repr. in *Collected Papers*, **262**.

274 ——. "Richard Robinson and the Stationers' Register." *MLR*, 50 (1955): 407-13. Repr. in *Collected Papers*, **262**.

275 ——. *Two Elizabethan Stage Abridgements*, The Battle of Alcazar *and* Orlando Furioso: *An Essay in Critical Bibliography*. Oxford U.P. for the Malone Society, 1923.

276   GUFFEY, George R. "Standardization of Photographic Reproductions for Mechanical Collation." *PBSA*, 62 (1968): 237-40.

277   HART, Alfred. "Acting Versions of Elizabethan Plays." *RES*, 10 (1934): 1-28. [About 2,400 lines, actable in about 2 hours.]

278   ——. "The Length of Elizabethan and Jacobean Plays." *RES*, 8 (1932): 139-54.

279   ——. "The Number of Lines in Shakespeare's Plays." *RES*, 8 (1932): 19-28.

280   ——. *Stolne and Surreptitious Copies: A Comparative Study of Shakespeare's Bad Quartos.* Melbourne U.P., 1942.

281   Canceled.

282   HEAWOOD, Edward. "Papers Used in England after 1600." *Library*, 11 (1930-31): 263-99, 466-98. [Watermarks.]

283   ——. "The Position on the Sheet of Early Watermarks." *Library*, 9 (1928-29): 38-47.

284   ——. *Watermarks Mainly of the 17th and 18th Centuries.* Monumenta Chartae Papyraceae Historiam Illustrantia, vol. 1. Hilversum: Paper Publication Society, 1950. [See review essay by Allan H. Stevenson in *PBSA*, 45 (1950): 23-36.]

285   HILL, Archibald A. "Some Postulates for Distributional Study of Texts." *SB*, 3 (1950-51): 63-95.

286   HILL, T. H. "Spelling and the Bibliographer." *Library*, 18 (1963): 1-28.

287   HINMAN, Charlton. "Mechanical Collation: A Preliminary Report." *PBSA*, 41 (1947): 99-106.

288   ——. "New Uses for Headlines as Bibliographical Evidence." *EIE 1941* (1942), pp. 207-22.

289   ——. "Principles Governing the Use of Variant Spellings as Evidence of Alternate Setting by Two Compositors." *Library*, 21 (1940-41): 78-103.

290   ——. "Shakespeare's Text—Then, Now, and Tomorrow." *ShS 18* (1965), pp. 23-33.

291   ——. *Six Variant Readings in the First Folio of Shakespeare.* U. of Kansas Libraries, 1961.

292   HONIGMANN, Ernst A. J. "On the Indifferent and One-Way Variants in Shakespeare." *Library*, 22 (1967): 189-204.

293   ——. *The Stability of Shakespeare's Text.* London: Edwin Arnold, 1965.

294   HOWARD, Edward J. "The Printer and Elizabethan Punctuation." *SP*, 27 (1930): 220-29.

295   HOWARD-HILL, Trevor H. "Ralph Crane's Parentheses." *N&Q*, 210 (1965): 334-40.

296 —. *Shakespearian Bibliography and Textual Criticism: A Bibliography.* Oxford U.P., 1971.

297 HUNTER, George K. "The Marking of *Sententiae* in Elizabethan Printed Plays, Poems, and Romances." *Library*, 6 (1951-52): 171-88. [*Luc, Ham* (1603, 1604/5), *Tro.*]

298 HUNTER, Mark. "Act- and Scene-Division in the Plays of Shakespeare." *RES*, 2 (1926): 295-310. [See also *RES* 3 (1927): 463-64 and **387**.]

299 HUTH, Alfred H. "On the Supposed False Dates in Certain Shakespeare Quartos." *Library*, 1 (1910): 36-45. [See pp. 46-53 for reply of Alfred W. Pollard.]

300 ISAACS, Jacob. "A Note on Shakespeare's Dramatic Punctuation." *RES*, 2 (1926): 461-63.

301 JACKSON, William A. *Bibliography and Literary Studies.* U. of California P., 1962.

302 —. "Some Limitations of Microfilm." *PBSA*, 35 (1941): 281-88.

303 JENKINSON, Hilary. "Elizabethan Handwritings: A Preliminary Sketch." *Library*, 3 (1922-23): 1-34, 12 plates.

304 JEWKES, Wilfred T. *Act-Division in Elizabethan and Jacobean Plays.* Hamden, Conn.: Shoe String P., 1958.

305 JOHNSON, Francis R. "Press Corrections and Presswork in the Elizabethan Printing Shop." *PBSA*, 40 (1946): 276-86.

306 —. "Printers' 'Copy Books' and the Black Market in the Elizabethan Book Trade." *Library*, 1 (1946-47): 97-105.

307 KABLE, William S. *The Pavier Quartos and the First Folio of Shakespeare.* Shakespeare Studies, Monograph Series 2. Dubuque, Iowa: W. C. Brown, 1970. [Enlarged from Kable, "The Influence of Justification on Spelling in Jaggard's Compositor B." *SB,* 20 (1967): 235-39; and "Compositor B, The Pavier Quartos, and Copy Spellings." *SB*, 21 (1968): 131-61.]

308 KIRSCHBAUM, Leo. "A Census of Bad Quartos." *RES*, 14 (1938): 20-43.

309 —. "An Hypothesis concerning the Origin of the Bad Quartos." *PMLA*, 60 (1945): 697-715.

310 —. "Is *The Spanish Tragedy* a Leading Case? Did a Bad Quarto of *LLL* Ever Exist?" *JEGP*, 37 (1938): 501-12.

311 —. *Shakespeare and the Stationers.* Ohio State U.P., 1955.

312 KLEIN, David. "Time Allotted for an Elizabethan Performance." *SQ*, 18 (1967): 434-38.

313 LEECH, Clifford. "On Editing One's First Play." *SB*, 23 (1970): 61-70.

314 McKENZIE, Donald F. *The Cambridge University Press, 1696-1712: A Bibliographical Study.* 2 vols. Cambridge U.P., 1966.

315   —. *An Early Printing House at Work: Some Notes for Bibliographers.* Wellington: Oliver & Boyd, 1964.

316   —. "A List of Printers' Apprentices, 1605-1640." *SB*, 13 (1960): 109-41. [John Leason may be Jaggard's compositor E, the "prentice hand."]

317   —. "Printers of the Mind: Some Notes on Bibliographical Theories and Printing-House Practices." *SB*, 22 (1969): 1-76. See also **314**.

318   —. "Shakespearian Punctuation—A New Beginning." *RES*, 10 (1959): 361-70.

319   McKERROW, Ronald B. "The Elizabethan Printer and Dramatic Manuscripts." *Library*, 12 (1931-32): 253-75. [Argues that many dramatic texts are bad because printed from the authors' foul sheets.]

320   —. "Elizabethan Printers and the Composition of Reprints." *Library*, 5 (1924-25): 357-64.

321   —. *Introduction to Bibliography for Literary Students.* See **72**.

322   —. "A Note on the 'Bad Quartos' of *2* and *3 H6* and the Folio Text." *RES*, 13 (1937): 64-72.

323   —. *Prolegomena for the Oxford Shakespeare.* Oxford U.P., 1939. [See Walter W. Greg, "McKerrow's Prolegomena Reconsidered." *RES*, 17 (1941): 139-49; Fredson T. Bowers, "McKerrow's Editorial Principles for Shakespeare Reconsidered." *SQ*, 6 (1955): 309-24.]

324   —. "A Suggestion regarding Shakespeare's Manuscripts." *RES*, 11 (1935): 459-65. [Variations in speech headings in certain plays and duplicated lines indicate certain quartos were printed from Shakespeare's holograph.]

324a McMANAWAY, James G. "Thomas Dekker: Further Textual Notes." *Library*, 19 (1938-39): 176-79. [The pattern of running-titles determines the relative priority of pages of text reprinted after type was pied.]

325   MALONE, Edmond. *An Inquiry into the Authenticity of Certain Miscellaneous Papers and Legal Instruments, Published . . . and Attributed to Shakespeare.* London: T. Cadell, Jr., 1796. [Ireland forgeries.]

326   MANLY, John M. "Cuts and Insertions in Shakespeare's Plays." *SP*, 14 (1917): 123-28.

327   MATTHEWS, William. "Peter Bales, Timothy Bright, and William Shakespeare." *JEGP*, 34 (1935): 483-510.

328   —. "Shakespeare and the Reporters." *Library*, 15 (1934-35): 481-98. [Elizabethan systems of shorthand were inadequate for reporting plays. See disagreement by Hereward T. Price, *Library*, 17 (1936-37): 225-30, and rejoinder by Matthews.]

329   —. "Shorthand and the Bad Shakespeare Quartos." *MLR*, 27 (1932): 243-62; 28 (1933): 81-83.

330   MORIARTY, W. D. "The Bearing on Dramatic Sequence of the Varia in *R3* and *Lr*." *MP*, 10 (1912-13): 451-71.

331 MURRAY, Peter B. "The Authorship of *The Revenger's Tragedy*." *PBSA*, 56 (1962): 195-218. [Spelling and authorship.]

331a ——. "The Collaboration of Dekker and Webster in *Northward Ho* and *Westward Ho*." *PBSA*, 56 (1962): 482-87.

332 NATHAN, Norman. "Compositor Haste in the First Folio." *SQ*, 8 (1957): 134-35. [Decries the evaluation of accuracy of composition in terms of haste.]

333 NEIDIG, William J. "The Shakespeare Quartos of 1619." *MP*, 8 (1910): 145-63, 5 plates. [See also Neidig, "False Dates on Shakspere Quartos: A New Method of Proof Applied to a Controversy of Scholars." *Century Magazine*, Oct. 1910, pp. 912-19.]

334 NORLAND, Howard B. "The Text of *The Maid's Tragedy*." *PBSA*, 61 (1967): 173-200.

335 ONG, Walter J. "Historical Backgrounds of Elizabethan and Jacobean Punctuation Theory." *PMLA*, 59 (1944): 349-60.

336 PERSHING, James H. "Storage of Printed Sheets in the Seventeenth Century." *Library*, 17 (1936-37): 468-71.

337 POLLARD, Alfred W. "Elizabethan Spelling as a Literary and Bibliographical Clue." *Library*, 4 (1923-24): 1-8.

338 ——. "False Dates in Shakespeare Quartos." *Library*, 2 (1911): 101-7.

339 ——. "The Foundations of Shakespeare's Text." Oxford U.P., 1923. [*PBA 1921-23*, 10 (1924): 379-94.]

340 ——. "The Manuscripts of Shakespeare's Plays." *Library*, 7 (1916): 198-226.

341 ——. *Shakespeare Folios and Quartos: A Study of the Bibliography of Shakespeare's Plays, 1594-1685.* London: Methuen, 1909.

342 ——. *Shakespeare's Fight with the Pirates and the Problems of the Transmission of His Text.* Shakespeare Problem Series, 1. London: A. Moring, 1917. 2nd ed. rev., Cambridge U.P., 1920; repr. 1937.

343 ——. "Shakespeare's Text." In *A Companion to Shakespeare Studies*, 2783.

344 POVEY, Kenneth. "The Optical Identification of First Formes." *SB*, 13 (1960): 189-90.

345 ——. "Working to Rule, 1600-1800: A Study of Pressmen's Practice." *Library*, 20 (1965): 13-54.

346 PRICE, George R. "Dividing the Copy for *Michaelmas Term*." *PBSA*, 60 (1966): 327-36.

347 ——. "Setting by Formes in the First Edition of *The Phoenix*." *PBSA*, 56 (1962): 414-27.

348 PRICE, Hereward T. "Another Shorthand Sermon." In *Essays and Studies in English and Comparative Literature by Members of the English Department.* U. of Michigan P., 1933.

349   —. "Author, Compositor, and Metre: Copy-Spelling in *Tit* and Other Elizabethan Printings." *PBSA*, 53 (1959): 160-87.

350   —. "Towards a Scientific Method of Textual Criticism for the Elizabethan Drama." *JEGP*, 36 (1937): 151-67.

351   SALMON, Vivian. "Early Seventeenth-Century Punctuation as a Guide to Sentence Structure." *RES*, 13 (1962): 347-60. [Theory and practice of Henry Clapham.]

352   SCHÄFER, Jürgen. "The Orthography of Proper Names in Modern-Spelling Editions of Shakespeare." *SB*, 23 (1970): 1-19.

353   SCHOLES, Robert E. "Dr. Johnson and the Bibliographical Criticism of Shakespeare." *SQ*, 11 (1960): 163-71.

354   SEN, Sailendra K. *Capell and Malone and Modern Critical Bibliography*. Calcutta: K. L. Mukhopadhyay, 1960.

355   SHAABER, Matthias A. "The Meaning of the Imprint in Early Printed Books." *Library*, 24 (1943-44): 120-41.

356   —. "Problems in the Editing of Shakespeare: Text." *EIE 1947* (1948), pp. 97-116.

357   SIMPSON, Percy. "The Bibliographical Study of Shakespeare." *Oxford Bibliog. Soc. Proceedings,* 1 (1922-23): 19-53.

358   —. "Literary Piracy in the Elizabethan Age." *Oxford Bibliog. Soc. Publications*, 1 (1947): 1-23.

359   —. *Proof-reading in the Sixteenth, Seventeenth, and Eighteenth Centuries.* Oxford U.P., 1935. [See 267.]

360   SISSON, Charles J. "Bibliographical Aspects of Some Stuart Dramatic Manuscripts." *RES*, 1 (1925): 421-30. [Mislined verse, repeated passages, "ghost" parts, and variant speech-headings.]

361   —. *New Readings in Shakespeare.* Shakespeare Problem Series, 8. 2 vols. Cambridge U.P., 1956. Repr. London: Dawson's, 1961.

362   SMITH, Gerald A. "Collating Machine, Poor Man's Mark VII." *PBSA*, 61 (1967): 110-13.

363   SMITH, Warren D. "Shakespeare's Exit Cues." *JEGP*, 61 (1962): 884-96.

364   STEVENSON, Allan H. "Chain-Indentations in Paper as Evidence." *SB*, 6 (1954): 181-95. [Helpful in identifying cancels.]

365   —. "New Uses of Watermarks as Bibliographical Evidence." *SB*, 1 (1948-49): 149-82.

366   —. *Observations on Paper as Evidence.* U. of Kansas Libraries, 1961.

367   —. "Shakespearian Dated Watermarks." *SB*, 4 (1951-52): 159-64.

368   —. "Watermarks Are Twins." *SB*, 4 (1951-52): 57-91.

369   STOKES, Roy. *The Function of Bibliography.* London: Deutsch, 1969. [Esp. chaps. 3 and 6.]

370 TANNENBAUM, Samuel A. "How Not to Edit Shakspere." *PQ*, 10 (1931): 97-137.

371 TANSELLE, G. Thomas. "The Identification of Type Faces in Bibliographical Description." *PBSA*, 60 (1966): 185-202.

372 —. "The Use of Type Damage as Evidence in Bibliographical Description." *Library*, 23 (1968): 328-51.

373 THEOBALD, Lewis. *Shakespeare Restored; or, A Specimen of the Many Errors . . . by Mr. Pope in His Late Edition.* London: R. Francklin, 1726. Repr. New York: AMS.

374 THORNDIKE, Ashley H. "Parentheses in Shakespeare." *SAB*, 9 (1934): 31-37. [A clue to identity of transcribers of texts in F1.]

375 THORPE, James. "The Aesthetics of Textual Criticism." *PMLA*, 80 (1965): 465-82.

375a —, and C. M. Simpson. *The Task of the Editor.* Los Angeles: William Andrews Clark Memorial Library, 1969.

376 TURNER, Robert K. "Analytical Bibliography and Shakespeare's Text." *MP*, 62 (1964): 51-58.

377 —. "The Printing of Beaumont and Fletcher's *The Maid's Tragedy* Q1 (1619)." *SB*, 13 (1960): 199-220. [Setting by formes; the order of formes sent to press.]

378 —. "Reappearing Types as Bibliographical Evidence." *SB*, 19 (1966): 198-209.

379 —. "Standing Type in Tomkis's *Albumazar*." *Library*, 13 (1958): 174-85. [*2H4* and *MV*.]

379a WALDER, Ernest. "The Text of Shakespeare." Chap. 11, vol. 5 of *Cam. Hist. Eng. Lit.*, 18a.

380 WALKER, Alice. "Compositor Determination and Other Problems in Shakespearian Texts." *SB*, 7 (1955): 3-15.

381 —. "Principles of Annotation: Some Suggestions for Editors of Shakespeare." *SB*, 9 (1957): 95-105.

382 WEITENKAMPF, Frank. "What Is a Facsimile?" *PBSA*, 37 (1943): 114-30.

383 WILLIAMS, George W. "Setting by Formes in Quarto Printing." *SB*, 11 (1958): 39-53. [*Contention* (1594) and part of *Rom* (1597) set by formes.]

384 WILLIAMS, Philip. "New Approaches to Textual Problems in Shakespeare." *SB*, 8 (1956): 3-14.

385 WILSON, Frank P. "Ralph Crane, Scrivener to the King's Players." *Library*, 7 (1926-27): 194-215, 5 plates.

386 —. "Shakespeare and the 'New Bibliography.' " In *The Bibliographical Society, 1892-1942: Studies in Retrospect.* Ed. Frank C. Francis. Oxford U.P. for the Bibliographical Society, 1945. Rev. ed., Oxford U.P., 1970 (ed. Helen Gardner). [See also Thomas M. Parrott, *Library*, 3 (1948-49): 63-65.]

387   WILSON, J. Dover. "Act- and Scene-Division in Shakespeare. A Rejoinder." *RES*, 3 (1927): 385-97.

388   —. "The New Way with Shakespeare's Texts: An Introduction for Lay Readers. I. The Foundations." *ShS* 7 (1954), pp. 48-56. "II. Recent Work on the Text of *Rom*." *ShS* 8 (1955), pp. 81-99. "III. In Sight of Shakespeare's Manuscripts." *ShS* 9 (1956), pp. 69-80. "IV. Towards the High Road." *ShS* 11 (1958), pp. 78-88.

389   —. "Thirteen Volumes of Shakespeare: A Retrospect." *MLR*, 25 (1930): 397-414.

390   WOLF, Edwin, 2nd. "Press Corrections in Sixteenth- and Seventeenth-Century Quartos." *PBSA*, 36 (1942): 187-98.

Shakespearean Publications

391 New Shakspere Society. *Publications.* 19 vols. Ser. 1-8. London: N. Trubner for the Society, 1874-92. Repr. Nendeln, Liechtenstein: Kraus-Thomson; New York: AMS; in microfiche and opaque, Washington, D.C.: NCR Microcard Editions.

392 *Ohio State University Theatre Bulletin.* Ohio State U. Theatre Collection, 1954–. [Occasional studies of Sh interest.]

393 *The Shakespeare Association Bulletin.* Ed. Paul Kaufman et al. New York: Shakespeare Association of America, 1924-49. 24 vols. Repr. New York: AMS; in microfiche, Washington, D.C.: NCR Microcard Editions.

394 *Shakespeare Jahrbuch.* Deutsche Shakespeare-Gesellschaft. Vols. 1-99. Ed. Friedrich Bodenstedt et al. Berlin: Georg Reimer et al., 1865-1963. *Gesamtverzeichnis für die Bände 1-99.* Heidelberg: Quelle & Meyer, 1964. Repr. vols. 1-71 (1865-1935) and index vols. 1-99, New York: AMS; vols. 1-50 (1865-1914) with index to vols. 1-16 in microfiche and opaque, Washington, D.C.: NCR Microcard Editions.

395 *Shakespeare Jahrbuch.* Deutsche Shakespeare-Gesellschaft. Vols. 100/101–. Ed. Anselm Schlösser and Armin-Gerd Kuckhoff. Weimar: Herman Böhlaus, 1965–. [See *Shakespeare Bibliographie für 1964-65,* ed. Peter Genzel, *Suppl.* to vol. 103, 1967 (Weimar: Herman Böhlaus, 1967).]

396 *Shakespeare Jahrbuch.* Deutsche Shakespeare-Gesellschaft West. Vols. 100–. Ed. Hermann Heuer et al. Heidelberg: Quelle & Meyer, 1964–.

397 *Shakespeare Newsletter.* Ed. Louis Marder. New York, 1951–. Repr. vols. 1-13 (1951-63), New York: AMS.

398 *Shakespeare Quarterly.* Ed. Robert M. Smith et al. New York: Shakespeare Association of America, 1950-72; Washington, D.C.: Folger Shakespeare Library, 1972–. Repr. New York: AMS; in microfilm, vols. 1-17 (1950-66), Washington, D.C.: NCR Microcard Editions. [*Cumulative Index to* Shakespeare Quarterly, *Vols. 1-15, 1950-1964,* ed. Martin Seymour-Smith (New York and London: AMS, 1969).]

399 Shakespeare Society of London. *Publications.* 20 vols. (i.e., nos. 1-48). London: for the Society, 1841-53. Repr. Nendeln, Liechtenstein: Kraus-Thomson; New York: AMS; in microfiche and opaque, Washington, D.C.: NCR Microcard Editions.

400 *Shakespeare Studies.* Ed. J. Leeds Barroll. Vols. 1-3, U. of Cincinnati, 1965-68; vols. 4-5, Vanderbilt U., Center for Shakespeare Studies, 1969-70; vol. 6–, U. of South Carolina, 1972–.

401 *Shakespeare Survey.* Ed. Allardyce Nicoll et al. Cambridge U.P., 1948–. Repr., vols. 1-20 (1948-67), New York: AMS. [Index vols. 1-10 in vol. 11; index vols. 11-20 in vol. 21.]

402 *SRO* [Shakespearean Research Opportunities]. Ed. William R. Elton. Department of English of the U. of California, Riverside, 1965-67; City U. of New York, 1968–.

Shakespeare Collections

No attempt has been made to include descriptions of every collection of Folios and Quartos. The locations of most of the copies of editions earlier than 1701 will be found in **14, 37, 85, 106, 107,** and **113**. See also **115, 116, 124,** and **126**.

403 ADAMS, Herbert M. "The Shakespeare Collection in the Library of Trinity College, Cambridge." *ShS 5* (1952), pp. 50-54.

404 ALDEN, John. "America's First Shakespeare Collection." *PBSA*, 58 (1964): 169-73. [Thomas P. Barton's, begun in 1834; now in the Boston Public Library.]

405 BALDWIN, Thomas W., and Isabelle Grant. *Shakespeare at Illinois.* U. of Illinois P., 1951. [Notes on the exhibition of the Ernest Ingold set of Folios.]

406 BARTLETT, Henrietta C. *Mr. William Shakespeare: Original and Early Editions of His Quartos and Folios, His Source Books, and Those Containing Contemporary Notices.* See **112**. [Library of W. A. White.]

407 "Les Collections shakespeariennes dans le monde." *ThR*, 5 (1963): 169-75.

408 DAVIES, Godfrey. "The Huntington Library." *ShS 6* (1953), pp. 53-63. [Esp. the Sh coll.]

409 FLEMING, John F. "The Rosenbach-Bodmer Shakespeare Folios and Quartos." *SQ*, 3 (1952): 257-59.

410 FOX, Levi. "The Heritage of Shakespeare's Birthplace." *ShS 1* (1948), pp. 79-88.

411 FRANCIS, Frank C. "The Shakespeare Collection in the British Museum." *ShS 3* (1950), pp. 43-57.

412 HANSON, Lawrence W. "The Shakespeare Collection in the Bodleian Library, Oxford." *ShS 4* (1951), pp. 78-96.

413 HUBBARD, James M. *Catalogue of the Works of William Shakespeare Original and Translated Together with the Shakespeariana Embraced in the Barton Collection in the Boston Public Library.* Boston: by the Trustees, 1880.

414 McMANAWAY, James G. "The Folger Shakespeare Library." *ShS 1* (1948), pp. 57-78. [Esp. the Sh coll.]

415   PATRICK, F. J.   "The Birmingham Shakespeare Memorial Library."
        ShS 7 (1954), pp. 90-94.

416   Rosenbach Company, Philadelphia. *William Shakespeare: A Collec-
        tion of First and Early Editions of His Works, 1594 to 1700.*
        Philadelphia: Rosenbach, 1951. [Acquired in 1951-52 by Dr. Martin
        Bodmer. See John Hayward, "The Rosenbach-Bodmer Shakespeare
        Collection." *BC*, 1 (1952): 112-16, and Georges A. Bonnard, "Shake-
        speare in the Bibliotheca Bodmeriana." *ShS* 9 (1956), pp. 81-85.]

417   *The Shakespeare Folios in the Cornell University Library Given by
        William G. Mennen.*   Cornell U. Library Association, 1954.

418   SMITH, Robert M.   *The Shakespeare Folios*   [in the Lehigh U. Li-
        brary] . . . *with a List of Original Folios in American Libraries.*
        Lehigh U., 1927.

419   SPARKS, Glenn.   *The William Luther Lewis Collection of English
        and American Literature Located at Texas Christian University.*
        Texas Christian U., 1955.   [Incl. 12 Sh quartos, F2-4, and complete
        vol. of 1619 quartos; on loan from Amon G. Carter Foundation.]

420   WILKINSON, Cyril H.   *A Handlist of English Plays and Masques
        Printed before 1750 in the Library of Worcester College, Oxford.*
        Oxford U.P.: for the Provost and Fellows of Worcester College, 1929.

Biography

LIFE

See also **137**, **2345**, and **3600**.

421 ADAMS, Joseph Q. *A Life of William Shakespeare*. Boston and New York: Houghton Mifflin, 1923.

422 ALDEN, Raymond M. *Shakespeare*. New York: Duffield, 1922. Repr. New York: AMS. [Incl. text of *Son*.]

423 Canceled.

424 ALEXANDER, Peter. *Shakespeare*. Oxford U.P., 1964.

425 —. *A Shakespeare Primer*. London: Nisbet, 1951.

426 —. *Shakespeare's Life and Art*. London: Nisbet, 1939. [NYU.]

427 BAGEHOT, Walter. *Shakespeare the Man*. New York: McClure, Phillips, 1901. Repr. in Bagehot, *Collected Works*. Ed. Norman St. John-Stevens. Vol. 1. Harvard U.P., 1965.

428 BAKER, Oliver. *In Shakespeare's Warwickshire and the Unknown Years*. London: Simpkin Marshall, 1937.

429 BEECHING, Henry C. *The Character of Shakespeare*. Oxford U.P., 1917. [*PBA 1917-18*, 8 (1918): 157-79.]

430 BENTLEY, Gerald E. *Shakespeare: A Biographical Handbook*. Yale Shakespeare Supplement. Yale U.P., 1961.

431 BRADLEY, Andrew C. "Shakespeare the Man." In *Oxford Lectures on Poetry*, **2883**.

432 BRANDES, Georg M. C. *William Shakespeare*. Trans. William Archer et al. London: Heinemann, 1898.

433 BROOKE, C. F. Tucker. *Shakespeare of Stratford*. Yale U.P., 1926. [Reprints documents.]

434 BROWN, Ivor. *Shakespeare: A Biography and an Interpretation*. London: Collins, 1949.

435 BULLOUGH, Geoffrey. *Shakespeare the Elizabethan*. Oxford U.P., 1964. [*PBA 1964*, 50 (1965): 121-41.]

436 CHAMBERS, Edmund K. *Sources for a Biography of Shakespeare*. Oxford U.P., 1946.

437 —. *William Shakespeare: A Study of Facts and Problems*. 2 vols. Oxford U.P., 1930. Repr. 1951. For Index, see **100**.

438   —. "William Shakespeare: An Epilogue." *RES*, 16 (1940): 385-401.

439   CHUTE, Marchette. *Shakespeare of London.* New York: Dutton, 1949.

440   DAWSON, Giles E. *The Life of William Shakespeare.* Washington, D.C.: Folger Shakespeare Library, 1958. Repr. in *Life and Letters*, **3958**.

441   DeGROOT, John H. *The Shakespeares and "The Old Faith."* New York: King's Crown, 1946.

442   ECCLES, Mark. *Shakespeare in Warwickshire.* U. of Wisconsin P., 1961.

443   EVERETT, A. L. "Shakspere in 1596." *SAB*, 14 (1939): 144-57. [Hunsdon's Men at Faversham.]

444   FLEMING, John F. "A Book from Shakespeare's Library Discovered by William Van Lennep." *SQ*, 15.2 (1964): 25-27, plates. Also in *Shakespeare 400*, **2793**. [*Songes and Sonnettes*, 1557.]

445   FOWLER, Elaine W. "The Earl of Bedford's 'Best' Bed." *SQ*, 18 (1967): 80. [Bequeathed to his youngest daughter, not to his widow.]

446   FOX, Levi. "An Early Copy of Shakespeare's Will." *ShS 4* (1951), pp. 69-77.

447   FRENCH, George R. *Shakespeareana Genealogica.* London: Macmillan, 1869. [Pt. 2, tables of descent of the Sh and Arden families.]

448   FRIPP, Edgar I., ed. *Minutes and Accounts of the Corporation of Stratford-upon-Avon and Other Records, 1533-1620.* Publications of the Dugdale Society, 1, 3, 5, 10. Oxford U.P. for the Dugdale Society, 1921, 1924, 1926, 1929.

449   —. *Shakespeare, Man and Artist.* 2 vols. Oxford U.P., 1938. Repr. 1964.

450   —. *Shakespeare Studies, Biographical and Literary.* Oxford U.P., 1930.

451   FRYE, Roland M. *Shakespeare's Life and Times: A Pictorial Record.* Princeton U.P., 1967.

452   GRAY, Joseph W. *Shakespeare's Marriage, His Departure from Stratford, and Other Incidents in His Life.* London: Chapman and Hall, 1905. Repr. New York: AMS.

453   Great Britain. Public Record Office. *Shakespeare in the Public Records.* Handbook 5. London: H. M. Stationery Office, [1964].

454   HALLIDAY, Frank E. *Life of Shakespeare.* London: Gerald Duckworth, 1961.

455   —. *Shakespeare: A Pictorial Biography.* London: Thames & Hudson, 1956.

456 HALLIWELL-PHILLIPPS, James O. *Outlines of the Life of Shakespeare.* 2 vols. 10th ed. London: Longmans, Green, 1898. Repr. of 1907 ed., New York: AMS.

457 HAMER, Douglas. "Was William Shakespeare William Shakeshafte?" *RES,* 21 (1970): 41-48.

458 HANLEY, Hugh A. "Shakespeare's Family in Stratford Records." *TLS,* 21 May 1964, p. 441. [Judith Shakespeare's marriage.]

459 HARRIS, Frank. *The Man Shakespeare and His Tragic Life-Story.* 2nd rev. ed. London: Palmer, 1911. [Horizon.]

460 HOTSON, Leslie. *I, William Shakespeare, Do Appoint Thomas Russell, Esquire.* London: Cape, 1937; New York: Oxford U.P., 1938.

461 —. *Shakespeare versus Shallow.* Boston: Little, Brown, 1931. [William Wayte petitions sureties of the peace against William Shakespeare, Francis Langley, et al., 1596.]

462 HUBLER, Edward L. "The Sunken Aesthete." *EIE 1950* (1951), pp. 32-56. [Writing biography.]

463 ISAACS, Jacob. "Shakespeare as a Man of the Theatre." In *A Series of Papers on Shakespeare and the Theatre,* **4133.**

464 —. *Shakespeare's Earliest Years in the Theatre.* Oxford U.P., 1953. [*PBA 1953,* 39 (1954): 119-38.]

465 KEEN, Alan, and Roger Lubbock. *The Annotator: The Pursuit of an Elizabethan Reader of Halle's Chronicle, Involving Some Surmises about the Early Life of William Shakespeare.* London: Putnam, 1954.

466 KITTREDGE, George L. "The Man Shakespeare." *SAB,* 11 (1936): 171-74. [The *opera* cannot be read as autobiography.]

467 LAW, Ernest. *Shakespeare as a Groom of the Chamber.* London: G. Bell, 1910.

468 LEE, Sidney. *A Life of William Shakespeare.* London: Macmillan, 1898. Repr. New York: AMS. Rewritten and enl. version, 2nd ed., 1916.

469 LEWIS, B. Roland. *The Shakespeare Documents: Facsimiles, Transliterations, Translations, and Commentary.* 2 vols. Stanford U.P., 1940.

470 McMANAWAY, James G. "John Shakespeare's 'Spiritual Testament.'" *SQ,* 18 (1967): 197-205.

471 —. "The License for Shakespeare's Marriage." *MLN,* 57 (1942): 450-51, 688-89.

472 MARCHAM, Frank. *William Shakespeare and His Daughter Susannah.* London: Grafton, 1931.

473 MASSON, David. *Shakespeare Personally.* London: Smith, Elder, 1914. Repr. New York: AMS.

474   MILWARD, Peter. "Some Missing Shakespeare Letters." *SQ*, 20 (1969): 84-87.

475   MORRIS, John. "The Name of Shakspere." *JEGP*, 30 (1931): 578-80.

476   MUTSCHMANN, Heinrich, and Karl Wentersdorf. *Shakespeare and Catholicism.* New York: Sheed and Ward, 1952.

477   OSBORN, James M. "The Search for English Literary Documents." *EIE 1939* (1940), pp. 31-55.

478   PARROTT, Thomas M. *William Shakespeare: A Handbook.* New York: Scribner's, 1934. [Rev. ed., SL 42 Scrib.]

479   PENNEL, Charles A. "The Authenticity of the *George a Greene* Title-Page Inscriptions." *JEGP*, 64 (1965): 668-76.

480   REESE, Max M. *Shakespeare: His World and His Work.* London: Arnold, 1953.

481   RIBNER, Irving. *William Shakespeare: An Introduction to His Life, Times, and Theatre.* Boston: Blaisdell, 1969.

482   ROWSE, Alfred L. "The Personality of Shakespeare." *HLQ*, 27 (1963-64): 193-210.

483   ——. *William Shakespeare: A Biography.* London and New York: Macmillan, 1963.

484   SCHELLING, Felix E. *Shakespeare Biography and Other Papers Chiefly Elizabethan.* U. of Pennsylvania P., 1937. Repr. New York: Books for Libraries.

485   SCHOENBAUM, S. "The Life of Shakespeare." In *A New Companion to Shakespeare Studies,* **2800.**

486   ——. "Shakespeare and Jonson: Fact and Myth." In *Elizabethan Theatre II,* **4010.**

487   ——. *Shakespeare's Lives.* Oxford U.P., 1970.

488   "Shakespeare's Deposition in the Belott-Mountjoy Suit." Transcribed by Arthur Brown and checked by Charles J. Sisson. *ShS 3* (1950), p. 13.

489   SIMPSON, Frank. "New Place: The Only Representation of Shakespeare's House, from an Unpublished Manuscript." *ShS 5* (1952), pp. 55-57.

490   SISSON, Charles J. *The Mythical Sorrows of Shakespeare.* Oxford U.P., 1934. [*PBA 1934*, 20 (1935): 45-70.]

491   ——. *Shakespeare.* London: Longmans, Green, 1955.

492   ——. "Studies in the Life and Environment of Shakespeare since 1900." *ShS 3* (1950), pp. 1-12.

493   SMART, John S. *Shakespeare: Truth and Tradition.* London: Arnold, 1928. Repr. Oxford U.P., 1966.

494   SMITH, James C. "Scott and Shakespeare." *E&S*, 24 (1938): 114-31. [Biog.]

495 SPENCER, Hazelton. *The Art and Life of William Shakespeare.* New York: Harcourt, Brace, 1940. Repr. New York: Barnes & Noble.

496 SUTHERLAND, Raymond C. "The Grants of Arms to Shakespeare's Father." *SQ*, 14 (1963): 379-85.

497 TANNENBAUM, Samuel A. "A Neglected Shakspere Document." *SAB*, 6 (1931): 111-12. [Bailbond of John Shakespeare and Thomas Jones in the amount of £10 each, dated 19 July 1587—not in Chambers.]

498 ——. "A New Study of Shakspere's Will." *SP*, 23 (1926): 117-41.

499 THALER, Alwin. "Shakspere's Income." *SP*, 15 (1918): 82-96.

500 WALLACE, Charles W. *Shakespeare and His London Associates As Revealed by Recently Discovered Documents.* University Studies, 10. U. of Nebraska, 1910. [Belott-Mountjoy suit.] See also **488**.

501 WENDELL, Barrett. "A Fantasy concerning the Epitaph of Shakspere." In *Anniversary Papers by Colleagues and Pupils of George Lyman Kittredge.* Boston: Ginn, 1919. [Sh wrote it.]

502 WESTFALL, Alfred V. "A New American Shakespeare Allusion." *MLN*, 63 (1948): 401-3. [In *New-York Gazette*, 16-23 March 1729, a legend about young Sh from Dryden.]

503 WHELER, Robert B. *Historical and Descriptive Account of the Birth-Place of Shakespeare.* Stratford-upon-Avon, 1824. Repr. Stratford-upon-Avon, 1863; New York: AMS.

504 ——. *History and Antiquities of Stratford-upon-Avon: Comprising a Description of the Collegiate Church, the Life of Shakespeare, and Copies of Several Documents . . . Never before Printed.* Stratford-upon-Avon: J. Ward, 1806. Repr. New York: AMS.

505 *Willowbie His Avisa.* London: J. Windet, 1594. Repr. Blackburn, Eng.: for subscribers, 1880; Manchester: The Spenser Society, 1886; and New York: Franklin, 1966 (ed. Alexander B. Grosart). Repr. London: Sherratt & Hughes, 1904 (ed. Charles Hughes); London: John Lane, and New York: Dutton, 1925 (ed. George B. Harrison [Bodley Head Quartos]).

506 WILSON, J. Dover. *The Essential Shakespeare.* Cambridge U.P., 1932.

EDUCATION

See also **1383, 2980, 3804, 3921, 3937,** and **3938.**

507 BALDWIN, Thomas W. *Shakspere's Petty School.* U. of Illinois P., 1943.

508 —. *William Shakspere's Small Latine and Lesse Greeke.* U. of Illinois P., 1944.

509 FARMER, Richard. *An Essay on the Learning of Shakespeare.* Cambridge: W. Thurlbourn & J. Woodyer, 1767. Repr. New York: AMS.

510 KERMODE, J. Frank. "On Shakespeare's Learning." *BJRL*, 48 (1965): 207-26.

511 LEACH, Arthur F. *English Schools at the Reformation, 1546-8.* Westminster: Constable, 1896.

512 MIRIAM Joseph, Sr. *Shakespeare's Use of the Arts of Language.* Columbia U.P., 1947. Repr. London and New York: Hafner. Abbrev. ed., *Rhetoric in Shakespeare's Time.* New York: Harcourt, Brace, and World, 1962.

513 PLIMPTON, George A. *The Education of Shakespeare: Illustrated from the Schoolbooks in Use in His Time.* Oxford U.P., 1933.

514 PRICE, Hereward T. "Shakespeare's Classical Scholarship." *RES*, 9 (1958): 54-55. [In the Folger Shakespeare Library copy of Lambarde's *Archaionomia* (1564) is the name William Shakespeare, apparently an autograph.]

515 SCHOENBAUM, S. "Shakespeare the Ignoramus." In *The Drama of the Renaissance*, **2763.**

516 STYLES, Philip. "Stratford on Avon Grammar School." In *Victoria History of the County of Warwick,* 2, 329-41. London: Constable, 1908.

517 WATSON, Foster. *The English Grammar Schools to 1660: Their Curriculum and Practice.* Cambridge U.P., 1908.

518 WHALLEY, Peter. *An Enquiry into the Learning of Shakespeare.* London: T. Waller, 1748. Repr. New York: AMS.

519 WILLCOCK, Gladys D. "Shakespeare and Rhetoric." *E&S*, 29 (1943): 50-61.

520 WILSON, Frank P. "Shakespeare's Reading." *ShS 3* (1950), pp. 14-21.

521 WILSON, J. Dover. "Shakespeare's 'Small Latin'–How Much?" *ShS 10* (1957), pp. 12-26.

HANDWRITING

See also **239**, **500**, **503**, and **677**.

522 ADAMS, Joseph Q. "A New Signature of Shakespeare?" *BJRL*, 27 (1943): 256-59. See also **239**.

523 BYRNE, M. St. Clare. "Elizabethan Handwriting for Beginners." *RES*, 1 (1925): 198-209.

524 DAWSON, Giles E., and Laetitia Kennedy-Skipton Yeandle. *Elizabethan Handwriting, 1500-1650: A Manual.* New York: Norton, 1963. Repr. 1966.

525 GREG, Walter W., ed. *English Literary Autographs.* 3 pts. Oxford U.P., 1925-32.

526 JENKINSON, Hilary. "Elizabethan Handwritings: A Preliminary Sketch." *Library*; see **303**.

527 KNIGHT, W. Nicholas. "The Seventh Shakespeare Signature." *ShN*, 21 (1971): 25.

528 McKERROW, Ronald B. "The Capital Letters in Elizabethan Handwriting." *RES*, 3 (1927): 28-36.

529 MADAN, Falconer. "Two Lost Causes." *Library*, 9 (1918): 89-105. [The "Shakespeare" signature in Ovid's *Metamorphoses* at the Bodleian Library.]

530 MADDEN, Frederic. *Observations on an Autograph of Shakspere and the Orthography of His Name.* London: T. Rodd, 1838. Repr. New York: AMS.

531 SCHULZ, Herbert C. "The Teaching of Handwriting in Tudor and Stuart Times." *HLQ*, 6 (1942-43): 381-425.

532 SIMPSON, Richard. "Are There Any Extant MSS. in Shakespeare's Handwriting?" *N&Q*, 8 (1871): 1-3. [First attribution of part of *More* to Sh.]

533 TANNENBAUM, Samuel A. *The Handwriting of the Renaissance.* Columbia U.P., 1930. Repr. New York: Ungar.

534 ——. *Problems in Shakspere's Penmanship.* New York: Modern Language Association of America, 1921.

535 ——. "Reclaiming One of Shakspere's Signatures." *SP*, 22 (1925): 392-411, 4 plates. [In Montaigne's *Essays*.]

536 THOMPSON, E. Maunde. *Shakespeare's Handwriting.* Oxford U.P., 1916.

537 ——. "Two Pretended Autographs of Shakespeare." *Library*, 8 (1917): 193-217, 5 plates. [In Montaigne's *Essays* at the British Museum and Ovid's *Metamorphoses* at the Bodleian.]

ICONOGRAPHY

538 BOADEN, James. *An Inquiry into the Authenticity of Various Pictures and Prints . . . Offered to the Public as Portraits of Shakespeare.* London: R. Triphook, 1824. Repr. New York: AMS.

539 DAWSON, Giles E. "The Arlaud-Duchange Portrait of Shakespeare." *Library*, 16 (1935-36): 290-94, 3 plates. [See also *Library*, 18 (1937-38): 342-44.]

540 ESDAILE, Katharine. "Some Fellow-Citizens of Shakespeare in Southwark." *E&S*, 5 (1952): 26-31. [Gerard Jannssen and the Stratford bust.]

541 FOX, Levi. "The Soest Portrait of Shakespeare." *ShS 15* (1962), p. 130 and plate.

542 GREENWOOD, George. *The Stratford Bust and the Droeshout Engraving.* London: Palmer, 1925.

543 HYDE, Mary C. "Shakespeare's Head." *SQ*, 16 (1965): 139-43 and plate. [Tonson's shop sign?]

544 McMANAWAY, James G. "The First American Engraving of Shakespeare." *SQ*, 12 (1961): 157-58, 1 plate. [In the *Columbian Magazine*, July 1787.]

545 MARDER, Louis. "The Stratford Bust: A New Authenticated Copy." *N&Q*, 212 (1967): 132-34. [See also p. 260.]

546 NEVINSON, John L. "Shakespeare's Dress in His Portraits." *SQ*, 18 (1967): 101-6, 6 plates.

547 NORRIS, J. Parker. *The Portraits of Shakespeare.* Philadelphia: R. M. Lindsay, 1885.

548 PIPER, David. *"O Sweet Mr. Shakespeare, I'll Have His Picture": The Changing Image of Shakespeare's Person, 1600-1800.* London: National Portrait Gallery, 1964.

549 POHL, Frederick J. "The Death-Mask." *SQ,* 12 (1961): 115-26.

550 ROE, F. G. "Elizabeth Barnard: A Shakespearian Problem Restated." *N&Q*, 15 (1968): 125-27.

551 SPIELMANN, Marion H. *The Title-Page of the First Folio of Shakespeare's Plays: A Comparative Study of the Droeshout Portrait and the Stratford Monument.* Oxford U.P., 1924. Incl. as "Shakespeare's Portraiture" in *Studies in the First Folio*, **705.**

552 STRONG, Roy. *Tudor and Jacobean Portraits.* 2 vols. London: H. M. Stationery Office, 1970. [Nine portraits of Sh.]

553 WIVELL, Abraham. *An Inquiry into the History, Authenticity, and Characteristics of the Shakspeare Portraits . . . Together with an Exposé of the Spurious Pictures and Prints.* London: the author, 1827. [In the same year, Wivell issued *A Supplement to an Inquiry*. Repr. New York: AMS.]

CIRCLE

See also **460, 461, 1935,** and **2345.**

554 AKRIGG, George P. V. *Shakespeare and the Earl of Southampton.* Harvard U.P., 1968.

555 CARMEL, Sr. Jean. "New Light on Robert Johnson, the King's Musician." *SQ*, 16 (1965): 233-35.

556 COLLIER, John P. *Memoirs of Edward Alleyn Founder of Dulwich College.* London: for the Shakespeare Society, 1841. Repr. Nendeln, Liechtenstein: Kraus-Thomson.

557 —. *Memoirs of the Principal Actors in the Plays of Shakespeare.* London: for the Shakespeare Society, 1846. Repr. Nendeln, Liechtenstein: Kraus-Thomson.

558 FRIPP, Edgar I. *Master Richard Quyny, Bailiff of Stratford-upon-Avon and Friend of William Shakespeare.* Oxford U.P., 1924.

559 KIRWOOD, Albert E. M. "Richard Field, Printer, 1589-1624." *Library*, 12 (1931-32): 1-39. [*Ven, Luc.*]

560 MASON, Alexandra. "The Social Status of Theatrical People." *SQ*, 18 (1967): 429-30. [In 1630 Cuthbert Burbage declined the offer of knighthood.]

561 MITCHELL, C. Martin. *The Shakespeare Circle: A Life of Dr. John Hall, Shakespeare's Son-in-Law.* Birmingham: Cornish, 1947.

562 NOSWORTHY, James M. "A Note on John Heminge." *Library*, 3 (1948-49): 287-88. [Tradition of acting with Sh.]

563 SISSON, Charles J. "Shakespeare's Friends: Hathaways and Burmans at Shottery." *ShS 12* (1959), pp. 95-106.

564 TAYLOR, Rupert. "Shakespeare's Cousin, Thomas Greene, and His Kin: Possible Light on the Shakespeare Family Background." *PMLA*, 60 (1945): 81-94.

565 WHITFIELD, Christopher. "Anthony and John Nash; Shakespeare's Legatees." *N&Q*, 212 (1967): 123-30.

566 —. "Four Town Clerks of Stratford on Avon, 1603-1625." *N&Q*, 209 (1964): 251-61.

567 —. "Some of Shakespeare's Contemporaries at the Middle Temple." *N&Q*, 211 (1966): 122-25, 283-87, 363-69, 443-48.

568 —. "Thomas Greene, Shakespeare's Cousin: A Biographical Sketch." *N&Q*, 209 (1964): 442-55. [See also *N&Q*, 210 (1965): 109.]

569 WILLIAMS, Franklin B. "Spenser, Shakespeare, and Zachary Jones." *SQ*, 19 (1968): 205-12.

Works

CANON

This section includes attribution, questions of authenticity, and apocrypha. See also *Cardenio, Cym, Edw3, H6, H8, Jn, Lr, Mac, More, PP, Per, Shr, Tim, Tit, Tmp, TNK.*

570 ASHLEY, Leonard R. N. *Authorship and Evidence.* Geneva: Droz, 1968. [Peele.]

571 BROOKE, C. F. Tucker, ed. *The Shakespeare Apocrypha.* Oxford U.P., 1918. Repr., 1967.

572 ERDMAN, David V., and Ephim G. Fogel, eds. *Evidence for Authorship: Essays on Problems of Attribution with an Annotated Bibliography of Selected Readings.* Cornell U.P., 1966. [*1, 2, 3 H6, Tit, Shr, H8, Edw3, More, Per, TNK.*]

573 EVERITT, Ephraim B. *The Young Shakespeare: Studies in Documentary Evidence.* Anglistica, 2. Copenhagen: Rosenkilde & Bagger, 1954.

574 —, and Ray L. Armstrong, eds. *Six Early Plays Related to the Shakespeare Canon.* Anglistica, 14. Copenhagen: Rosenkilde & Bagger, 1965.

575 FARMER, John S., ed. *The First Part of the True and Honorable History of the Life of Sir John Oldcastle . . . 1600.* Tudor Facs. Texts. Amersham: Farmer, 1913. Repr. New York: AMS.

576 —, ed. *The Lamentable and True Tragedie of M. Arden of Feversham . . . 1592.* Tudor Facs. Texts. Amersham: Farmer, 1913. Repr. New York: AMS.

577 —, ed. *The Lamentable Tragedie of Locrine . . . 1595.* Tudor Facs. Texts. Amersham: Farmer, 1913. Repr. New York: AMS.

578 —, ed. *The London Prodigall . . . 1605.* Tudor Facs. Texts. Amersham: Farmer, 1913. Repr. New York: AMS.

579 —, ed. *The Puritaine; or, The Widow of Watling Street . . . 1607.* Tudor Facs. Texts. Amersham: Farmer, 1913. Repr. New York: AMS.

580 —, ed. *The True Chronicle Historie of the Whole Life and Death of Thomas Lord Cromwell . . . 1602.* Tudor Facs. Texts. Amersham: Farmer, 1913. Repr. New York: AMS.

581 —, ed. *A Yorkshire Tragedy . . . 1608*. Tudor Facs. Texts. Amersham: Farmer, 1913. Repr. New York: AMS.

582 GREG, Walter W. "Author Lists." In *Bibliography*, **37**, 3:1304-62.

583 —. "The Date of the Earliest Play-Catalogues." *Library*, 2 (1947-48): 190-91. [See also Greg, "Authorship Attributions in the Early Play-Lists, 1656-1671." *Trans. Edinburgh Bibliog. Soc.*, 2 (1946): 303-29.]

584 —. "Shakespeare and *Arden of Feversham.*" *RES*, 21 (1945): 134-36.

585 HOPKINSON, Arthur F., ed. *The First Part of Sir John Oldcastle*. London: M. E. Sims [pseud.], 1899.

586 —, ed. *The Puritan; or, The Widow of Watling Street*. London: M. E. Sims [pseud.], 1894.

587 —. *Shakespeare's Doubtful Plays*. London: M. E. Sims [pseud.], 1900.

588 HUNTER, George K. *John Lyly: The Humanist as Courtier*. London: Routledge & Kegan Paul, 1962. [Authorship of songs in Lyly's plays.]

589 LEECH, Clifford. *The John Fletcher Plays*. Harvard U.P., 1962. [*H8, TNK.*]

590 MACARTHUR, John R., ed. *The First Part of Sir John Oldcastle*. Chicago: Scott, Foresman, 1907.

591 MacDONALD, Hugh, and D. Nichol Smith, eds. *Arden of Feversham*. Oxford U.P. for the Malone Society, 1947.

592 McKERROW, Ronald B., ed. *The Tragedy of Locrine, 1595*. Oxford U.P. for the Malone Society, 1908.

593 MAXWELL, Baldwin. "Conjectures on *The London Prodigal.*" In *Studies in Honor of T. W. Baldwin*, **2760**.

594 —. *Studies in the Shakespeare Apochrypha*. New York: King's Crown, 1956.

595 MAXWELL, James C. "Peele and Shakespeare: A Stylometric Test." *JEGP*, 49 (1950): 557-61.

596 MUIR, Kenneth. *Shakespeare as Collaborator*. London: Methuen, 1960. [*Edw3, Per, TNK, Cardenio.*]

597 PITCHER, Seymour M. *The Case for Shakespeare's Authorship of The Famous Victories*. University Publishers for the State of New York, 1961. [Reprints *The Famous Victories of Henry the Fifth*.]

598 PRIOR, Moody E. "Imagery as a Test of Authorship." *SQ*, 6 (1955): 381-86.

599 ROBERTSON, John M. *The Shakespeare Canon*. 5 vols. London: Routledge, 1922-32.

600   SCHOENBAUM, S. *Internal Evidence and Elizabethan Dramatic Authorship.* Northwestern U.P.; London: Arnold, 1966. [See also Thomas Clayton, "Review Article." *ShakS 4 1968* (1969), pp. 350-76.]

601   SHAPIRO, I. A. "Shakespeare and Mundy." *ShS 14* (1961), pp. 25-33. [Do scenarios by Munday lie behind *Famous Victories, Troublesome Raigne, Leir, A Shrew*?]

602   SIMPSON, Percy, ed. *The Life of Sir John Oldcastle, 1600.* London: C. Whittingham for the Malone Society, 1908.

603   STEVENSON, Warren. "Shakespeare's Hand in *The Spanish Tragedy,* 1602." *SEL,* 8 (1968): 307-21.

604   SYKES, Henry D. *The Authorship of* The Taming of a Shrew, The Famous Victories of Henry V, *and the Additions to Marlowe's* Faustus. Oxford U.P., 1935.

605   TAYLOR, George C. "Did Shakespeare, Actor, Improvise in *Every Man in His Humour?*" In *Adams Memorial Studies*, **2794**.

CHRONOLOGY

With the possible exception of *Luc*, the date of composition of every title in the canon is more or less controversial. In addition to the general discussions listed here, see also **437** and **4288**.

606   BARROLL, J. Leeds. "The Chronology of Shakespeare's Jacobean Plays and the Dating of *Ant*." In *Essays on Shakespeare*, **2813**.

607   FURNIVALL, Frederick J. *The Succession of Shakspere's Works and the Use of Metrical Tests in Settling It*. London: Smith, Elder, 1874. Repr. New York: AMS. [Appeared as Introd. to Georg G. Gervinus, *Shakespeare Commentaries*, trans. Fanny E. Bunnètt.]

608   GRAY, Henry D. "Chronology of Shakespeare's Plays." *MLN*, 46 (1931): 147-50.

609   LAW, Robert A. "Shakespeare's Earliest Plays." *SP*, 28 (1931): 631-38.

610   McMANAWAY, James G. "Recent Studies in Shakespeare's Chronology." *ShS 3* (1950), pp. 22-33.

611   MINCOFF, Marco. "The Chronology of Shakespeare's Early Works." *SJ* (East), 100/101 (1965): 253-65.

612   WENTERSDORF, Karl. "Shakespeare Chronology and the Metrical Tests." In *Shakespeare-Studien . . . für Heinrich Mutschmann*, **2778**.

COLLECTED EDITIONS

Editions of great historical importance published before 1930 are included, and also widely used modern editions.

613   ALEXANDER, Peter, ed. *Complete Works.* London and Glasgow: Collins, 1951; New York: Random House, 1952.

614   BARNET, Sylvan, gen. ed. *Complete Signet Classic Shakespeare.* New York: Harcourt Brace Jovanovich, 1972. [1 vol. ed. of 40 vols. issued in paperback (C.D. 160, etc.), 1963-68, with various editors.]

615   *Bell's Edition of Shakespeare's Plays, As They Are Now Performed at the Theatres Royal in London, Regulated from the Prompt Books of Each House.* With Notes . . . by [Francis Gentleman] . 9 vols. London: John Bell, 1773-74. Repr. London: Cornmarket. [Also includes Poems.]

616   BOSWELL, James. *Plays and Poems: . . . A Life of the Poet and an Enlarged History of the Stage by the Late Edmund Malone.* 21 vols. London: F. C. & J. Rivington, 1821. Repr. New York: AMS.

617   CAMPBELL, Oscar J., ed. *The Living Shakespeare: Twenty-two Plays and the Son.* New York: Macmillan, 1949.

618   —, ed. *The Son, Songs, and Poems of Shakespeare.* New York: Schocken, 1964.

619   CAPELL, Edward. *Mr. William Shakespeare: His Comedies, Histories, and Tragedies.* 10 vols. London: J. & R. Tonson, 1767-68. Repr. New York: AMS. [The holograph manuscript is in Trinity College, Cambridge, Library.]

620   CLARK, William G., and W. Aldis Wright, eds. *The Works.* Globe. London: Macmillan, 1864. Repr. New York: AMS. [Glossary incl. in 1873 repr.; New Glossary in 1891 repr.]

621   —, and John Glover [and W. Aldis Wright] , eds. *The Works.* Cambridge. 9 vols. London: Macmillan, 1863-66. Rev. ed., 1891-95; repr. New York: AMS. [George R. French, *Shakespeare Genealogica* was added in 1869 to some sets.]

622   CRAIG, Hardin, ed. *Complete Works.* Chicago: Scott, Foresman, 1961.

623   CRAIG, William J., ed. *The Complete Works.* Oxford. London: H. Frowde, 1892. Often repr.; ed. of 1904 repr. New York: AMS.

624   — (1899-1904), Robert H. Case (1909-44), Una Ellis-Fermor (1944-58), Harold F. Brooks and Harold Jenkins (1959–), gen. eds. *The Works.* Arden. 39 vols. London: Methuen, 1899–. [Individual editors for each title. Rev. eds. began in 1944, some of which have been further rev.]

625   *Dramatic Works . . . Johnson's Preface and Notes.* 16 nos. = 8 vols. 2nd American ed. Boston: Munroe & Francis, 1802-4. Repr. 1807, 1810-12. [The Poems were added in the 1807 ed., making 18 nos.]

626 FARJEON, Herbert, ed. *The Works.* 7 vols. London: Nonesuch; New York: Random House, 1929-33. Repr. in 4 vols., 1953.

627 FURNESS, Horace H. (1871-1907), H. H. Furness, Jr. (1908-31), eds.; Joseph Q. Adams (1932-48), Hyder E. Rollins (1949-54), James G. McManaway (1954–), gen. eds. *A New Variorum Edition of Shakespeare.* Philadelphia: Lippincott, 1871-1928; New York: Modern Language Association, 1929–. First 14 titles (1871-1912) repr. New York: American Scholar. [Dover.]

628 FURNIVALL, Frederick J., and Walter G. Boswell-Stone, eds. *The Old-Spelling Shakespeare.* Shakespeare Library. London: Chatto & Windus; New York: Duffield, 1908-9. [40 vols. announced; 13 traced. *LLL* is the remaindered sheets, with new title page and page of corrections, of an edition printed for Furnivall in 1904 by Alexander Moring.]

629 HALLIWELL-PHILLIPPS, James O., ed. *Works.* 16 vols. London: for the ed. by C. & J. Allard, 1853-65. [Extensive background information; 142 plates.]

630 HANMER, Thomas, ed. *Works.* 6 vols. Oxford U.P., 1744-46. Repr. New York: AMS.

631 HARBAGE, Alfred, gen. ed. *The Complete Works.* Pelican. Baltimore: Penguin Books, 1969. [Rev. ed. in 1 vol. of 38 titles issued in paperback (AB 1-38), 1956-67, each with separate editor.]

632 HARRISON, George B., ed. *Complete Works.* New York: Harcourt, Brace, 1952.

633 JOHNSON, Samuel, ed. *Plays.* 8 vols. London: J. & R. Tonson, 1765. Repr. New York: AMS.

634 KITTREDGE, George L., ed. *Complete Works.* Boston: Ginn, *ca.* 1936. Rev. ed., Waltham, Mass.: Ginn, 1971 (ed. Irving Ribner). [1 vol. ed. of single plays issued in paper (Blaisdell), 1965–.]

635 —, ed. *Sixteen Plays of Shakespeare.* Preface and annotation by Arthur C. Sprague. Boston: Ginn, 1946.

636 KÖKERITZ, Helge, and Charles T. Prouty, gen. eds. *Yale Shakespeare.* Yale U.P., 1957–. [Supersedes the old Yale ed., Wilbur L. Cross, C. F. Tucker Brooke, and Willard H. Durham, gen. eds., 50 vols., 1917-27.]

637 MALONE, Edmond, ed. *Plays and Poems.* 10 vols. London: J. Rivington & Son, 1790. Repr. New York: AMS.

638 —, ed. *Supplement to the Edition of . . . 1778.* London: C. Bathurst, 1780.

639 MUNRO, John, ed. *The London Shakespeare.* Introd. by Glynne Wickham. 6 vols. London: Eyre & Spottiswoode; New York: Simon & Schuster, 1957.

640 NEILSON, William A., ed. *The Complete Works.* Boston: Houghton, Mifflin, 1904. Rev. ed., 1942 (with Charles J. Hill).

641   PARROTT, Thomas M., Edward L. Hubler, and R. S. Telfer, eds. *Shakespeare: 23 Plays and the Son.* Rev. ed. New York: Scribner, 1953.

642   *Plays and Poems . . . Notes by S. Johnson.* 8 vols. 1st American ed. Philadelphia: Bioren & Madan, 1795-96.

643   POPE, Alexander, ed. *Works.* 6 vols. London: J. Tonson, 1723-25. Repr. New York: AMS.

644   REED, Isaac, ed. *Plays . . . Notes by Samuel Johnson and G. Steevens.* 2nd ed., rev. 10 vols. London: C. Bathurst, 1778. [Includes Malone's attempt to fix the chronology of the plays.]

645   RIDLEY, Maurice R., ed. *The Complete Works.* New Temple. 41 vols. London: Dent; New York: Dutton, 1934-36.

646   ROWE, Nicholas, ed. *Works.* 6 vols. London: J. Tonson, 1709. Repr., incl. Charles Gildon's *Volume the Seventh* (1710), New York: AMS. ["Life" by Rowe; first illustrated edition. Incl. apocryphal plays.]

647   SISSON, Charles J., ed. *Complete Works.* London: Odhams, 1954.

648   SPENCER, Terence J. B., gen. ed. *The New Penguin Shakespeare.* Harmondsworth: Penguin, 1967–. [One play to a vol.; various eds. Paper.]

649   STEEVENS, George, ed. *Dramatic Works.* 18 parts = 9 vols. London: J. & J. Boydell, 1791-1802. [With 100 engravings. The original paintings comprised the Boydell Shakespeare Gallery.]

650   —, ed. *Twenty of the Plays of Shakespeare, Being the Whole Number Printed during His Life-time.* 4 vols. London: J. & R. Tonson, 1766. Repr. New York: AMS.

651   THEOBALD, Lewis, ed. *Works.* 7 vols. London: A. Bettesworth & C. Hitch, J. Tonson, 1733. Repr. New York: AMS.

652   WARBURTON, William, ed. *Works.* 8 vols. London: J. & P. Knapton, 1747. Repr. New York: AMS.

653   WILSON, J. Dover, and Arthur T. Quiller-Couch, eds. *The Works.* 39 vols. Cambridge U.P., 1921-66. Issued in paper, 1968–. [Assisted by several special editors. Some vols. revised.]

EDITIONS, EDITORS: COMMENTARY

See also **354** and **2959**.

654 BLACK, Matthew W., and Matthias A. Shaaber. *Shakespeare's Seventeenth-Century Editors, 1632-85*. New York: Modern Language Association of America, 1937. Repr. New York: Kraus.

655 BROWN, Arthur. *Edmond Malone and English Scholarship*. London: University College, 1964.

CAPELL, Edward. See **677**.

656 DAWSON, Giles E. "Robert Walker's Editions of Shakespeare." In *Studies in . . . Memory of Karl Julius Holzknecht*, **2762**.

657 —. "Warburton, Hanmer, and the 1745 Edition of Shakespeare." *SB*, 2 (1949-50): 35-48.

658 EASTMAN, Arthur M. "The Texts from Which Johnson Printed His Shakespeare." *JEGP*, 49 (1950): 182-91.

659 EDDY, Donald D. "Samuel Johnson's Editions of Shakespeare (1765)." *PBSA*, 56 (1962): 428-44.

660 EVANS, G. Blakemore. "The Text of Johnson's *Shakespeare* (1765)." *PQ*, 28 (1949): 425-28.

661 FARR, Henry. "Notes on Shakespeare's Printers and Publishers with Special Reference to the Poems and *Ham*." *Library*, 3 (1922-23): 225-60.

662 HART, John A. "Pope as Scholar-Editor." *SB*, 23 (1970): 45-59.

663 JACKSON, Alfred. "Rowe's Edition of Shakespeare." *Library*, 10 (1929-30): 455-73. See also **666**.

664 JONES, Richard F. *Lewis Theobald, His Contribution to English Scholarship*. Columbia U.P., 1919.

665 LOUNSBURY, Thomas R. *The Text of Shakespeare: Its History from the Publication of the Quartos and Folios down to and Including the Publication of the Editions of Pope and Theobald*. New York: Scribner's, 1906. Repr. New York: AMS. Pub. as *First Editors of Shakespeare*. London: Nutt, 1906.

666 McKERROW, Ronald B. "Rowe's Shakespeare, '1709.'" *TLS*, 8 March 1934, p. 168. [Two editions.]

667 —. *The Treatment of Shakespeare's Text by His Earlier Editors, 1709-1768*. Oxford U.P., 1933. [*PBA 1933*, 19 (1934): 89-122.] Repr. in *Studies in Shakespeare*, **2759**.

668 MONAGHAN, T. J. "Johnson's Additions to His *Shakespeare* for the Edition of 1773." *RES*, 4 (1953): 234-48. [Also surveys periodical criticism and evaluates the contributions of Steevens.]

669 NICOLL, Allardyce. "The Editors of Shakespeare from First Folio to Malone." In *Studies in the First Folio*, **705**.

670 OSBORN, James M. "Edmond Malone: Scholar-Collector." *Library*, 19 (1964): 11-37.

671 PERRIN, Noel. "The Real Bowdler." *N&Q*, 13 (1966): 141-42. [Not Thomas, but his sister, Henrietta Maria Bowdler.]

672 SCHERZER, Jane. "American Editions of Shakespeare, 1753-1866." *PMLA*, 22 (1907): 633-96.

673 SEN, Sailendra K. *Capell and Malone and Modern Critical Bibliography*. See **354**.

674 SHERBO, Arthur. *Samuel Johnson, Editor of Shakespeare*. U. of Illinois P., 1956. [See also Arthur Eastman, "In Defense of Dr. Johnson." *SQ*, 8 (1957): 493.]

675 —. "Warburton and the 1745 Shakespeare." *JEGP*, 51 (1952): 71-82.

676 SINGER, Samuel W. *The Text of Shakespeare Vindicated from the Interpretations and Corrections Advocated by John Payne Collier*. London: W. Pickering, 1853. Repr. New York: AMS.

677 TAYLOR, George C. "The Date of Edward Capell's *Notes and Various Readings to Shakespeare, Volume II*." *RES*, 5 (1929): 317-19. See **231**.

678 THEOBALD, Lewis. *Shakespeare Restored; or, A Specimen of the Many Errors As Well Committed As Unamended by Mr. Pope in His Late Edition of This Poet*. London: Francklin, 1726.

679 WALKER, Alice. *Edward Capell and His Edition of Shakespeare*. Oxford U.P., 1962. [*PBA 1960*, 46 (1961): 131-45.] Repr. in *Studies in Shakespeare*, **2759**.

680 WHEATLEY, Henry B. *Notes on the Life of J. P. Collier, with a Complete List of His Works and an Account of Such Shakespeare Documents As Are Believed to Be Spurious*. London: L. Stock, 1884.

FOLIOS: COMMENTARY

681 BALDWIN, Thomas W. *On Act and Scene Division in the Shakespere First Folio*. Southern Illinois U.P., 1965.

682 BOWERS, Fredson T. "Robert Roberts: A Printer of Shakespeare's Fourth Folio." *SQ*, 2 (1951): 241-46.

683 CRAVEN, Alan E. "Justification of Prose and Jaggard Compositor B." *ELN*, 3 (1965): 15-17.

684 DAWSON, Giles E. "A Bibliographical Problem in the First Folio of Shakespeare." *Library*, 22 (1941-42): 25-33. [*Tro.*]

685 ——. "Some Bibliographical Irregularities in the Shakespeare Fourth Folio." *SB*, 4 (1951-52): 93-103.

686 FARR, Henry. "Philip Chetwind and the Allott Copyrights." *Library*, 15 (1934-35): 129-60. [Sh Folios, pp. 130, 159-60.]

687 FLATTER, Richard. *Shakespeare's Producing Hand: A Study of His Marks of Expression to Be Found in the First Folio*. London: Heinemann, 1948.

688 ——. "Some Instances of Line-Division in the First Folio." *SJ*, 92 (1956): 184-96.

689 GREG, Walter W. "The First Folio and Its Publishers." In *Studies in the First Folio*, **705**.

690 ——. *The Shakespeare First Folio: Its Bibliographical and Textual History*. Oxford U.P., 1955.

691 HASTINGS, William T. " 'Shakespeare' Ireland's First Folio." *Colophon*, New Graphic Series, 1 (1939): 75-86.

692 HINMAN, Charlton. "Cast-off Copy for the First Folio of Shakespeare." *SQ*, 6 (1955): 259-73.

693 ——. *The Printing and Proof-reading of the First Folio of Shakespeare*. 2 vols. Oxford U.P., 1963.

694 ——. "Variant Readings in the First Folio of Shakespeare." *SQ*, 4 (1953): 279-88.

695 HORROX, Reginald. "Tables for the Identification and Collation of the Shakespeare Folios." *Book Handbook*, 1 (1947-50): 105-12, 113-28, 129-76.

696 LEE, Sidney. *A Supplement to the Reproduction in Facsimile of the First Folio Edition (1623)... Containing a Census of Extant Copies with Some Account of Their History and Condition*. Oxford U.P., 1902. See **726**. [See also Lee, *Notes and Additions to the Census* (Oxford U.P., 1906; repr. from *Library*, 7 [1906] : 113-39), and "A Survey of First Folios" in *Studies in the First Folio*, **705**.]

697 LENNAM, Trevor N. S. "Sir Edward Dering's Collection of Playbooks, 1619-1624." *SQ*, 16 (1965): 145-53, 2 illus. [Incl. 2 copies of F1(?), one of which may be the copy now in Padua.]

698 McMANAWAY, James G. "The Colophon of the Second Folio of Shakespeare." *Library*, 9 (1954): 199-200.

699 —. "A Miscalculation in the Printing of the Third Folio." *Library*, 9 (1954): 129-33.

700 MADAN, Falconer, G. M. R. Turbutt, and Strickland Gibson. *The Original Bodleian Copy of the First Folio of Shakespeare*. Oxford U.P., 1905.

701 RHODES, R. Crompton. "The First Folio and the Elizabethan Stage." In *Studies in the First Folio*, **705**.

702 —. *The Shakespeare First Folio*. Oxford U.P., 1922.

703 —. *Shakespeare's First Folio*. Oxford: Blackwell, 1923. [Actors' names in Sh texts.]

704 SECORD, Arthur W. "I. M. of the First Folio Shakespeare and Other Mabbe Problems." *JEGP*, 47 (1948): 374-81.

705 Shakespeare Association. *1623-1923: Studies in the First Folio . . . in Celebration of the First Folio Tercentenary*. Introd. by Israel Gollancz. Oxford U.P., 1924.

706 SHROEDER, John W. *The Great Folio of 1623: Shakespeare's Plays in the Printing House*. Hamden, Conn.: Shoe String P., 1956.

707 SMITH, Robert M. "Fly-Specks and Folios." *Colophon*, New Series, 1 (1935): 25-32.

708 —. *The Variant Issues of Shakespeare's Second Folio and Milton's First Published English Poem: A Bibliographical Problem*. Lehigh University Publications, 2. Lehigh U., 1928.

709 —. "Why a First Folio Shakespeare Remained in England." *RES*, 15 (1939): 257-64. [The Bodleian-Turbutt-Bodleian copy.]

710 STECK, James S. "Center Rules in Folio Printing: A New Kind of Bibliographical Evidence." *SB*, 1 (1948-49): 188-91.

711 TAYLOR, Dick. "The Earl of Montgomery and the Dedicatory Epistle of Shakespeare's First Folio." *SQ*, 10 (1959): 121-23.

712 TODD, William B. "The Issues and States of the Second Folio and Milton's Epitaph on Shakespeare." *SB*, 5 (1952-53): 81-108.

713 WALKER, Alice. *Textual Problems of the First Folio* R3, Lr, Tro, 2H4, Ham, Oth. Shakespeare Problem Series, 7. Cambridge U.P., 1953.

714 WILLOUGHBY, Edwin E. *The Printing of the First Folio of Shakespeare*. London: Bibliographical Society, 1932.

715 WILSON, Frank P. "The Jaggards and the First Folio of Shakespeare." *TLS*, 5 Nov. 1925, p. 737. [See also "The First Folio of Shakespeare." *TLS*, 12 Nov. 1925, p. 756.]

716 WILSON, J. Dover. "The Task of Heminge and Condell." In *Studies in the First Folio*, **705**.

717 WOOD, E. R. "Cancels and Corrections in *A Discovery of Errors*, 1622." *Library*, 13 (1958): 124-27. [The accuracy of Jaggard's printing.]

EDITIONS TO 1700; FOLIO FACSIMILES;
SERIES OF QUARTO FACSIMILES

The original editions (quarto and folio), meticulously described in Greg's *Bibliography* (37), are not listed. See individual titles for facsimiles of single works.

718   BARTLETT, Henrietta C. "First Editions of Shakespeare's Quartos." *Library*, 16 (1935-36): 166-72.

719   BOOTH, Lionel, ed. *Shakespeare As Put Forth in 1623.* London: Lionel Booth, 1864. [Remarkably accurate type facs. of F1.]

720   FURNIVALL, Frederick J., ed. *Shakspere-Quarto Facsimiles.* 44 vols. London: C. Praetorius [or William Griggs], 1880-89. Repr. in microfiche and opaque, Washington, D.C.: NCR Microcard Editions. [Photolithographs; vols. 1-6, 6a, 7-13, 17 by Griggs, vols. 14-16, 18-43 by Praetorius.]

721   GREG, Walter W. (1939-59), and Charlton Hinman (1959–), eds. *Shakespeare Quarto Facsimiles.* London: Shakespeare Association and Sidgwick & Jackson, 1939-52; Oxford U.P., 1957–. Rev. ed. of *Lr* and *Ham* (1604-5), 1964. [*Lr* (1608), *MV* (1600), *Wiv* (1602), *Ham* (1604-5), *Per* (1609), *Rom* (1599), *Ham* (1603), *Tro* (1609), *H5* (1600), *LLL* (1598), *The True Tragedy* (1595), *R3* (1597), *R2* (1597), *1H4* (1598).]

722   HALLIWELL PHILLIPPS, James O., ed. *A Collection of Lithographic Facsimiles of the Early Quarto Editions of the Separate Works of Shakespeare.* Lithography, Edmund W. Ashbee. 48 vols. London: n.p., 1861-71.

723   —, ed. *The Works.* London: Chatto & Windus, 1875. [Reduced facs. Comedies and Histories to middle of *1H4* from Bridgewater copy of F1 (Lee No. 86 = Folger 33); the rest from Stanton facs. See Charlton Hinman, "The 'Halliwell-Phillipps Facsimile' of the First Folio." *SQ*, 5 (1954): 395-401.]

724   HINMAN, Charlton, ed. *The First Folio of Shakespeare.* New York: Norton, 1968. [Collotype facs.]

725   KÖKERITZ, Helge, ed. *Mr. William Shakespeare's Comedies, Histories, and Tragedies: A Facsimile Edition.* Introd. Charles T. Prouty. Yale U.P., 1954. [See also Fredson T. Bowers, "The Yale Folio Facsimile and Scholarship." *MP*, 53 (1955-56): 50-57.]

726   LEE, Sidney, ed. *Shakespeares Comedies, Histories and Tragedies, Being a Reproduction in Facsimile . . . with Introduction and Census of Copies.* Oxford U.P., 1902. See also **696**. [Chatsworth copy, now in Huntington Library. See also Lee, *Notes and Additions to the Census* (Oxford U.P., 1906; repr. from *Library*, 7 [1906]: 113-39), and "A Survey of First Folios" in *Studies in the First Folio*, **705**.]

727   MORGAN, J. Appleton, gen. ed. *The Comedies, Histories, and Tragedies*. Bankside. 22 vols. New York: Shakespeare Society of New York; London: Trübner, 1888-1906. Repr. New York: AMS. [Parallel texts of all the plays printed in quarto format except *Edw3*, *TNK*, *Mac*, *JC*.]

728   RADIN, Paul, ed. *William Shakespeare: Facsimile Reproduction of First Folio 1623, Sutro Library Copy*. San Francisco: California State Library, 1940. [*TN*, *Mac*, *Ant*.]

729   SHAKESPEARE, William. *Comedies, Histories, and Tragedies Faithfully Reproduced in Facsimile from the Edition of 1623*. London: Methuen, 1910. [See John H. P. Pafford, "The Methuen Facsimile, 1910, of the First Folio, 1623." *N&Q*, 13 (1966): 126-27.]

730   —. *Comedies, Histories, and Tragedies Faithfully Reproduced in Facsimile from the Edition of 1632*. London: Methuen, 1909.

731   —. *Comedies, Histories, and Tragedies Faithfully Reproduced in Facsimile from the Edition of 1664*. London: Methuen, 1905.

732   —. *Comedies, Histories, and Tragedies Faithfully Reproduced in Facsimile from the Edition of 1685*. London: Methuen, 1904.

733   [Shakespeare Quarto Facsimiles.] *Ham* (1605), *1H4* (1599), *2H4* (1600), *H5* (1600), *Lr* (1608), *R2* (1597), *R3* (1597), *LLL* (1598), *MV* (1600), *Wiv* (1602), *MND* (1600), *Ado* (1600), *Oth* (1622), *Per* (1609), *Rom* (1599), *Tit* (1594), *Tro* (1609). London: University Microfilms, 1964. [Xerox prints, separately bound.]

734   STAUNTON, Howard, ed. *Mr. William Shakespeares Comedies, Histories, and Tragedies . . . Copied by Photo-zincography*. Southampton: Ordnance Survey Office, 1862. [Complete through *MND*. 30 copies printed. Based on Lee 75, 51, and possibly 1.]

735   —, ed. *Shakespeare: The First Collected Edition of the Dramatic Works, . . . A Reproduction in Exact Facsimile*. Lithography, R. W. Preston. London: Day, 1866. [First complete facs.; photolithographed. Said to reproduce the Ellesmere (Lee 51) and British Museum (prob. Lee 1) copies. But see Gilbert R. Redgrave (*Library*, 6 [1925-26]: 314-15), who says 866 pp. repr. from Sir Henry Dryden's copy (Lee 75).]

736   WHEATLEY, Henry B. "Post-Restoration Quartos of Shakespeare's Plays." *Library*, 4 (1913): 237-69. [Also notes on some 18th-cent. adaptations.]

737   WILLIAMS, Franklin B. "Photo-Facsimiles of *STC* Books: A Cautionary Check List." *SB*, 21 (1968): 109-30. [See also Williams, "A Sequel." *SB*, 23 (1970): 252-53.]

ADAPTATIONS

See also under individual plays, especially **943**, **1024**, **1085**, and **1700**.

738 *Acting Versions of Shakespeare's Plays from the Restoration to the Death of David Garrick: Seventy-eight Rare Texts from the Birmingham Shakespeare Library Reprinted.* 86 vols. London: Cornmarket, 1969. [Incl. Bell's ed., 1774, and, as no. 79, *Dramatic Characters*, plates showing contemporary stage costume.]

739 BRANAM, George C. *Eighteenth-Century Adaptations of Shakespearean Tragedy.* U. of California P., 1956. [Check-list, 1660-1820. Excludes shortened versions and acting texts of unaltered Sh plays.]

740 CREIZENACH, Wilhelm M. A. *Die Schauspiele der englischen Komödianten.* Berlin and Stuttgart: W. Spemann, [1889]. [Plays related to *Tit*, *TN*, *Ham*, scenario of *Lr* in Breslau in 1692.]

741 ELSON, John J., ed. *The Wits; or, Sport upon Sport.* Cornell U.P.; Oxford U.P., 1932. [Pre-Restoration drolls, incl. *Ham*, *MND*.]

742 *Engelische Comedien und Tragedien.* N.p., n.p., 1620. Repr. 1624. [*Tit*, *TGV*.] See also **764** and **768**.

743 EVANS, G. Blakemore. "The Douai Manuscript—Six Shakespearean Transcripts (1694-95)." In *Studies . . . Presented to Baldwin Maxwell*, **2824**.

744 MERCHANT, W. Moelwyn. "Shakespeare 'Made Fit.'" *Restoration Theatre.* Stratford-upon-Avon Studies, 6. London: Arnold, 1965.

745 MORGAN, J. Appleton, and Willis Vickery, eds. *The Plays of Mr. William Shakespeare as Re-written or Re-arranged by His Successors of the Restoration Period . . . with the First Folio.* Bankside Shakespeare. 5 vols. New York: Shakespeare Society of New York, 1907-8. [*Tim*, *Tmp*, *Ham*, *MM*, *Ant*.]

746 NICOLL, Allardyce. *Dryden as an Adapter of Shakespeare.* Oxford U.P., 1922.

747 POLLARD, Alfred W. "The Improvers of Shakespeare." *Library*, 7 (1916): 265-90.

748 SHARP, Robert F. "Travesties of Shakespeare's Plays." *Library*, 1 (1920-21): 1-20. [See also W. Davenport Adams, *A Book of Burlesque* (London, 1891), chap. 6, "Burlesque of Shakespeare."]

749 SISSON, Charles J. *Shakespeare in India: Popular Adaptations on the Bombay Stage.* Oxford U.P., 1926.

750 SPENCER, Christopher, ed. *Five Restoration Adaptations of Shakespeare.* U. of Illinois P., 1965.

751 SPENCER, Hazelton. *Shakespeare Improved.* Harvard U.P., 1927. Repr. New York: Ungar.

752 SUMMERS, Montague, ed. *Shakespeare Adaptations:* Tmp, The Mock Tempest, *and* Lr. London: J. Cape, 1922. Repr. New York: Blom.

753 WELLS, Stanley. "Shakespearian Burlesques." *SQ*, 16 (1965): 49-61.

PROMPTBOOKS

See also under individual plays, especially **895, 1100, 1134, 1172, 1186, 1423, 1912, 1916, 2204, 2250, 4210, 4254, 4255,** and **4260.**

754 BALD, R. Cecil. "Shakespeare on the Stage in Restoration Dublin." *PMLA*, 56 (1941): 369-78. [Surviving promptbooks extracted from F3.]

755 CASSON, Leslie F. "Notes on a Shakespearean First Folio in Padua." *MLN*, 51 (1936): 417-23.

756 EVANS, G. Blakemore. "New Evidence on the Provenence of the Padua Prompt-Books of Shakespeare's *Mac, MM,* and *WT.*" *SB,* 20 (1967): 239-42.

757 —, ed. *Shakespeare Promptbooks of the Seventeenth Century.* Charlottesville: Bibliographical Society of the U. of Virginia, 1960—. [Vol. 1, pts. 1 and 2, *Mac*; vol. 2, pts. 1 and 2, *MM, WT*; vol. 3, pts. 1 and 2, *Err, MND*; vol. 4, pts. 1 and 2, *Ham.* Facs. and text.]

758 FLOOD, William H. G. "Early Shakespearian Representations in Dublin." *RES,* 2 (1926): 92-95. [15 plays between 1622-1740.]

759 McMANAWAY, James G. "Additional Prompt-Books of Shakespeare from the Smock Alley Theatre." *MLR*, 45 (1949): 64-65.

760 SHATTUCK, Charles H. *The Shakespeare Promptbooks: A Descriptive Catalogue.* U. of Illinois P., 1965. [See also Shattuck, "The Shakespeare Promptbooks: First Supplement." *TN,* 24 (1969): 5-17.]

761 VAN LENNEP, William. "The Smock Alley Players of Dublin." *ELH*, 13 (1946): 216-22.

TRANSLATIONS

A few French and German translations are listed. A very rich collection of translations is in the Shakespeare Library of the Birmingham, Eng., Reference Library. See also **1192** and **2550**.

762   BONNEFOY, Yves. "Comment traduire Shakespeare." In *EA*, 17, **2776**.

763   BRANDL, Alois, ed. *Dramatische Werke*. Trans. August W. von Schlegel and Ludwig Tieck. 10 vols. 2nd crit. rev. ed. Leipzig: Bibliographisches Institut, n.d.

764   BRENNECKE, Ernest, and Henry Brennecke. *Shakespeare in Germany, 1590-1700*. U. of Chicago P., 1964. [Trans. from Ger. of five plays based on *Tit, MND, MV, TN, Ham*.] See also **742** and **768**.

765   BROCK-SULZER, Elisabeth. "André Gide als Übersetzer Shakespeares." In *SJ*, 92, **793**.

766   CANDIDUS, Irmentraud, and Erika Roller. "*MND* in deutscher Übersetzung von Wieland bis Flatter." In *SJ*, 92, **793**.

767   CHEN-HSIEN, Chang. "Shakespeare in China." *ShS* 6 (1953), pp. 112-16.

768   COHN, Albert. *Shakespeare in Germany in the Sixteenth and Seventeenth Centuries: An Account of English Actors in Germany and the Netherlands and of the Plays Performed by Them during the Same Period*. London: Asher, 1865. [Original texts, with trans., of *Tmp, Ado, TGV, Tit, Ham, Rom*.]

769   COLLISON-MORLEY, Lacy. *Shakespeare in Italy*. Stratford-upon-Avon: Shakespeare Head, 1916. Repr. New York: Blom.

770   DARGAN, Edwin P. "Shakespeare and Ducis." *MP*, 10 (1912-13): 137-78. [Earliest French versions of Sh.]

771   DAVRIL, Robert. "Shakespeare in French Garb." In *SJ*, 92, **793**.

772   ECKHOFF, Lorentz. "Shakespeare in Norwegian Translations." In *SJ*, 92, **793**.

773   FORT, Joseph B., ed. *Théâtre Complet*. Trans. François V. Hugo. 3 vols. Paris: Garnier, 1961-64.

774   HILTY, Hans Rudolf. "Zur Behandlung der Eigennamen in Shakespeare-Übersetzungen." In *SJ*, 92, **793**.

775   HOFFMANN, Friedrich. "Stefan Georges Übertragung der Shakespeare-*Son*." In *SJ*, 92, **793**.

776   HORN-MONVAL, Madeleine. *Les Traductions françaises de Shakespeare à l'occasion du quatrième centenaire de sa naissance, 1564-1964*. Paris: Centre National de la Recherche Scientifique, 1963.

777 HUGO, François V., trans. *Oeuvres.* Rev. and annotated by Christine and René Lalou. Paris: Cluny, 1938.

778 JOSTEN, Walter. "Schwierigkeiten der Shakespeare-Übersetzung." In *SJ*, 92, **793**.

779 KACHLER, K. G. "Weshalb immer noch die Shakespeare-Übertragungen der Romantiker vorzuziehen sind." In *SJ*, 92, **793**.

780 KORNINGER, Siegfried. "Shakespeare und seine deutschen Übersetzer." In *SJ*, 92, **793**.

781 LEVIDOVA, Inna M. *W. Shakespeare: A Bibliography of Russian Translations and Literature on Shakespeare in Russian, 1748-1962.* Ed. Mikhail P. Alekseev. Moscow: Publishing House "Kniga," 1964. [In Russian.]

782 LÜDEKE, Henry. "Gundolf, Flatter und Shakespeares *Mac.*" In *SJ*, 92, **793**.

783 MARK, Thomas R. "The First Hungarian Translation of Shakespeare." *SQ*, 9 (1958): 471-78. [*Ham* by Francis Kazinczy, 1790.]

784 ———. "The First Hungarian Translation of Shakespeare's Complete Works." *SQ*, 16 (1965): 105-15. [By Michael Vörösmarty et al., beginning in 1848. In 1845 Emilia Lemouton published the first of five plays in prose translation.]

785 MESSIAEN, Pierre, trans. *Les Comedies; Les Tragédies; Les Drames historiques et les poemes.* 3 vols. Paris, Bruges: Désclée, 1959.

786 MOLIN, Nils. "Shakespeare Translated into Swedish." In *SJ*, 92, **793**.

787 PRAGER, Leonard. "Shakespeare in Yiddish." *SQ*, 19 (1968): 149-63. [Bibliog. of trans., actors, etc.]

788 PRAZ, Mario. "Shakespeare Translations in Italy." In *SJ*, 92, **793**.

789 PURDIE, Edna. "Observations on Some Eighteenth-Century German Versions of the Witches Scenes in *Mac.*" In *SJ*, 92, **793**.

790 SCHALLER, Rudolf. "Gedanken zur Übertragung Shakespeares in unsere Sprache." In *SJ*, 92, **793**.

791 SCHWARZ, Hedwig. "Arbeit für Shakespeare durch Shakespeare-Bearbeitungen." In *SJ*, 92, **793**.

792 SHACKLETON, Robert. "Shakespeare in French Translation." *Modern Languages*, 23 (1941): 15-21. [18th cent.]

793 *SJ*, 92 (1956). [16 papers on translations and problems of translation.]

794 STRICKER, Käthe. "Deutsche Shakespeare-Übersetzungen im letzten Jarhhundert." In *SJ*, 92, **793**.

Individual Works

For bibliographical descriptions through 1700, see **27**. For other facsimiles, see **718-37**. For parallel texts, see **745**. New Variorum editions (see **627**) are listed under title. For other modern separate editions of individual plays and poems, see **614, 624, 631, 634, 636, 645, 648,** and **653**. See also Editions to 1700 (**718-37**), Adaptations (**738-53**), Promptbooks (**754-61**), and Translations (**762-94**).

ALL'S WELL THAT ENDS WELL

Commentary

See also The Comedies (**3444-3549**), The History Plays (**3550-3615**), and The Problem Plays (after **3734**); **2870, 2937, 3130, 3383, 3387, 3394, 3735, 3760, 3785,** and **4407**.

795   ADAMS, John F. "*AWW:* The Paradox of Procreation." *SQ,* 12 (1961): 261-70.

796   ARTHOS, John. "The Comedy of Generation." *EIC,* 5 (1955): 97-117.

797   BENNETT, Josephine W. "New Techniques of Comedy in *AWW.*" *SQ,* 18 (1967): 337-62.

798   BRADBROOK, Muriel C. "Virtue Is the True Nobility: A Study of the Structure of *AWW.*" *RES,* 1 (1950): 289-301.

799   CALDERWOOD, James L. "The Mingled Yarn of *AWW.*" *JEGP,* 62 (1963): 61-76.

800   —— "Styles of Knowing in *AWW.*" *MLQ,* 25 (1964): 272-94.

801   CARTER, Albert H. "In Defence of Bertram." *SQ,* 7 (1956): 21-31.

802   HALIO, Jay L. "*AWW.*" *SQ,* 15.1 (1964): 33-43.

803   HAPGOOD, Robert. "The Life of Shame: Parolles and *AWW.*" *EIC,* 15 (1965): 269-78.

804 KING, Walter N. "Shakespeare's 'Mingled Yarn.' " *MLQ*, 21 (1960): 33-44.

805 KRAPP, George P. "Parolles." In *Shaksperian Studies*, **2798**.

806 LA GUARDIA, Eric. *Nature Redeemed: The Imitation of Order in Three Renaissance Poems.* The Hague: Mouton, 1966.

807 LEECH, Clifford. "The Theme of Ambition in *AWW*." *ELH*, 21 (1954): 17-29.

808 LEGOUIS, Émile H. "La Comtesse de Roussillon." *English*, 1 (1937): 399-404.

809 NAGARAJAN, S. "The Structure of *AWW*." *EIC*, 10 (1960): 24-31.

810 PRICE, Joseph G. *The Unfortunate Comedy: A Study of* AWW *and Its Critics.* U. of Toronto P., 1969.

811 SCHOFF, Francis G. "Claudio, Bertram, and a Note on Interpretation." *SQ*, 10 (1959): 11-23.

812 TURNER, Robert Y. "Dramatic Conventions in *AWW*." *PMLA'* 75 (1960): 497-502.

813 WARREN, Roger. "Why Does It End Well? Helena, Bertram, and *Son*." In *ShS 22*, **3530**.

814 WILSON, Harold S. "Dramatic Emphasis in *AWW*." *HLQ*, 13 (1949-50): 217-40.

ANTONY AND CLEOPATRA

Editions

815   FURNESS, Horace H., ed. *Ant.* New Variorum. Philadelphia: Lippincott, 1907.

816   WILSON, J. Dover, ed. *Ant.* London: Faber & Gwyer, [1929]. [Facs. from Grenville copy of F1 in the British Museum.]

Textual Commentary

See also **745**.

817   HOSLEY, Richard. "The Staging of the Monument Scenes in *Ant.*" *Library Chronicle* (U. of Pennsylvania), 30 (1964): 62-71.

818   JENKIN, Bernard. "*Ant:* Some Suggestions on the Monument Scenes." *RES,* 21 (1945): 1-14.

819   THOMAS, Mary O. "The Repetitions in Antony's Death Scene." *SQ,* 9 (1958): 153-57.

Commentary

See also The Tragedies (**3616-3734**), The Roman Plays (after **3734**), and The Problem Plays (after **3734**); **161, 606, 728, 2803, 2834, 2871, 2887, 2902, 2972, 3035, 3082, 3108, 3137, 3177, 3293, 3294, 3326, 3354, 3684, 3694, 3735, 3744,** and **3757**.

820   BARROLL, J. Leeds. "*Ant* and Pleasure." *JEGP,* 57 (1958): 708-20.

821   —. "Shakespeare and the Art of Character: A Study of Anthony." *ShakS 5 1969* (1970), pp. 159-235.

822   BINDER, Rudolf. *Der Dramatische Rhythmus in Shakespeare's* Ant. Würzburg-Aumühle: Triltsch, 1939.

823   BLISSETT, William. "Dramatic Irony in *Ant.*" *SQ,* 18 (1967): 151-66.

824   BRADLEY, Andrew C. "*Ant.*" In *Oxford Lectures on Poetry,* **2883**.

825   BROWN, John R., ed. *Shakespeare:* Ant; *A Casebook.* London: Macmillan, 1968. [28 sel. from prev. pub. wks., 1616 to modern.]

826   BUCK, Eva. "Cleopatra, eine Charakterdeutung." *SJ,* 74 (1938): 101-22.

827   CAPUTI, Anthony. "Shakespeare's *Ant:* Tragedy without Terror." *SQ,* 16 (1965): 183-92.

828 CHARNEY, Maurice. "Shakespeare's Antony: A Study of Image Themes." *SP*, 54 (1957): 149-61.

829 COUCHMAN, Gordon W. *"Ant* and the Subjective Convention." *PMLA*, 76 (1961): 420-25.

830 CUNNINGHAM, Dolora G. "The Characterization of Shakespeare's Cleopatra." *SQ*, 6 (1955): 9-17.

831 DAICHES, David. "Imagery and Meaning in *Ant.*" *ES*, 43 (1962): 343-58.

832 DANBY, John F. *"Ant:* A Shakespearian Adjustment." In *Poets on Fortune's Hill*, **2956**.

833 ——. "The Shakespearean Dialectic." *Scrutiny*, 16 (1949): 196-213.

834 DONNO, Elizabeth S. "Cleopatra Again." *SQ*, 7 (1956): 227-33.

835 DORAN, Madeleine. " 'High Events as These': The Language of Hyperbole in *Ant.*" *QQ*, 72 (1965): 26-51.

836 FITCH, Robert E. "No Greater Crack?" *SQ*, 19 (1968): 3-17.

837 HARBAGE, Alfred [pseud. Thomas Kyd]. "Cosmic Card Game." *ASch*, 20 (1951): 325-33.

838 HOMAN, Sidney R. "Divided Response and the Imagination in *Ant.*" *PQ*, 49 (1970): 460-68.

839 JORGENSEN, Paul A. "Antony and the Protesting Soldiers: A Renaissance Tradition for the Structure of *Ant.*" In *Essays on Shakespeare*, **2813**.

840 KAULA, David. "The Time Sense of *Ant.*" *SQ*, 15.3 (1964): 211-23.

841 KIRSCHBAUM, Leo. "Shakspere's Cleopatra." *SAB*, 19 (1944): 161-71.

842 LEAVIS, Frank R. *"Ant* and *All for Love:* A Critical Exercise." *Scrutiny*, 5 (1936-37): 158-69.

843 LLOYD, Michael. "Antony and the Game of Chance." *JEGP*, 61 (1962): 548-54.

844 ——. "Cleopatra as Isis." *ShS 12* (1959), pp. 88-94.

845 ——. "The Roman Tongue." *SQ*, 10 (1959): 461-68.

846 LONG, John H. *"Ant:* A Double Critical Reversal." In *RenP 1964*, **2785**.

847 McMANAWAY, James G. "Notes on Act V of *Ant.*" *Shakespeare Studies* (Japan), 1 (1962): 1-5. Repr. in *Studies in Shakespeare, Bibliography, and Theater*, **3174**.

848 MacMULLEN, Katherine V. "Death Imagery in *Ant.*" *SQ*, 14 (1963): 399-410.

849 MARKELS, Julian. *The Pillar of the World: Ant in Shakespeare's Development.* Ohio State U.P., 1968.

850 MAXWELL, James C. "Shakespeare's Roman Plays: 1900-1956." *ShS 10* (1957), pp. 1-11.

851 MILLS, Laurens J. *The Tragedies of Shakespeare's* Ant. Indiana U.P., 1964. [Slightly modified chap. on "Cleopatra's Tragedy" repr. from *SQ*, 11 (1960): 147-62.]

852 MOORE, John R. "The Enemies of Love: The Example of Antony and Cleopatra." *KR*, 31 (1969): 646-74.

853 NANDY, Dipak. "The Realism of Antony and Cleopatra." In *Shakespeare in a Changing World*, **2792.**

854 NELSON, C. E. "*Ant* and the Triumph of Rome." *UR*, 32 (1966): 199-203.

855 NEVO, Ruth. "The Masque of Greatness." *ShakS 3 1967* (1968), pp. 111-28.

856 ORNSTEIN, Robert T. "The Ethic of the Imagination: Love and Art in *Ant.*" In *Later Shakespeare*, **2767.**

857 QUILLER-COUCH, Arthur T. "*Ant.*" In *Studies in Literature, Second Series.* Cambridge U.P., 1922.

858 ROERECKE, Edith M. "Baroque Aspects of *Ant.*" In *Essays on Shakespeare*, **2813.**

859 ROSE, Paul L. "The Politics of *Ant.*" *SQ*, 20 (1969): 379-89.

860 SEATON, Ethel. "*Ant* and the *Book of Revelation.*" *RES*, 22 (1946): 219-24.

861 SHAPIRO, Stephen A. "The Varying Shore of the World: Ambivalence in *Ant.*" *MLQ*, 27 (1966): 18-32.

862 SIMMONS, Joseph L. "The Comic Pattern and Vision in *Ant.*" *ELH*, 36 (1969): 493-510.

863 SPENCER, Benjamin T. "*Ant* and the Paradoxical Metaphor." *SQ*, 9 (1958): 373-78.

864 STEIN, Arnold. "The Image of Antony: Lyric and Tragic Imagination." *KR*, 21 (1959): 586-606.

865 STEMPEL, Daniel. "The Transmigration of the Crocodile." *SQ*, 7 (1956): 59-72.

866 STIRLING, Brents. "Cleopatra's Scene with Seleucus: Plutarch, Daniel, and Shakespeare." *SQ*, 15.2 (1964): 299-311. Also in *Shakespeare 400*, **2793.**

867 STOLL, Elmer E. "Cleopatra." *MLR*, 23 (1928): 145-63.

868 STROUP, Thomas B. "The Structure of *Ant.*" *SQ*, 15.2 (1964): 289-98. Also in *Shakespeare 400*, **2793.**

869 THOMAS, Mary O. "Cleopatra and the 'Mortal Wretch.'" *SJ*, 99 (1963): 174-83.

870 WAITH, Eugene M. "Manhood and Valor in Two Shakespearean Tragedies." *ELH*, 17 (1950): 262-73. [*Ant* and *Mac*.]

871 WILCOX, John. "Love in *Ant.*" *PMASAL,* 21 (1935): 531-44.

872 WILLIAMSON, Marilyn L. "Fortune in *Ant.*" *JEGP*, 67 (1968): 423-29.

873 ——. "Patterns of Development in *Ant.*" *TSL*, 14 (1969): 129-39.

874 WILSON, Elkin C. "Shakespeare's Enobarbus." In *Adams Memorial Studies,* 2794.

875 WIMSATT, William K. "Poetry and Morals." *Thought*, 23 (1948): 281-99. Repr. in Wimsatt, *The Verbal Icon.* U. of Kentucky P., 1954.

AS YOU LIKE IT

Editions

876   FURNESS, Horace H., ed. *AYL*. New Variorum. Philadelphia: Lippincott, 1890.

877   WILSON, J. Dover, ed. *AYL*. London: Faber & Gwyer, 1929. [Facs. from Grenville copy of F1 in the British Museum.]

Commentary

See also The Comedies (**3444-3549**) and The Romances (after **3734**); **3085, 3382, 3425**, and **4407**.

878   BABB, Lawrence. "On the Nature of Elizabethan Psychological Literature." In *Adams Memorial Studies*, **2794**.

879   BARBER, Cesar L. "The Use of Comedy in *AYL*." *PQ*, 21 (1942): 353-67.

880   BARNET, Sylvan. "'Strange Events': Improbability in *AYL*." *ShakS 4 1968* (1969), pp. 119-31.

881   BRADBY, Godfrey F. "Jacques." In *Short Studies in Shakespeare*. London: J. Murray, 1929. [Also *Son, H4, H5, R2, Mac, Ham.*]

882   CAMPBELL, Oscar J. "Jaques." *Huntington Library Bulletin*, 8 (1935): 71-102.

883   CHEW, Samuel C. "'This Strange Eventful History.'" In *Adams Memorial Studies*, **2794**.

884   DRAPER, R. P. "Shakespeare's Pastoral Comedy." *EA*, 11 (1958): 1-17.

885   FINK, Zera S. "Jaques and the Malcontent Traveler." *PQ*, 14 (1935): 237-52.

886   GARDNER, Helen. "*AYL*." In *More Talking of Shakespeare*, **2780**.

887   HALIO, Jay L. "'No Clock in the Forest': Time in *AYL*." *SEL*, 2 (1962): 197-207.

888   —, ed. *Twentieth-Century Interpretations of* AYL. Englewood Cliffs, N.J.: Prentice-Hall, 1968. [14 prev. pub. essays.]

889   JAMIESON, Michael. *Shakespeare: AYL*. London: Arnold, 1965.

890   JENKINS, Harold. "*AYL*." *ShS 8* (1955), pp. 40-51.

891   KNOWLES, Richard. "Myth and Type in *AYL*." *ELH*, 33 (1966): 1-22.

892   KREIDER, Paul V. "Genial Literary Satire in the Forest of Arden." *SAB*, 10 (1935): 212-31.

893 MINCOFF, Marco. "What Shakespeare Did to *Rosalynde*." *SJ*, 96 (1960): 78-89.

894 PALMER, D. J. "Art and Nature in *AYL*." *PQ*, 49 (1970): 30-40.

895 SHATTUCK, Charles H. *Mr. William Charles Macready Produces AYL: A Promptbook Study*. U. of Illinois P., 1962.

896 SHAW, John. "Fortune and Nature in *AYL*." *SQ*, 6 (1955): 45-50.

897 SMITH, James C. "*AYL*." *Scrutiny*, 9 (1940-41): 9-32.

898 SPENCER, Theodore. "The Elizabethan Malcontent." In *Adams Memorial Studies*, **2794**.

899 STAEBLER, Warren. "Shakespeare's Play of Atonement." *SAB*, 24 (1949): 91-105.

900 STOLL, Elmer E. "Jaques and the Antiquaries." *MLN*, 54 (1939): 79-85.

901 TOLMAN, Albert H. "Shakespeare's Manipulation of His Sources in *AYL*." *MLN*, 37 (1922): 65-76.

902 WILLIAMSON, Marilyn L. "The Masque of Hymen in *AYL*." *CompD*, 2 (1968): 248-58.

CARDENIO

Commentary

See also Canon (**570-605**); **596** and **2701**.

903   CADWALLADER, John.   "Theobald's Alleged Shakespeare Manu-
       script." *MLN*, 55 (1940): 108-9.

904   FRAZIER, Harriet C.   "Theobald's *The Double Falsehood:* A Revi-
       sion of Shakespeare's *Cardenio*?"   *CompD*, 1 (1967): 219-33.

905   FREEHAFER, John.   "*Cardenio*, by Shakespeare and Fletcher."
       PMLA, 84 (1969): 501-13.

906   MUIR, Kenneth. "*Cardenio*." *EA*, 11 (1958): 202-9. [Evidence
       inconclusive.]

THE COMEDY OF ERRORS

Commentary

See also The Comedies (**3444-3549**); **757**, **3487**, and **4407**.

907 ARTHOS, John. "Shakespeare's Transformation of Plautus." *CompD*, 1 (1967): 239-53.

908 BALDWIN, Thomas W. "*Err* and Marprelate." In *Studies in Honor of DeWitt T. Starnes*, **2784**.

909 —. *On the Compositional Genetics of* Err. U. of Illinois P., 1965.

910 —. "Three Homilies in *Err*." In *Essays . . . in Honor of Hardin Craig*, **2786**.

911 —. *William Shakespeare Adapts a Hanging*. Princeton U.P., 1931.

912 BARBER, Cesar L. "Shakespearean Comedy in *Err*." *CE*, 25 (1964): 493-97.

913 BLAND, Desmond, ed. *Gesta Grayorum; or, The History of the High and Mighty Prince Henry, Prince of Purpoole, Anno Domini 1594*. English Repr. Series No. 22. Liverpool U.P., 1968.

914 BROOKS, Harold F. "Themes and Structures in *Err*." In *Early Shakespeare*, **2766**.

915 BROWN, Basil. *Law Sports at Gray's Inn (1594)*. New York: for the author, 1921. [*Gesta Grayorum.*]

916 ELLIOTT, George R. "Weirdness in *Err*." *UTQ*, 9 (1939): 95-106.

917 FERGUSSON, Francis. "*Err* and *Ado*." *SR*, 62 (1954): 24-37. Repr. in *The Human Image in Dramatic Literature*, **3000**.

918 GILL, Erma M. "The Plot-Structure of *Err* in Relation to Its Sources." *TxSE*, No. 10 (1930), pp. 13-65.

919 GREG, Walter W., ed. *Gesta Grayorum, 1688*. Oxford U.P. for the Malone Society, 1914.

920 LANGHAM, Michael. "*Err* and *Luc*." *KR*, 26 (1964): 556-59.

921 THOMAS, Sidney. "The Date of *Err*." *SQ*, 7 (1956): 377-84.

922 WILLIAMS, Gwyn. "*Err* Rescued from Tragedy." *REL*, 5 (1964): 63-71.

CORIOLANUS

Editions

923 FURNESS, Horace H., Jr., ed. *Cor.* New Variorum. Philadelphia: Lippincott, 1928.

924 WILSON, J. Dover, ed. *Cor.*   London: Faber & Gwyer, [1928] [Facs. from Grenville copy of F1 in the British Museum.]

Commentary

See also The Tragedies (**3616-3734**) and The Roman Plays (after **3734**); **3035, 3038, 3137, 3238, 3274, 3293, 3694,** and **3951**.

925 BAUMGARTEN, Eduard. "Gemeinschaft und Gewissen in Shakespeares *Cor.*" *NS*, 43 (1935): 363-84, 413-25.

926 BOWDEN, William R. "The 'Unco Guid' and Shakespeare's *Cor.*" *SQ*, 13 (1962): 41-48.

927 BRADLEY, Andrew C. *Cor.* Oxford U.P., 1912. [*PBA 1911-12*, 5 (1913): 457-73.]   Repr. in *A Miscellany*, **2882**, and *Studies in Shakespeare*, **2759**.

928 BRITTIN, Norman A. "Coriolanus, Alceste, and Dramatic Genres." *PMLA*, 71 (1956): 799-807.

929 BROWNING, Ivor R. "Coriolanus: Boy of Tears." *EIC*, 5 (1955): 18-31.

930 BURKE, Kenneth. "*Cor*—and the Delights of Faction." *Arts in Society*, 2, no. 3 (1963). Repr. in *HudR*, 19 (1966): 185-202.

931 BYRNE, M. St. Clare. "Classical Coriolanus." *National Review*, 96 (1931): 426-30.

932 CALDERWOOD, James L. "*Cor:* Wordless Meanings and Meaningless Words." *SEL*, 6 (1966): 211-24.

933 CARR, W. I. "'Gracious Silence'—A Selective Reading of *Cor.*" *ES*, 46 (1965): 221-43.

934 CHARNEY, Maurice. "The Dramatic Use of Imagery in Shakespeare's *Cor.*" *ELH*, 23 (1956): 183-93.

935 COLMAN, E. A. M. "The End of Coriolanus." *ELH*, 34 (1967): 1-20.

936 CRAIG, Hardin. "*Cor:* Interpretation." In *Pacific Coast Studies in Shakespeare*, **2796**.

937 DEAN, Leonard F. "Voice and Deed in *Cor.*" *UR*, 21 (1955): 177-84.

938 ELLIS-FERMOR, Una. "*Cor.*" In *Shakespeare the Dramatist*, **2984**.

939 —. "Some Functions of Verbal Music in Drama." *SJ*, 90 (1954): 37-48.

940 ENRIGHT, D. J. "*Cor:* Tragedy or Debate?" *EIC*, 4 (1954): 1-19.

941 FABER, M. D. "Freud and Shakespeare's Mobs." *L&P*, 15 (1965): 238-55.

942 FRYE, Dean. "Commentary in Shakespeare: The Case of *Cor.*" *ShakS 1* (1965), pp. 105-17.

943 FURNESS, Horace H., Jr., ed. *The Ingratitude of a Common-Wealth; or, The Fall of Caius Martius Coriolanus.* By N. Tate. [Philadelphia: n.p., 1930.] [Play by Tate; omitted from New Variorum ed. and 25 copies printed.]

944 GORDON, Donald J. "Name and Fame: Shakespeare's Coriolanus." In *Papers Mainly Shakespearean*, **2775**.

945 HEUER, Hermann. "From Plutarch to Shakespeare: A Study of *Cor.*" *ShS 10* (1957), pp. 50-59.

946 —. "Shakespeare and Plutarch." *Anglia*, 62 (1938): 321-46.

947 HILL, R. F. "*Cor:* Violentest Contrariety." *E&S*, 17 (1964): 12-23.

948 HODGSON, Geraldine. "*Cor* and Shakespeare's 'Tragic Course.'" *CQR*, 117 (1934): 292-303.

949 HOFLING, Charles K. "An Interpretation of Shakespeare's *Cor.*" *AI*, 14 (1957): 407-35.

950 HONIG, Edwin. "*Sejanus* and *Cor:* A Study in Alienation." *MLQ*, 12 (1951): 407-21.

951 JORGENSEN, Paul A. "Shakespeare's Coriolanus: Elizabethan Soldier." *PMLA*, 64 (1949): 221-35.

952 KNIGHTS, Lionel C. "Shakespeare and Political Wisdom: A Note on the Personalism of *JC* and *Cor.*" *SR*, 61 (1953): 43-55.

953 LEES, F. N. "*Cor*, Aristotle, and Bacon." *RES*, 1 (1950): 114-25.

954 McCANLES, Michael. "The Dialectic of Transcendence in Shakespeare's *Cor.*" *PMLA*, 82 (1967): 44-53.

955 MAXWELL, James C. "Animal Imagery in *Cor.*" *MLR*, 42 (1947): 417-21.

956 MITCHELL, Charles. "*Cor:* Power as Honor." *ShakS 1* (1965), pp. 199-226.

957 MÜNCH, W. "Aufidius." *SJ*, 42 (1906): 127-47.

958 MUIR, Kenneth. "The Background of *Cor.*" *SQ*, 10 (1959): 137-45.

959 MURRY, John Middleton. "*Cor.*" In *Discoveries*, **3217**; repr. in *John Clare and Other Studies*, **3218**.

960 —. "A Neglected Heroine of Shakespeare." In *Countries of the Mind*, **3215**.

961 NEUMEYER, Peter F. "Ingratitude Is Monstrous: An Approach to *Cor.*" *CE*, 25 (1964): 192-98.

962 —. "Not Local Habitation nor a Name: Coriolanus." *UR*, 32 (1966): 195-98.

963 OLIVER, Harold J. "Coriolanus as Tragic Hero." *SQ*, 10 (1959): 53-60.

964 PETTET, Ernest C. "*Cor* and the Midlands Insurrection of 1607." *ShS 3* (1950), pp. 34-42.

965 PROSER, Matthew N. "*Cor:* The Constant Warrior and the State." *CE*, 24 (1963): 507-12.

966 RABKIN, Norman. "*Cor:* The Tragedy of Politics." *SQ*, 17 (1966): 195-212.

967 RIBNER, Irving. "The Tragedy of *Cor.*" *ES*, 34 (1953): 1-9.

968 ROUDA, F. H. "*Cor*–A Tragedy of Youth." *SQ*, 12 (1961): 103-6.

969 SEN, Sailendra K. "What Happens in *Cor.*" *SQ*, 9 (1958): 331-45.

970 SHANKER, Sidney. "Some Clues for *Cor.*" *SAB*, 24 (1949): 209-13.

971 STOCKHOLDER, Katherine. "The Other Coriolanus." *PMLA*, 85 (1970): 228-36.

972 TOLMAN, Albert H. "The Structure of Shakespeare's Tragedies with Special Reference to *Cor.*" *MLN*, 37 (1922): 449-58.

973 TRAVERSI, Derek A. "*Cor.*" *Scrutiny*, 6 (1937-38): 43-58.

974 WILSON, Emmett. "Coriolanus: The Anxious Bridegroom." *AI*, 25 (1968): 224-41.

975 ZEEVELD, W. Gordon. "*Cor* and Jacobean Politics." *MLR*, 57 (1962): 321-34.

CYMBELINE

Editions

976   FURNESS, Horace H., Jr., ed. *Cym.* New Variorum. Philadelphia: Lippincott, 1913.

Commentary

See also The Comedies (**3444-3549**), The Roman Plays (after **3734**), and The Romances (after **3734**); **2886**, **3035**, **3326**, **3354**, **3728**, **3760**, and **4429**.

977   BROCKBANK, J. P. "History and Histrionics in *Cym.*" *ShS 11* (1958), pp. 42-49.

978   CAMDEN, Carroll C. "The Elizabethan Imogen." *Rice Institute Pamphlet*, 38 (1951): 1-17.

979   GESNER, Carol. "*Cym* and the Greek Romances." In *Studies ... Dedicated to John Earle Uhler,* **2795**.

980   HARRIS, Bernard. "'What's Past Is Prologue': *Cym* and *H8*." In *Later Shakespeare*, **2767**.

981   HOENIGER, F. David. "Irony and Romance in *Cym.*" *SEL*, 2 (1962): 219-28.

982   HOFLING, Charles K. "Notes on Shakespeare's *Cym.*" *ShakS 1* (1965), pp. 118-36.

983   JONES, Emrys. "Stuart *Cym.*" *EIC*, 11 (1961): 84-99.

984   KIRSCH, Arthur C. "*Cym* and Coterie Dramaturgy." *ELH*, 34 (1967): 285-306.

985   MARSH, Derick R. C. *The Recurring Miracle: A Study of* Cym *and the Last Plays.* Pietermaritzburg: U. of Natal P., 1962. Repr. New York: AMS.

986   MOFFET, Robin. "*Cym* and the Nativity." *SQ*, 13 (1962): 207-18.

987   MOWAT, Barbara A. "*Cym:* Crude Dramaturgy and Aesthetic Distance." *RenP 1966* (1967), pp. 39-48.

988   NOSWORTHY, James M. "The Integrity of Shakespeare: Illustrated from *Cym.*" *ShS 8* (1955), pp. 52-56.

989   RIBNER, Irving. "Shakespeare and Legendary History: *Lr* and *Cym.*" *SQ*, 7 (1956): 47-52.

990   SHAHEEN, Naseeb. "The Use of Scripture in *Cym.*" *ShakS 4 1968* (1969), pp. 294-315.

991   SMITH, Warren D. "Cloten with Caius Lucius." *SP*, 49 (1952): 185-94.

992   STAMM, Rudolf. "George Bernard Shaw and Shakespeare's *Cym.*" In *Studies in Honor of T. W. Baldwin*, **2760**.

993   STEPHENSON, A. A. "The Significance of *Cym*." *Scrutiny*, 10 (1941-42): 329-38.

994   SWANDER, Homer D. "*Cym* and the 'Blameless Hero.'" *ELH*, 31 (1964): 259-70.

995   —. "*Cym*: Religious Idea and Dramatic Design." In *Pacific Coast Studies in Shakespeare*, **2796**.

996   THORNE, William B. "*Cym*: 'Lopp'd Branches' and the Concept of Regeneration." *SQ*, 20 (1969): 143-59.

997   TINKLER, F. C. "*Cym*." *Scrutiny*, 7 (1938-39): 5-20.

998   WILSON, Harold S. "*Philaster* and *Cym*." *EIE 1951* (1952), pp. 146-67.

999   WOODRUFF, Neal. "*Cym*." In *Shakespeare: Lectures on Five Plays*. Carnegie Series in English, 4. Pittsburgh: Carnegie Institute of Technology, 1958.

EDWARD 3

Editions

1000 COLLIER, John P., ed. *Edw3: A Historical Play.* London: Richards, 1874.

1001 FARMER, John S., ed. *Edw3 . . . 1896.* Tudor Facs. Texts. Amersham: Farmer, 1913. Repr. New York: AMS.

1002 HOPKINSON, Arthur F., ed. *Edw3.* London: M. E. Sims [pseud.], 1891. Enl. ed., 1911.

1003 SMITH, George C. M., ed. *Edw3.* Temple Dramatists. London: Dent, 1897.

1004 WARNKE, Karl, and L. Proescholdt, eds. *Edw3.* Halle: Niemeyer, 1884.

Commentary

See also Canon **(570-605)** and The History Plays **(3550-3615)**; **596, 2701,** and **3088.**

1005 GOLDING, S. R. "The Authorship of *Edw3.*" *N&Q,* 154 (1928): 313-15.

1006 JACKSON, Macdonald P. "*Edw3,* Shakespeare, and Pembroke's Men." *N&Q,* 12 (1965): 329-31.

1007 MUIR, Kenneth. "A Reconsideration of *Edw3.*" *ShS* 6 (1953), pp. 39-48.

1008 SMITH, Robert M. "*Edw3:* A Study of the Authorship of the Drama in the Light of a New Source." *JEGP,* 10 (1911): 90-104.

1009 WENTERSDORF, Karl. "The Date of *Edw3.*" *SQ,* 16 (1965): 227-31.

HAMLET

Editions

1010   ADAMS, Joseph Q., ed. *Ham.* Boston: Houghton Mifflin, 1929.

1011   CAMPBELL, Oscar J., ed. *Shakespeare's Ham: The First Quarto 1603.* Harvard U.P.,1931. [Facs. of Huntington Library copy;last page from British Museum copy.]

1012   —. *Shakespeare's* Ham:*The Second Quarto 1604.* San Marino, Calif.: Huntington Library, 1938. [Facs.]

1013   FURNESS, Horace H., ed. *Ham.* New Variorum. 2 vols. London and Philadelphia: Lippincott, 1877.

1014   HOY, Cyrus, ed. *Ham.* New York: Norton, 1963. [Text, introd., sel. from sources, sel. from criticism 18th cent. to modern.]

1015   SHAKESPEARE, William. *Ham: The Text of the First Folio, 1623; Ham: First Quarto, 1603; Ham: Second Quarto.* 3 vols. Menston, Yorks., Eng.: Scolar, 1969. [Facs.]

1016   TIMMINS, Samuel, ed. *Ham, 1603; Ham, 1604.* London: S. Low, Sons, 1860. [Parallel texts.]

1017   VIËTOR, Wilhelm, ed. *Ham: Parallel Texts of the First and Second Quartos and the First Folio.* Shakespeare Reprints, 2. Marburg: N. G. Elwert'sche Verlagsbuchhandlung, 1891. [Text of Qq 1, 2 from Griggs facs.; of F1 from Halliwell-Phillipps reduced facs.]

1018   WEINER, Albert B., ed. *William Shakespeare:* Ham, *The First Quarto 1603.* Great Neck, N.Y.: Barron, 1962.

Textual Commentary

See also **224, 297, 661,** and **713.**

1019   ALEXANDER, Peter. "The Text of *Ham.*" *RES*, 12 (1936): 385-400. [Objects to J. Dover Wilson's punctuation in his New Sh ed.]

1020   BOWERS, Fredson T. "The Printing of *Ham* Q2." *SB*, 7 (1955): 41-50. [See also Bowers, "Addendum...." *SB*, 8 (1956): 267-69.]

1021   —. "The Textual Relation of Q2 to Q1 *Ham* (I)." *SB*, 8 (1956): 39-66.

1022   DeMENT, Joseph W. "A Possible 1594 Reference to *Ham.*" *SQ*, 15 (1964): 446-47. [To a passage in *Ham* considered original with Sh.]

1023   DUTHIE, George Ian. *The "Bad" Quarto of* Ham: *A Critical Study.* Shakespeare Problem Series, 6. Cambridge U.P., 1941.

1024   GLICK, Claris. "*Ham* in the English Theatre—Acting Texts, 1676-1963." *SQ*, 20 (1969): 17-35.

1025   GRAY, Henry D. "The *Ham* First Quarto Pirate." *PQ*, 16 (1937): 394-401.

1026 HANDLEMAN, Celia, and R. Weston Babcock. "'One Part Wisdom,' and Ever Two Parts–?" *SAB*, 11 (1936): 191-225. [Q1 and F1 of *Ham* are reworkings of a two-part play.]

1027 HART, Alfred. "The Vocabulary of the First Quarto of *Ham*." *RES*, 12 (1936): 18-30. [Q1 a derivative text.]

1028 JENKINS, Harold. "Playhouse Interpolations in the Folio Text of *Ham*." *SB*, 13 (1960): 31-47.

1029 ——. "The Relation between the Second Quarto and the Folio Text of *Ham*." *SB*, 7 (1955): 69-83.

1030 KANE, Robert J. "Hamlet's Apotheosis of Man—Its Punctuation." *RES*, 14 (1938): 67-68. [The apotheosis of woman in Marston's *Malcontent* (Q 1604) is punctuated as Hamlet's is in F1.]

1031 KIRSCHBAUM, Leo. "The Sequence of Scenes in *Ham*." *MLN*, 55 (1940): 382-87.

1032 SCHÜCKING, Levin L. "The Churchyard-Scene in Shakespeare's *Ham*, V. i. An Afterthought?" *RES*, 11 (1935): 129-38.

1033 STABLER, Arthur P. "The Source of the German *Ham*." *ShakS 5 1969* (1970), pp. 97-105. [Belleforest.]

1034 SULLIVAN, Mary I. "*Ham* and Dr. Timothy Bright." *PMLA*, 41 (1926): 667-79.

1035 WALKER, Alice. "Collateral Substantive Texts (with Special Reference to *Ham*)." *SB*, 7 (1955): 51-67.

1036 ——. "The Textual Problem of *Ham:* A Reconsideration." *RES*, 2 (1951): 328-38.

1037 WILSON, J. Dover. *The Manuscripts of Shakespeare's* Ham *and the Problems of Its Transmission*. Shakespeare Problem Series, 4. 2 vols. Cambridge U.P., 1934. Repr. 1963 with foreword by George Ian Duthie.

Commentary

See also The Tragedies (3616-3734) and The Problem Plays (after 3734); 721, 733, 740, 741, 745, 757, 764, 768, 783, 881, 2832, 2870, 2876, 2879, 2971, 3003, 3006, 3024, 3035, 3038, 3043, 3085, 3106, 3142, 3173, 3177, 3201, 3230, 3247, 3248, 3284, 3354, 3370, 3383, 3387, 3420, 3757, 3807, 3951, 4207, 4280, 4407, and 4432.

1038 ALEXANDER, Peter. *Hamlet: Father and Son*. Oxford U.P., 1955.

1039 ALTICK, Richard D. "*Ham* and the Odor of Mortality." *SQ*, 5 (1954): 167-76.

1040 BABCOCK, R. Weston. *Ham: A Tragedy of Errors*. Purdue U.P., 1961.

1041   BAILEY, Helen P. Ham *in France from Voltaire to Laforgue.*
        Geneva: Droz, 1964.

1042   BAKER, Joseph E. "The Philosophy of Hamlet." In *Essays . . . in
        Honor of T. M. Parrott,* 2771.

1043   BATTENHOUSE, Roy W. "The Ghost in *Ham:* A Catholic 'Linch-
        pin'?" *SP,* 48 (1951): 161-92.

1044   —. "The Significance of Hamlet's Advice to the Players." In *The
        Drama of the Renaissance,* 2763.

1045   BENCHETTRIT, Paul. "*Ham* at the Comédie Française: 1769-1896."
        In *ShS 9,* 1174.

1046   BENNETT, Josephine W. "Characterization in Polonius' Advice to
        Laertes." *SQ,* 4 (1953): 3-9.

1047   BEVINGTON, David M., ed. *Twentieth-Century Interpretations of*
        Ham. Englewood Cliffs, N.J.: Prentice-Hall, 1968. [16 prev.pub.
        essays.]

1048   BOAS, Frederick S. "The Date of *Ham* and Gabriel Harvey's *Margi-
        nalia.*" In *Shakespeare and the Universities and Other Studies in
        Elizabethan Drama.* Oxford: Blackwell, 1923. Repr. New York:
        Blom.

1049   BOKLUND, Gunnar. "Judgment in *Ham.*" In *Essays on Shake-
        speare,* 2813.

1050   BONJOUR, Adrien. "Hamlet and the Phantom Clue." *ES,* 35
        (1954): 253-59.

1051   —. "The Question of Hamlet's Grief." *ES,* 43 (1962): 336-43.

1052   BOOTH, Stephen. "On the Value of *Ham.*" In *Reinterpretations
        of Elizabethan Drama,* 2806.

1053   BOWERS, Fredson T. "The Death of Hamlet." In *Studies . . . in
        Memory of Karl Julius Holzknecht,* 2762.

1054   —. "Dramatic Structure and Criticism: Plot in *Ham.*" *SQ,* 15.2
        (1964): 207-18. Also in *Shakespeare 400,* 2793.

1055   —. "Hamlet as Minister and Scourge." *PMLA,* 70 (1955): 740-49.

1056   BRADDY, Haldeen. *Hamlet's Wounded Name.* Texas Western Col-
        lege P., 1964.

1057   BROCK, James H. E. *The Dramatic Purpose of* Ham. Cambridge:
        Heffer, 1935.

1058   BROWN, John R., and Bernard Harris, eds. *Ham.* Stratford-upon-
        Avon Studies, 5. London: Arnold, 1963. Repr. New York: St.
        Martin's; Schocken. [10 essays, incl. A Reader's Guide.]

1059   BROWNE, E. Martin. "English Hamlets of the Twentieth Century."
        In *ShS 9,* 1174.

1060   BUNDY, Murray W. "A Record of Edwin Booth's *Ham.*" *SQ,* 2
        (1951): 99-102, 2 plates. [Journal of Charles W. Clark, 1870.]

1061 CALHOUN, Jean S. *"Ham* and the Circumference of Action." *RN,* 15 (1962): 281-98.

1062 CAMDEN, Carroll C. "On Ophelia's Madness." *SQ,* 15.2 (1964): 247-55. Also in *Shakespeare 400,* **2793.**

1063 CAMPBELL, Lily B. "Polonius: The Tyrant's Ears." In *Adams Memorial Studies,* **2794.**

1064 CHAMBERS, Edmund K. "The Date of *Ham."* In *Shakespearean Gleanings,* **2913.**

1065 CHARNEY, Maurice. *Style in* Ham. Princeton U.P., 1969.

1066 CHILDS, Herbert E. "On the Elizabethan Staging of *Ham." SQ,* 13 (1962): 463-74, 2 plates.

1067 CONKLIN, Paul. *A History of* Ham *Criticism, 1601-1821.* Oxford U.P.; New York: King's Crown, 1947. Repr. London: Routledge & Kegan Paul, 1957; New York: Humanities P.

1068 COOPERMAN, Stanley. "Shakespeare's Anti-Hero: Hamlet and the Underground Man." *ShakS 1* (1965), pp. 37-63.

1069 CRAIG, Hardin. "Hamlet as a Man of Action." *HLQ,* 27 (1963-64): 229-37.

1070 —. "Hamlet's Book." *Huntington Library Bulletin,* 6 (1934): 17-37.

1071 DESSEN, Alan C. "Hamlet's Poisoned Sword: A Study in Dramatic Imagery." *ShakS 5 1969* (1970), pp. 53-69.

1072 DETMOLD, George. "Hamlet's 'All but Blunted Purpose.'" *SAB,* 24 (1949): 23-36.

1073 DIAMOND, William. "Wilhelm Meister's Interpretation of *Ham."* *MP,* 23 (1925-26): 89-101.

1074 DORAN, Madeleine. "The Language of *Ham." HLQ,* 27 (1963-64): 259-78.

1075 DRAPER, John W. *The* Ham *of Shakespeare's Audience.* Duke U.P., 1938. Repr. New York: Octagon.

1076 ELIOT, Thomas S. "Hamlet and His Problems." In *The Sacred Wood.* London: Methuen, 1920. Repr. in *Elizabethan Essays,* **3817,** and *Selected Essays.* London: Faber & Faber, 1934.

1077 ELLIOTT, George R. *Scourge and Minister: A Study of* Ham *as Tragedy of Revengefulness and Justice.* Duke U.P., 1951. Repr. New York: AMS.

1078 EMPSON, William. *"Ham* When New." *SR,* 61 (1953): 15-42; 185-205.

1079 FALK, Doris V. "Proverbs and the Polonius Destiny." *SQ,* 18 (1967): 23-36.

1080 FERGUSSON, Francis. *"Ham:* The Analogy of Action." In *The Idea of a Theater.* Princeton U.P., 1949.

1081   FLATTER, Richard. "The Dumb-Show in *Ham*." *SQ* (London), 1 (1948): 26-49.

1082   —. *Hamlet's Father.* London: Heinemann, 1949.

1083   FOAKES, Reginald A. "*Ham* and the Court of Elsinore." In *ShS* 9, **1174.**

1084   FORKER, Charles R. "Shakespeare's Theatrical Symbolism and Its Function in *Ham*." *SQ*, 14 (1963): 215-29.

1085   FREUDENSTEIN, Reinhold. *Der bestrafte Brudermord: Shakespeares* Ham *auf der Wanderbühne des 17. Jahrhunderts.* Hamburg: Cram, de Gruyter, 1958.

1086   GARDNER, Helen. "The Historical Approach.   In *The Business of Criticism,* **3021.**

1087   GILDER, Rosamond. *John Gielgud's Hamlet.* New York: Oxford U.P.; Toronto, Methuen, 1937. [Incl. John Gielgud, "The *Ham* Tradition: Some Notes on Costume, Scenery, and Stage Business" and text of play with Gilder's description of Gielgud's performance.]

1088   GRAY, Henry D. "The Date of *Ham*." *JEGP*, 31 (1932): 51-61.

1089   GREBANIER, Bernard D. *The Heart of* Ham: *The Play Shakespeare Wrote.* New York: Crowell, 1960. [Apollo-A141.]

1090   GREEN, Andrew J. "The Cunning of the Scene." *SQ*, 4 (1953): 395-404.

1091   HALIO, Jay L. "Hamlet's Alternative." *TSLL*, 8 (1966): 169-88.

1092   HAMILTON, William. "Hamlet and Providence." *Christian Scholar*, 47 (1964): 193-207.

1093   HANKINS, John E. *The Character of Hamlet and Other Essays.* U. of North Carolina P., 1941. [8 essays on *Ham* and rel. topics.]

1094   HAPGOOD, Robert. "*Ham* Nearly Absurd: The Dramaturgy of Delay." *TDR*, 9 (1965): 132-45.

1095   HARDISON, Osborne B. "The Dramatic Triad in *Ham*." *SP*, 57 (1960): 144-64.

1096   HOGREFE, Pearl. "Artistic Unity in *Ham*." *SP*, 46 (1949): 184-95.

1097   HOLMES, Martin. *The Guns of Elsinore.* London: Chatto & Windus, 1964.

1098   HONIGMANN, Ernst A. J. "The Date of *Ham*." In *ShS* 9, **1174.**

1099   HUNTER, George K. "Isocrates' Precepts and Polonius' Character." *SQ*, 8 (1957): 501-6.

1100   ISAACS, Jacob, ed. *Fratricide Punished: William Poel's Prompt Book.* London: Society for Theatre Research, 1956.

1101   JACK, Adolphus A. *Young Hamlet: A Conjectural Resolution of Some of the Difficulties in the Plotting of Shakespeare's Play.* Aberdeen: The U.P., 1950.

1102   JAMES, David G. *The Dream of Learning: An Essay on the Advancement of Learning,* Ham, *and* Lr. Oxford U.P., 1951.

1103   JANARO, Richard P. "Dramatic Significance in *Ham.*" In *Studies in Shakespeare,* 2797.

1104   JENKINS, Harold. *Hamlet and Ophelia.* Oxford U.P., 1964. [*PBA 1963,* 49 (1964): 135-51.]

1105   ——. "*Ham* Then till Now." *ShS 18* (1965), pp. 34-45.

1106   JOHNSON, Samuel F. "The Regeneration of Hamlet." *SQ,* 3 (1952): 187-207.

1107   JONES, Ernest. *Hamlet and Oedipus.* London: V. Gollancz, 1949.

1108   ——. "The Problem of Hamlet and the Oedipus-Complex." In Ham *by William Shakespeare with a Psycho-analytical Study.* London: Vision, 1947.

1109   JORGENSEN, Paul A. "*Ham* and the Restless Renaissance." In *Shakespearean Essays,* 2819.

1110   ——. "Hamlet's Therapy." *HLQ,* 27 (1963-64): 239-58.

1111   JOSEPH, Bertram L. *Conscience and the King: A Study of* Ham. London: Chatto & Windus, 1953.

1112   ——. "*The Spanish Tragedy* and *Ham:* Two Exercises in English Seneca." In *Classical Drama and Its Influence: Essays Presented to H. D. F. Kitto,* ed. M. J. Anderson. New York: Barnes & Noble, 1965.

1113   JUMP, John D., ed. *Shakespeare:* Ham, *a Casebook.* London: Macmillan, 1968. [37 sel. from prev. pub. wks., 1710-1964.]

1114   KIRSCHBAUM, Leo. "The Date of Shakespeare's *Ham.*" *SP,* 34 (1937): 168-75.

1115   ——. "Hamlet and Ophelia." *PQ,* 35 (1956): 376-93.

1116   KITTO, H. D. F. "*Ham.*" In *Form and Meaning in Drama.* London: Methuen, 1956.

1117   KNIGHTS, Lionel C. *An Approach to* Ham. Stanford U.P., 1961. Repr. in *Some Shakespearean Themes; An Approach to* Ham. Stanford U.P., 1966. [SP 23.]

1118   KOTT, Jan. "Hamlet and Orestes." Trans. Boleslaw Taborski. *PMLA,* 82 (1967): 303-13.

1119   LAW, Robert A. "Belleforest, Shakespeare, and Kyd." In *Adams Memorial Studies,* 2794.

1120   LAWLOR, John J. "The Tragic Conflict in *Ham.*" *RES,* 1 (1950): 97-113.

1121   LAWRENCE, William W. "Ophelia's Heritage." *MLR,* 42 (1947): 409-16. [See *MLR,* 44 (1949): 236 for "Correction."]

1122   LAWRY, Jon S. "'Born to Set It Right': Hal, Hamlet, and Prospero." *BSUF,* 5 (1964): 16-24.

1123   LEAVENWORTH, Russell E. *Interpreting* Ham: *Materials for Analysis.* San Francisco: Chandler, 1960. [Chandler.]

1124   LeCOMTE, Edward S. "The Ending of *Ham* as a Farewell to Essex." *ELH*, 17 (1950): 87-114.

1125   LEECH, Clifford. "Studies in *Ham*, 1901-1955." In *ShS 9*, **1174.**

1126   LEVENSON, Jacob C., ed. *Discussions of* Ham. Boston: Heath, 1960. [12 prev. pub. sel., Dryden to present.]

1127   LEVIN, Harry. *The Question of* Ham. New York: Oxford U.P., 1959. [Viking C78.]

1128   LEVITSKY, Ruth M. "Rightly to Be Great." *ShakS 1* (1965), pp. 142-67.

1129   LEWIS, Charlton M. *The Genesis of* Ham. New York: Holt, 1907. Repr. Port Washington, N.Y.: Kennikat.

1130   LEWIS, Clive S. *Hamlet: The Prince or the Poem?* Oxford U.P., 1942. [*PBA 1942*, 28 (1943): 139-54.] Repr. in *Studies in Shakespeare*, **2759.**

1131   McALINDON, Thomas. "Indecorum in *Ham." ShakS 5 1969* (1970), pp. 70-96.

1132   McGINN, Donald J. *Shakespeare's Influence on the Drama of His Age, Studied in* Ham. Rutgers U.P., 1938. Repr. New York: Octagon.

1133   MACK, Maynard. "The World of Hamlet." *YR*, 41 (1952): 502-23. Repr. in *Essays on Shakespeare*, **2770.**

1134   McMANAWAY, James G. "The Two Earliest Prompt Books of *Ham." PBSA*, 43 (1949): 288-320. Repr. in *Studies in Shakespeare, Bibliography, and Theater*, **3174.**

1135   MADARIAGA, Salvador de. *On* Ham. London: Hollis & Carter, 1948. Repr. London: Frank Cass, 1964.

1136   MÄDE, Hans D. "*Ham* und das Problem des Ideals." *SJ* (East), 102 (1966): 7-22.

1137   MANDER, Raymond, and Joe Mitchenson. Ham *through the Ages: A Pictorial Record from 1709.* London: Rockliff, 1952.

1138   MAXWELL, Baldwin. "Hamlet's Mother." *SQ*, 15.2 (1964): 235-46. Also in *Shakespeare 400*, **2793.**

1139   MENDEL, Sydney. "The Revolt against the Father: The Adolescent Hero in *Ham* and *The Wild Duck." EIC*, 14 (1964): 171-78.

1140   MIRIAM Joseph, Sr. "Discerning the Ghost in *Ham." PMLA*, 76 (1961): 493-502.

1141   —. "*Ham*, A Christian Tragedy." *SP*, 59 (1962): 119-40.

1142   *Miscellaneous Observations on* The Tragedy of Ham, Prince of Denmark. London: W. Clarke, 1752.

1143   MORRIS, Harry. "*Ham* as a *memento mori* Poem." *PMLA*, 85 (1970): 1035-40.

1144   MUIR, Kenneth. "Imagery and Symbolism in *Ham.*" In *EA*, 17, **2776**.

1145   —. *Shakespeare: Ham.* London: Arnold, 1963.

1146   MUSCHG, Walter. "Deutschland ist *Ham.*" *SJ 1965* (West), pp. 32-58.

1147   MYRICK, Kenneth. "Kittredge on *Ham.*" *SQ*, 15.2 (1964): 219-34. Also in *Shakespeare 400*, **2793**.

1148   NEWELL, Alex. "The Dramatic Context and Meaning of Hamlet's 'To Be or Not to Be' Soliloquy." *PMLA*, 80 (1965): 38-50.

1149   OLIVE, W. J. "Sejanus and Hamlet." In *A Tribute to George Coffin Taylor*, **2822**.

1150   ORNSTEIN, Robert T. "Historical Criticism and the Interpretation of Shakespeare." *SQ*, 10 (1959): 3-9.

1151   —. "The Mystery of Hamlet: Notes toward an Archetypal Solution." *CE*, 21 (1959): 30, 35-36.

1152   ØSTERBERG, V. "Nashe's 'Kid in AEsop': A Danish Interpretation." *RES*, 18 (1942): 385-94. [J. Dover Wilson's free rendering of the gist of Østerberg's argument that Kyd wrote the *Ur-Hamlet* in 1588.]

1153   PARIS, Jean. *Hamlet; ou, Les Personnages du fils.* Paris: Éditions du Seuil, 1953.

1154   PATERSON, John. "The Word in *Ham.*" *SQ*, 2 (1951): 47-55.

1155   PEARLMAN, E. "The Hamlet of Robert Wilks." *TN*, 24 (1970): 125-33.

1156   PHIALAS, Peter G. "Hamlet and the Grave-Maker." *JEGP*, 63 (1964): 226-34.

1157   POLLIN, Burton R. "Hamlet, a Successful Suicide." *ShakS 1* (1965), pp. 240-60.

1158   POTTS, Abbie F. "Hamlet and Gloriana's Knights." *SQ*, 6 (1955): 31-43. Repr. in *Shakespeare and* The Faerie Queene, **3248**.

1159   PRIOR, Moody E. "The Thought of *Ham* and the Modern Temper." *ELH*, 15 (1948): 261-85.

1160   PROSER, Matthew N. "Hamlet and the Name of Action." In *Essays on Shakespeare*, **2813**.

1161   PROSSER, Eleanor A. Ham *and Revenge.* Stanford U.P., 1967.

1162   RAVEN, Anton A. *A* Ham *Bibliography and Reference Guide, 1877-1935.* Chicago U.P., 1936. Repr. New York: Russell & Russell.

1163   REID, B. L. "The Last Act of *Ham.*" *YR*, 54 (1964): 59-80.

1164   REYNOLDS, George F. "*Ham* at the Globe." In *ShS 9*, **1174**.

1165   RUSSELL, D. A. "Hamlet Costumes from Garrick to Gielgud." In *ShS 9*, **1174**.

1166   SACKS, Claire, and Edgar Whan, eds. *Ham: Enter Critic.*   New York: Appleton-Century-Crofts, 1960. [Sel. from prev. pub. wks., 1736-1959.]

1167   SANFORD, Wendy C. *Theater as Metaphor in* Ham. Harvard U.P. , 1967.

1168   SCHÜCKING, Levin L. *Der Sinn des* Ham. Leipzig: Quelle & Meyer, 1936. Trans. Graham Rawson, *The Meaning of* Ham. Oxford U.P., 1937; repr. New York: Barnes & Noble.

1169   SEMPER, Isidore J. "The Ghost in *Ham:* Pagan or Christian?" *The Month*, 9 (1953): 222-34.

1170   —. *Hamlet without Tears: A Study of Hamlet as a Thomist Philosopher.* Dubuque, Iowa: Loras College P., 1946.

1171   SENG, Peter J. "Ophelia's Songs in *Ham.*" *DUJ*, 25 (1964): 77-85.

1172   SHATTUCK, Charles H. *The Hamlet of Edwin Booth.* Illinois U.P., 1970. [See also Shattuck, "Edwin Booth's *Ham:* A New Promptbook." *HLB*, 15 (1967): 20-48.]

1173   SHOEMAKER, Neille. "The Aesthetic Criticism of *Ham* from 1692-1699." *SQ*, 16 (1965): 99-103.

1174   *ShS 9* (1956). [8 essays on *Ham.*]

1175   SISSON, Charles J. "The Mouse-trap Again." *RES*, 16 (1940): 129-36. [The Elizabethan method of staging the Dumb Show.]

1176   SKULSKY, Harold. "Revenge, Honor, and Conscience in *Ham.*" *PMLA*, 85 (1970): 78-87.

1177   *Some Remarks on* The Tragedy of Ham, Prince of Denmark. London: W. Wilkins, 1736. Repr. Ann Arbor, Mich.: Augustan Reprint Society, 1947 (ser. 3, no. 3); New York: AMS. [Often attrib. to Thomas Hanmer; but see C. D. Thorp, "Thomas Hanmer and the Anonymous Essay on *Ham.*" *MLN*, 49 (1934): 493-98.]

1178   SPAETH, J. Duncan. "Horatio's Hamlet." *SAB*, 24 (1949): 37-47.

1179   SPENCER, Hazelton. "Seventeenth-Century Cuts in Hamlet's Soliloquies." *RES*, 9 (1933): 257-65.

1180   SPENCER, Theodore. "Hamlet and the Nature of Reality." *ELH*, 5 (1938): 253-77.

1181   SPEVACK, Marvin. "Hamlet and Imagery: The Mind's Eye." *NS*, 25 (1966): 203-12.

1182   STABLER, Arthur P. "The Source of the German *Ham.*" *ShakS 5* ; see 1033.

1183   STIRLING, Brents. "Theme and Character in *Ham.*" *MLQ*, 13 (1952): 323-32.

1184   STOLL, Elmer E. *Ham: An Historical and Comparative Study.* U. of Minnesota P., 1919. Repr. New York: Gordian.

1185   —   *Hamlet the Man.* Oxford U.P., 1935.

1186   STONE, George W. "Garrick's Long Lost Alteration of *Ham.*" *PMLA*, 49 (1934): 890-921.

1187   THOMAS, Sidney. *The Antic Hamlet and Richard III.* New York: King's Crown, 1943.

1188   Canceled.

1189   TOLMAN, Albert H. *The Views about* Ham *and Other Essays.* Boston: Houghton, Mifflin, 1904. [2 essays on *Ham.*]

1190   TRENCH, Wilbraham F. *Shakespeare's* Ham. London: Smith, Elder, 1913.

1191   TURGENEV, Ivan S. *Hamlet and Don Quixote.* Trans. Robert Nichols. London: Hendersons, 1930.

1192   VANDERHOOF, Mary B. "*Ham*—A Tragedy Adapted from Shakespeare (1770) by Jean François Ducis: A Critical Edition." *PAPS*, 97 (1953): 88-142. [See also Willard B. Pope, "Ducis's *Ham.*" *SQ*, 5 (1954): 209-11.]

1193   VAN LAAN, Thomas F. "Ironic Reversal in *Ham.*" *SEL*, 6 (1966): 247-62.

1194   VENABLE, Emerson. *The* Ham *Problem and Its Solution.* Cincinnati: Stewart & Kidd, 1912. Abridged ed., Los Angeles: Oxford P., 1954.

1195   WALDOCK, Arthur J. A. *Ham: A Study in Critical Method.* Cambridge U.P., 1931.

1196   WALKER, Roy O. *The Time Is Out of Joint: A Study of* Ham. London: Dakers, 1948.

1197   WALLEY, Harold R. "The Dates of *Ham* and Marston's *The Malcontent.*" *RES*, 9 (1933): 397-409. [*Ham* precedes *Malcontent.* See also Elmer E. Stoll, "The Date of *The Malcontent:* A Rejoinder." *RES*, 11 (1935): 42-50. About 1600 and thus not necessarily derived from *Ham.*]

1198   WARHAFT, Sidney. "The Mystery of *Ham.*" *ELH*, 30 (1963): 193-208.

1199   WEIGAND, Hermann J. "Hamlet's Consistent Inconsistency." In *Essays in Honor of Robert W. Babcock*, **2810.**

1200   WEITZ, Morris. Ham *and the Philosophy of Literary Criticism.* U. of Chicago P., 1964.

1201   WERTHAM, Frederic. *Dark Legend: A Study in Murder.* London: Gollancz, 1947.

1202   WEST, Rebecca. *The Court and the Castle.* Yale U.P., 1957. [Chaps. 2 and 3 on *Ham.*]

1203   WEST, Robert H. "King Hamlet's Ambiguous Ghost." *PMLA*, 70 (1955): 1107-17.

1204   WILLIAMSON, Claude C. H., ed. *Readings on the Character of Hamlet, 1661-1947.* London: Allen & Unwin, 1950. [Sel. from over 300 prev. pub. wks.]

1205   WILSON, J. Dover. *What Happens in* Ham. Cambridge U.P., 1935. Rev. ed., 1951. [CUP 109.]

1206   WORMHOUDT, Arthur. *Hamlet's Mousetrap: A Psychoanalytic Study of the Drama.* New York: Philosophical Library, 1956. Repr. New York: AMS.

1207   YEARSLEY, Percival M. *The Sanity of Hamlet.* London: Bale & Danielsson, 1932.

HENRY 4

Editions

1208   HALLIWELL-PHILLIPPS, James O., ed. *Shakespeare's Play of* 1H4 *Printed from a Contemporary Manuscript.* London: The Shakespeare Society, 1845.

Textual Commentary

1209   FARMER, John S., ed. *The Famous Victories of Henry the Fifth . . . 1598.* Tudor Facs. Texts. Amersham: Farmer, 1913. Repr. New York: AMS.

Commentary

See also The History Plays (**3550-3615**); **881, 2166, 2214, 2928, 2952, 3006, 3142, 3445, 3547,** and **3567.**

1210   AVERY, Emmett L. "*1H4* and *2H4* during the First Half of the Eighteenth Century." *JEGP,* 44 (1945): 89-90.

1211   BARBER, Charles L. "Prince Hal, Henry V, and the Tudor Monarchy." In *The Morality of Art,* **2789.**

1212   BARISH, Jonas A. "The Turning Away of Prince Hal." *ShakS 1* (1965), pp. 9-17.

1213   BASS, Eben. "Falstaff and the Succession." *CE,* 24 (1963): 502-6.

1214   BECK, Richard J. *Shakespeare: H4.* London: Arnold, 1965.

1215   BERMAN, Ronald S. "The Nature of Guilt in the *H4* Plays. *ShakS 1* (1965), pp. 18-28.

1216   BOUGHNER, Daniel C. "Traditional Elements in Falstaff." *JEGP,* 43 (1944): 417-28.

1217   ——. "Vice, Braggart, and Falstaff." *Anglia,* 72 (1954): 35-61.

1218   BRADLEY, Andrew C. "The Rejection of Falstaff." In *Oxford Lectures on Poetry,* **2883.**

1219   BRYANT, Joseph A. "Prince Hal and the Ephesians." *SR,* 67 (1959): 204-19.

1220   CAIN, H. Edward. "Further Light on the Relation of *1* and *2 H4.*" *SQ,* 3 (1952): 21-38.

1221   CHARLTON, Henry B. "Falstaff." *BJRL,* 19 (1935): 46-89. Repr. U. of Manchester P., 1935.

1222   CRAIG, Hardin. "The Dering Version of Shakespeare's *H4.*" *PQ,* 35 (1956): 218-19.

1223 DICKINSON, Hugh. "The Reformation of Prince Hal." *SQ*, 12 (1961): 33-46.

1224 DORAN, Madeleine. "Imagery in *R2* and *H4*." *MLR*, 37 (1942): 113-22.

1225 DRAPER, John W. "Sir John Falstaff." *RES*, 8 (1932): 414-24.

1226 EMPSON, William. "Falstaff and Mr. Dover Wilson." *KR*, 15 (1953): 213-62.

1227 —. "They That Have Power." In *Some Versions of Pastoral.* London: Chatto & Windus, 1950.

1228 EVANS, G. Blakemore. "The 'Dering MS' of Shakespeare's *H4* and Sir Edward Dering." *JEGP*, 54 (1955): 498-503.

1229 EVANS, Gareth L. "The Comical-Tragical-Historical Method: *H4*." In *Early Shakespeare*, **2766**.

1230 FISH, Charles. "*H4:* Shakespeare and Holinshed." *SP*, 61 (1964): 205-18.

1231 HAPGOOD, Robert. "Falstaff's Vocation." *SQ*, 16 (1965): 91-98.

1232 HEMINGWAY, Samuel B. "On Behalf of that Falstaff." *SQ*, 3 (1952): 307-11.

1233 HUNTER, George K. "*H4* and the Elizabethan Two-Part Play." *RES*, 5 (1954): 236-48.

1234 —. "Shakespeare's Politics and the Rejection of Falstaff." *CritQ*, 1 (1959): 229-36.

1235 JENKINS, Harold. *The Structural Problem in Shakespeare's* H4. London: Methuen, 1956.

1236 KNOWLTON, Edgar C. "Falstaff Redux." *JEGP*, 25 (1926): 193–215.

1237 KRIS, Ernst. "Prince Hal's Conflict." *Psychoanalytical Quarterly,* 17 (1948): 487-506.

1238 LANDT, D. B. "The Ancestry of Sir John Falstaff." *SQ*, 17 (1966): 69-76.

1239 LAWRY, Jon S. "'Born to Set It Right': Hal, Hamlet, and Prospero." *BSUF*; see **1122**.

1240 McLUHAN, Herbert M. "*H4*, a Mirror for Magistrates." *UTQ*, 17 (1947): 152-60.

1241 McNAMARA, Anne M. "*H4:* The King as Protagonist." *SQ*, 10 (1959): 423-31.

1241a MAXWELL, Baldwin. "The Original of Sir John Falstaff—Believe It or Not." *SP*, 27 (1930): 230-32. Repr. in *Evidence for Authorship,* **572**.

1242 MONAGHAN, James. "Falstaff and His Forebears." *SP*, 18 (1921): 353-61.

1243   MORGANN, Maurice. *An Essay on the Dramatic Character of Sir John Falstaff.* London: T. Davies, 1777. Repr. New York: AMS. See also **3351.**

1244   MURRY, John Middleton. "The Creation of Falstaff." In *John Clare and Other Studies*, **3218.**

1245   NEWMAN, Franklin B. "The Rejection of Falstaff and the Rigorous Charity of the King." *ShakS 2 1966* (1967), pp. 153-61.

1246   OLIVER, Leslie M. "Sir John Oldcastle: Legend or Literature?" *Library*, 1 (1946-47): 179-83.

1247   PALMER, D. J. "Casting off the Old Man: History and St. Paul in *H4.*" *CritQ*, 12 (1970): 267-83.

1248   RICHARDSON, William. *Essays on Shakespeare's Dramatic Character of Sir John Falstaff, and on His Imitation of Female Characters.* London: J. Murray, 1788.

1249   SCOUFOS, Alice L. "The 'Martyrdom' of Falstaff." *ShakS 2 1966* (1967), pp. 174-91.

1250   SCOUTEN, Arthur H., and Leo Hughes. "A Calendar of Performances of *1H4* and *2H4* during the First Half of the Eighteenth Century." *JEGP*, 43 (1944): 23-41.

1251   SENG, Peter J. "Songs, Time, and the Rejection of Falstaff." *ShS 15* (1962), pp. 31-40.

1252   SHAABER, Matthias A. "The Unity of *H4.*" In *Adams Memorial Studies*, **2794.**

1253   SHIRLEY, John W. "Falstaff, an Elizabethan Glutton." *PQ*, 17 (1938): 271-87.

1254   SMALL, Samuel A. "The Reflective Element in Falstaff." *SAB*, 14 (1939): 108-21, 131-43.

1255   SPARGO, John W. "An Interpretation of Falstaff." *Washington University Studies*, 9, Humanistic Series 2 (1922): 119-33.

1256   SPIVACK, Bernard. "Falstaff and the Psychomachia." *SQ*, 8 (1957): 449-59.

1257   TAVE, Stuart M. "Notes on the Influence of Morgann's Essay on Falstaff." *RES*, 3 (1952): 371-75.

1258   TOLIVER, Harold E. "Falstaff, the Prince, and the History Play." *SQ*, 16 (1965): 63-80.

1259   WILLIAMS, Philip. "The Birth and Death of Falstaff Reconsidered." *SQ*, 8 (1957): 359-65.

1260   WILSON, J. Dover. *The Fortunes of Falstaff.* Cambridge U.P.; New York: Macmillan, 1944. [CUP 246.]

1261   —. "The Origins and Development of Shakespeare's *H4.*" *Library*, 26 (1945-46): 2-16.

1262   —. "The Political Background of Shakespeare's *R2* and *H4.*" *SJ*, 75 (1939): 36-51.

1 HENRY 4

Editions

1263   EVANS, G. Blakemore, ed. *Supplement to* 1H4. New Variorum ed. New York: Shakespeare Association of America, 1956. [Also pub. as *SQ*, 7.3 (1956).]

1264   HEMINGWAY, Samuel B., ed. *1H4*. New Variorum. Philadelphia: Lippincott, 1936.

1265   SANDERSON, James, ed. *1H4*. New York: Norton, 1962. Rev. ed., 1969. [Text, cultural contexts, sel. from sources, criticism.]

Textual Commentary

1266   WALKER, Alice. "The Folio Text of *1H4*." *SB*, 6 (1954): 45-59.

Commentary

See also The History Plays (**3550-3615**); **721, 733, 2345, 3247, 3293, 3444, 3744, 3757**, and **4407**.

1267   BERKELEY, David, and Donald Eidson. "The Theme of *1H4*." *SQ*, 19 (1968): 25-31.

1268   BOWERS, Fredson T. "Theme and Structure in *1H4*." In *The Drama of the Renaissance*, **2763**.

1269   KNOEPFLMACHER, U. C. "The Humors as Symbolic Nucleus in *1H4*." *CE*, 24 (1963): 497-501.

1270   LA BRANCHE, Anthony. "'If Thou Wert Sensible of Courtesy': Private and Public Virtue in *1H4*." *SQ*, 17 (1966): 371-82.

1271   LEVIN, Harry. "The Shakespearean Overplot." *RenD*, 8 (1965): 63-72.

1272   McGUIRE, Richard L. "The Play-within-the-Play in *1H4*." *SQ*, 18 (1967): 47-52.

1273   McNEIR, Waldo F. "Structure and Theme in the First Tavern Scene of *1H4*." In *Pacific Coast Studies in Shakespeare,* **2796**, and *Essays on Shakespeare,* **2813**.

1274   RENO, Raymond H. "Hotspur: The Integration of Character and Theme." *RenP 1962* (1963), pp. 17-26.

1275   SCOUFOS, Alice L. "Gads Hill and the Structure of Comic Satire." *ShakS 5 1969* (1970), pp. 25-52.

1276   SHAW, John. "The Staging of Parody and Parallels in *1H4*." *ShS 20*, (1967), pp. 61-73.

1277 SHUCHTER, J. D. "Prince Hal and Francis: The Imitation of an Action." *ShakS 3 1967* (1968), pp. 129-37.

1278 SPRAGUE, Arthur C. "Gadshill Revisited." *SQ*, 4 (1953): 125-37.

1279 ZEEVELD, W. Gordon. " 'Food for Powder'–'Food for Worms.' " *SQ*, 3 (1952): 249-53.

2 HENRY 4

Editions

1280   SHAABER, Matthias A., ed. *2H4*. New Variorum. Philadelphia: Lippincott, 1940.

Textual Commentary

See also **254, 379,** and **713.**

1281   FUSILLO, Robert J. "'Enter Prince John.' Quarto or Folio?" *SQ*, 14 (1963): 179-82.

1282   HART, Alfred. "Was the Second Part of *H4* Censored?" In *Shakespeare and the Homilies*, **3063.**

1283   McMANAWAY, James G. "The Cancel in the Quarto of *2H4*." In *Studies in Honor of A. H. R. Fairchild*, **2804.**

1284   SHAABER, Matthias A. "The Folio Text of *2H4*." *SQ*, 6 (1955): 135-44.

1285   SMITH, John H. "The Cancel in the Quarto of *2H4* Revisited." *SQ*, 15.3 (1964): 173-78.

1286   TAYLOR, Neil. "Variants in the Quarto of *2H4*." *Library*, 25 (1970): 249-50.

1287   WALKER, Alice. "The Cancelled Lines in *2H4*, IV.i.93, 95." *Library*, 6 (1951-52): 115-16.

1288   ——. "Quarto 'Copy' and the 1623 Folio: *2H4*." *RES*, 2 (1951): 217-25.

Commentary

See also The History Plays **(3550-3615)**; **733, 1234, 1994, 3053, 3137, 3247, 3293, 3744,** and **3757.**

1289   HOTSON, Leslie. "Ancient Pistol." *YR*, 38 (1948): 51-66. Repr. in *Shakespeare's Son Dated*, **2345.**

1290   KNOWLES, Richard. "Unquiet and the Double Plot of *2H4*." *ShakS 2 1966* (1967), pp. 133-40.

1291   LEECH, Clifford. "The Unity of *2H4*." *ShS 6* (1953), pp. 16-24.

1292   PIERCE, R. B. "The Generations in *2H4*." In *Twentieth-Century Interpretations of* 2H4, **1294.**

1293   YATES, Frances A. "English Actors in Paris during the Lifetime of Shakespeare." *RES*, 1 (1925): 392-403. [The Dauphin saw three performances in 1604 and later used phrases corresponding to lines in *2H4* or, possibly, *R3*.]

1294   YOUNG, David P., ed. *Twentieth-Century Interpretations of* 2H4 . Englewood Cliffs, N.J.: Prentice-Hall, 1968. [12 sel. from prev. pub. wks. and one new essay by R. B. Pierce.]

HENRY 5

Editions

1295   NICHOLSON, Brinsley, and Peter A. Daniel, eds.   *H5: Parallel Texts of the First Quarto (1600) and First Folio (1623) Editions.*   London: for the New Shakspere Society by N. Trübner, 1877.

1296   PITCHER, Seymour M.   *The Case for Shakespeare's Authorship of* The Famous Victories *with the Complete Text of the Anonymous Play*.   State U. of New York, 1961.

1297   ROMAN, Ernest, ed.   *H5: . . . Parallel Texts of the First and Third Quartos and First Folio.*   London: Nutt, 1908.

1298   WILSON, J. Dover, ed.   *H5.*   London: Faber & Faber, [1931].   [Facs. from Grenville copy of F1 in the British Museum.]

Textual Commentary

See also **1209**.

1299   CAIRNCROSS, Andrew S.   "Quarto Copy for Folio *H5.*"   *SB*, 8 (1956): 67-93.

1300   CRAIG, Hardin.   "The Relation of the First Quarto Version to the First Folio Version of Shakespeare's *H5.*"   *PQ*, 6 (1927): 225-34.

1301   DUTHIE, George Ian.   "The Quarto of Shakespeare's *H5.*"   In *Papers Mainly Shakespearean*, **2775**.

1302   OKERLUND, Gerda.   "The Quarto Version of *H5* as a Stage Adaptation."   *PMLA*, 49 (1934): 810-34.

1303   PRICE, Hereward T.   "The Quarto and Folio Texts of *H5.*"   *PQ*, 12 (1933): 24-32.

1304   ——.   *The Text of* H5.   Newcastle-under-Lyme: Mandley & Unett, 1921.

1305   SIMISON, Barbara D.   "Stage-Directions: A Test for the Playhouse Origin of the First Quarto of *H5.*"   *PQ*, 11 (1932): 39-56.

1306   SMITH, Warren D.   "The *H5* Choruses in the First Folio."   *JEGP*, 53 (1954): 38-57.

1307   WALKER, Alice.   "Some Editorial Principles (with Special Reference to *H5*)."   *SB*, 8 (1956): 95-111.

1308   WALTER, J. H.   " 'With Sir John in It.' "   *MLR*, 41 (1946): 237-45.

1309   WARD, Bernard M.   "*The Famous Victories of Henry V:* Its Place in Elizabethan Dramatic Literature."   *RES*, 4 (1928): 270-94.   [Suggests the Earl of Oxford wrote it about 1573; its relation to *H5.*]

1310   WILKINSON, Allan.   "A Note on *H5*, Act IV."   *RES*, 1 (1950): 345-46.   [IV.vii.117-viii.73 possibly an interpolation.]

Commentary

See also The History Plays (**3550-3615**); **601, 604, 721, 733, 881, 1122, 1289, 2928, 3165, 3238, 3567, 3736, 3744**, and **3757**.

1311   BARBER, Charles L. "Prince Hal, Henry V, and the Tudor Monarchy." In *The Morality of Art*, **2789**.

1312   BATTENHOUSE, Roy W. "*H5* as Heroic Comedy." In *Essays . . . in Honor of Hardin Craig*, **2786**.

1313   BERMAN, Ronald S. "Shakespeare's Alexander: Henry V." *CE*, 23 (1962): 532-39.

1314   —, ed. *Twentieth-Century Interpretations of* H5. Englewood Cliffs, N.J.: Prentice-Hall, 1968. [15 sel. from prev. pub. wks.]

1315   BOUGHNER, Daniel C. "Pistol and the Roaring Boys." *SAB*, 11 (1936): 226-37.

1316   BRADDY, Haldeen. "Shakespeare's *H5* and the French Nobility." *TSLL*, 3 (1961): 189-96.

1317   BURNS, Landon C. "Three Views of King Henry V." *DramS*, 1 (1962): 278-300.

1318   CUNLIFFE, John W. "The Character of Henry V as Prince and King." In *Shaksperian Studies*, **2798**.

1319   DRAPER, John W. "The Humor of Corporal Nym." *SAB*, 13 (1938): 131-38.

1320   EGAN, Robert. "A Muse of Fire: *H5* in the Light of *Tamburlaine*." *MLQ*, 29 (1968): 15-28.

1321   FLEISSNER, Robert F. "Falstaff's Green Sickness unto Death." *SQ*, 12 (1961): 47-55.

1322   GILBERT, Allan H. "Patriotism and Satire in *H5*." In *Studies in Shakespeare*, **2797**.

1323   HOBDAY, C. H. "Imagery and Irony in *H5*." *ShS 21* (1968), pp. 107-13.

1324   JORGENSEN, Paul A. "Accidental Judgments, Casual Slaughters, and Purposes Mistook: Critical Reactions to Shakspere's *H5*." *SAB*, 22 (1947): 51-61.

1325   —. "The Courtship Scene in *H5*." *MLQ*, 11 (1950): 180-88.

1326   LEVER, Julius W. "Shakespeare's French Fruits." *ShS 6* (1953), pp. 79-90.

1327   MAXWELL, James C. "Simple or Complex?" *DUJ*, 46 (1954): 112-13.

1328   MENDILOW, A. A. "Falstaff's Death of a Sweat." *SQ*, 9 (1958): 479-83.

1329   MERCHANT, W. Moelwyn. "The Status and Person of Majesty." *SJ*, 90 (1954): 285-89.

1330   MITCHELL, Charles. "Henry V: The Essential King." In *Shakespearean Essays*, **2819**.

1331   PHIALAS, Peter G. "Shakespeare's *H5* and the Second Tetralogy." *SP*, 62 (1965): 155-75.

1332   RADOFF, M. L. "Influence of the French Farce in *H5* and *Wiv.*" *MLN*, 48 (1933): 427-35.

1333   STŘIBRNÝ, Zdeněk. "Henry V and History." In *Shakespeare in a Changing World*, **2792**.

1334   TOLMAN, Albert H. "The Epic Character of Henry V." *MLN*, 34 (1919): 7-16.

1335   WILLIAMS, Charles. "*H5*." In *Shakespeare Criticism, 1919-35*, **2807**.

1336   WILLIAMSON, Marilyn L. "The Episode with Williams in *H5*." *SEL*, 9 (1969): 275-82.

1337   WILSON, J. Dover. "Martin Marprelate and Shakespeare's Fluellen." *Library*, 3 (1912): 113-51, 241-76.

1338   ZIMBARDO, Rose A. "The Formalism of *H5*." In *Shakespeare Encomium*, **2802**.

HENRY 6

Editions

See also Canon **(570-605).**

1339 HALLIWELL-PHILLIPPS, James O., ed. *The First Sketches of* 2, 3 H6. London: The Shakespeare Society, 1843. [*Contention; True Tragedy.*]

Textual Commentary

1340 ALEXANDER, Peter. *Shakespeare's* H6 *and* R3. Shakespeare Problem Series, 3. Cambridge U.P., 1929.

1341 DORAN, Madeleine. 2 *and* 3 H6: *Their Relation to* The Contention *and* The True Tragedy. U. of Iowa P., 1928.

1342 GREER, Clayton A. "More about the Actor-Reporter Theory in *The Contention* and *The True Tragedy.*" *N&Q*, 202 (1957): 52-53.

1343 ——. "The York and Lancaster Quarto-Folio Sequence." *PMLA*, 48 (1933): 655-704.

1344 McKERROW, Ronald B. "A Note on the 'Bad Quartos' of 2 and *3 H6* and the Folio Text." *RES*; see **322.**

Commentary

See also The History Plays **(3550-3615)** and **3585.**

1345 BERMAN, Ronald S. "Fathers and Sons in the *H6* Plays." *SQ*, 13 (1962): 487-97.

1346 BROCKBANK, J. P. "The Frame of Disorder: *H6.*" In *Early Shakespeare,* **2766.**

1347 KNICKERBOCKER, William S. "Shakespearean Excursion: Who Wrote 2 and 3 *H6?*" *SR*, 45 (1937): 328-42.

1348 LAW, Robert A. "The Chronicles and the Three Parts of *H6.*" *TxSE,* 33 (1954): 13-32.

1349 LEE, Jane. "On the Authorship of 2 and *3 H6* and Their Originals." *Trans. New Shakspere Soc.,* Series 1, no. 4 (1875-76): 219-313.

1350 LEECH, Clifford. "The Two-Part Play: Marlowe and the Early Shakespeare." *SJ*, 94 (1958): 90-100.

1351 McNEAL, Thomas H. "Margaret of Anjou." *SQ*, 9 (1958): 1-10.

1352 MESSIAEN, Pierre. "La Trilogie de *H6.*" *Revue des Cours et Conferences*, 39 (1938): 137-56.

1353 PRATT, Samuel M. "Shakespeare and Humphrey Duke of Gloucester: A Study in Myth." *SQ*, 16 (1965): 201-16.

1354   RICKS, Don M.   *Shakespeare's Emergent Form: A Study of the Structure of the* H6 *Plays.*   Utah State U.P., 1968.

1355   SWAYNE, Mattie.   "Shakespeare's Henry VI as a Pacifist."   *CE*, 3 (1941): 143-49.

1 HENRY 6

Textual Commentary

See also Canon (**570-605**).

1356   DENNY, Charles F. "The Sources of *1H6* as an Indication of Revision." *PQ*, 16 (1937): 225-48.

1357   GREER, Clayton A. "Revision and Adaptation in *1H6*." *TxSE*, No. 4226 (1942), pp. 110-20.

Commentary

See also The History Plays (**3550-3615**).

1358   BEVINGTON, David M. "The Domineering Female in *1H6*." *ShakS 2 1966* (1967), pp. 51-58.

1359   BOAS, Frederick S. "Joan of Arc in Shakespeare, Schiller, and Shaw." *SQ*, 2 (1951): 35-45.

1360   BURCKHARDT, Sigurd. "'I Am But Shadow of Myself': Ceremony and Design in *1H6*." *MLQ*, 28 (1967): 139-58. Repr. in *Shakespearean Meanings*, **2901**.

1361   FRENCH, A. L. "Joan of Arc and *H6*." *ES*, 49 (1968): 425-29.

1362   GAW, Allison. *The Origin and Development of* 1H6 *in Relation to Shakespeare, Marlowe, Peele, and Greene.* U. of Southern California P., 1926. Repr. New York: AMS.

1363   GREER, Clayton A. "The Place of *1H6* in the York-Lancaster Tetralogy." *PMLA*, 53 (1938): 687-701.

1364   HARLOW, C. G. "A Source for Nashe's *Terrors of the Night*, and the Authorship of *1H6*." *SEL*, 5 (1965): 31-47, 269-81.

1365   KIRSCHBAUM, Leo. "The Authorship of *1H6*." *PMLA*, 67 (1952): 809-22.

1366   MINCOFF, Marco. "The Composition of *1H6*." *SQ*, 16 (1965): 279-87.

2 HENRY 6

Editions

1367   FARMER, John S., ed. *The First Part of the Contention . . . 1594.*
        Tudor Facs. Texts. Amersham: Farmer, 1913. Repr. New York:
        AMS.

Textual Commentary

See also Canon (**570-605**); **221, 254, 322, 383**, and **1340-44**.

1368   FREEMAN, Arthur. "Notes on the Text of *2H6* and the 'Upstart
        Crow.'" *N&Q*, 15 (1968): 128-30.

1369   JORDAN, John E. "The Reporter of *2H6*." *PMLA*, 64 (1949):
        1089-1113.

1370   McKERROW, Ronald B. "A Note on *2H6* and *The Contention of
        York and Lancaster*." *RES*, 9 (1933): 157-69.   [See pp. 315-16
        for correction of a detail.]

1371   McMANAWAY, James G. "*The Contention* and *2H6*." In *Studies
        in English Language and Literature*. Ed. Siegfried Korninger. Stutt-
        gart: Braumüller, 1957.

1372   PROUTY, Charles T. The Contention *and Shakespeare's* 2H6: *A
        Comparative Study*. Yale U.P.; Oxford U.P., 1954.

Commentary

See also The History Plays (**3550-3615**) and **2215**.

1373   AUSTIN, Warren B. "A Supposed Contemporary Allusion to Shake-
        speare as a Plagiarist." *SQ*, 6 (1955): 373-80.

1374   CALDERWOOD, James L. "Shakespeare's Evolving Imagery: *2H6*."
        ES, 48 (1967): 481-93.

1375   RINGLER, William A. "Spenser, Shakespeare, Honor, and Worship."
        RN, 14 (1961): 159-61. [Chettle's "Divers of worship" refers to
        people of the rank of gentleman or knight.]

1376   THOMAS, Sidney. "The Meaning of Greene's Attack on Shake-
        speare." *MLN*, 66 (1951): 483-84.

1377   WILSON, J. Dover. "Malone and the Upstart Crow." *ShS 4* (1951),
        pp. 56-68.

3 HENRY 6

Editions

1378 FARMER, John S., ed. *The True Tragedie of Richarde Duke of Yorke ... 1600.* Tudor Facs. Texts. Amersham: Farmer, 1913. Repr. New York: AMS.

Textual Commentary

See also Canon **(570-605); 322** and **1340-44.**

1379 GREG, Walter W., ed. *The True Tragedy of Richard the Third, 1594.* Oxford U.P. for the Malone Society, 1929.

Commentary

See also The History Plays **(3550-3615)** and **2235.**

1380 KERNAN, Alvin B. "A Comparison of the Imagery in *3H6* and *Richard, Duke of York.*" *SP*, 51 (1954): 431-42.

1381 MINCOFF, Marco. "*3H6* and *The True Tragedy.*" *ES*, 42 (1961): 273-88.

HENRY 8

Textual Commentary

See also Canon (**570-605**) and **589**.

1382   FOAKES, Reginald A. "On the First Folio Text of *H8*." *SB*, 11 (1958): 55-60.

Commentary

See also The History Plays (**3550-3615**) and The Romances (after **3734**); **3085**, **4236** and **4407**.

1383   ALEXANDER, Peter. "Conjectural History; or, Shakespeare's *H8*." *E&S*, 16 (1930): 85-120. [Sh's education: authorship of *H8*.]

1384   BERMAN, Ronald S. "*H8:* History and Romance." *ES*, 48 (1967): 112-21.

1385   CLARK, Cumberland. *A Study of Shakespeare's* H8. London: Golden Vista, 1931.

1386   CUTTS, John P. "Shakespeare's Song and Masque Hand in *H8*." *SJ*, 99 (1963): 184-95.

1387   FELPERIN, Howard. "Shakespeare's *H8:* History as Myth." *SEL*, 6 (1966): 225-46.

1388   HARRIS, Bernard. " 'What's Past Is Prologue': *Cym* and *H8*." In *Later Shakespeare*, **2767**.

1389   HOY, Cyrus. "The Shares of Fletcher and His Collaborators in the Beaumont and Fletcher Canon (VII)." *SB*, 15 (1962): 71-90.

1390   KERMODE, J. Frank. "What Is Shakespeare's *H8* About?" *DUJ*, 40 (1947): 48-55.

1391   KNIGHT, G. Wilson. "A Note on *H8*." *Criterion*, 15 (1936): 228-36.

1392   LAW, Robert A. "The Double Authorship of *H8*." *SP*, 56 (1959): 471-88.

1393   —. "Holinshed and *H8*." *TxSE*, 36 (1957): 3-11.

1394   MAXWELL, Baldwin. *Studies in Beaumont, Fletcher, and Massinger*. U. of North Carolina P., 1939.

1395   MINCOFF, Marco. "*H8* and Fletcher." *SQ*, 12 (1961): 239-60.

1396   OMAN, C. W. C. "The Personality of Henry VIII." *QR*, 269 (1937): 88-104.

1397   ORAS, Ants. " 'Extra Monosyllables' in *H8* and the Problem of Authorship." *JEGP*, 52 (1953): 198-213.

1398   PARKER, A. A. "Henry VIII in Shakespeare and Calderón." *MLR*, 43 (1948): 327-52.

1399   PARTRIDGE, Astley C. *The Problem of* H8 *Reopened: Some Linguistic Criteria for the Two Styles Apparent in the Play.* Cambridge: Bowes & Bowes, 1949.

1400   RICHMOND, Hugh M. "Shakespeare's *H8:* Romance Redeemed by History." *ShakS 4 1968* (1969), pp. 334-49.

1401   TILLYARD, Eustace M. W. "Why Did Shakespeare Write *H8*?" *CQ*, 3 (1961): 22-27.

1402   WAITH, Eugene M. *The Pattern of Tragicomedy in Beaumont and Fletcher.* Yale U.P., 1952.

1403   WILEY, Paul L. "Renaissance Exploitation of Cavendish's *Life of Wolsey*." *SP*, 43 (1946): 121-46.

KING JOHN

Editions

Since there is disagreement about whether *The Troublesome Raigne* is a source play or a text derived from Shakespeare, it is listed here.

1404   FARMER, John S., ed. *The Troublesome Raigne of John King of England . . . 1591.* Tudor Facs. Texts. Amersham: Farmer, 1913. Repr. New York: AMS.

1405   —, ed. *The Second Part of the Troublesome Raigne of King John . . . 1591.* Tudor Facs. Texts. Amersham: Farmer, 1913. Repr. New York: AMS.

1406   FURNESS, Horace H., Jr., ed. *Jn.* New Variorum. Philadelphia: Lippincott, 1919.

1407   FURNIVALL, Frederick J., and John Munro, eds. *The Troublesome Reign of King John: Being the Original of Shakespeare's* Jn. London: Chatto & Windus; New York: Duffield, 1913.

Commentary

See also The History Plays (**3550-3615**); **601, 2288, 3585, 4247,** and **4407**.

1408   ASH, D. F. "Anglo-French Relations in *Jn.*" *EA*, 3 (1939): 349-58.

1409   BONJOUR, Adrien. "Bastinado for the Bastard?" *ES*, 45 Supplement (1964): 169-76.

1410   —. "Le Problème du héros et la structure du *Roi Jean.*" *EdL*, 22 (1950): 3-15.

1411   —. "The Road to Swinstead Abbey: A Study of the Sense and Structure of *Jn.*" *ELH*, 18 (1951): 253-74.

1412   BURCKHARDT, Sigurd. "*Jn:* The Ordering of This Present Time." *ELH*, 33 (1966): 133-53. Repr. in *Shakespearean Meanings,* **2901.**

1413   CALDERWOOD, James L. "Commodity and Honour in *Jn.*" *UTQ*, 29 (1960): 341-56.

1414   ELLIOTT, John R. "Shakespeare and the Double Image of King John." *ShakS 1* (1965), pp. 64-84.

1415   ELSON, John J. "Studies in the King John Plays." In *Adams Memorial Studies,* **2794.**

1416   GREENEWALD, Gerard M. *Shakespeare's Attitude toward the Catholic Church in* Jn. Catholic U. of America P., 1938.

1417   LAW, Robert A. "On the Date of *Jn.*" *SP*, 54 (1957): 119-27.

1418 MATCHETT, William H. "Richard's Divided Heritage in *Jn.*" *EIC*, 12 (1962): 231-53.

1419 ORTEGO, Philip D. "Shakespeare and the Doctrine of Monarchy in *Jn.*" *CLAJ*, 13 (1970): 392-401.

1420 PETIT-DUTAILLIS, Charles E. *Le Roi Jean et Shakespeare.* Paris: Gallimard, 1944.

1421 PETTET, Ernest C. "Hot Irons and Fever: A Note on Some of the Imagery of *Jn.*" *EIC*, 4 (1954): 128-44.

1422 SALTER, F. M. "The Problem of *Jn.*" *Trans. Royal Soc. of Canada*, 43 (1949): 115-36.

1423 SHATTUCK, Charles H., ed. *William Charles Macready's* Jn: *A Facsimile Prompt Book.* U. of Illinois P., 1962.

1424 SIBLY, John. "The Anomalous Case of *Jn.*" *ELH*, 33 (1966): 415-21.

1425 SIMMONS, Joseph L. "Shakespeare's *Jn* and Its Source: Coherence, Pattern, and Vision." *TSE*, 17 (1969): 53-72.

1426 STEVICK, Robert D. "'Repentant Ashes': the Matrix of 'Shakespearean' Poetic Language." *SQ*, 13 (1962): 366-70.

1427 VAN der WATER, Julia C. "The Bastard in *Jn.*" *SQ*, 11 (1960): 137-46.

JULIUS CAESAR

Editions

1428   FURNESS, Horace H., Jr., ed. *JC.* New Variorum. Philadelphia: Lippincott, 1913.

1429   WILSON, J. Dover, ed. *JC.* London: Faber & Gwyer, [1929]. [Facs. from Grenville copy of F1 in the British Museum.]

Textual Commentary

1430   BARTLETT, Henrietta C. "Quarto Editions of *JC.*" *Library*, 4 (1913): 122-32.

1431   EVANS, G. Blakemore. "The Problem of Brutus: An Eighteenth-Century Solution." In *Studies in Honor of T. W. Baldwin*, **2760.**

1432   ——. "Shakespeare's *JC*–a Seventeenth-Century Manuscript." *JEGP*, 41 (1942): 401-17.

1433   SMITH, Warren D. "The Duplicate Revelation of Portia's Death." *SQ*, 4 (1953): 153-61.

1434   STIRLING, Brents. "Brutus and the Death of Portia." *SQ*, 10 (1959): 211-17. [Stirling reverses this interpretation on decisive bibliographical evidence in "*JC* in Revision." *SQ*, 13 (1962): 187-205.]

1435   VELZ, John W. "The Text of *JC* in the Second Folio." *SQ*, 20 (1969): 95-98.

Commentary

See also The Tragedies (**3616-3734**), The Roman Plays (after **3734**), and The Problem Plays (after **3734**); **2866, 2879, 3006, 3035, 3053, 3065, 3165, 3238, 3274, 3294, 3744, 3757, 4407,** and **4436.**

1436   ANDERSEN, Peter S. "Shakespeare's *Caesar:* The Language of Sacrifice." *CompD*, 3 (1969): 3-26.

1437   ANSON, John S. "*JC:* The Politics of the Hardened Heart." *ShakS* *2 1966* (1967), pp. 11-33.

1438   BELLRINGER, A. W. "*JC:* Room Enough." *CritQ*, 12 (1970): 31-48.

1439   BONJOUR, Adrien. *The Structure of* JC. Liverpool U.P., 1958.

1440   BOWDEN, William R. "The Mind of Brutus." *SQ*, 17 (1966): 57-67.

1441   BREWER, D. S. "Brutus' Crime: A Footnote to *JC.*" *RES*, 3 (1952): 51-54.

1442 BREYER, Bernard R. "A New Look at *JC*." In *Essays in Honor of W. C. Curry.* Vanderbilt U.P., 1954.

1443 BRUMEAU, Jean. "La Figure de Jules César de Dante à Shakespeare." In *EA*, 17, **2776.**

1444 BURKE, Kenneth. "Antony in Behalf of the Play." *SoR*, 1 (1935): 308-19. Repr. in Burke, *The Philosophy of Literary Form.* Louisiana State U.P., 1941. Repr. New York: Vintage, 1957.

1445 CHANG, Joseph S. M. J. "*JC* in the Light of Renaissance Historiography." *JEGP*, 69 (1970): 63-71.

1446 CONNOLLY, Thomas F. "Shakespeare and the Double Man." *SQ*, 1 (1950): 30-35.

1447 COURSEN, Herbert R. "The Fall and Decline of *JC*." *TSLL*, 4 (1962): 241-51.

1448 CRAIK, George L. *The English of Shakespeare; Illustrated in a Philological Commentary on His* JC. Ed. W. J. Rolfe from 3rd rev. London ed. (1864). Boston: Ginn, 1869. Repr. 1902. Repr. New York: AMS.

1449 DEAN, Leonard F., ed. *Twentieth-Century Interpretations of* JC. Englewood Cliffs, N.J.: Prentice-Hall, 1968. [Introd. and 18 sel. from prev. pub. wks.]

1450 DEUTSCHBEIN, Max. "Die Tragik in Shakespeares *JC*." *Anglia*, 62 (1938): 306-20.

1451 FELDMAN, Harold. "Unconscious Envy in Brutus." *AI*, 9 (1952): 307-35.

1452 FELHEIM, Marvin. "The Problem of Time in *JC*." *HLQ*, 13 (1949-50): 399-405.

1453 FOAKES, Reginald A. "An Approach to *JC*." *SQ*, 5 (1954): 259-70.

1454 FORTIN, Rene E. "*JC*: An Experiment in Point of View." *SQ*, 19 (1968): 341-47.

1455 FOWLER, W. Warde. "The Tragic Element in Shakespeare's *JC.*" *Trans. Royal Soc. of Literature*, 30 (1910): 31-58. Repr. in Fowler, *Roman Essays and Interpretations.* Oxford U.P., 1920.

1456 HALL, Vernon. "*JC*: A Play without Political Bias." In *Studies ... in Memory of Karl Julius Holzknecht*, **2762.**

1457 HAPGOOD, Robert. "Speak Hands for Me: Gesture as Language in *JC*." *DramS* 5 (1966): 162-70.

1458 HARTSOCK, Mildred E. "The Complexity of *JC*." *PMLA*, 81 (1966): 56-62.

1459 HUNTER, Mark. "Politics and Character in Shakespeare's *JC*." *EDH*, 10 (1931): 109-40.

1460   KIRSCHBAUM, Leo. "Shakespeare's Stage Blood and Its Critical Significance." *PMLA*, 64 (1949): 517-29.

1461   KLEIN, David. "Has Cassius Been Misinterpreted?" *SAB*, 14 (1939): 27-36.

1462   KNIGHTS, Lionel C. "Personality and Politics in *JC*." *Anglica*, 5 (1964): 1-24. Repr. in *Further Explorations*, **3132**.

1462a   —. "Shakespeare and Political Wisdom: A Note on the Personalism of *JC* and *Cor*." *SR*; see **952**.

1463   LLOYD, Michael. "Antony and the Game of Chance." *JEGP*; see **843**.

1464   LUNDHOLM, Helge. "Mark Antony's Speech and the Psychology of Persuasion." *Character and Personality*, 6 (1938): 293-305.

1465   McDOWELL, John H. "Analyzing *JC* for Modern Production." *QJS*, 31 (1945): 303-14.

1466   McNAMEE, Lawrence F. "The First Production of *JC* on the German Stage." *SQ*, 10 (1959): 409-21. [Trans. in 1741; produced in 1785 by Baron Wolfgang von Dalberg.]

1467   MARKELS, Julian, ed. *Shakespeare's* JC. New York: Scribner's, 1961. [Incl. text, 9 sel. from prev. pub. crit. wks., mostly modern.]

1468   MORSBACH, Lorenz. *Shakespeares Cäsarbild*. Halle: Niemeyer, 1935.

1469   MUSGROVE, Sydney. *JC*. Sydney: Australian English Association, 1941.

1470   ORNSTEIN, Robert T. "Seneca and the Political Drama of *JC*." *JEGP*, 57 (1958): 51-56.

1471   PAOLUCCI, Anne. "The Tragic Hero in *JC*." *SQ*, 11 (1960): 329-33.

1472   PETERSON, Douglas L. "'Wisdom Consumed in Confidence': An Examination of Shakespeare's *JC*." *SQ*, 16 (1965): 19-28.

1473   PRIOR, Moody E. "The Search for a Hero in *JC*." *RenD*, 2 (1969): 81-101.

1474   RABKIN, Norman. "Structure, Convention, and Meaning in *JC*." *JEGP*, 63 (1964): 240-54.

1475   REES, Joan. "*JC*—An Earlier Play and an Interpretation." *MLR*, 50 (1955): 135-41.

1476   RIBNER, Irving. "Political Issues in *JC*." *JEGP*, 56 (1957): 10-22.

1477   SANDERS, Norman. "The Shift of Power in *JC*." *REL*, 5 (1964): 24-35.

1478   SCHANZER, Ernest. "The Problem of *JC*." *SQ*, 6 (1955): 297-308.

1479   —. "The Tragedy of Shakespeare's Brutus." *ELH*, 22 (1955): 1-15.

1480 SMITH, Gordon R. "Brutus, Virtue, and Will." *SQ*, 10 (1959): 367-79.

1481 STIRLING, Brents. "'Or Else This Were a Savage Spectacle.'" *PMLA*, 66 (1951): 765-74. [Later version in *Unity in Shakespearian Tragedy*, 3724.]

1482 TASSIN, Algernon D. "*JC*." In *Shaksperian Studies*, 2798.

1483 UHLER, John E. "*JC:* A Morality of Respublica." In *Studies in Shakespeare*, 2797.

1484 VELZ, John W. "Clemency, Will, and Just Cause in *JC*." *ShS 22* (1969), pp. 109-18.

1485 —. "'If I Were Brutus Now . . .': Role-playing in *JC*." *ShakS 4 1968* (1969), pp. 149-59.

1486 —. "Undular Structure in *JC*." *MLR*, 66 (1971): 21-30.

1487 WICKERT, Maria. "Antikes Gedankengut in Shakespeares *JC*." *SJ*, 82/83 (1948): 11-33.

1488 WILKINSON, Andrew M. "A Psychological Approach to *JC*." *REL*, 7 (1966): 65-78.

1489 WILSON, J. Dover. "Ben Jonson and *JC*." *ShS 2* (1949), pp. 36-43.

1490 ZANDVOORT, Reinard W. "Brutus's Forum Speech in *JC*." *RES*, 16 (1940): 62-66. Repr. in Zandvoort, *Collected Papers*. Groningen: Wolters, 1954.

KING LEAR

Editions

1491   DUTHIE, George Ian, ed. *Shakespeare's* Lr: *A Critical Edition.* Oxford: Blackwell, 1949.

1492   FURNESS, Horace H., ed. *Lr.* New Variorum. Philadelphia: Lippincott, 1880.

1493   HARRISON, George B., and Robert F. McDonnell, eds. *Lr: Text, Sources, Criticism.* New York: Harcourt, Brace and World, 1962. [HB&W.] [Incl. portion of Tate's *Lr*, sel. from prev. pub. crit. wks.]

1494   VIËTOR, Wilhelm, ed. *Lr: Parallel Texts of the First Quarto and the First Folio.* Shakespeare Reprints 1. Marburg: N. G. Elwert'sche Verlagsbuchhandlung, 1892. [Text of Q1 from Praetorius facs.; of F1 from Halliwell-Phillipps reduced facs., supplemented by references to Booth facs.]

1495   WILSON, J. Dover, ed. *Lr.* London: Faber & Faber, [1931]. [Facs. from Grenville copy of F1 in the British Museum.]

Textual Commentary

See also **268** and **713**.

1496   ADAMS, Joseph Q. "The Quarto of *Lr* and Shorthand." *MP*, 31 (1933-34): 135-63.

1497   BOWERS, Fredson T. "An Examination of the Method of Proof Correction in *Lr*." *Library*, 2 (1947-48): 20-44.

1498   CAIRNCROSS, Andrew S. "The Quartos and the Folio Text of *Lr*." *RES*, 6 (1955): 252-58.

1499   CAUTHEN, Irby B. "Compositor Determination in the First Folio *Lr*." *SB*, 5 (1952-53): 73-80.

1500   CRAIG, Hardin. "The Composition of *Lr*." *RenP 1961* (1962), pp. 57-61.

1501   DORAN, Madeleine. "Elements in the Composition of *Lr*." *SP*, 30 (1933): 34-58.

1502   ——. "The Quarto of *Lr* and Bright's Shorthand." *MP*, 33 (1935): 139-57.

1503   ——. *The Text of* Lr. Stanford U.P., 1931. Repr. New York: AMS.

1504   DUTHIE, George Ian. *Elizabethan Shorthand and the First Quarto of* Lr. Oxford: Blackwell, 1949.

1505   FARMER, John S., ed. *The True Chronicle History of King Leir . . . 1605.* Tudor Facs. Texts. Amersham: Farmer, 1913. Repr. New York: AMS.

1506 GREG, Walter W. "The Date of *Lr* and Shakespeare's Use of Earlier Versions of the Story." *Library*, 20 (1939-40): 377-400.

1507 —. "The Function of Bibliography in Literary Criticism Illustrated in a Study of the Text of *Lr.*" *Neophil;* see **268.**

1508 —. "*Lr*–Mislineation and Stenography." *Library*, 17 (1936-37): 172-83.

1509 —. "The Staging of *Lr.*" *RES*, 16 (1940): 300- 303. [Folio text may preserve act and scene division of the original production. But see radical revision of this idea in Greg, *RES*, 22 (1946): 229.]

1510 —. *The Variants in the First Quarto of* Lr: *A Bibliographical and Literary Inquiry.* London: Bibliographical Society, 1940.

1511 —, and R. Warwick Bond, eds. *The History of King Leir 1605.* Oxford U.P. for the Malone Society, 1907.

1512 HOGAN, Jeremiah J. "Cutting His Text According to His Measure: A Note on the Folio *Lr.*" In *Studies . . . Presented to Baldwin Maxwell,* **2824.** [Justification of lines.]

1513 HONIGMANN, Ernst A. J. "Spelling Tests and the First Quarto of *Lr.*" *Library*, 20 (1965): 310-15.

1514 HUBLER, Edward L. "The Verse Lining in the First Quarto of *Lr.*" In *Essays . . . in Honor of T. M. Parrott,* **2771.**

1515 KIRSCHBAUM, Leo. "How Jane Bell Came to Print the Third Quarto of Shakespeare's *Lr.*" *PQ*, 17 (1938): 308-11.

1516 —. *The True Text of* Lr. Johns Hopkins U.P., 1945.

1517 LEE, Sidney, ed. The Chronicle History of King Leir: *The Original of Shakespeare's* Lr. London: Chatto & Windus, 1909.

1518 SMIDT, Kristian. "The Quarto and the Folio *Lr:* Another Look at the Theories of Textual Deviation." *ES*, 45 (1964): 149-62.

1519 WILLIAMS, George W. "A Note on *Lr*, III.ii.1-3." *SB*, 2 (1949-50): 175-82.

1520 WILLIAMS, Philip. "The Compositor of the 'Pied Bull' *Lr.*" *SB*, 1 (1948-49): 59-68.

1521 —. "Two Problems in the Folio Text of *Lr.*" *SQ*, 4 (1953): 451-60.

Commentary

See also The Tragedies (3616-3734); **55, 151, 330, 601, 721, 733, 740, 750, 752, 1728, 2866, 2886, 3035, 3082, 3137, 3142, 3173, 3284, 3293, 3317, 3326, 3370, 3412, 3420, 3631, 3695, 3757, 3807, 4114, 4205, 4207, 4407,** and **4437.**

1522 ADAMS, John C. "The Original Staging of *Lr.*" In *Adams Memorial Studies,* **2794.**

1523   ALPERS, Paul J. "*Lr* and the Theory of the 'Sight Pattern.'" In *In Defense of Reading*. Ed. Reuben A. Brower and Richard Poirier. New York: Dutton, 1962.

1524   ANSHUTZ, H. L. "Cordelia and the Fool." *RS*, 32 (1964): 240-60.

1525   BALD, R. Cecil. "'Thou Nature, Art My Goddess': Edmund and Renaissance Free-Thought." In *Adams Memorial Studies*, **2794**.

1526   BARISH, Jonas A., and Marshall Waingrow. "'Service' in *Lr*." *SQ*, 9 (1958): 347-55.

1527   BARNET, Sylvan. "Some Limitations of a Christian Approach to Shakespeare." *ELH*, 22 (1955): 81-92.

1528   BAUER, Robert J. "Despite of Mine Own Nature: Edmund and the Orders, Cosmic and Moral." *TSLL*, 10 (1968): 359-66.

1529   BENNETT, Josephine W. "The Storm Within: The Madness of Lear." *SQ*, 13 (1962): 137-55.

1530   BERGEMANN, Otto. "Zum Aufbau von *Lr*." In *SJ*, 90, **3327**.

1531   BICKERSTETH, Geoffrey L. *The Golden World of* Lr. Oxford U.P., 1947. [*PBA 1946*, 32 (1947): 147-71.]

1532   BLOCK, Edward A. "*Lr*: A Study in Balanced and Shifting Sympathies." *SQ*, 10 (1959): 499-512.

1533   BLOK, Alexander. "Shakespeare's *Lr*." In *Shakespeare in the Soviet Union*, **2809**.

1534   BLUNDEN, Edmund C. *Shakespeare's Significances*. Oxford U.P., 1929.

1535   BONHEIM, Helmut W., ed. *The* Lr *Perplex*. San Francisco: Wadsworth, 1960. [71 sel. from prev. pub. wks., Nahum Tate to William Elton.]

1536   BRANSOM, James S. H. *The Tragedy of King Lear*. Oxford: Blackwell, 1934.

1537   BROOKE, C. F. Tucker. "*Lr* on the Stage." *SR*, 21 (1913): 88-98. Rep. in *Essays on Shakespeare and Other Elizabethans*, 2688.

1538   BROOKE, Nicholas. "The Ending of *Lr*." In *Shakespeare, 1564-1964*, **2764**.

1539   ——. *Shakespeare: Lr*. London: Arnold, 1963.

1540   BURKE, Kenneth. "*Lr*: Its Form and Psychosis." *Shenandoah*, 21 (1969): 3-18.

1541   CAMPBELL, Oscar J. "The Salvation of Lear." *ELH*, 15 (1948): 93-109.

1542   CHAMBERS, Raymond W. *Lr*. Glasgow: Jackson, 1940.

1543   CHAPLIN, William H. "Form and Psychology in *Lr*." *L&P*, 19 (1969): 31-45.

1544   CRAIG, Hardin. "The Ethics of *Lr*." *PQ*, 4 (1925): 97-109.

1545 DANBY, John F. *"Lr* and Christian Patience: A Culmination." In *Poets on Fortune's Hill,* **2956.**

1546 —. *Shakespeare's Doctrine of Nature: A Study of* Lr. London: Faber & Faber, 1949.

1547 DONNELLY, John. "Incest, Ingratitude, and Insanity: Aspects of the Psychopathology of *Lr." PsyR,* 40 (1953): 149-55.

1548 DRAPER, John W. "The Old Age of King Lear." *JEGP,* 39 (1940): 527-40.

1549 DUNN, E. Catherine. "The Storm in *Lr." SQ,* 3 (1952): 329-33.

1550 DYE, Harriet. "The Appearance-Reality Theme in *Lr." CE,* 25 (1964): 514-17.

1551 ELTON, William R. Lr *and the Gods.* San Marino, Calif.: Huntington Library, 1966.

1552 EMPSON, William. "Fool in *Lr."* In *The Structure of Complex Words.* London: Chatto & Windus; New York: New Directions, 1951.

1553 EVERETT, Barbara. "The New King Lear." *CQ,* 2 (1960): 325-39.

1554 FRASER, Russell A. *Shakespeare's Poetics in Relation to* Lr. London: Routledge & Kegan Paul, 1962.

1555 FRENCH, Carolyn S. "Shakespeare's 'Folly': *Lr." SQ,* 10 (1959): 523-29.

1556 FREUD, Sigmund. "The Theme of the Three Caskets." In vol. 12, *The Standard Edition of the Complete ... Works.* Ed. James Strachey. London: Hogarth, 1953–.

1557 FRICKER, Robert. "Shakespeare und das Drama des Absurden." *SJ 1966* (West), pp. 7-29.

1558 FROST, William. "Shakespeare's Rituals and the Opening of *Lr." HudR,* 10 (1958): 577-85.

1559 FRYE, Dean. "The Context of Lear's Unbuttoning." *ELH,* 32 (1965): 17-31.

1560 GARDNER, Helen. *Lr.* London: Athlone, 1967.

1561 GREENFIELD, Thelma N. "The Clothing Motif in *Lr." SQ,* 5 (1954): 281-86.

1562 HEILMAN, Robert B. "The Lear World." In *EIE 1948,* **2979.**

1563 —. *This Great Stage: Image and Structure in* Lr. Louisiana State U.P., 1948. 2nd ed., U. of Washington P., 1963. [WP9.]

1564 HENDERSON, W. B. Drayton. "Montaigne's *Apologie of Raymond Sebond,* and *Lr." SAB,* 14 (1939): 209-25; 15 (1940): 40-54.

1565 HOCKEY, Dorothy C. "The Trial Pattern of *Lr." SQ,* 10 (1959): 389-95.

1566   HOLE, Sandra. "The Background of Divine Action in *Lr*." *SEL*, 8 (1968): 217-33.

1567   HUTCHENS, Eleanor N. "The Transfer of Power in *Lr* and *Tmp*." *REL*, 4 (1963): 82-93.

1568   ISENBERG, Arnold. "Cordelia Absent." *SQ*, 2 (1951): 185-94.

1569   JACKSON, Esther M. "*Lr:* The Grammar of Tragedy." *SQ*, 17 (1966): 25-40.

1570   JAFFA, Harry V. "The Limits of Politics." *American Political Science Review*, 51 (1957): 405-27. [I.i.]

1570a   JAMES, David G. *The Dream of Learning: An Essay on the Advancement of Learning, Ham and* Lr.   See **1102**.

1571   —. "Keats and *Lr*." In *ShS 13*, **1625**.

1572   JAYNE, Sears. "Charity in *Lr*." *SQ*, 15.2 (1964): 277-88. Also in *Shakespeare 400*, **2793**.

1573   JORGENSEN, Paul A. *Lear's Self-Discovery.* U. of California P., 1967.

1574   KAHN, Sholom J. "'Enter Lear Mad.'" *SQ*, 8 (1957): 311-29.

1575   KANZER, Mark. "Imagery in *Lr*." *AI*, 22 (1965): 3-13.

1576   KEAST, W. R. "Imagery and Meaning in the Interpretation of *Lr*." *MP*, 47 (1949): 45-64.

1577   KERNAN, Alvin B. "Formalism and Realism in Elizabethan Drama: The Miracles in *Lr*." *RenD*, 9 (1966): 59-66.

1578   KERNODLE, George R. "The Symphonic Form of *Lr*." In *Elizabethan Studies . . . in Honor of George F. Reynolds*, **2821**.

1579   KIRSCHBAUM, Leo. "Albany." In *ShS 13*, **1625**.

1580   —. "Banquo and Edgar: Character or Function?" In *EIC;* see **1746**.

1581   KNIGHTS, Lionel C. "*Lr* as Metaphor." In *Further Explorations*, **3132**.

1582   KREIDER, Paul V. "Gloucester's Eyes." *SAB*, 8 (1933): 121-32 .

1583   LAW, Robert A. "Holinshed's Leir Story and Shakespeare's." *SP*, 47 (1950): 42-50.

1584   —. "*Lr* and *Leir*." In *Studies in Honor of T. W. Baldwin*, **2760**.

1585   LEVIN, Harry. "The Heights and Depths: A Scene from *Lr*." In *More Talking of Shakespeare*, **2780**.

1586   LOTHIAN, John M. *Lr: A Tragic Reading of Life.* Toronto: Clarke, Irwin, 1949.

1587   LUMIANSKY, Robert M., and Herschel Baker, eds. *Critical Approaches to Six Major English Works:* Beowulf *through* Paradise Lost. U. of Pennsylvania P., 1968. [E. W. Talbert on *Lr*.]

1588   McCLOSKEY, John C. "The Emotive Use of Animal Imagery in *Lr*." *SQ*, 13 (1962): 321-25.

1589   McCULLEN, Joseph T. "Edgar: The Wise Bedlam." In *Shakespeare in the Southwest*, **2817**.

1590   MACK, Maynard. Lr *in Our Time*. U. of California P., 1968.

1591   MacLEAN, Hugh. "Disguise in *Lr*." *SQ*, 11 (1960): 49-54.

1592   MacLEAN, Norman. "Episode, Scene, Speech, and Word: The Madness of Lear." In *Critics and Criticism*. Ed. Ronald S. Crane. U. of Chicago P., 1952.

1593   McNEIR, Waldo F. "The Role of Edmund in *Lr*." *SEL*, 8 (1968): 187-216.

1594   MARKELS, Julian. "Shakespeare's Confluence of Tragedy and Comedy: *TN* and *Lr*." *SQ*, 15.2 (1964): 75-88. Also in *Shakespeare 400*, **2793**.

1595   MARKS, Carol L. " 'Speak What We Feel': The End of *Lr*." *ELN*, 5 (1968): 163-71.

1596   MAXWELL, James C. "The Technique of Invocation in *Lr*." *MLR*, 45 (1950): 142-47.

1597   MENDONÇA, Barbara H. C. de. "The Influence of *Gorboduc* on *Lr*." In *ShS 13*, **1625**.

1598   MERCHANT, W. Moelwyn. "Costume in *Lr*." In *ShS 13*, **1625**.

1599   MORRIS, Ivor. "Cordelia and Lear." *SQ*, 8 (1957): 141-58.

1600   MORTENSEN, Peter. "The Role of Albany." *SQ*, 16 (1965): 217-25.

1601   MUIR, Edwin. *The Politics of* Lr. Glasgow: Jackson, 1947.

1602   MUIR, Kenneth. "Madness in *Lr*." In *ShS 13*, **1625**.

1603   —. "Samuel Harsnett and *Lr*." *RES*, 2 (1951): 11-21.

1604   MYRICK, Kenneth. "Christian Pessimism in *Lr*." In *Shakespeare, 1564-1964*, **2764**.

1605   NOWOTTNY, Winifred M. T. "Lear's Questions." *ShS 10* (1957), pp. 90-97.

1606   —. "Some Aspects of the Style of *Lr*." In *ShS 13*, **1625**.

1607   OPPEL, Horst. *Die Gerichtsszene in* Lr. Mainz: Steiner, 1968.

1608   ORWELL, George. "Lear, Tolstoy, and the Fool." In *Shooting an Elephant and Other Essays*. London: Martin Secker & Warburg; New York: Harcourt Brace and World, 1950.

1609   PAUNCZ, Arpad. "Psychopathology of Shakespeare's *Lr*." *AI*, 9 (1952): 57-78.

1610   PECK, Russell A. "Edgar's Pilgrimage: High Comedy in *Lr*." *SEL*, 7 (1967): 219-37.

1611   PERKINSON, Richard H. "Is This the Promised End?" *EStn*, 73 (1939): 202-11.

1612   —. "Shakespeare's Revision of the Lear Story and the Structure of *Lr*." *PQ*, 22 (1943): 315-29.

1613   PRESSON, Robert K. "Boethius, King Lear, and 'Maystresse Philosophie.'" *JEGP*, 64 (1965): 406-24.

1614   PROVOST, Foster. "On Justice and the Music in *R2* and *Lr*." *AnM*, 2 (1961): 55-71.

1615   PYLE, Fitzroy. "*TN, Lr*, and *Arcadia*." *MLR*, 43 (1948): 449-55.

1616   REYNOLDS, George F. "Two Conventions of the Open Stage (As Illustrated in *Lr*)." *PQ*, 41 (1962): 82-95.

1617   RIBNER, Irving. "The Gods Are Just." *TDR*, 2 (1958): 34-54.

1618   —. "Shakespeare and Legendary History: *Lr* and *Cym*." *SQ*; see **989**.

1619   —. "Sidney's *Arcadia* and the Structure of *Lr*." *ShN*, 24 (1952): 63-68.

1620   ROSIER, James L. "The Lex Aeterna and *Lr*." *JEGP*, 53 (1954): 574-80.

1621   ROSINGER, Lawrence. "Gloucester and Lear: Men Who Act Like Gods." *ELH*, 35 (1968): 491-504.

1622   RUSCHE, Harry. "Edmund's Conception and Nativity in *Lr*." *SQ*, 20 (1969): 161-64.

1623   SCHOFF, Francis G. "King Lear: Moral Example or Tragic Protagonist?" *SQ*, 13 (1962): 157-72.

1624   SEWALL, Richard B. *The Vision of Tragedy*. Yale U.P., 1959. [One chap. on *Lr*.]

1625   *ShS 13* (1960). [9 essays on *Lr*.]

1626   SIEGEL, Paul N. "Adversity and the Miracle of Love in *Lr*." *SQ*, 6 (1955): 325-36.

1627   SKULSKY, Harold. "*Lr* and the Meaning of Chaos." *SQ*, 17 (1966): 3-17.

1628   SMITH, Robert M. "A Good Word for Oswald." In *A Tribute to George Coffin Taylor*, **2822**.

1629   SNYDER, Susan. "*Lr* and the Prodigal Son." *SQ*, 17 (1966): 361-69.

1630   SOENS, A. L. "Cudgels and Rapiers: The Staging of the Edgar-Oswald Fight in *Lr*." *ShakS 5 1969* (1970), pp. 149-58.

1631   STAMPFER, J. "The Catharsis of *Lr*." In *ShS 13*, **1625**.

1632   STETNER, Sam C. V., and Oscar B. Goodman. "Lear's Darker Purpose." *L&P*, 18 (1968): 82-90.

1633   STEVENSON, Warren. "Albany as Archetype in *Lr*." *MLQ*, 26 (1965): 257-64.

1634   STEWART, John I. M. "The Blinding of Gloster." *RES*, 21 (1945): 264-70.

1635 STOCKHOLDER, Katherine. "The Multiple Genres of *Lr:* Breaking the Archetypes." *BuR,* 16 (1968): 40-63.

1636 STONE, George W. "Garrick's Production of *Lr:* A Study in the Temper of the Eighteenth-Century Mind." *SP,* 45 (1948): 89-103.

1637 STUART, Betty K. "Truth and Tragedy in *Lr.*" *SQ,* 18 (1967): 167-80.

1638 SWINBURNE, Algernon C. *"Lr."* In *Three Plays of Shakespeare*. New York: Harper, 1909. [*Lr, Oth, R2.*]

1639 SZYFMAN, Arnold. *"Lr* on the Stage." In *ShS 13*, **1625**.

1640 TALBERT, Ernest W. "Lear the King: A Preface to a Study of Shakespeare's Tragedy." In *Medieval and Renaissance Studies.* Proceedings of the Southeastern Institute of Medieval and Renaissance Studies, Summer 1965. Ed. O. B. Hardison. U. of North Carolina P., 1966. See also **1587**.

1641 TOLSTOY, Leo. "Tolstoy on Shakespeare and the Drama." *Fortnightly Review,* 80 (1906): 963-83.

1642 TRAVERSI, Derek A. *"Lr."* *Scrutiny,* 19 (1952-53): 43-64, 126-42, 206-30.

1643 VICKERS, Brian. *"Lr* and Renaissance Paradoxes." *MLR,* 63 (1968): 305-14.

1644 WALTON, James K. "Lear's Last Speech." In *ShS 13*, **1625**.

1645 WEIDHORN, Manfred. "Lear's Schoolmasters." *SQ,* 13 (1962): 305-16.

1646 WEST, Robert H. "Sex and Pessimism in *Lr.*" *SQ,* 11 (1960): 55-60.

1647 WILLIAMS, George W. "The Poetry of the Storm in *Lr.*" *SQ,* 2 (1951): 57-71.

A LOVER'S COMPLAINT

Commentary

See also Poems (**2153-62**).

1648   JACKSON, Macdonald P. *LC: Its Date and Authenticity*.   Auckland, New Zealand: Dobbie, 1965.

1649   MUIR, Kenneth. "*LC:* A Reconsideration."   In *Shakespeare, 1564-1964,* **2764**.

LOVE'S LABOUR'S LOST

Editions

1650   FURNESS, Horace H., ed. *LLL*. New Variorum. Philadelphia: Lippincott, 1904.

Textual Commentary

See also **310**.

1651   CUNNINGHAM, James V. "'With That Facility': False Starts and Revisions in *LLL*." In *Essays on Shakespeare*, **2770**.

Commentary

See also The Comedies (**3444-3549**); **628, 721, 733, 3035, 3405, 3465,** and **3476**.

1652   AGNEW, Gates K. "Berowne and the Progress of *LLL*." *ShakS 4 1968* (1969), pp. 40-72.

1653   BABCOCK, R. Weston. "Fools, Fowls, and Perttaunt-like in *LLL*." *SQ*, 2 (1951): 211-19.

1654   BARTON, Anne (Roesen). "*LLL*." *SQ*, 4 (1953): 411-26.

1655   BERRY, Ralph. "The Words of Mercury." In *ShS 22*, **3530**.

1656   BOUGHNER, Daniel C. "Don Armado and the *Commedia dell'Arte*." *SP*, 37 (1940): 201-24.

1657   ——. "Don Armado as a Gallant." *Revue Anglo-Américaine*, 13 (1935-36): 18-28.

1658   BRADBROOK, Muriel C. *The School of Night.* Cambridge U.P., 1936.

1659   BROWNE, Ray B. "The Satiric Use of 'Popular' Music in *LLL*." *SFQ*, 23 (1959): 137-49.

1660   CALDERWOOD, James L. "*LLL:* A Wantoning with Words." *SEL*, 5 (1965): 317-32.

1661   COURSEN, Herbert R. "*LLL* and the Comic Truth." *PLL*, 6 (1970): 316-22.

1662   DRAPER, John W. "Tempo in *LLL*." *ES*, 29 (1948): 129-37.

1663   GODSHALK, William L. "Pattern in *LLL*." *RenP 1968* (1969), pp. 41-48.

1664   GRAY, Austin K. "The Secret of *LLL*." *PMLA*, 39 (1924): 581-611.

1665   HARBAGE, Alfred. "*LLL* and the Early Shakespeare." *PQ*, 41 (1962): 18-36. Also in *Studies... Presented to Baldwin Maxwell*, **2824**, and *Stratford Papers on Shakespeare, 1961*, **2787**.

1666   HASLER, Jörg. "Enumeration in *LLL*." *ES*, 50 (1969): 176-85.

1667   HOY, Cyrus. "*LLL* and the Nature of Comedy." *SQ*, 13 (1962): 31-40.

1668   LEFRANC, Abel. Les Éléments français de *Peines d'amour perdues* de Shakespeare." *Revue Historique*, 178 (1937): 411-32.

1669   LEVER, Julius W. "Three Notes on Shakespeare's Plants." *RES,* 3 (1952): 117-29. [Indebtedness to Gerard's *Herbal* (1597) affects dating of *LLL*.]

1670   McLAY, Catherine M. "The Dialogues of Spring and Winter: A Key to the Unity of *LLL*." *SQ*, 18 (1967): 119-27.

1671   MATTHEWS, William. "Language in *LLL*." *E&S*, 17 (1964): 1-11.

1672   PARSONS, Philip. "Shakespeare and the Mask." *ShS 16* (1963), pp.121-31.

1673   PHELPS, John. "The Source of *LLL*." *SAB*, 17 (1942): 97-102 .

1674   SCHRICKX, W. *Shakespeare's Early Contemporaries: The Background of the Harvey-Nashe Polemic and* LLL. Antwerp: Nederlandsche Boekhandel, 1956. Repr. New York: AMS.

1675   SPENS, Janet. "Notes on *LLL*." *RES*, 7 (1931): 331-34. [Rev. *ca.* 1593-94, augmented in 1597.]

1676   SPEVACK, Marvin. "Shakespeare's Early Use of Wordplay: *LLL*." In *Festschrift für Edgar Mertner.* Ed. Bernhard F. Fabian and Ulrich Suerbaum. Munich: Fink, 1969.

1677   STRATHMANN, Ernest A. "The Textual Evidence for 'The School of Night.'" *MLN*, 56 (1941): 176-86.

1678   STRATTON, Lowell D. "The Nine Worthies." *Ashland Studies in Shakespeare*, 2 (1956): 67-99.

1679   TAYLOR, Rupert. *The Date of* LLL. Columbia U.P., 1932. Repr. New York: AMS.

1680   WESTLUND, Joseph. "Fancy and Achievement in *LLL*." *SQ*, 18 (1967): 37-46.

1681   YATES, Frances A. *A Study of* LLL. Shakespeare Problem Series, 5. Cambridge U.P., 1936.

LOVE'S LABOUR'S WON

Commentary

See also **2345**.

682   BALDWIN, Thomas W. *Shakspere's* Love's Labor's Won: *New Evidence from the Account Book of an Elizabethan Bookseller.* Southern Illinois U.P., 1957.

683   TOLMAN, Albert H. *What Has Become of Shakespeare's Play* Love's Labour's Won? U. of Chicago, 1902. Repr. New York: AMS.

MACBETH

Editions

See also Canon (**570-605**) and **728**.

1684   ADAMS, Joseph Q., ed. *Mac*. Boston: Houghton Mifflin, [1931]

1685   FURNESS, Horace H., ed. *Mac*. New Variorum. Philadelphia: Lip‑
        pincott, 1873. Rev. ed., 1903.

1686   WILSON, J. Dover, ed. *Mac*. London: Faber & Gwyer, [1928]
        [Facs. from Grenville copy of F1 in the British Museum.]

Textual Commentary

1687   AMNÉUS, Daniel A. "The Cawdor Episode in *Mac*." *JEGP*, 63
        (1964): 185-90.

1688   ——. "A Missing Scene in *Mac*." *JEGP*, 60 (1961): 435-40.

1689   DREES, L., and H. de Vocht, eds. *The Witch*. Louvain: Ch. Uyst
        pruyst, 1945.

1690   FLATTER, Richard. "Hecate, 'The Other Three Witches,' and Their
        Songs." *SJ*, 95 (1959): 225-37.

1691   ——. "The Latest Edition of *Mac*." *MP*, 49 (1951-52): 124-32
        [New Sh.]

1692   ——. "Who Wrote the Hecate-Scene?" *SJ*, 93 (1957): 196-210.
        [See also John P. Cutts, "Who Wrote the Hecate-Scene?" *SJ*, 94
        (1958): 202-9.]

1693   GREG, Walter W. "Some Notes on Crane's Manuscript of *The
        Witch*." *Library*, 22 (1941-42): 208-22.

1694   ——, and Frank P. Wilson, eds. The Witch *by Thomas Middleton*.
        Oxford U.P. for the Malone Society, 1950. [2 songs interpolated
        in *Mac*.]

1695   LYLE, E. B. "The Speech-Heading 'I' in Act IV, Scene I, of the
        Folio Text of *Mac*." *Library*, 25 (1970): 150-51.

1696   NOSWORTHY, James M. "The Bleeding Captain Scene in *Mac*."
        RES, 22 (1946): 126-30. [Supports attribution to Sh. See also
        Holger Nørgaard, *RES*, 6 (1955): 395-96.]

1697   ——. "The Hecate Scenes in *Mac*." *RES*, 24 (1948): 138-39. [Au‑
        thorship.]

1698   ——. "*Mac* at the Globe." *Library*, 2 (1947-48): 108-18. [Omitted
        scenes.]

1699   ——. "Shakespeare and the Siwards." *RES*, 24 (1948): 139-41.
        [The genuineness of at least 20 of the last 40 lines of *Mac*.]

1700   SPENCER, Christopher. *Davenant's* Mac *from the Yale Manuscript: An Edition, with a Discussion of the Relation of Davenant's Text to Shakespeare*. Yale U.P., 1961.

1701   THALER, Alwin. "The 'Lost' Scenes of *Mac*." *PMLA*, 49 (1934): 835-47.

Commentary

See also The Tragedies (3616-3734); 151, 750, 756, 757, 782, 789, 881, 2245, 2803, 2858, 2952, 2971, 3003, 3038, 3106, 3137, 3165, 3177, 3201, 3230, 3284, 3290, 3326, 3354, 3420, 3551, 3552, 3608, 3655, 3695, 3744, 3757, 3951, 4207, 4407, and 4438.

1702   ANDERSON, Ruth L. "The Pattern of Behavior Culminating in *Mac*." *SEL*, 3 (1963): 151-73.

1703   ARTHOS, John. "The Naive Imagination and the Destruction of Macbeth." *ELH*, 14 (1947): 114-26.

1704   AUDEN, Wystan H. "The Dyer's Hand." *The Listener*, 53 (June 1955): 1063-66.

1705   BALD, R. Cecil. "*Mac* and the 'Short' Plays." *RES*, 4 (1928): 429-31.

1706   BARTHOLOMEUSZ, Dennis. *Macbeth and the Players*. Cambridge U.P., 1969.

1707   BERNAD, Miguel A. "The Five Tragedies in *Mac*." *SQ*, 13 (1962): 49-61.

1708   BLISSETT, William. " 'The Secret'st Man of Blood': A Study of Dramatic Irony in *Mac*." *SQ*, 10 (1959): 397-408.

1709   BOOTH, Wayne. "Macbeth as Tragic Hero." *JGE*, 6 (1951): 17-25. Rev. version in *Shakespeare's Tragedies*, 3689.

1710   BRADBROOK, Muriel C. "The Sources of *Mac*." *ShS 4* (1951), pp. 35-48.

1711   BROOKS, Cleanth. "The Naked Babe and the Cloak of Manliness." In *The Well-Wrought Urn*. New York: Reynal & Hitchcock, 1947.

1712   BROWN, John R. *Shakespeare: Mac*. London: Arnold, 1963.

1713   BURRELL, Margaret D. "*Mac:* A Study in Paradox." *SJ*, 90 (1954): 167-90.

1714   BYRNE, M. St. Clare. "The Stage Costuming of *Mac* in the Eighteenth Century." In *Studies in English Theatre History in Memory of Gabrielle Enthoven*. London: Society for Theatre Research, 1952.

1715   CHAMBERS, David L. *The Metre of* Mac. Princeton U.P., 1903. Repr. New York: AMS.

1716   COLLMER, Robert G. "An Existentialist Approach to *Mac*." *Person*, 41 (1960): 484-91.

1717   COURSEN, Herbert R. "In Deepest Consequence: *Mac*." *SQ*, 18 (1967): 375-88.

1718   CUNNINGHAM, Dolora G. *"Mac:* The Tragedy of the Hardened Heart." *SQ*, 14 (1963): 39-47.

1719   CURRY, Walter C. "The Demonic Metaphysics of *Mac*." *SP*, 30 (1933): 395-426. Repr. in *Shakespeare's Philosophical Patterns*, **2953**.

1720   —. "Macbeth's Changing Character." *JEGP*, 34 (1935): 311-38. Repr. in *Shakespeare's Philosophical Patterns*, **2953**.

1721   CUTTS, John P. "The Original Music to Middleton's *The Witch*." *SQ*, 7 (1956): 203-9.

1722   DAVID, Richard. "The Tragic Curve." *ShS 9* (1956), pp. 122-31.

1723   DEAN, Leonard F. *"Mac* and Modern Criticism." *EJ*, 47 (1958): 57-67.

1724   DONOHUE, Joseph W. "Kemble and Mrs. Siddons in *Mac:* The Romantic Approach to Tragic Character." *TN*, 22 (1968): 65-86.

1725   DORAN, Madeleine. "That Undiscovered Country." *PQ*, 20 (1941): 413-27.

1726   DUTHIE, George Ian. "Antithesis in *Mac*." In *ShS 19*, **1766**.

1727   DYSON, J. P. "The Structural Function of the Banquet Scene in *Mac*." *SQ*, 14 (1963): 369-78.

1728   ELLIOTT, George R. *Dramatic Providence in* Mac. Princeton U.P., 1958. Repr. New York: Greenwood. [Also essay on *Lr*.]

1729   EMPSON, William. "Dover Wilson on *Mac*." *KR*, 14 (1952): 84-102.

1730   EWBANK, Inga-Stina. "The Fiend-like Queen: A Note on *Mac* and Seneca's *Medea*." In *ShS 19*, **1766**.

1731   FERGUSSON, Francis. *"Mac* as the Imitation of an Action." In *The Human Image in Dramatic Literature*, **3000**.

1732   FERGUSSON, James. *The Man behind Macbeth and Other Studies*. London: Faber & Faber, 1969.

1733   FREUD, Sigmund. "Those Wrecked by Success." In vol. 14, *The Standard Edition of the Complete . . . Works*. Ed. James Strachey. London: Hogarth, 1953–.

1734   FRYE, Roland M. *"Mac* and the Powers of Darkness." *EUQ*, 8 (1952): 164-74.

1735   GARDNER, Helen. "Interpretations." In *The Business of Criticism*, **3021**.

1736   HALIO, Jay L. *Approaches to* Mac. Belmont, Calif.: Wadsworth, 1966. [26 sel. from prev. pub. wks., Aristotle to present.]

1737   HARDING, D. W. "Women's Fantasy of Manhood: A Shakespearian Theme." *SQ*, 20 (1969): 245-53.

1738 HEILMAN, Robert B. "The Criminal as Tragic Hero." In *ShS 19*, **1766**.

1739 HUNTER, George K. "*Mac* in the Twentieth Century." In *ShS 19*, **1766**.

1740 HUNTLEY, Frank L. "*Mac* and the Background of Jesuitical Equivocation." *PMLA*, 79 (1964): 390-400.

1741 JAARSMA, Richard J. "The Tragedy of Banquo." *L&P*, 17 (1967): 87-94.

1742 JACK, Jane H. "*Mac*, King James, and the Bible." *ELH*, 22 (1955): 173-93.

1743 JOHNSON, Samuel. *Miscellaneous Observations on* Mac ... *to Which Is Affix'd, Proposals for a New Edition of Shakeshear* [sic] *with a Specimen*. London: E. Cave, 1745.

1744 KANTAK, V. Y. "An Approach to Shakespearian Tragedy: The 'Actor' Image in *Mac*." *ShS 16* (1963), pp. 42-52.

1745 KEMBLE, John P. Mac *Reconsidered*. London: T. & J. Egerton, 1786. Repr. New York: AMS.

1746 KIRSCHBAUM, Leo. "Banquo and Edgar: Character or Function?" *EIC*, 7 (1957): 1-21.

1747 KNIGHTS, Lionel C. "On the Background of Shakespeare's Use of Nature in *Mac*." *SR*, 64 (1956): 207-17.

1748 LAW, Robert A. "The Composition of *Mac* with Reference to Holinshed." *TxSE,* 31 (1952): 35-41.

1749 LAWLOR, John J. "Mind and Hand: Some Reflections on the Study of Shakespeare's Imagery." *SQ*, 8 (1957): 179-93.

1750 LEECH, Clifford. "The Dark Side of *Mac*." *Literary Half-Yearly*, 8 (1967): 27-34.

1751 McGEE, Arthur R. "*Mac* and the Furies." In *ShS 19*, **1766**.

1752 MAETERLINCK, Maurice. "*Mac*." *Fortnightly Review*, 93 (1910): 696-99.

1753 MERCHANT, W. Moelwyn. " 'His Fiend-like Queen.' " In *ShS 19*, **1766**.

1754 MOORE, Robert E. "The Music to *Mac*." *Musical Quarterly*, 47 (1961): 22-40.

1755 MOROZOV, Mikhail M. "The Individualization of Shakespeare's Characters through Imagery." *ShS 2* (1949), pp. 83-106.

1756 MUIR, Kenneth. "Image and Symbol in *Mac*." In *ShS 19*, **1766**.

1757 MURRAY, W. A. "Why Was Duncan's Blood Golden?" In *ShS 19*, **1766**.

1758 NEILSON, Francis. *A Study of* Mac *for the Stage*. Mineola, N.Y.: Davenport, 1952.

1759 NIELSEN, Elizabeth. "*Mac*: The Nemesis of the Post-Shakespearian Actor." *SQ*, 16 (1965): 193-99.

1760   PACK, Robert. "*Mac:* The Anatomy of Loss." *YR*, 45 (1956): 533-48.

1761   PAOLUCCI, Anne. "*Mac* and *Oedipus Rex:* A Study in Paradox." In *Shakespeare Encomium,* 2802.

1762   PAUL, Henry N. *The Royal Play of* Mac. New York: Macmillan, 1950.

1763   REID, B. L. "*Mac* and the Play of Absolutes." *SR*, 73 (1965): 19-46.

1764   RIBNER, Irving. "*Mac:* the Pattern of Idea and Action." *SQ*, 10 (1959): 147-59.

1765   ——. "Political Doctrine in *Mac*." *SQ*, 4 (1953): 202-5.

1766   *ShS 19* (1966). [9 articles on *Mac*.]

1767   SMIDT, Kristian. "Two Aspects of Ambition in Elizabethan Tragedy: *Doctor Faustus* and *Mac*." *ES*, 50 (1969): 235-48.

1768   SMITH, Fred M. "The Relationship of *Mac* to *R3*." *PMLA*, 60 (1945): 1003-20.

1769   SPARGO, John W. "The Knocking at the Gate in *Mac*." In *Adams Memorial Studies*, 2794.

1770   SPENCER, Christopher. "*Mac* and Davenant's *The Rivals*." *SQ*, 20 (1969): 225-29.

1771   SPENDER, Stephen. "Time, Violence, and *Mac*." *Penguin New Writing*, 3 (1940-41): 115-26.

1772   STEIN, Arnold. "*Mac* and Word-Magic." *SR*, 59 (1951): 271-84.

1773   STIRLING, Brents. "The Unity of *Mac*." *SQ*, 4 (1953): 385-94.

1774   STOLL, Elmer E. "Source and Motive in *Mac* and *Oth*." *RES*, 19 (1943): 25-32.

1775   STONE, George W. "Garrick's Handling of *Mac*." *SP*, 38 (1941): 609-28.

1776   TOPPEN, Willem H. *Conscience in Shakespeare's* Mac. Groningen: Wolters, 1962.

1777   VESZY-WAGNER, L. "*Mac:* 'Fair Is Foul and Foul Is Fair.'" *AI*, 25 (1968): 242-57.

1778   WAITH, Eugene M. "Manhood and Valor in Two Shakespearean Tragedies." *ELH*; see 870. [*Mac* and *Ant*.]

1779   WALKER, Roy O. *The Time Is Free: A Study of* Mac. London: Dakers, 1949.

1780   WALTON, James K. "*Mac*." In *Shakespeare in a Changing World*, 2792.

1781   WICKHAM, Glynne. "Hell-Castle and Its Door-Keeper." In *ShS 19*, 1766.

MEASURE FOR MEASURE

Editions

1782   LEISI, Ernst, ed. *MM: An Old-Spelling and Old-Meaning Edition.* Heidelberg: C. Winter, 1964.

Textual Commentary

1783   MUIR, Kenneth. "The Duke's Soliloquies in *MM*." *N&Q*, 13 (1966): 135-36.

1784   MUSGROVE, Sydney. "Some Composite Scenes in *MM*." *SQ*, 15.1 (1964): 67-74.

1785   WASSON, John. "*MM:* A Text for Court Performance?" *SQ*, 21 (1970): 17-24.

Commentary

See also The Comedies (**3444-3549**) and The Problem Plays (after **3734**); **745, 756, 757, 2870, 2937, 3006, 3085, 3248, 3294, 3383, 3387, 3394, 3476, 3735, 3760, 3785,** and **4407.**

1786   BACHE, William B. MM *as Dialectical Art.* Purdue U., 1969.

1787   BALL, Robert H. "Cinthio's *Epitia* and *MM*." In *Elizabethan Studies . . . in Honor of George F. Reynolds,* **2821.**

1788   BATTENHOUSE, Roy W. "*MM* and Christian Doctrine of the Atonement." *PMLA*, 61 (1946): 1029-59.

1789   BECKERMAN, Bernard. "A Shakespearean Experiment: The Dramaturgy of *MM*." In *Elizabethan Theatre II,* **4010.**

1790   BENNETT, Josephine W. MM *as Royal Entertainment.* Columbia U.P., 1966.

1791   BERMAN, Ronald S. "Shakespeare and the Law." *SQ*, 18 (1967): 141-50.

1792   BIRJE-PATIL, J. "Marriage Contracts in *MM*." *ShakS 5 1969* (1970), pp. 106-11.

1793   BRADBROOK, Muriel C. "Authority, Truth, and Justice in *MM*." *RES*, 17 (1941): 385-99.

1794   CAPUTI, Anthony. "Scenic Design in *MM*." *JEGP*, 60 (1961): 423-34.

1795   CHAMBERS, Raymond W. *The Jacobean Shakespeare and* MM. Oxford U.P., 1938. [*PBA 1937*, 23 (1938): 135-92.] Repr. in *Man's Unconquerable Mind.* London: Cape, 1939. Repr. 1952.

1796   COGHILL, Nevill. "Comic Form in *MM*." *ShS 8* (1955), pp. 14-27.

1797 COLE, Howard C. "The 'Christian' Context of *MM*." *JEGP*, 64 (1965): 425-51.

1798 CRAIG, David. "Love and Society: *MM* and Our Own Time." In *Shakespeare in a Changing World*, **2792**.

1799 DICKINSON, John W. "Renaissance Equity and *MM*." *SQ*, 13 (1962): 287-97.

1800 Canceled.

1801 DUNKEL, Wilbur D. "Law and Equity in *MM*." *SQ*, 13 (1962): 275-85.

1802 DURHAM, Willard H. "*MM* as Measure for Critics." In *Essays in Criticism*. U. of California P., 1929.

1803 —. "What Are Thou, Angelo?" In *Studies in the Comic*. U. of California P., 1941.

1804 EMPSON, William. "Sense in *MM*." In *The Structure of Complex Words*, **2992**.

1805 FAIRCHILD, Hoxie N. "The Two Angelo's." *SAB*, 6 (1931): 53-59.

1806 FERGUSSON, Francis. "Philosophy and Theatre in *MM*." *KR*, 14 (1952): 103-20.

1807 GECKLE, George L., ed. *Twentieth-Century Interpretations of* MM. Englewood Cliffs, N.J.: Prentice-Hall, 1970. [Coll. prev. pub. essays.]

1808 HAMBURGER, Michael P. "Besonderheiten der Herzogfigur in *MM*." *SJ* (East), 105 (1969): 158-67.

1809 HARDING, Davis P. "Elizabethan Betrothals and *MM*." *JEGP*, 49 (1950): 139-58.

1810 HARRISON, John L. "The Convention of 'Heart and Tongue' and the Meaning of *MM*." *SQ*, 5 (1954): 1-10.

1811 HETHMON, Robert H. "The Theatrical Design of *MM*." *DramS*, 1 (1962): 261-77.

1812 KAUFMANN, Ralph J. "Bond Slaves and Counterfeits: Shakespeare's *MM*." *ShakS 3 1967* (1968), pp. 85-97.

1813 KNIGHTS, Lionel C. "The Ambiguity of *MM*." *Scrutiny*, 10 (1941-42): 222-33.

1814 KRIEGER, Murray. "*MM* and Elizabethan Comedy." *PMLA*, 66 (1951): 775-84.

1815 LASCELLES, Mary M. *Shakespeare's* MM. London: Athlone, 1953.

1816 LAWRENCE, William W. "*MM* and Lucio." *SQ*, 9 (1958): 443-53.

1817 LEAVIS, Frank R. "The Greatness of *MM*." *Scrutiny*, 10 (1941-42): 234-47. Repr. in *The Common Pursuit*, **3151**.

1818 LEECH, Clifford. "The 'Meaning' of *MM*." *ShS 3* (1950), pp. 66-73.

1819 LEVER, Julius W. "The Date of *MM*." *SQ*, 10 (1959): 381-88.

1820   McGINN, Donald J. "The Precise Angelo." In *Adams Memorial Studies*, **2794**.

1821   MACKAY, Eileen. *"MM." SQ*, 14 (1963): 109-13.

1822   MANSELL, Darrel. " 'Seemers' in *MM." MLQ*, 27 (1966): 270-84.

1823   MARSH, Derick R. C. "The Mood of *MM." SQ*, 14 (1963): 31-38.

1824   MAXWELL, James C. *"MM:* A Footnote to Recent Criticism." *DownR*, 65 (1947): 45-59.

1825   MERCHANT, W. Moelwyn. *"MM:* An Essay in Visual Interpretation." In *Shakespeare and the Artist*, **4461**.

1826   MILLET, Stanton. "The Structure of *MM." BUSE*, 2 (1956): 207-17.

1827   MINCOFF, Marco. *"MM:* A Question of Approach." *ShakS 2 1966* (1967), pp. 141-52.

1828   NAGARAJAN, S. *"MM* and Elizabethan Betrothals." *SQ*, 14 (1963): 115-19.

1829   NATHAN, Norman. "The Marriage of Duke Vincentio and Isabella." *SQ*, 7 (1956): 43-45.

1829a· NOWOTTNY, Winifred M. T. (Dodds). "The Character of Angelo in *MM." MLR*, 41 (1946): 246-55.

1830   NUTTALL, Anthony D. *"MM:* Quid pro Quo?" *ShakS 4 1968* (1969), pp. 231-51.

1831   ORNSTEIN, Robert T. "The Human Comedy." *UKCR*, 24 (1957): 15-22.

1832   POPE, Elizabeth M. "The Renaissance Background of *MM." ShS 2* (1949), pp. 66-82.

1833   POTTS, Abbie F. *"MM* and the Book of Justice." In *Shakespeare and* The Faerie Queene, **3248**.

1834   PRICE, Jonathan R. *"MM* and the Critics: Towards a New Approach." *SQ*, 20 (1969): 179-204.

1835   PROUTY, Charles T. "George Whetstone and the Sources of *MM." SQ*, 15.2 (1964): 131-45. Also in *Shakespeare 400*, **2793**.

1836   REIMER, Christian J. *Der Begriff der Gnade in Shakespeares* MM. Düren: Reimer, 1937.

1837   ROSCELLI, William J. "Isabella, Sin, and Civil Law." *UR*, 28 (1962): 215-27.

1838   SALE, Roger. "The Comic Mode of *MM." SQ*, 19 (1968): 55-61.

1839   SCHANZER, Ernest. "The Marriage-Contracts in *MM." ShS 13* (1960), pp. 81-89.

1840   SIEGEL, Paul N. *"MM:* The Significance of the Title." *SQ*, 4 (1953): 317-20.

1841   SKULSKY, Harold. "Pain, Law, and Conscience in *MM." JHI*, 25 (1964): 147-68.

1842   SMITH, Gordon R. "Isabella and Elbow in Varying Contexts of Interpretation." *JGE*, 17 (1965): 63-78.

1843   SMITH, Robert M. "Interpretations of *MM*." *SQ*, 1 (1950): 208-18.

1844   SMITH, Warren D. "More Light on *MM*." *MLQ*, 23 (1962): 309-22.

1845   SOELLNER, Rolf, and Samuel Bertsche, eds. MM: *Text, Source, and Criticism.* Boston: Houghton Mifflin, 1966. [Incl. 21 sel. from prev. pub. wks., Aristotle to present.]

1846   SOUTHALL, Raymond. "*MM* and the Protestant Ethic." *EIC*, 11 (1961): 10-33.

1847   STEVENSON, David L. *The Achievement of Shakespeare's* MM. Cornell U.P., 1966.

1848   —. "Design and Structure in *MM:* A New Appraisal." *ELH*, 23 (1956): 256-78.

1849   —. "The Role of James I in Shakespeare's *MM*." *ELH*, 26 (1959): 188-208.

1850   SYPHER, Wylie. "Shakespeare as Casuist: *MM*." *SR*, 58 (1950): 262-80.

1851   TRAVERSI, Derek A. "*MM*." *Scrutiny*, 11 (1942-43): 40-58.

1852   WASSON, John. "*MM:* A Play of Incontinence." *ELH*, 27 (1960): 262-75.

1853   WEIL, Herbert S. "Form and Contexts in *MM*." *CritQ*, 12 (1970): 55-72.

1854   WILSON, Harold S. "Action and Symbol in *MM* and *Tmp*." *SQ*, 4 (1953): 375-84.

1855   WILSON, Robert H. "The Mariana Plot of *MM*." *PQ*, 9 (1930): 341-50.

THE MERCHANT OF VENICE

.ditions

856 FURNESS, Horace H., ed. *MV*. New Variorum. Philadelphia: Lip pincott, 1888.

.extual Commentary

ee also 224 and 379.

857 McKENZIE, Donald F. "Compositor B's Role in *MV* Q2 (1619)." *SB*, 12 (1959): 75-90.

.ommentary

ee also The Comedies (3444-3549); 151, 733, 750, 764, 2043, 2866, 2887, 006, 3035, 3038, 3082, 3085, 3165, 3247, 3317, 3436, 3757, 3760, 4236, 407, and 4442.

858 ANDREWS, Mark E. *Law versus Equity in* MV. Colorado U.P., 1965.

859 BARNET, Sylvan, ed. *Twentieth-Century Interpretations of* MV. Englewood Cliffs, N.J.: Prentice-Hall, 1970. [Coll. prev. pub. essays.]

860 BASKERVILL, Charles R. "Bassanio as an Ideal Lover." In *The Manly Anniversary Studies in Language and Literature*. U. of Chicago P., 1923.

861 BLOOM, Allan. "Shakespeare on Jew and Christian: An Interpretation of *MV*." *SocR*, 30 (1963): 1-22.

862 BRONSTEIN, Herbert. "Shakespeare, the Jews, and *MV*." *SQ*, 20 (1969): 3-10.

863 BROWN, Beatrice D. "Mediaeval Prototypes of Lorenzo and Jessica." *MLN*, 44 (1929): 227-32.

864 BROWN, John R. "The Realization of Shylock: A Theatrical Criticism." In *Early Shakespeare*, **2766**.

865 BURCKHARDT, Sigurd. "*MV*: The Gentle Bond." *ELH*, 29 (1962): 239-62. Repr. in *Shakespearean Meanings*, **2901**.

866 CARDOZO, Jacob L. "The Background of Shakespeare's *MV*." *ES*, 14 (1932): 177-86.

867 —. *The Contemporary Jew in the Elizabethan Drama*. Amsterdam: H. J. Paris, 1925.

868 CARNOVSKY, Morris. "Mirror of Shylock." *TDR*, 3 (1959): 35-45.

1869   DONOW, Herbert S. "Shakespeare's Caskets: Unity in *MV*." *ShakS 4 1968* (1969), pp. 86-93.

1870   DRAPER, John W. "Shakespeare's Antonio and the Queen's Finance." *Neophil*, 51 (1967): 178-85.

1871   FELHEIM, Marvin. "*MV*." *ShakS 4 1968* (1969), pp. 94-108

1872   FODOR, A. "Shakespeare's Portia." *AI*, 16 (1959): 49-64.

1873   FREUD, Sigmund. "The Theme of the Three Caskets." In *Complete Works*; see **1556**.

1874   FRIEDLANDER, Gerald. *Shakespeare and the Jew*. London: Routledge; New York: Dutton, 1921.

1875   FUJIMARA, Thomas H. "Mode and Structure in *MV*." *PMLA*, 81 (1966): 499-511.

1876   GOLLANCZ, Israel. *Allegory and Mysticism in Shakespeare: A Medievalist on* MV. London: Jones, 1931.

1877   GRAHAM, Cary B. "Standards of Value in *MV*." *SQ*, 4 (1953) 145-51.

1878   GREBANIER, Bernard D. *The Truth about Shylock*. New York Random House, 1962.

1879   HAPGOOD, Robert. "Portia and the Merchant of Venice: The Gentle Bond." *MLQ*, 28 (1967): 19-32.

1880   HOLADAY, Allan. "Antonio and the Allegory of Salvation." *ShakS 4 1968* (1969), pp. 109-18.

1881   HURRELL, John D. "Love and Friendship in *MV*." *TSLL*, 3 (1961): 328-41.

1882   LANDA, Myer J. *The Shylock Myth*. London: Allen, 1942.

1883   LELYVELD, Toby B. *Shylock on the Stage*. P. of Western Reserve U., 1960.

1884   LEVER, Julius W. "Shylock, Portia, and the Values of Shakespearian Comedy." *SQ*, 3 (1952): 383-86. [See also Norman Nathan, "Rejoinder." *SQ*, 3 (1952): 386-88.]

1885   LEWALSKI, Barbara K. "Biblical Allusion and Allegory in *MV*." *SQ*, 13 (1962): 327-43.

1886   MIDGLEY, Graham. "*MV:* A Reconsideration." *EIC*, 10 (1960) 119-33.

1887   MITCHELL, Charles. "The Conscience of Venice: Shakespeare' Merchant." *JEGP*, 63 (1964): 214-25.

1888   MOODY, Anthony D. *Shakespeare:* MV. London: Arnold, 1964

1889   NATHAN, Norman. "Shylock, Jacob, and God's Judgment." *SQ* 1 (1950): 255-59.

1890   ——. "Three Notes on *MV*." *SAB*, 23 (1948): 152-73.

1891   NIEMEYER, Theodor. *Der Rechtsspruch gegen Shylock im Kaufmann von Venedig*. Munich and Leipzig: Duncker & Humblot, 1912

1892 PETTET, Ernest C. "*MV* and the Problem of Usury." *E&S*, 31 (1945): 19-33.

1893 PLOWMAN, Max. "Money and *The Merchant*." *The Adelphi*, 2 (1931): 508-13.

1894 ROSENBERG, Edgar. "The Jew in Western Drama." In *The Jew in English Drama: An Annotated Bibliography*. Ed. Edward D. Coleman. New York: New York Public Library and KTAV, 1970.

1895 ROTH, Cecil. "The Background of Shylock." *RES*, 9 (1933): 148-56.

1896 SIEGEL, Paul N. "Shylock the Puritan." *CUF*, (1962): 14-19.

1897 SIEMON, James E. "*MV:* Act V as Ritual Reiteration." *SP*, 67 (1970): 201-9.

1898 SINSHEIMER, Hermann. *Shylock: The History of a Character; or, The Myth of a Jew*. London: Gollancz, 1947. Repr. New York: Blom.

1899 SISK, John P. "Bondage and Release in *MV*." *SQ*, 20 (1969): 217-23.

1900 SISSON, Charles J. "A Colony of Jews in Shakespeare's London." *E&S*, 23 (1938): 38-51.

1901 SMALL, Samuel A. *The Return to Shakspere: The Historical Realists*. Johns Hopkins U.P., 1927. Repr. New York: AMS. Also in *Shaksperean Character Interpretation: MV*, **1902**.

1902 ——. *Shaksperean Character Interpretation: MV*. Göttingen: Vandenhoeck & Ruprecht; Johns Hopkins U.P., 1927.

1903 SMITH, John H. "Shylock: 'Devil Incarnation' or 'Poor Man . . . Wronged'?" *JEGP*, 60 (1961): 1-21.

1904 SMITH, Warren D. "Shakespeare's Shylock." *SQ*, 15.3 (1964): 193-99.

1905 STONEX, Arthur B. "The Usurer in Elizabethan Drama." *PMLA*, 31 (1916): 190-210.

1906 TEETER, Louis. "Scholarship and the Art of Criticism." *ELH*, 5 (1938): 173-94.

1907 TILLYARD, Eustace M. W. "The Trial Scene in *MV*." *REL*, 2 (1961): 51-59.

1908 WALLEY, Harold R. "Shakespeare's Portrayal of Shylock." In *Essays . . . in Honor of T. M. Parrott*, **2771**.

1909 WENGER, Berta V. "Shylocks Pfund Fleisch." *SJ*, 65 (1929): 92-174.

1910 WILSON, John H. "Granville's 'Stock-jobbing Jew.'" *PQ*, 13 (1934): 1-15.

1911 WOOD, Frederick T. "*MV* in the Eighteenth Century." *ES*, 15 (1933): 209-18.

THE MERRY WIVES OF WINDSOR

Editions

1912   DALY, Augustin. *Shakespeare's* Wiv: *A Fac-Simile in Photo-Lithography of the First Quarto (1602), Together with a Reprint of the Prompt-Copy Prepared for Use.* Introd. William Winter. New York: A. Daly, 1886. [Repr. of Griggs facs.]

1913   GREG, Walter W., ed. *Shakespeare's* Wiv *1602.* Tudor and Stuart Library. Oxford U.P., 1910. [Type facs.]

1914   HALLIWELL-PHILLIPPS, James O., ed. *The First Sketch of Shakespeare's* Wiv. London: The Shakespeare Society, 1842.

Textual Commentary

See also **191**.

1915   GREEN, William. *Shakespeare's* Wiv. Princeton U.P., 1962.

1916   HALLIWELL-PHILLIPPS, James O. *An Account of the Only Known Manuscript of Shakespeare's . . .* Wiv *Obtained from a Playhouse Copy of that Play Recently Discovered.* London: J. R. Smith, 1843. Repr. New York: AMS. [Part of a Smock Alley promptbook.]

1917   LONG, John H. "Another Masque for *Wiv.*" *SQ*, 3 (1952): 39-43.

1918   WHITE, David M. "An Explanation of the *Brook-Broome* Question in Shakespeare's *Wiv.*" *PQ*, 25 (1946): 280-83.

Commentary

See also The Comedies (**3444-3549**); **733, 1289, 2879, 3024,** and **3230**.

1919   BENNETT, A. L. "The Sources of Shakespeare's *Wiv.*" *RenQ*, 23 (1970): 429-33.

1920   BOUGHNER, Daniel C. "Traditional Elements in Falstaff." *JEGP*; see **1216**.

1921   BRUCE, Dorothy H. "*Wiv* and *Two Brethren.*" *SP*, 39 (1942): 265-78.

1922   CAMPBELL, Oscar J. "The Italianate Background of *Wiv.*" *Essays and Studies in English and Comparative Literature.* (Ann Arbor, Mich.), 8 (1932): 81-117.

1923   CHARLTON, Henry B. "Falstaff." *BJRL*; see **1221**.

1924   CROFTS, John E. V. *Shakespeare and the Post Horses.* Bristol: Arrowsmith, 1937.

1925   DRAPER, John W. "Falstaff and the Plautine Parasite." *CJ*, 33 (1938): 390-401.

1926   —. "Falstaff's Robin and Other Pages." *SP*, 36 (1939): 476-90.

1927   —. "The Humor of Corporal Nym." *SAB*; see **1319**.

1928   FORSYTHE, Robert S. "Two New Analogues of *Wiv.*" *PQ*, 7 (1928): 390-98.

1929   GRAY, Henry D. "The Rôles of William Kemp." *MLR*, 25 (1930): 261-73. [Reporter of *Wiv* (1602)?]

1930   GRINDON, Rosa L. *In Praise of Shakespeare's* Wiv. Manchester: Sherratt & Hughes, 1902.

1931   HALLER, Eleanor J. "The Realism of the Merry Wives." *West Virginia U. Studies*, 3 (1937): 32-38.

1932   HAPGOOD, Robert. "Falstaff's Vocation." *SQ*; see **1231**.

1933   HEMINGWAY, Samuel B. "On Behalf of That Falstaff." *SQ*; see **1232**.

1934   HOTSON, Leslie. "Ancient Pistol." *YR*; see **1289**.

1935   —. *Shakespeare versus Shallow.* See **461**.

1936   MURRY, John Middleton. "The Creation of Falstaff." In *Discoveries*, **3217**; repr. in *John Clare and Other Studies*, **3218**.

1937   RADOFF, M. L. "Influence of the French Farce in *H5* and *Wiv.*" *MLN*; see **1332**.

1938   REIK, Theodor. "Comedy of Intrigue." In *The Secret Self.* New York: Farrar, Straus, & Young, 1952.

1938a   ROBERTS, Jeanne A. "*Wiv:* Suitably Shallow, but neither Simple nor Slender." *ShakS 6 1970* (1972), pp. 109-23.

1939   SEWELL, Sallie. "The Relation between *Wiv* and Jonson's *Every Man in His Humour.*" *SAB*, 16 (1941): 175-89.

1940   SHIRLEY, John W. "Falstaff, an Elizabethan Glutton." *PQ*; see **1253**.

1941   SPARGO, John W. "An Interpretation of Falstaff." *Washington University Studies*; see **1255**.

1942   STEADMAN, John M. "Falstaff as Actaeon: A Dramatic Emblem." *SQ*, 14 (1963): 230-44.

1943   WEST, E. J. "On Master Slender." *CE*, 8 (1947): 228-30.

A MIDSUMMER NIGHT'S DREAM

Editions

1944   FURNESS, Horace H., ed. *MND.* New Variorum. Philadelphia: Lippincott, 1895.

Textual Commentary

1945   TURNER, Robert K. "Printing Methods and Textual Problems in *MND* Q1." *SB*, 15 (1962): 33-55. [Setting by formes.]

1945a   WIDMANN, R. L. "Use of the Computer in Historical Collation of *MND.*" In *The Computer in Literary and Linguistic Research.* Ed. R. A. Wisbey. Cambridge U.P., 1971.

Commentary

See also The Comedies (**3444-3549**) and The Romances (after **3734**); **733, 741, 757, 764, 3247, 3444, 3465, 3951, 4407,** and **4443.**

1946   ALLEN, John A. "Bottom and Titania." *SQ*, 18 (1967): 107-17.

1947   BERRY, Ralph. "No Exit from Arden." *MLR*, 66 (1971): 11-20.

1948   BETHURUM, Dorothy. "Shakespeare's Comment on Mediaeval Romance in *MND.*" *MLN*, 60 (1945): 85-94.

1949   BONNARD, Georges A. "Shakespeare's Purpose in *MND.*" *SJ*, 92 (1956): 268-79.

1950   BRADDY, Haldeen. "Shakespeare's Puck and Froissart's Orthon." *SQ*, 7 (1956): 276-80.

1951   BRIGGS, Katharine M. *The Anatomy of Puck.* London: Routledge & Kegan Paul, 1959.

1952   CALDERWOOD, James L. "*MND:* The Illusion of Drama." *MLQ*, 26 (1965): 506-22.

1953   CAMBILLARD, C. "*Le Songe d'une nuit d'été:* Thème astrologique." *EA*, 3 (1939): 118-26.

1954   CHAMBERS, Edmund K. "The Occasion of *MND.*" In *A Book of Homage to Shakespeare*, **2782**; repr. in *Shakespearean Gleanings*, **2913**.

1955   DENT, Robert W. "Imagination in *MND.*" *SQ*, 15.2 (1964): 115-29. Also in *Shakespeare 400*, **2793**.

1956   DILLINGHAM, William B. "Bottom: the Third Ingredient." *EUQ*, 12 (1956): 230-37.

1957   DORAN, Madeleine. "Pyramus and Thisbe Once More." In *Essays... in Honor of Hardin Craig*, **2786**.

1958   DRAPER, John W. "The Date of *MND*." *MLN*, 53 (1938): 266-68.

1959   FENDER, Stephen. *Shakespeare: MND*. London: Arnold, 1968.

1960   FISHER, Peter F. "The Argument of *MND*." *SQ*, 8 (1957): 307-10.

1961   GENEROSA, Sister M. "Apuleius and *MND*: Analogue or Source, Which?" *SP*, 42 (1945): 198-204.

1962   GREEN, Roger L. "Shakespeare and the Fairies." *Folklore* (London), 73 (1962): 89-103.

1963   GREENFIELD, Thelma N. "*MND* and *The Praise of Folly*." *CL*, 20 (1968): 236-44.

1964   GUI, Weston A. "Bottom's Dream." *AI*, 9 (1952): 251-305.

1965   HALLIWELL-PHILLIPPS, James O. *Illustrations of the Fairy Mythology of* MND. London: for the Shakespeare Society, 1845. Repr. Nendeln, Liechtenstein: Kraus-Thomson; New York: AMS.

1966   HOMAN, Sidney R. "The Single World of *MND*." *BuR*, 17 (1969): 72-84.

1967   KERSTEN, Dorelies. "Shakespeare's Puck." *SJ*, 98 (1962): 189-200.

1968   LAW, Robert A. "The Pre-Conceived Pattern of *MND*." *TxSE* (1943): 5-14.

1969   LEGOUIS, Émile H. "La Psychologie dans *Le Songe d'une nuit d'été*." *EA*, 3 (1939): 113-17.

1970   MERCHANT, W. Moelwyn. "*MND*: A Visual Re-creation." In *Early Shakespeare*, **2766**.

1971   MILLER, Donald C. "Titania and the Changeling." *ES*, 22 (1940): 66-70.

1972   MUIR, Kenneth. "Pyramus and Thisbe: A Study in Shakespeare's Method." *SQ*, 5 (1954): 141-53.

1973   NEMEROV, Howard. "The Marriage of Theseus and Hippolyta." *KR*, 18 (1956): 633-41.

1974   OLSEN, Paul A. "*MND* and the Meaning of Court Marriage." *ELH*, 24 (1957): 95-119.

1975   POIRIER, Michel. "Sidney's Influence upon *MND*." *SP*, 44 (1947): 483-89.

1976   REYNOLDS, Lou A., and Paul Sawyer. "Folk Medicine and the Four Fairies of *MND*." *SQ*, 10 (1959): 513-21.

1977   ROBINSON, J.W. "Palpable Hot Ice: Dramatic Burlesque in *MND*." *SP*, 61 (1964): 192-204.

1978   ROBINSON, James E. "The Ritual and Rhetoric of *MND*." *PMLA*, 83 (1968): 380-91.

1979   SCHANZER, Ernest. "The Central Theme of *MND*." *UTQ*, 20 (1951): 233-38.

1980   ——. "*MND.*" In *Shakespeare, the Comedies*, **3514**. [A shortened English version of an essay which first appeared in *Oeuvres complètes de Shakespeare*, ed. Pierre Leyris and Henri Evans (Paris, 1958).]

1981   ——. "The Moon and the Fairies in *MND.*" *UTQ*, 24 (1955): 234-46.

1982   SIEGEL, Paul N. "*MND* and the Wedding Guests." *SQ*, 4 (1953): 139-44. Repr. in *Shakespeare in His Time and Ours*, **3317**.

1983   TAYLOR, Michael. "The Darker Purpose of *MND.*" *SEL*, 9 (1969): 259-73.

1984   THOMAS, Sidney. "The Bad Weather in *MND.*" *MLN*, 64 (1949): 319-22. [1596?]

1985   WATKINS, Ronald. *Moonlight at the Globe*. London: Joseph, 1946.

1986   WEIL, Herbert S. "Comic Structure and Tonal Manipulation in Shakespeare and Some Modern Plays." In *ShS 22*, **3530**.

1987   YOUNG, David P. *Something of a Great Constancy: The Art of MND*. Yale U.P., 1966.

1988   ZITNER, Sheldon P. "The Worlds of *MND.*" *SAQ*, 59 (1960): 397-403.

MUCH ADO ABOUT NOTHING

Editions

1989 FURNESS, Horace H., ed. *Ado*. New Variorum. Philadelphia: Lippincott, 1899.

1990 NEWCOMER, Alphonsus G., ed. *Ado*. Parallel Passage Edition. Stanford U.P., 1929. Repr. New York: AMS. [On facing pages are the text and parallel phrases or passages from elsewhere in the canon. The book was completed by Henry D. Gray.]

1991 *Shakespeare's Comedy of* Ado. London: Day & Son, 1864. [Photolithograph of Ellesmere Q1 under supervision of Howard Staunton.]

Textual Commentary

See also **254** and **259**.

1992 BRERETON, J. LeGay. "*Ado* IV.i.145-60." *RES*, 4 (1928): 84-86. [Probably an insertion and also an omission of text.]

1993 GILBERT, Allan H. "Two Margarets: The Composition of *Ado*." *PQ*, 41 (1962): 61-71. Also in *Studies . . . Presented to Baldwin Maxwell*, **2824**.

1994 SMITH, John H. "The Composition of the Quarto of *Ado*." *SB*, 16 (1963): 9-26. [Printing may have been interrupted to print the cancel sheet of *2H4*.]

Commentary

See also The Comedies (**3444-3549**); **733, 768, 2886, 3082, 3317, 3476, 3695, 3735,** and **4444**.

1995 CRAIK, Thomas W. "*Ado*." *Scrutiny*, 19 (1952-53): 297-316.

1996 DAVIS, Walter R., ed. *Twentieth-Century Interpretations of* Ado. Englewood Cliffs, N.J.: Prentice-Hall, 1969. [18 sel. from prev. pub. wks.]

1997 EVERETT, Barbara. "*Ado*." *CritQ*, 3 (1961): 319-35.

1998 FERGUSSON, Francis. "*Err* and *Ado*." *SR*; see **917**.

1999 HARTLEY, Lodwick. "Claudio and the Unmerry War." *CE*, 26 (1965): 609-14.

2000 HOCKEY, Dorothy C. "Notes, Notes, Forsooth." *SQ*, 8 (1957): 353-58.

2001 JORGENSEN, Paul A. "*Ado*." *SQ*, 5 (1954): 287-95.

2002 KING, Walter N. "Much Ado about *Something*." *SQ*, 15.3 (1964): 143-55.

2003   LEWALSKI, Barbara K. "Love, Appearance, and Reality: Much Ado about Something." *SEL*, 8 (1968): 235-51.

2004   McCOLLOM, William G. "The Role of Wit in *Ado.*" *SQ*, 19 (1968): 165-74.

2005   MUESCHKE, Paul, and Miriam Mueschke. "Illusion and Metamorphosis in *Ado.*" *SQ*, 18 (1967): 53-65.

2006   MULRYNE, J. R. *Shakespeare: Ado.* London: Arnold, 1965.

2007   NEILL, J. Kerby. "More Ado about Claudio: An Acquittal for the Slandered Groom." *SQ*, 3 (1952): 91-107.

2008   PAGE, Nadine. "Beatrice: My Lady Disdain." *MLN*, 50 (1935): 494-99.

2009   ——. "The Public Repudiation of Hero." *PMLA*, 50 (1935): 739-44.

2010   PROUTY, Charles T. *The Sources of* Ado. Yale U.P., 1950.

2011   ROSE, Steven. "Love and Self-Love in *Ado.*" *EIC*, 20 (1970): 143-50.

2012   SMITH, James C. "*Ado.*" *Scrutiny*, 13 (1944-46): 242-57.

2013   STOREY, Graham. "The Success of *Ado.*" In *More Talking of Shakespeare*, **2780**.

2014   SYPHER, Wylie. "Nietzche and Socrates in Messina." *PR*, 16 (1949): 702-13.

2015   WAIN, John. "The Shakespearean Lie-Detector: Thoughts on *Ado.*" *CritQ*, 9 (1967): 27-42.

2016   WEST, E. J. "Much Ado about an Unpleasant Play." *SAB*, 22 (1947): 30-34.

2017   WEY, James J. "'To Grace Harmony': Musical Design in *Ado.*" *BUSE*, 4 (1960): 181-88.

OTHELLO

Editions

2018   FURNESS, Horace H., ed. *Oth*. New Variorum. Philadelphia: Lippincott, 1886.

2019   SCHRÖER, M. M. Arnold, ed. *Oth: Paralleldruck der ersten Quarto und der ersten Folio mit den Lesarten der zweiten Quarto*. Heidelberg: Carl Winter, 1949. [Texts of play in English.]

Textual Commentary

See also **713**.

2020   BRENNECKE, Ernest. " 'Nay, That's Not Next!': The Significance of Desdemona's 'Willow Song.' " *SQ*, 4 (1953): 35-58.

2021   CAMERON, Kenneth W. "*Oth*, Quarto 1, Reconsidered." *PMLA*, 47 (1932): 671-83.

2022   —. "The Text of *Oth:* An Analysis." *PMLA*, 49 (1934): 762-96.

2023   HINMAN, Charlton. "The 'Copy' for the Second Quarto of *Oth*." In *Adams Memorial Studies*, **2794**.

2024   —. "A Proof-Sheet in the First Folio of Shakespeare." *Library*, 23 (1942-43): 101-7. [*Oth*.]

2025   MUIR, Kenneth. "The Text of *Oth*." *ShakS 1* (1965), pp. 227-39.

Commentary

See also The Tragedies (3616-3734); **151, 733, 2832, 2853, 2866, 2886, 3006, 3024, 3035, 3201, 3326, 3370, 3420, 3436, 3744, 3757, 3760, 4122, 4205, 4207, 4407**, and **4445**.

2026   ADAMOWSKI, T. H. "The Aesthetic Attitude and Narcissism in *Oth*." *L&P*, 18 (1968): 73-81.

2027   ALLEN, Ned B. "The Source of *Oth*." *Delaware Notes*, 21 (1948): 71-96.

2028   —. "The Two Parts of *Oth*." In *ShS 21*, **2094**.

2029   ARTHOS, John. "The Fall of Othello." *SQ*, 9 (1958): 93-104.

2030   BETHELL, Samuel L. "Shakespeare's Imagery: The Diabolic Images in *Oth*." *ShS 5* (1952), pp. 62-80.

2031   BODKIN, Maud. "The Hero and the Devil." *Archetypal Patterns in Poetry*. Oxford U.P., 1934.

2032   BONNARD, Georges A. "Are Othello and Desdemona Innocent or Guilty?" *ES*, 30 (1949): 175-84.

2033   BROOKE, C. F. Tucker. "The Romantic Iago." *YR*, 7 (1917): 349-59. Repr. in *Essays on Shakespeare and Other Elizabethans*, **2888**.

2034   BURKE, Kenneth. "*Oth:* An Essay to Illustrate a Method." *HudR*, 4 (1951): 165-203.

2035   CAMDEN, Carroll C. "Iago on Women." *JEGP*, 48 (1949): 57-71.

2036   CARRÈRE, Félix. "Deux Motifs sur l'*Oth* de Shakespeare: Le Monologue,–l'amour et la jalousie." *Annales publiées par la Faculté des Lettres de Toulouse: Littératures,* 2 (1953): 15-30.

2037   DEAN, Leonard F., ed. *A Casebook on* Oth. New York: Crowell, 1961. [Incl. text and 13 sel. from prev. pub. wks., Rymer to present.]

2038   DE SMET, Robert. "*Oth* in Paris and Brussels." *ShS 3* (1950), pp. 98-106.

2039   DORAN, Madeleine. "Good Name in *Oth*." *SEL*, 7 (1967): 195-217.

2040   ——. "Iago's 'If': An Essay on the Syntax of *Oth*." In *The Drama of the Renaissance*, **2763**.

2041   DRAPER, John W. "Honest Iago." *PMLA*, 46 (1931): 724-37.

2042   ——. *The* Oth *of Shakespeare's Audience*. Paris: Didier, 1952. Repr. New York: Octagon.

2043   ——. "Shakespeare and the Doge of Venice." *JEGP,* 46 (1947): 75-81.

2044   ELLIOTT, George R. *Flaming Minister: A Study of* Oth *as Tragedy of Love and Hate*. Duke U.P., 1953. Repr. New York: AMS.

2045   EMPSON, William. "Honest in *Oth*." In *The Structure of Complex Words*, **2992**.

2046   EVANS, K. W. "The Racial Factor in *Oth*." *ShakS 5 1969* (1970), pp. 124-40.

2047   FLATTER, Richard. *The Moor of Venice*. London: Heinemann, 1950.

2048   GARDNER, Helen. *The Noble Moor*. Oxford U.P., 1956. [*PBA 1955,* 41 (1956): 189-205.]

2049   ——. "*Oth:* A Retrospect, 1900-67." In *ShS 21*, **2094**.

2050   GERARD, Albert S. "'Egregiously an Ass': The Dark Side of the Moor, a View of Othello's Mind." *ShS 10* (1957), pp. 98-106.

2051   ——. "The Loving Killers: The Rationale of Righteousness in Baroque Tragedy." *CLS*, 2 (1965): 209-32.

2051a   GOLL, August. "Criminal Types in Shakespeare." Trans. J. Moritzen. *Journal of Criminal Law*, 30 (1939): 22-51. [Iago and Richard III.]

2052   HALLSTEAD, R. N. "Idolatrous Love: A New Approach to *Oth*." *SQ*, 19 (1968): 107-24.

2053 HALSTEAD, William L. "Artifice and Artistry in *R2* and *Oth*." In *Sweet Smoke of Rhetoric: A Collection of Renaissance Essays*. Ed. Natalie G. Lawrence and Jack A. Reynolds. U. of Miami P., 1964.

2054 HAPGOOD, Robert. "The Trial of Othello." In *Pacific Coast Studies in Shakespeare*, **2796**.

2055 HAWKES, Terence. "Iago's Use of Reason." *SP*, 58 (1961): 160-69.

2056 HEILMAN, Robert B. *Magic in the Web*. U. of Kentucky P., 1956.

2057 HIBBARD, George R. "*Oth* and the Pattern of Shakespearian Tragedy." In *ShS 21*, **2094**.

2058 HOMAN, Sidney R. "Iago's Aesthetics: *Oth* and Shakespeare's Portrait of an Artist." *ShakS 5 1969* (1970), pp. 141-48.

2059 HOSLEY, Richard. "The Staging of Desdemona's Bed." *SQ*, 14 (1963): 57-65.

2060 HUBLER, Edward L. "The Damnation of Othello: Some Limitations on the Christian View of the Play." *SQ*, 9 (1958): 295-300.

2061 HUNTER, George K. "Othello and Colour Prejudice." Oxford U.P., 1968. [*PBA 1967*, 53 (1968): 139-63.]

2062 HYMAN, Stanley E. *Iago: Some Approaches to the Illusion of His Motivation*. New York: Atheneum, 1970.

2063 JONES, Eldred D. *Othello's Countrymen: The African in English Renaissance Drama*. Oxford U.P., 1965.

2064 JORDAN, Hoover H. "Dramatic Illusion in *Oth*." *SQ*, 1 (1950): 146-52.

2065 JORGENSEN, Paul A. "*Honesty* in *Oth*." *SP*, 47 (1950): 557-67.

2066 —. "'Perplex'd in the Extreme': The Role of Thought in *Oth*." *SQ*, 15.2 (1964): 265-75. Also in *Shakespeare 400*, **2793**.

2067 KAULA, David. "Othello Possessed: Notes on Shakespeare's Use of Magic and Witchcraft." *ShakS 2 1966* (1967), pp. 112-32.

2068 KIRSCHBAUM, Leo. "The Modern Othello." *ELH*, 11 (1944): 283-96.

2069 LEAVIS, Frank R. "Diabolic Intellect and the Noble Hero." In *The Common Pursuit*, **3151**.

2070 LERNER, Laurence. "The Machiavel and the Moor." *EIC*, 9 (1959): 339-60.

2071 LEVIN, Harry. "*Oth* and the Motive-Hunters." *CentR*, 8 (1964): 1-16.

2072 McCULLEN, Joseph T. "Iago's Use of Proverbs for Persuasion." *SEL*, 4 (1964): 247-62.

2073 McGEE, Arthur R. "Othello's Motive for Murder." *SQ*, 15.1 (1964): 45-54.

2074   MATTHEWS, G. M. "Othello and the Dignity of Man." In *Shakespeare in a Changing World*, **2792**.

2074a   MENDONÇA, Barbara H. C. de. "*Oth:* A Tragedy Built on a Comic Structure." In *ShS 21*, **2094**.

2075   MERCER, Peter. "*Oth* and the Form of Heroic Tragedy." *CritQ*, 11 (1969): 45-61.

2076   MONEY, John. "Othello's 'It Is the Cause . . .': An Analysis." *ShS 6* (1953), pp. 94-105.

2077   MOORE, John R. "The Character of Iago." In *Studies in Honor of A. H. R. Fairchild*, **2804**.

2078   —. "Othello, Iago, and Cassio as Soldiers." *PQ*, 31 (1952): 189-94.

2079   MUIR, Kenneth. "The Jealousy of Iago." *EM*, 2 (1951): 65-83.

2080   NOWOTTNY, Winifred M. T. "Justice and Love in *Oth*." *UTQ*, 21 (1951-52): 330-44.

2081   POIRIER, Michel. "Le 'Double Temps' dans *Oth*." *EA*, 5 (1952): 107-16.

2082   PRIOR, Moody E. "Character in Relation to Action in *Oth*." *MP*, 44 (1947): 225-37.

2083   RANALD, Margaret L. "The Indiscretions of Desdemona." *SQ*, 14 (1963): 127-39.

2084   RAND, Frank P. "The Over Garrulous Iago." *SQ*, 1 (1950): 155-61.

2085   REID, Stephen. "Othello's Jealousy." *AI*, 25 (1968): 274-93.

2086   ROGERS, Robert. "Endopsychic Drama in *Oth*." *SQ*, 20 (1969): 205-15.

2087   ROSENBERG, Marvin. *The Masks of Othello*. U. of California P., 1961.

2088   ROSS, Lawrence J. "Shakespeare's 'Dull Clown' and Symbolic Music." *SQ*, 17 (1966): 107-28.

2089   —. "The Use of a 'Fit-Up' Booth in *Oth*." *SQ*, 12 (1969): 359-70.

2090   SCHWARTZ, Elias. "Stylistic 'Impurity' and the Meaning of *Oth*." *SEL*, 10 (1970): 297-313.

2091   SCRAGG, Leah. "Iago—Vice or Devil?" In *ShS 21*, **2094**.

2092   SHAFFER, Elinor S. "Iago's Malignity Motivated: Coleridge's Unpublished 'Opus Magnum.'" *SQ*, 19 (1968): 195-203.

2093   SHAPIRO, Stephen A. "Othello's Desdemona." *L&P*, 14 (1964): 56-61.

2094   *ShS 21* (1968). [9 essays on *Oth*.]

2095   SIEGEL, Paul N. "The Damnation of Othello." *PMLA*, 68 (1953): 1068-78.

2096   SPENCER, Theodore. "The Elizabethan Malcontent." In *Adams Memorial Studies*, **2794**.

2097   STANISLAVSKY [Alekseev, Konstantin S]. *Stanislavsky Produces Oth*. Trans. Helen Nowak. London: Bles, 1948.

2098   STEMPEL, Daniel. "The Silence of Iago." *PMLA*, 84 (1969): 252-63.

2099   STIRLING, Brents. "Psychology in *Oth*." *SAB*, 19 (1944): 135-44.

2100   STOLL, Elmer E. "Another *Oth* Too Modern." In *Adams Memorial Studies*, **2794**.

2101   —. "Iago Not a 'Malcontent.'" *JEGP*, 51 (1952): 163-67.

2102   —. "An *Oth* All-Too Modern." *ELH*, 13 (1946): 46-58.

2103   —. *Oth: An Historical and Comparative Study*. U. of Minnesota, 1915.

2104   —. "Slander in Drama." *SQ*, 4 (1953): 433-50.

2105   —. "Source and Motive in *Mac* and *Oth*." *RES*; see **1774**.

2106   SWINBURNE, Algernon C. "*Oth*." In *Three Plays of Shakespeare*. New York: Harper, 1909.

2107   TANNENBAUM, Samuel A. "The Wronged Iago." *SAB*, 12 (1937): 57-62.

2108   WALTON, James K. " 'Strength's Abundance': A View of *Oth*." *RES*, 11 (1960): 8-17.

2109   WARNKEN, Henry L. "Iago as a Projection of Othello." In *Shakespeare Encomium*, **2802**.

2110   WATTS, Robert A. "The Comic Scenes in *Oth*." *SQ*, 19 (1968): 349-54.

2111   WEBB, Henry J. "The Military Background in *Oth*." *PQ*, 30 (1951): 40-52.

2112   WEST, Robert H. "The Christianness of *Oth*." *SQ*, 15 (1964): 333-43.

2113   WILCOX, John. "Othello's Crucial Moment." *SAB*, 24 (1949): 181-92.

THE PASSIONATE PILGRIM

Editions

See also Poems (**2153-62**) and Canon (**570-605**).

2114   ADAMS, Joseph Q., ed. *PP.* New York and London: Scribner's for
        the Trustees of Amherst College, 1939. [Facs. incl. the unique
        fragment of first ed.]

2115   LEE, Sidney, ed. *PP, Being a Reproduction in Facsimile of the First
        Edition 1599 from the Copy in the Christie Miller Library at Britwell.*
        Oxford U.P., 1905. [Original now in Huntington Library. 2nd ed.,
        not first.]

2116   *PP.* Cambridge: E. & E. Plumbridge, 1964. [Facs. of the copy in
        Trinity College, Cambridge; 2nd ed., 1599.]

2117   ROLLINS, Hyder E., ed. *PP: The Third Edition, 1612.* New York
        and London: Scribner's for the Trustees of Amherst College, 1940.
        [Facs.]

PERICLES

Editions

2118 LEE, Sidney, ed. *Shakespeares* Per, *Being a Reproduction in Facsimile of the First Edition 1609 from the Copy in the Malone Collection in the Bodleian Library*. Oxford U.P., 1905.

Textual Commentary

See also Canon (**570-605**) and The Romances (after **3734**).

2119 EDWARDS, Philip. "An Approach to the Problem of *Per*." *ShS 5* (1952), pp. 25-49.

2120 LAKE, D. J. "The *Per* Candidates—Heywood, Rowley, Wilkins." *N&Q*, 17 (1970): 135-41. [Favors Wilkins.]

2121 SCHIFFHORST, Gerald J. "The Imagery of *Per* and What It Tells Us." *BSUF*, 8 (1967): 61-70. [One author.]

2122 WOOD, James O. "The Running Image in *Per*." *ShakS 5 1969* (1970), pp. 240-52.

Commentary

See also The Comedies (**3444-3549**) and The Romances (after **3734**); **596, 721, 733**, and **2701**.

2123 ARTHOS, John. "*Per:* A Study in the Dramatic Use of Romantic Narrative." *SQ*, 4 (1953): 257-70.

2124 BARBER, Cesar L. "'Thou That Beget'st Him That Did Thee Beget': Transformation in *Per* and *WT*." In *ShS 22*, **3530**.

2125 BARKER, Gerard A. "Themes and Variations in Shakespeare's *Per*." *ES*, 44 (1963): 401-14.

2126 CRAIG, Hardin. "*Per* and the *Painfull Adventures*." *SP*, 45 (1948): 600-605.

2127 CUTTS, John P. "Pericles' 'Downright Violence.'" *ShakS 4 1968* (1969), pp. 275-93.

2128 DICKSON, George B. "The Identity of George Wilkins." *SAB*, 14 (1939): 195-207.

2129 FELPERIN, Howard. "Shakespeare's Miracle Play." *SQ*, 18 (1967): 363-74.

2130 GREENFIELD, Thelma N. "A Re-Examination of the 'Patient' Pericles." *ShakS 3 1967* (1968), pp. 51-61.

2131 HASTINGS, William T. "*Exit* George Wilkins?" *SAB*, 11 (1936): 67-83.

2132   ——. "Shakspere's Part in *Per*." *SAB*, 14 (1939): 67-85.

2133   HOENIGER, F. David. "How Significant Are Textual Parallels? A New Author for *Per*?" *SQ*, 11 (1960): 27-37.

2134   McMANAWAY, Mary R. "Poets in the Parish of St. Giles, Cripplegate." *SQ*, 9 (1958): 561-62. [Data about George Wilkins and Richard Hathaway.]

2135   MUIR, Kenneth.   "The Problem of *Per*." *ES*, 30 (1949): 65-83.

2136   PARROTT, Thomas M. "*Per:* The Play and the Novel." *SAB*, 23 (1948): 105-13.

2137   SPIKER, Sina. "George Wilkins and the Authorship of *Per*." *SP*, 30 (1933): 551-70.

2138   TOMPKINS, J. M. S. "Why *Per*?" *RES*, 3 (1952): 315-24.

2139   WILKINS, George. *The Painfull Adventures of Pericles Prince of Tyre, Being the True History of the Play of* Pericles*, As It Was Lately Presented by the Worthy and Ancient Poet John Gower.* Ed. Kenneth Muir. U.P. of Liverpool, 1953.

THE PHOENIX AND THE TURTLE

Editions

See Poems (2153-62).

Commentary

See also 347, 2351, and 2358.

2140   ALVAREZ, A. "Shakespeare: *PhT*." In *Interpretations*. Ed. John Wain. London: Routledge & Kegan Paul, 1955.

2141   BATES, Ronald. "Shakespeare's *PhT*." *SQ*, 6 (1955): 19-30.

2142   BONAVENTURE, S. M. "The Phoenix Renewed." *BSUF*, 5 (1964): 72-76.

2143   BRADBROOK, Muriel C. "*PhT*." *SQ*, 6 (1955): 356-58.

2144   COPLAND, Murray. "The Dead Phoenix." *EIC*, 15 (1965): 279-87.

2145   CUNNINGHAM, James V. "'Essence' and *PhT*." *ELH*, 19 (1952): 265-76.

2146   ELLRODT, Robert. "The Anatomy of *PhT*." In *ShS 15*, 2161.

2147   EMPSON, William. "*PhT*." *EIC*, 16 (1966): 147-53.

2148   MATCHETT, William H. *PhT: Shakespeare's Poem and Chester's Loves Martyr*. The Hague: Mouton; New York: Humanities P., 1965.

2149   O'BRIEN, A. P. "Tension in Poetry and Shakespeare's *PhT*." *Criticism and Research* (Banaras Hindu U.) (1964), pp. 1-9.

2150   ONG, Walter J. "Metaphor and the Twinned Vision (*PhT*)." *SR*, 63 (1955): 193-201.

2151   SCHWARTZ, Elias. "Shakespeare's Dead Phoenix." *ELN*, 7 (1969): 25-32.

2152   STRAUMANN, Heinrich. *Phönix und Taube*. Zurich: Artemis, 1953.

POEMS

Editions

See also **618**. For concordance, see **166**.

2153   *A Collection of Poems.* London: B. Lintott, [1709]. [Repr. of
              Ven, 1630; *Luc*, 1632; *PP*, 1599. *Son*, 1609, added in a separate
              volume *ca.* 1711.]

2154   N., S. [Charles Gildon], ed. *Works...Volume the Seventh.* Lon-
              don: E. Curll & E. Sanger, 1710. Repr. as part of Rowe (1709),
              New York: AMS. [Issued to match Nicholas Rowe's *Works* (1709).
              A modernized repr. of Lintott's *Ven*; of *Luc* from *Poems on Affairs
              of State* (1707), vol. 4; of *Son* from Benson's ed. of 1640.]

2155   ROLLINS, Hyder E., ed. *Poems.* New Variorum. Philadelphia:
              Lippincott, 1938. [*Ven, Luc, PP, PhT, LC.*]

2155a *Shakespeare's Poems:* Ven, Luc, PP, PhT, Son, LC, *a Facsimile of
              the Earliest Editions.* Ed. James M. Osborn, Louis L. Martz, Eugene
              M. Waith. Yale U.P. for the Elizabethan Club, 1964.

Textual Commentary

See also **661**.

2156   SWAN, Marshall W. S. "Shakespeare's 'Poems': The First Three
              Boston Editions." *PBSA*, 36 (1942): 27-36.

Commentary

See also **2329, 2374,** and **4452**.

2157   ALDEN, Raymond M. "The Lyrical Conceit of the Elizabethans."
              SP, 14 (1917): 129-52.

2157a ALPERS, Paul J., ed. *Elizabethan Poetry: Modern Essays in Criti-
              cism.* Oxford U.P., 1967. [3 prev. pub. essays: *Son, Ven.*]

2158   BROWN, John R., and Bernard Harris, eds. *Elizabethan Poetry.*
              Stratford-upon-Avon Studies, 2. London: Arnold, 1960. Repr. New
              York: St. Martin's. [10 essays, 1 on *Son.*]

2159   LEVER, Julius W. "Shakespeare's Narrative Poems." In *A New
              Companion to Shakespeare Studies,* **2800**.

2160   ——. "Twentieth-Century Studies in Shakespeare's Poems." In *ShS
              15,* **2161**.

2161   *ShS 15* (1962). [6 essays on Poems.]

2162   SMITH, Hallett. "'No Cloudy Stuffe to Puzzell Intellect': A Testi-
              monial Misapplied to Shakespeare." *SQ*, 1 (1950): 18-21. [Benson's
              Epistle in *Poems* (1640).]

THE RAPE OF LUCRECE

Editions

See also Poems (**2153-62**).

2163   LEE, Sidney, ed. *Shakespeare's* Luc, *Being a Reproduction in Facsimile of the First Edition from the Copy in the Malone Collection in the Bodleian Library.* Oxford U.P., 1905.

2164   *Luc (1594).* Menston, Yorks., Eng.: Scolar, 1968. [Facs. of Bodleian copy.]

Commentary

See also **297, 559, 2358, 3048, 3247,** and **4452.**

2165   ALLEN, Don C. "Some Observations on *Luc.*" In *ShS 15,* **2161.** Also in 2nd ed. of *Image and Meaning,* **3769.**

2166   "Commonplace-Book from the Time of Shakespeare." *British Museum Quarterly,* 29 (News Supplement No. 12) (1965): 6-7. [Contains a poem corresponding to *Luc* ll. 764-1036, except for two lines; ante 1597. Also allusions to *R3* and *H4*.]

2167   FRYE, Roland M. "Shakespeare's Composition of *Luc:* New Evidence." *SQ,* 16 (1965): 289-96.

2168   HYNES, Sam. "The Rape of Tarquin." *SQ,* 10 (1959): 451-53.

2169   LANGHAM, Michael. "*Err* and *Luc.*" *KR;* see **920.**

2170   MONTGOMERY, Robert L. "Shakespeare's Gaudy: The Method of *Luc.*" In *Studies in Honor of DeWitt T. Starnes,* **2784.**

2171   MUIR, Kenneth. "*Luc.*" *Anglica,* 5 (1964): 25-40.

2172   SYLVESTER, Bickford. "Natural Mutability and Human Responsibility: Form in Shakespeare's *Luc.*" *CE,* 26 (1965): 505-11.

2173   WALLEY, Harold R. "*Luc* and Shakespearean Tragedy." *PMLA,* 76 (1961): 480-87.

RICHARD 2

Editions

2174   BLACK, Matthew W., ed. *R2*. New Variorum. Philadelphia: Lippincott, 1955.

2175   POLLARD, Alfred W., ed. *A New Shakespeare Quarto: R2, 1598*. London: Quaritch, 1916. [Facs.]

Textual Commentary

2176   HASKER, Richard E. "The Copy for the First Folio *R2*." *SB*, 5 (1952-53): 53-72.

Commentary

See also The History Plays (**3550-3615**); **161, 721, 733, 881, 1048, 2902, 2928, 3038, 3053, 3177, 3238, 3284, 3290, 3585, 3591, 3757, 3951**, and **4290**.

2177   ALTICK, Richard D. "Symphonic Imagery in *R2*." *PMLA*, 62 (1947): 339-65.

2178   BLACK, Matthew W. "The Sources of Shakespeare's *R2*." In *Adams Memorial Studies*, **2794**.

2179   BOGARD, Travis. "Shakespeare's Second Richard." *PMLA*, 70 (1955): 192-209.

2180   BONNARD, Georges A. "The Actor in *R2*." *SJ*, 87/88 (1951-52): 87-101.

2181   BRERETON, J. LeGay. "Shakespeare's *R2*." In *Writings on Elizabethan Drama*. Melbourne U.P., 1948. Repr. New York: AMS.

2182   BRYANT, Joseph A. "The Linked Analogies of *R2*." *SR*, 65 (1957): 420-33.

2183   DEAN, Leonard F. "*R2*: The State and the Image of the Theater." *PMLA*, 67 (1952): 211-18.

2184   DORAN, Madeleine. "Imagery in *R2* and *H4*." *MLR*; see **1224**.

2185   DORIUS, Raymond J. "A Little More Than a Little: Prudence and Excess in *R2* and the Histories." *SQ*; see **3567**.

2186   DRAPER, John W. "The Character of Richard II." *PQ*, 21 (1942): 228-36.

2187   ELLIOTT, John R. "History and Tragedy in *R2*." *SEL*, 8 (1968): 253-71.

2188   ——. "*R2* and the Medieval." *RenP 1965* (1966), pp. 25-34.

2189 FRIJLINCK, Wilhelmina, ed. *The First Part of the Reign of King Richard the Second; or, Thomas of Woodstock.* Oxford U.P. for the Malone Society, 1929.

2190 GREG, Walter W. "Samuel Harsnett and Hayward's *Henry IV.*" *Library*, 11 (1956): 1-10. [Essex conspiracy and *R2.*]

2191 HALLIWELL-PHILLIPPS, James O., ed. *A Tragedy of King Richard the Second.* London: Richards, 1870. [*Woodstock.*]

2192 HALSTEAD, William L. "Artifice and Artistry in *R2* and *Oth.*" In *Sweet Smoke of Rhetoric*; see 2053.

2193 HAPGOOD, Robert. "Three Eras in *R2.*" *SQ*, 14 (1963): 281-83.

2194 HENINGER, Simeon K. "The Sun-King Analogy in *R2.*" *SQ*, 11 (1960): 319-27.

2195 HILL, R. F. "Dramatic Techniques and Interpretation in *R2.*" In *Early Shakespeare*, 2766.

2196 HOCKEY, Dorothy C. "A World of Rhetoric in *R2.*" *SQ*, 15.3 (1964): 179-91.

2197 HUMPHREYS, Arthur R. *Shakespeare: R2.* London: Arnold, 1967.

2198 JEFFARES, A. Norman. "In One Person Many People: *R2.*" In *The Morality of Art*, 2789.

2199 JORGENSEN, Paul A. "Vertical Patterns in *R2.*" *SAB*, 23 (1948): 119-34.

2200 KANTOROWICZ, Ernst H. "Shakespeare: *R2.*" In *The King's Two Bodies: A Study in Mediaeval Political Theology.* Princeton U.P., 1957.

2201 KLIGER, Samuel. "The Sun Imagery in *R2.*" *SP*, 45 (1948): 196-202.

2202 LAMBRECHTS, G. "Sur deux prétendues sources de *R2.*" *EA*, 20 (1967): 118-39. [Thinks *R2* preceded Daniel's *Civil Wars* and probably *Woodstock.*]

2203 LAW, Robert A. "Deviations from Holinshed in *R2.*" *TxSE*, 29 (1950): 91-101.

2204 McMANAWAY, James G. "*R2* at Covent Garden." *SQ*, 15.2 (1964): 161-75, 4 plates. Also in *Shakespeare 400,* 2793, and *Studies in Shakespeare, Bibliography, and Theater,* 3174. [Drawings of the stage setting of two scenes. 1738.]

2205 McPEEK, James A. S. "Richard and His Shadow World." *AI*, 15 (1958): 195-212.

2206 MONTGOMERY, Robert L. "The Dimensions of Time in *R2.*" *ShakS 4 1968* (1969), pp. 73-85.

2207 PHIALAS, Peter G. "The Medieval in *R2.*" *SQ*, 12 (1961): 305-10.

2208 ——. "*R2* and Shakespeare's Tragic Mode." *TSLL*, 5 (1963): 344-55.

2209   PROVOST, Foster. "On Justice and the Music in *R2* and *Lr*." *AnM;* see **1614**.

2210   —. "The Sorrows of Shakespeare's Richard II." In *Studies . . . Dedicated to John Earle Uhler,* **2795**.

2211   QUINN, Michael. " 'The King Is Not Himself': The Personal Tragedy of Richard II." *SP*, 56 (1959): 169-86.

2212   REED, Robert R. *R2: From Mask to Prophet.* Pennsylvania State U.P., 1968.

2213   REIMAN, Donald H. "Appearance, Reality, and Moral Order in *R2*." *MLQ*, 25 (1964): 34-45.

2214   RIBNER, Irving. "Bolingbroke, a True Machiavellian." *MLQ*, 9 (1948): 177-84. [Also *H4*.]

2215   ROSSITER, Arthur P., ed. *Woodstock, a Moral History.* London: Chatto & Windus, 1946. [Infl. *R2, 2H6*.]

2216   SHAPIRO, I. A. "*R2* or *R3* or . . .?" *SQ*, 9 (1958): 204-6. [Sir Edward Hoby's letter of Dec. 1595.]

2217   SPEAIGHT, Robert. "Shakespeare and the Political Spectrum As Illustrated by *R2*." In *Stratford Papers on Shakespeare, 1964*, **2787**.

2218   STIRLING, Brents. "Bolingbroke's 'Decision.' " *SQ*, 2 (1951): 27-34.

2219   SUZMAN, Arthur. "Imagery and Symbolism in *R2*." *SQ*, 7 (1956): 355-70.

2220   SWINBURNE, Algernon C. "*R2*." In *Three Plays of Shakespeare.* New York: Harper, 1909.

2221   THOMPSON, Karl F. "Richard II, Martyr." *SQ*, 8 (1957): 159-66.

2222   TROUSDALE, Marion. "Reality and Illusion in the Theatre." *CritQ*, 11 (1969): 347-59.

2223   TYLER, Parker. "Phaethon: The Metaphysical Tension between Ego and the Universe in English Poetry." *Accent*, 16 (1956): 29-44.

2224   URE, Peter. "The Looking-Glass of Richard II." *PQ*, 34 (1955): 219-24.

2225   WILSON, J. Dover. "The Political Background of Shakespeare's *R2* and *H4*." *SJ*; see **1262**.

RICHARD 3

Editions

2226 FARMER, John S., ed. *R3 . . . 1597*. Tudor Facs. Texts. Amersham: Farmer, 1913. Repr. New York: AMS.

2227 FURNESS, Horace H., ed. *R3*. New Variorum. Philadelphia: Lippincott, 1908.

2228 SMIDT, Kristian, ed. *R3: Parallel Texts of the First Quarto and the First Folio with Variants of the Early Quartos*. Oslo: Universitetsforlaget; New York: Humanities P., 1969.

Textual Commentary

See also **713**.

2229 BABCOCK, Robert W. "An Introduction to the Study of the Text of *R3*." *SP*, 24 (1927): 243-60.

2230 BOWERS, Fredson T. "The Copy for the Folio *R3*." *SQ*, 10 (1959): 541-44.

2231 CAIRNCROSS, Andrew S. "Coincidental Variants in *R3*." *Library*, 12 (1957): 187-90. [See James K. Walton's rejoinder, *Library*, 13 (1958): 139-40.]

2232 ——. "The Quartos and the Folio Text of *R3*." *RES*, 8 (1957): 225-33.

2233 FIELD, Barron, ed. *The True Tragedy of Richard the Third, to Which Is Appended the Latin Play of* Richardus Tertius, *by Dr. Thomas Legge*. London: for the Shakespeare Society, 1844. Repr. Nendeln, Liechtenstein: Kraus-Thomson.

2234 FUSILLO, Robert J. "Tents on Bosworth Field." *SQ*, 6 (1955): 193-94. [See also Richard Hosley, "More about 'Tents' on Bosworth Field." *SQ*, 7 (1956): 458-59; and Albert B. Weiner, "Two Tents in *R3*?" *SQ*, 13 (1962): 258-60.]

2235 GREER, Clayton A. "The Relation of *R3* to *The True Tragedy of Richard Duke of York* and *3H6*." *SP*, 29 (1932): 543-50.

2236 GREG, Walter W. "*R3*–Q5 (1612)." *Library*, 17 (1936-37): 88-97.

2237 GRIFFIN, William J. "An Omission in the Folio Text of *R3*." *RES*, 13 (1937): 329-32. [The "Clock" passage. See correction of a detail by Hazelton Spencer, *RES*, 14 (1938): 205.]

2238 HONIGMANN, Ernst A. J. "The Text of *R3*." *ThR*, 7 (1965): 48-55.

2239 MAAS, Paul. "Two Passages in *R3*." *RES*, 18 (1942): 315-17, [Considers Q2's lines I.i.101-2 an actor's gag.]

2240 PATRICK, David L. *The Textual History of* R3. Stanford U.P.; Oxford U.P., 1936. Repr. New York: AMS.

2241 SMIDT, Kristian. *Injurious Impostors and* R3. Oslo: Norwegian Universities P.; New York: Humanities P., 1964.

2242   WALTON, James K. *The Copy for the Folio Text of R3.* Auckland, N.Z.: Pilgrim P., 1955.

2243   ———. "The Quarto Copy for the Folio *R3.*" *RES*, 10 (1959): 127-40.

2244   WILSON, J. Dover. "Shakespeare's *R3* and *The True Tragedy of Richard the Third*, 1594." *SQ*, 3 (1952): 299-306.

Commentary

See also The History Plays (3550-3615); 330, 721, 733, 750, 1293, 1340, 2166, 2216, 2952, 2971, 3238, 3284, 3290, 3757, 4280, and 4407.

2245   ARNOLD, Aerol. "The Recapitulation Dream in *R3* and *Mac.*" *SQ*, 6 (1955): 51-62.

2246   BEGG, Edleen. "Shakespeare's Debt to Hall and to Holinshed in *R3.*" *SP*, 32 (1935): 189-96.

2247   BROOKE, Nicholas. "Reflecting Gems and Dead Bones: Tragedy versus History in *R3.*" *CQ*, 7 (1965): 123-34.

2248   CLEMEN, Wolfgang. *Kommentar zu Shakespeares R3.* Göttingen: Vandenhoeck & Ruprecht, 1957. Trans. Jean Bonheim as *A Commentary of Shakespeare's* R3. London: Methuen, 1968. [Eng. version greatly shortened.]

2249   ———. "Tradition and Originality in Shakespeare's *R3.*" *SQ*, 5 (1954): 247-57.

2250   DOWNER, Alan S., ed. *Oxberry's 1822 Edition of R3, with the Descriptive Notes Recording Kean's Performance by James H. Hackett.* London: Society for Theatre Research, 1956-57.

2251   FRENCH, A. L. "The World of *R3.*" *ShakS 4 1968* (1969), pp. 25-39.

2252   GOLL, August. "Criminal Types in Shakespeare." *Journal of Criminal Law;* see 2051a. [Iago and Richard III.]

2253   HAEFFNER, Paul. *A Critical Commentary on Shakespeare's* R3. London: Macmillan, 1966.

2254   HEILMAN, Robert B. "Satiety and Conscience: Aspects of *R3.*" *Antioch Review*, 24 (1964): 57-73.

2255   KENDALL, Paul M., ed. *Richard III: The Great Debate.* New York: Norton; London: Folio Society, 1965. [Incl. Thomas More's *History of Richard III* and Horace Walpole's *Historic Doubts on the Life and Reign of Richard III.*]

2256   ROSSITER, Arthur P. "The Structure of *R3.*" *DUJ*, 31 (1938): 44-75.

2257   SMITH, Fred M. "The Relationship of *Mac* to *R3.*" *PMLA;* see 1768.

2257a   THOMAS, Sidney. *The Antic Hamlet and Richard III.* See 1187.

2258   WILLIAMS, Philip. "*R3:* The Battle Orations." In *English Studies in Honor of James S. Wilson*, 2765.

2259   WOOD, Alice I. P. *The Stage History of Shakespeare's* R3. Columbia U.P.; Oxford U.P., 1909. Repr. New York: AMS.

ROMEO AND JULIET

Editions

2260 DANIEL, Peter A., ed. *Rom: Parallel Texts of the First Two Quartos.* London: for the New Shakspere Society by N. Trübner, 1874.

2260a FURNESS, Horace H., ed. *Rom.* New Variorum. Philadelphia: Lippincott, 1871.

2261 MOMMSEN, Tycho, ed. *Shakespeare's* Romeo und Julia: *Eine kritische Ausgabe des überlieferten Doppeltextes mit vollständiger Varia Lectio bis auf Rowe.* Oldenberg: Gerhard Stalberg; London: Williams & Norgate, 1859.

2262 WILLIAMS, George W., ed. *Rom: A Critical Edition.* Duke U.P., 1964.

Textual Commentary

See also **259**, **383**, and **388**.

2263 CANTRELL, Paul L., and George W. Williams. "The Printing of the Second Quarto of *Rom* (1599)." *SB*, 9 (1957): 107-28.

2264 DUTHIE, George Ian. "The Text of Shakespeare's *Rom.*" *SB*, 4 (1951-52): 3-29.

2265 HINMAN, Charlton. "The Proof-reading of the First Folio Text of *Rom.*" *SB*, 6 (1954): 61-70.

2266 HOPPE, Harry R. *The Bad Quarto of* Rom: *A Bibliographical and Textual Study.* Cornell U.P., 1948.

2267 HOSLEY, Richard. "The Corrupting Influence of the Bad Quarto on the Received Text of *Rom.*" *SQ*, 4 (1953): 11-34. [See also Clifford Leech, "Notes on . . . the Received Text of *Rom.*" *SQ*, 5 (1954): 94-95.]

2268 ——. "Quarto Copy for Q2 *Rom.*" *SB*, 9 (1957): 129-41.

2269 LAVIN, Joseph A. "John Danter's Ornament Stock." *SB*, 23 (1970): 21-44. [Argues *Rom* Q1 was set by formes and printed simultaneously by Danter and Allde.]

2270 THOMAS, Sidney. "The Bibliographical Links between the First Two Quartos of *Rom.*" *RES*, 25 (1949): 110-14.

2271 ——. "Henry Chettle and the First Quarto of *Rom.*" *RES*, 1 (1950): 8-16. [Chettle possibly the author of the un-Shakespearean lines.]

2272 WILLIAMS, George W. "The Printer and the Date of *Rom* Q4." *SB*, 18 (1965): 253-54.

2273 WILSON, J. Dover. "Recent Work on the Text of *Rom.*" *ShS 8;* see **388**.

Commentary

See also The Tragedies (**3616-3734**); **151, 721, 733, 768, 3035, 3177, 3405, 3629, 3735, 3744, 3760**, and **4446**.

2274   ADAMS, Barry B. "The Prudence of Prince Escalus." *ELH*, 35 (1968): 32-50.

2275   ADAMS, John C. "*Rom:* As Played on Shakespeare's Stage." *Theatre Arts,* 20 (1936): 896-904.

2276   ——. "Shakespeare's Use of the Upper Stage in *Rom* III.v." *SQ,* 7 (1956): 145-52.

2277   BONNARD, Georges A. "*Rom:* A Possible Significance?" *RES,* 2 (1951): 319-27.

2278   BOWLING, Lawrence E. "The Thematic Framework of *Rom.*" *PMLA,* 64 (1949): 208-20.

2279   CAIN, H. Edward. "*Rom:* A Reinterpretation." *SAB,* 22 (1947): 163-92.

2280   CHANG, Joseph S. M. J. "The Language of Paradox in *Rom.*" *ShakS 3 1967* (1968), pp. 22-42.

2281   CHARLTON, Henry B. *Rom as an Experimental Tragedy.* Oxford U.P., 1940. [*PBA 1939*, 25 (1940): 143-85.]

2282   COLE, Douglas, ed. *Twentieth-Century Interpretations of* Rom. Englewood Cliffs, N.J.: Prentice-Hall, 1970. [Coll. 15 sel. from prev. pub. wks.]

2283   DRAPER, John W. "The Date of *Rom.*" *RES,* 25 (1949): 55-57. [Astrological references suggest 1596.]

2284   DRIVER, Tom F. "The Shakespearean Clock: Time and the Vision of Reality in *Rom* and *Tmp.*" *SQ,* 15 (1964): 363-70.

2285   ERSKINE, John. "*Rom.*" In *Shaksperian Studies,* **2798.**

2286   EVANS, Bertrand. "The Brevity of Friar Laurence." *PMLA,* 65 (1950): 841-65.

2287   EVANS, Robert O. *The Osier Cage: Rhetorical Devices in* Rom. Kentucky U.P., 1966.

2288   FREEMAN, Arthur. "Shakespeare and *Solyman and Perseda.*" *MLR,* 58 (1963): 481-87. [Dating *Rom* and *Jn.*]

2289   HARTLEY, Lodwick. " 'Mercy but Murders': A Subtheme in *Rom.*" *PELL,* 1 (1965): 259-64.

2290   HOLLAND, Norman N. "Mercutio, Mine Own Son the Dentist." In *Essays on Shakespeare,* **2813.**

2291   HOSLEY, Richard. "The Use of the Upper Stage in *Rom.*" *SQ,* 5 (1954): 371-79.

2292   LAIRD, David. "The Generation of Style in *Rom.*" *JEGP,* 63 (1964): 204-13.

2293 LAWLOR, John J. *"Rom."* In *Early Shakespeare*, **2766**.

2294 LEIMBERG, Inge. *Shakespeares* Romeo und Julia: *Von der Sonett-dichtung zur Liebestragödie.* Munich: Wilhelm Fink, 1968.

2295 LEVIN, Harry. "Form and Formality in *Rom.*" *SQ*, 11 (1960): 1-11.

2296 McARTHUR, Herbert. "Romeo's Loquacious Friend." *SQ*, 10 (1959): 35-44.

2297 McGRADY, Donald. *"Rom* Has No Spanish Source." *ShakS 5 1969* (1970), pp. 20-24.

2298 MOORE, Olin H. *The Legend of* Rom. Ohio State U.P., 1950.

2299 NEVO, Ruth. "Tragic Form in *Rom.*" *SEL*, 9 (1969): 241-58.

2300 NOSWORTHY, James M. "The Two Angry Families of Verona." *SQ*, 3 (1952): 219-26.

2301 PARKER, Douglas H. "Light and Dark Imagery in *Rom.*" *QQ*, 75 (1968): 663-74.

2302 PARSONS, Philip. "Shakespeare and the Mask." *ShS 16*; see **1672**.

2303 PEARCE, Thomas M. *"Rom* as Situation Ethics." In *Shakespeare in the Southwest*, **2817**.

2304 PETERSON, Douglas L. *"Rom* and the Art of Moral Navigation." In *Pacific Coast Studies in Shakespeare*, **2796**.

2305 PETTET, Ernest C. "The Imagery of *Rom.*" *English*, 8 (1950): 121-26.

2306 RIBNER, Irving. " 'Then I Denie You Starres': A Reading of *Rom.*" In *Studies in . . . Memory of Karl Julius Holzknecht*, **2762**.

2307 SIEGEL, Paul N. "Christianity and the Religion of Love in *Rom.*" *SQ*, 12 (1961): 371-92. Repr. in *Shakespeare in His Time and Ours*, **3317**.

2308 SMITH, Gordon R. "The Balance of Themes in *Rom.*" In *Essays on Shakespeare*, **2813**.

2309 SMITH, Warren D. "Romeo's Final Dream." *MLR*, 62 (1967): 579-83.

2310 SNYDER, Susan. *"Rom:* Comedy into Tragedy." *EIC*, 20 (1970): 391-402.

2311 STEVENS, Martin. "Juliet's Nurse: Love's Herald." *PLL*, 2 (1966): 195-206.

2312 STEWART, Stanley. *"Rom* and Necessity." In *Pacific Coast Studies in Shakespeare*, **2796**.

2313 STONE, George W. *"Rom:* The Source of Its Modern Stage Career." *SQ*, 15.2 (1964): 191-206. Also in *Shakespeare 400*, **2793**.

2314 TANSELLE, G. Thomas. "Time in *Rom.*" *SQ*, 15 (1964): 349-61.

2315 ZASLOVE, Jerald. "Romeo and Juliet—The Rites of Disciplined Youth." *Paunch* (Buffalo, N.Y.), 27 (1965): 10-17.

SONNETS

Editions

See also Poems (**2153-62**) and **618**. For concordances, see **163** and **166**.

2316   ALDEN, Raymond M., ed. Son *of Shakespeare: From the Quarto of 1609 with Variorum Readings and Commentary.* Boston and New York: Houghton Mifflin, 1916.

2317   BROOKE, C. F. Tucker, ed. *Shakespeare's* Son. Oxford U.P., 1936.

2318   DOUGLAS, Noel, ed. *William Shakespeare's* Son. London: P. L. Humphries, 1926. [Facs.]

2319   INGRAM, W. G., and Theodore Redpath. *Shakespeare's* Son. New York: Barnes & Noble, 1965. Repr. New York: Barnes & Noble. [*B&N* 448.]   [Text and commentary.]

2320   LEE, Sidney, ed. *Shakespeares* Son *Faithfully Reproduced in Facsimile of the First Edition 1609 from the Copy in the Malone Collection in the Bodleian Library.* Oxford U.P., 1905.

2321   ROLLINS, Hyder E., ed. *Son.* New Variorum. 2 vols. Philadelphia: Lippincott, 1944.

2322   ROWSE, Alfred L., ed. *Son.* London: Macmillan, 1964.

2323   *Shakespeare's* Son. London: Lovell Reeve, 1862. [Photo-zincograph facs.]

2324   *Shake-speares* Son, *1609.* Menston, Yorks., Eng.: Scolar, 1970. [Facs.]

2325   SMITH, Barbara H., ed. *William Shakespeare:* Son. New York U.P., 1969.

Textual Commentary

2326   BENNETT, Josephine W. "Benson's Alleged Piracy of *Shake-speares Son* and of Some of Jonson's Works." *SB,* 21 (1968): 235-48.

2327   CARTER, Albert H. "The Punctuation of Shakespeare's *Son* of 1609." In *Adams Memorial Studies,* **2794**.

2328   STIRLING, Brents. "More Shakespeare Sonnet Groups." In *Essays . . . in Honor of Hardin Craig,* **2786**.

Commentary

See also **151, 422, 813, 881, 2358, 2858, 3137, 3177,** and **4448.**

2329   BALDWIN, Thomas W. *On the Literary Genetics of Shakespeare's Poems and* Son. U. of Illinois P., 1950.

2330   BATES, Paul A. "Shakespeare's *Son* and Pastoral Poetry." *SJ* (East), 103 (1967): 81-96.

2331   BATESON, Frederick W. "Elementary, My Dear Hotson! A Caveat for Literary Detectives." *EIC*, 1 (1951): 81-88.

2332   BOOTH, Stephen. *An Essay on Shakespeare's* Son. Yale U.P., 1969.

2333   CHAMBERS, Edmund K. "The Order of the *Son*"; "The 'Youth' of the *Son*"; "The 'Mortal Moon' Sonnet." In *Shakespearean Gleanings*, **2913**.

2334   COOK, I. R. W. "William Hervey and Shakespeare's *Son*." *ShS 21* (1968), pp. 97-106.

2335   CRUTTWELL, M. J. Patrick. "A Reading of the *Son*." *HudR*, 5 (1953): 554-70.

2336   EMPSON, William. "They That Have Power." In *Some Versions of Pastoral*; see **1227**.

2337   FORT, James A. "The Order and Chronology of Shakespeare's *Son*." *RES*, 9 (1933): 19-23.

2338   GOLDSMITH, Ulricht K. "Words Out of a Hat? Alliteration and Assonance in Shakespeare's *Son*." *JEGP*, 49 (1950): 33-48.

2339   GRAVES, Robert, and Laura Riding. "A Study in Original Punctuation and Spelling." In *The Common Asphodel*. London: Hamish Hamilton, 1949. [Rev. version of "William Shakespeare and E. E. Cummings," in *A Survey of Modernist Poetry*. London: Heinemann, 1927.]

2340   GREEN, A. Wigfall. "Significant Words in Shakespeare's *Son*." *U. of Mississippi Studies in English*, 3 (1962): 95-113.

2341   GRUNDY, Joan. "Shakespeare's *Son* and the Elizabethan Sonneteers." In *ShS 15*, **2374**.

2342   HARBAGE, Alfred. "The Dating of Shakespeare's *Son*." *SQ*, 1 (1950): 57-63.

2343   HERRNSTEIN, Barbara, ed. *Discussions of Shakespeare's* Son. Boston: Heath, 1964.

2344   HOTSON, Leslie. *Mr. W. H.* London: Rupert Hart-Davis, 1964.

2345   —. *Shakespeare's* Son *Dated, and Other Essays*. New York: Oxford U.P., 1949.

2346   HUBLER, Edward L., ed. *The Riddle of Shakespeare's* Son. New York: Basic Books, 1962.

2347   —. *The Sense of Shakespeare's* Son. Princeton U.P., 1952.

2348   KAULA, David. "'In War with Time': Temporal Perspectives in Shakespeare's *Son*." *SEL*, 3 (1963): 45-57.

2349   KLEIN, David. "Foreign Influence on Shakespeare's *Son*." *SR*, 13 (1905): 454-74.

2350   KNIGHT, G. Wilson. *Gold-Dust: A Sequence on the Theme of Shakespeare's* Son *with Other Poetry*. New York: Barnes & Noble, 1968.

2351   ——. *The Mutual Flame: On Shakespeare's* Son *and* PhT. London: Methuen, 1955. Repr. 1962.

2352   KRIEGER, Murray. "The Innocent Insinuations of Wit: The Strategy of Language in Shakespeare's *Son*." In *The Play and Place of Criticism*. Johns Hopkins U.P., 1967.

2353   ——. *A Window to Criticism: Shakespeare's* Son *and Modern Poetics*. Princeton U.P., 1964.

2354   LANDRY, Hilton. *Interpretations in Shakespeare's* Son. U. of California P., 1963.

2355   LEE, Sidney. "Ovid and Shakespeare's *Son*." *QR*, 210 (1909): 455-76.

2356   LEISHMAN, James B. *Themes and Variations in Shakespeare's* Son. New York: Hillary House; London: Hutchinson, 1961. [TB 1259.]

2357   LEVER, Julius W. *The Elizabethan Love Sonnet*. London: Methuen, 1956. Repr. 1966. [UP 176.] [100 pp. on Sh.]

2358   LEWIS, Clive S. *English Literature in the Sixteenth Century, Excluding Drama*. Oxford U.P., 1954. [Incl. *Son, PhT, Ven, Luc.*]

2359   MACKENZIE, Barbara A. *Shakespeare's* Son: *Their Relation to His Life*. Capetown: Maskew Miller, 1946. Repr. New York: AMS.

2360   MASSON, David I. "Free Phonetic Patterns in Shakespeare's *Son*." *Neophil*, 38 (1954): 277-89.

2361   MIZENER, Arthur. "The Structure of Figurative Language in Shakespeare's *Son*." *SoR*, 5 (1940): 730-47.

2362   MUIR, Kenneth. "Biographical Red Herrings and Shakespeare's *Son*." *Literary Half-Yearly*, 6 (1965): 61-69.

2363   MURRY, John Middleton. "Problems of the *Son*." In *Countries of the Mind, Second Series*, **3216**.

2364   NEJGEBAUER, A. "Twentieth-Century Studies in Shakespeare's *Son*." In *ShS 15*, **2374**.

2365   NOWOTTNY, Winifred M. T. "Formal Elements in Shakespeare's *Son:* Sonnets I-VI." *EIC*, 2 (1952): 76-84.

2366   NOYES, Alfred. "The Origin of Shakespeare's *Son*." *Bookman*, 67 (1924): 159-62.

2367   PARKER, David. "Verbal Moods in Shakespeare's *Son*." *MLQ*, 30 (1969): 331-39.

2368   PEARSON, Lu E. *Elizabethan Love Conventions*. U. of California P., 1933. Repr. New York: Barnes & Noble.

2369   PETERSON, Douglas L. "Shakespeare's *Son*." In *The English Lyric from Wyatt to Donne*. Princeton U.P., 1967.

2370 PIRKHOFER, Anton M. " 'A Pretty Pleasing Pricket'—On the Use of Alliteration in Shakespeare's *Son.*" *SQ*, 14 (1963): 3-14.

2371 RANSOM, John C. "A Postscript on Shakespeare's *Son.*" *KR*, 30 (1968): 523-31.

2372 —. "Shakespeare at Sonnets." *SoR*, 3 (1938): 531-53. Also in Ransom, *The World's Body*. New York: Scribner, 1938.

2373 ROSTENBERG, Leona. "Thomas Thorpe, Publisher of *Shake-Speares Son.*" *PBSA*, 54 (1960): 16-37.

2374 *ShS 15* (1962). [3 essays on *Son.*]

2375 STIRLING, Brents. *The Shakespeare Sonnet Order.* U. of California P., 1969.

2376 STONE, Walter B. "Shakespeare and the Sad Augurs." *JEGP*, 52 (1953): 457-79.

2377 WILLEN, Gerald, and Victor B. Reed, eds. *A Casebook on Shakespeare's* Son. New York: Crowell, 1964. [Text and prev. pub. essays.]

2378 WILSON, J. Dover. *An Introduction to the* Son *of Shakespeare.* Cambridge U.P., 1963. Repr. as Introd. to New Cambridge Shakespeare, **653.**

2379 WINNY, James. *The Master-Mistress: A Study of Shakespeare's* Son. New York: Barnes & Noble, 1968.

2380 YOUNG, Henry M. *The* Son *of Shakespeare: A Psycho-sexual Analysis.* Menasha, Wis.: George Banta, 1937.

THE TAMING OF THE SHREW

Textual Commentary

See also Canon (**570-605**).

2381   ALEXANDER, Peter. "The Original Ending of *Shr.*" *SQ*, 20 (1969): 111-16.

2382   ——. "*The Taming of a Shrew.*" *TLS*, 16 Sept. 1926, p. 614.

2383   AMYOT, Thomas, ed. *The Old* Taming of a Shrew, *upon Which Shakespeare Founded His Comedy, Reprinted from the Edition of 1594, and Collated with the Subsequent Editions of 1596 and 1607.* London: The Shakespeare Society, 1844. [Incl. "The Wife Lapped in Morels Skin."]

2384   ASHTON, Florence H. "The Revision of the Folio Text of *Shr.*" *PQ*, 6 (1927): 151-60.

2385   BOAS, Frederick S., ed. *The Taming of a Shrew.* London: Chatto & Windus; New York: Duffield, 1908.

2386   CRAIG, Hardin. "*Shr* and *A Shrew.*" In *Elizabethan Studies... in Honor of George F. Reynolds*, **2821**.

2387   DUTHIE, George Ian. "*The Taming of a Shrew* and *Shr.*" *RES*, 19 (1943): 337-56. [Derives them from postulated lost play.]

2388   FARMER, John S., ed. *A Pleasant Conceited Historie, Called the Taming of a Shrew... 1594.* Tudor Facs. Texts. Amersham: Farmer, 1913. Repr. New York: AMS.

2389   GRAY, Henry D. "*The Taming of a Shrew.*" *PQ*, 20 (1941): 325-33.

2390   HOSLEY, Richard. "Was There a 'Dramatic Epilogue' to *Shr?*" *SEL*, 1.2 (1961): 17-34.

2391   PARROTT, Thomas M. "*The Taming of a Shrew*—A New Study of an Old Play." In *Elizabethan Studies... in Honor of George F. Reynolds*, **2821**.

2392   SHROEDER, John W. "*The Taming of a Shrew* and *Shr:* A Case Reopened." *JEGP*, 57 (1958): 424-43.

Commentary

See also The Comedies (**3444-3549**); **601, 604, 3247, 3744,** and **4449.**

2393   ALEXANDER, Peter. "A Case of Three Sisters." *TLS*, 8 July 1965, p. 588.

2394   BERGERON, David M. "The Wife of Bath and Shakespeare's *Shr.*" *UR*, 35 (1969): 279-86.

2395   BRADBROOK, Muriel C. "Dramatic Role as Social Image: A Study of *Shr*." *SJ*, 94 (1958): 132-50.

2396   BRUNVAND, Jan H. "The Folktale Origin of *Shr*." *SQ*, 17 (1966): 345-59.

2397   DRAPER, John W. "Kate the Curst." *JNMD*, 89 (1939): 757-64.

2398   GREENFIELD, Thelma N. "The Transformation of Christopher Sly." *PQ*, 33 (1954): 34-42.

2399   HEILMAN, Robert B. "The *Taming* Untamed; or, The Return of the Shrew." *MLQ*, 27 (1966): 147-61.

2400   HIBBARD, George R. "*Shr*: A Social Comedy." In *Shakespearean Essays*, **2819**.

2401   HOSLEY, Richard. "Sources and Analogues of *Shr*." *HLQ*, 27 (1963-64): 289-308.

2402   HOUK, Raymond A. "The Evolution of *Shr*." *PMLA*, 57 (1942): 1009-38.

2403   —. "The Integrity of Shakespeare's *Shr*." *JEGP*, 39 (1940): 222-29.

2404   —. "Shakspere's Heroic Shrew." *SAB*, 18 (1943): 121-32, 175-86.

2405   —. "Strata in *Shr*." *SP*, 39 (1942): 291-301.

2406   JAYNE, Sears. "The Dreaming of *The Shrew*." *SQ*, 17 (1966): 41-56.

2407   KING, Thomson. "*Shr*." *SAB*, 17 (1942): 73-79.

2408   LONG, John H. "Shakespeare and Thomas Morley." *MLN*, 65 (1950): 17-22. [Date of *Shr*.]

2409   MOORE, William H. "An Allusion in 1593 to *Shr*?" *SQ*, 15.1 (1964): 55-60.

2410   RIBNER, Irving. "The Morality of Farce: *Shr*." In *Essays in American and English Literature Presented to Bruce R. McElderry*. Ed. Max F. Schulz et al. Ohio U.P., 1968.

2411   SERONSY, Cecil C. "'Supposes' as the Unifying Theme in *Shr*." *SQ*, 14 (1963): 15-30.

2412   SHROEDER, John W. "A New Analogue and Possible Source for *Shr*." *SQ*, 10 (1959): 251-55.

2413   TAYLOR, George C. "Two Notes on Shakespeare." *PQ*, 20 (1941): 371-76. [The second treats of authorship of *A Shrew*.]

2414   THOMAS, Sidney. "A Note on *Shr*." *MLN*, 64 (1949): 94-96. [Date.]

2415   THORNE, William B. "Folk Elements in *Shr*." *QQ*, 75 (1968): 482-96.

2416   WALDO, Tommy R., and T. Walter Herbert. "Musical Terms in *Shr*: Evidence of Single Authorship." *SQ*, 10 (1959): 185-99.

2417   WENTERSDORF, Karl. "The Authenticity of *Shr*." *SQ*, 5 (1954): 11-32.

THE TEMPEST

Editions

2418   FURNESS, Horace H., ed. *Tmp*. New Variorum. Philadelphia: Lippincott, 1892.

2419   WILSON, J. Dover, ed. *Tmp*. London: Faber & Gwyer, [1928]. [Facs. from Grenville copy of F1 in the British Museum.]

Textual Commentary

2420   CHAMBERS, Edmund K. "The Integrity of *Tmp*." In *Shakespearean Gleanings*, **2913**.

2421   SMITH, Irwin. "Ariel and the Masque in *Tmp*." *SQ*, 21 (1970): 213-22.

Commentary

See also The Comedies (**3444-3549**) and The Romances (after **3734**); **745**, **750**, **752**, **768**, **2834**, **3082**, **3412**, **3420**, **3547**, **3719**, **3745**, **4236**, **4407**, and **4450**.

2422   ADAMS, John C. "The Staging of *Tmp*, III.iii." *RES*, 14 (1938): 404-19.

2423   ALLEN, Don C. "*Tmp*." In *Image and Meaning*, **3769**.

2424   BAUM, Bernard. "*Tmp* and *Hairy Ape:* The Literary Incarnation of Mythos." *MLQ*, 14 (1953): 258-73.

2425   BERGER, Harry. "Miraculous Harp: A Reading of Shakespeare's *Tmp*." *ShakS 5 1969* (1970), pp. 253-83.

2426   BROWER, Reuben A. "The Heresy of Plot." *EIE 1951* (1952), pp. 44-69.

2427   —. "The Mirror of Analogy: *Tmp*." In *The Fields of Light: An Experiment in Critical Reading.* New York: Oxford U.P., 1951.

2428   BROWN, John R. *Shakespeare: Tmp.* London: Arnold, 1969.

2429   CAMDEN, Carroll C. "Songs and Choruses in *Tmp*." In *Studies . . . Presented to Baldwin Maxwell*, **2824**. [Possibly from the unpublished adaptation by R. B. Sheridan about 1777.]

2430   COLLINS, J. Churton. "Poetry and Symbolism: A Study of *Tmp*." *Contemporary Review*, 93 (Jan. 1908): 65-83.

2431   COURSEN, Herbert R. "Prospero and the Drama of the Soul." *ShakS 4 1968* (1969), pp. 316-33.

2432   CRAIG, Hardin. "Magic in *Tmp*." *PQ*, 47 (1968): 8-15.

2433 CURRY, Walter C. "Sacerdotal Science in Shakespeare's *Tmp*." In *Shakespeare's Philosophical Patterns,* **2953**.

2434 DAVIDSON, Frank. "*Tmp:* An Interpretation." *JEGP*, 62 (1963): 501-17.

2435 DEVEREUX, E. J. "Sacramental Imagery in *Tmp*." *HAB*, 19.1 (1968): 50-62.

2436 DOBRÉE, Bonamy. "*Tmp*." *E&S*, 5 (1952): 13-25.

2437 DRIVER, Tom F. "The Shakespearean Clock: Time and the Vision of Reality in *Rom* and *Tmp*." *SQ;* see **2284**.

2438 EBNER, Dean. "*Tmp:* Rebellion and the Ideal State." *SQ*, 16 (1965): 161-73.

2439 GESNER, Carol. "*Tmp* as Pastoral Romance." *SQ*, 10 (1959): 531-39.

2440 GILBERT, Allan H. "*Tmp:* Parallelism in Characters and Situations." *JEGP*, 14 (1915): 63-74.

2441 GOHN, Ernest. "*Tmp:* Theme and Structure." *ES*, 45 (1964): 116-25.

2442 GOLDSMITH, Robert H. "The Wild Man on the English Stage." *MLR*, 53 (1958): 481-91.

2443 HANKINS, John E. "Caliban the Bestial Man." *PMLA*, 62 (1947): 793-801.

2444 HART, Jeffrey P. "Prospero and Faustus." *BUSE*, 2 (1956): 197-206.

2445 HAYWOOD, Charles. "*The Songs and Masque in the New Tempest:* An Incident in the Battle of the Two Theatres, 1674." *HLQ*, 19 (1955-56): 39-56. [Libretto of Duffett's *The Mock Tempest.*]

2446 HEUER, Hermann. "Traumwelt und Wirklichkeit in der Sprache des *Tmp*." *SJ*, 90 (1954): 210-28.

2447 HOENIGER, F. David. "Prospero's Storm and Miracle." *SQ*, 7 (1956): 33-38.

2448 HOTSON, Leslie. "Sir Dudley Digges and *Tmp*." In *I, William Shakespeare,* **460**.

2449 HOWARTH, Robert G. *Shakespeare's* Tmp. Sydney: Australasian Medical P., 1936. Rev. and abridged ed., 1947. [Sources.]

2450 HUNT, John D. *A Critical Commentary on Shakespeare's* Tmp. London: Macmillan, 1968.

2451 HUTCHENS, Eleanor N. "The Transfer of Power in *Lr* and *Tmp*." *REL;* see **1567**.

2452 JAMES, David G. *The Dream of Prospero*. Oxford U.P., 1967.

2453 JEWKES, Wilfred T. "Excellent Dumb Discourse: The Limits of the Language in *Tmp*." In *Essays on Shakespeare,* **2813**.

2454 JOHNSON, Wendell S. "The Genesis of Ariel." *SQ*, 2 (1951): 205-10.

2455   KIPLING, Rudyard. *How Shakespeare Came to Write* Tmp. New York: Columbia Dramatic Museum, 1916.

2456   KNOX, Bernard. "*Tmp* and the Ancient Comic Tradition." *EIE 1954* (1955), pp. 52-73.

2457   KOSZUL, A. "Ariel." *ES*, 19 (1937): 200-204.

2458   LAWRY, Jon S. " 'Born to Set It Right': Hal, Hamlet, and Prospero." *BSUF;* see **1122.**

2459   LEVIN, Harry. "Two Magian Comedies: *Tmp* and *The Alchemist.*" In *ShS 22*, **3530.**

2460   McMANAWAY, James G. "Songs and Masques in *Tmp.*" In *Theatre Miscellany.* Luttrell Society Reprints, 14. Oxford: Blackwell for the Luttrell Society, 1953. Repr. in *Studies in Shakespeare, Bibliography, and Theater*, **3174.** [Libretto of the operatic *Tmp* of 1674.]

2461   McPEEK, James A. S. "The Genesis of Caliban." *PQ*, 25 (1946): 378-81.

2462   MERTON, Stephen. "*Tmp* and *Tro.*" *CE*, 7 (1945): 143-50.

2463   NOSWORTHY, James M. "The Narrative Sources of *Tmp.*" *RES* 24 (1948): 281-94.

2464   NUTTALL, Anthony D. *Two Concepts of Allegory: A Study of Shakespeare's* Tmp *and the Logic of Allegorical Expression.* New York: Barnes & Noble, 1967.

2465   ORGEL, Stephen K. "New Uses of Adversity: Tragic Experience in *Tmp.*" In *In Defense of Reading.* Ed. Reuben A. Brower and Richard Poirier. New York: Dutton, 1962.

2466   PHILLIPS, James E. "*Tmp* and the Renaissance Idea of Man." *SQ*, 15.2 (1964): 147-59. Also in *Shakespeare 400*, **2793.**

2467   REED, Robert R. "The Probable Origin of Ariel." *SQ*, 11 (1960): 61-65.

2468   RICKEY, Mary E. "Prospero's Living Drolleries." In *RenP 1964*, **2785.**

2469   ROBINSON, James E. "Time and *Tmp.*" *JEGP*, 63 (1964): 255-67.

2470   RYKEN, Leland. "The Temptation Theme in *Tmp* and the Question of Dramatic Suspense." *TSL*, 14 (1969): 119-27.

2471   SEIDEN, Melvin. "Utopianism in *Tmp.*" *MLQ*, 31 (1970): 3-21.

2472   SISSON, Charles J. "The Magic of Prospero." In *ShS 11*, **3529.**

2473   SMITH, Hallett, ed. *Twentieth-Century Interpretations of* Tmp. Englewood Cliffs, N.J.: Prentice-Hall, 1969. [Introd. and 16 sel. from prev. pub. wks.]

2474   STILL, Colin. *Shakespeare's Mystery Play: A Study of* Tmp. London: Palmer, 1921. Enlarged and clarified as *The Timeless Theme.* London: Nicholson & Watson, 1936.

2475   STOLL, Elmer E. *"Tmp."* *PMLA*, 47 (1932): 699-726.

2476   STONE, George W. "Shakespeare's *Tmp* at Drury Lane during Garrick's Management." *SQ*, 7 (1956): 1-7.

2477   TRAVERSI, Derek A. *"Tmp."* *Scrutiny*, 16 (1949): 127-57.

2478   WAGNER, Emma B. *Shakespeare's* Tmp: *An Allegorical Interpretation.* Antioch P., 1933.

2479   WEST, Robert H. "Ceremonial Magic in *Tmp*." In *Shakespearean Essays*, **2819**.

2480   WILLIAM, David. *"Tmp* on the Stage." In *Jacobean Theatre*, **3795**.

2481   WILSON, Harold S. "Action and Symbol in *MM* and *Tmp*." *SQ;* see **1854**.

2482   WILSON, J. Dover. *The Meaning of* Tmp. Newcastle upon Tyne: Literary and Philosophical Society, 1936.

2483   ZIMBARDO, Rose A. "Form and Disorder in *Tmp*." *SQ*, 14 (1963): 49-56.

SIR THOMAS MORE

Editions

See also Canon (**570-605**) and Handwriting (**522-37**).

2484   CLAYTON, Thomas, ed. *The "Shakespearean" Addition in The Booke of Sir Thomas Moore* [*sic*] : *Some Aids to Scholarly and Critical Shakespearean Studies.* Shakespeare Studies Monograph Series, 1. Dubuque, Iowa: W. C. Brown, 1969. [Transcription; modernized text; index verborum; index litterarum; concordance.]

2485   DYCE, Alexander, ed. *More: A Play; Now First Printed.* London: for the Shakespeare Society, 1844. Repr. Nendeln, Liechtenstein: Kraus & Thomson.

2486   FARMER, John S., ed. *More.* Tudor Facs. Texts. Amersham: Farmer, 1913. Repr. New York: AMS.

2487   GREG, Walter W., ed. *More.* Oxford U.P. for the Malone Society, 1911. Repr. 1961. [Reprint has Harold Jenkins's "Supplement to the Introduction," which was reprinted in Malone Society *Collections*, 6 (1961): 179-92.]

2488   HOPKINSON, Arthur F., ed. *More.* London: M. E. Sims, 1902.

2488a   SHIRLEY, John W., ed. *More.* Canterbury: Goulden, 1920.

Commentary

See also **151**.

2489   BALD, R. Cecil. "Addition III of *More.*" *RES*, 7 (1931): 67-69. [Attributes to Sh.]

2490   CHAMBERS, Raymond W. "Shakespeare and the Play of *More.*" In *Man's Unconquerable Mind.* London: Cape, 1939. Repr. 1952.

2491   COLLINS, Douglas C. "On the Date of *More.*" *RES*, 10 (1934): 401-11. [About 1601.]

2492   DEUTSCHBERGER, Paul. "Shakespere and *More.*" *SAB*, 18 (1943): 75-91, 99-108, 156-67.

2493   GREENWOOD, George. *The Shakespere Signatures and* More. London: Cecil Palmer, 1924.

2494   MAAS, Paul. "Henry Finch and Shakespeare." *RES*, 4 (1953): 142.

2495   McMILLIN, Scott. "*More:* A Theatrical View." *MP*, 68 (1970): 10-24.

2496   NOSWORTHY, James M. "Hand B in *More.*" *Library*, 11 (1956): 47-50. [Not Thomas Heywood's.]

2497   ——. "Shakespeare and *More.*" *RES*, 6 (1955): 12-25. [Dates Addition II about 1601-2; also Addition III.]

2498   OLIPHANT, Ernest H. C. *"More."* *JEGP*, 18 (1919): 226-35.

2499   SCHÜCKING, Levin L. "Shakespeare and *More.*" *RES*, 1 (1925): 40-59. [Doubts attribution to Sh.]

2500   *Shakespeare's Hand in the Play of* More. Shakespeare Problem Series, 2. Cambridge U.P., 1923. [Papers by Alfred W. Pollard, Walter W. Greg, E. Maunde Thompson, J. Dover Wilson, Raymond W. Chambers, with the text of the Ill May Day Scenes edited by Greg.]

2501   SIMPSON, Percy. "The Play of *More* and Shakespeare's Hand in It." *Library*, 8 (1917): 79-96.

2502   SPURGEON, Caroline F. E. "Imagery in the *More* Fragment." *RES*, 6 (1930): 257-70.

2503   TANNENBAUM, Samuel A. "Shakspere's Unquestioned Autographs and the Additions to *More.*" *SP*, 22 (1925): 133-60, 6 plates.

2504   THOMPSON, E. Maunde. "The Autograph Manuscripts of Anthony Munday." *Trans. Bibliog. Soc.* (London), 14 (1917): 325-53.

TIMON OF ATHENS

Commentary

See also The Tragedies (**3616-3734**); **745**, **2879**, **3293**, and **3394**.

2505   ANDERSON, Ruth L. "Excessive Goodness a Tragic Fault." *SAB*, 19 (1944): 85-96.

2506   BACQUET, Paul. "Réflexions sur la technique dramatique de Shakespeare dans *Tim*." *BFLS*, 63 (1965): 147-55.

2507   BERGERON, David M. "Alchemy and *Tim*." *CLAJ*, 13 (1970): 364-73.

2507a   ——. "*Tim* and Morality Drama." *CLAJ*, 10 (1967): 181-88.

2508   BOND, R. Warwick. "Lucian and Boiardo in *Tim*." *MLR*, 26 (1931): 52-68.

2509   BONNARD, Georges A. "Note sur les sources de *Tim*." *EA*, 7 (1954): 59-69.

2510   BRADBROOK, Muriel C. "The Comedy of Timon." *RenD*, 9 (1966): 83-103.

2511   ——. *The Tragic Pageant of* Tim. Cambridge U.P., 1966. Repr. as "Blackfriars: The Pageant of *Tim*" in *Shakespeare the Craftsman*, **2879**.

2512   BUTLER, Francelia. *The Strange Critical Fortunes of Shakespeare's* Tim. Iowa State U.P., 1966.

2513   CLEMONS, W. H. "The Sources of *Tim*." *Princeton U. Bulletin*, 15 (1903-4): 208-23.

2514   COLLINS, A. S. "*Tim*: A Reconsideration." *RES*, 22 (1946): 96-108.

2515   COOK, David. "*Tim*." *ShS 16* (1963), pp. 83-94.

2516   DRAPER, John W. "Patterns of Tempo in Shakespeare's *Tim*." *SAB*, 23 (1948): 188-94.

2517   ——. "The Theme of *Tim*." *MLR*, 29 (1934): 20-31.

2518   DRAPER, R. P. "*Tim*." *SQ*, 8 (1957): 195-200.

2519   DYCE, Alexander, ed. *Timon: A Play; Now First Printed*. London: The Shakespeare Society, 1842. [Anon.; *ca.* 1581-90?]

2520   ELLIS-FERMOR, Una. "*Tim*: An Unfinished Play." *RES*, 18 (1942): 270-83.

2521   EMPSON, William. "Timon's Dog." In *The Structure of Complex Words*, **2992**.

2522   FARNHAM, Willard E. "The Beast Theme in Shakespeare's *Tim*." *Essays and Studies, U. of California*, 14 (1943): 49-56.

2523 GOLDSMITH, Robert H. "Did Shakespeare Use the Old Timon Comedy?" *SQ*, 9 (1958): 31-38.

2524 GOLDSTEIN, Leonard. "Alcibiades' Revolt in *Tim*." *ZAA*, 15 (1967): 256-78.

2525 GOMME, Andor. "*Tim*." *EIC*, 9 (1959): 107-25.

2526 HAUG, Ralph A. "The Authorship of *Tim*." *SAB*, 15 (1940): 227-48.

2527 HONIGMANN, Ernst A. J. "*Tim*." *SQ*, 12 (1961): 3-20.

2528 KNIGHT, G. Wilson. "*Tim* and Its Dramatic Descendants." *REL*, 2 (1961): 9-18. Also in *Stratford Papers on Shakespeare, 1963*, 2787.

2529 KNIGHTS, Lionel C. "*Tim*." In *The Morality of Art*, 2789.

2530 MAXWELL, James C. "*Tim*." *Scrutiny*, 15 (1948): 195-208.

2531 MERCHANT, W. Moelwyn. "*Tim* and the Conceit of Art." *SQ*, 6 (1955): 249-57.

2532 MORSBERGER, Robert E. "*Tim:* Tragedy or Satire?" In *Shakespeare in the Southwest*, 2817.

2533 MUIR, Kenneth. "*Tim* and the Cash-Nexus." *Modern Quarterly Miscellany*, 1 (1946): 57-76.

2534 NOWOTTNY, Winifred M. T. "Acts IV and V of *Tim*." *SQ*, 10 (1959): 493-97.

2535 PAULIN, Bernard. "La Mort de Timon d'Athènes." In *EA*, 17, 2776.

2536 PETTET, Ernest C. "*Tim:* The Disruption of Feudal Morality." *RES*, 23 (1947): 321-36.

2537 SPENCER, Terence J. B. "Shakespeare Learns the Value of Money: The Dramatist at Work on *Tim*." *ShS* 6 (1953), pp. 75-78.

2538 SWIGG, R. "*Tim* and the Growth of Discrimination." *MLR*, 62 (1967): 387-94.

2539 WAGGONER, George R. "*Tim* and the Jacobean Duel." *SQ*, 16 (1965): 303-11.

2540 WILLIAMS, Stanley T. "Some Versions of *Tim* on the Stage." *MP*, 18 (1920-21): 269-85.

2541 WOODS, Andrew H. "Syphilis in Shakespeare's Tragedy of *Tim*." *American Journal of Psychiatry*, 91 (1934): 95-107.

TITUS ANDRONICUS

Editions

2542 ADAMS, Joseph Q., ed. *Shakespeare's* Tit: *The First Quarto 1594 Reproduced in Facsimile.* New York and London: Scribner's for The Trustees of Amherst College, 1936.

Textual Commentary

See also **349**.

2543 ADAMS, John C. "Shakespeare's Revisions in *Tit.*" *SQ*, 15.2 (1964): 177-90. Also in *Shakespeare 400,* **2793**.

2544 BOLTON, Joseph S. G. "The Authentic Text of *Tit.*" *PMLA*, 44 (1929): 765-88. [Q2 printed from a defective copy of Q1.]

2545 CANTRELL, Paul L., and George W. Williams. "Roberts' Compositors in *Tit* Q2." *SB*, 8 (1956): 27-38.

2546 KRAMER, Joseph E. "*Tit:* The 'Fly-Killing' Incident." *ShakS 5 1969* (1970), pp. 9-19. [Not Sh.]

2547 McKERROW, Ronald B. "A Note on *Tit.*" *Library*, 15 (1934-35): 49-53. [Q2 printed from a defective copy of Q1.]

2548 PRICE, Hereward T. "Author, Compositor, and Metre: Copy-Spelling in *Tit* and Other Elizabethan Printings." *PBSA*, 53 (1959): 160-87.

2549 ——. "The First Quarto of *Tit.*" *EIE 1947* (1948), pp. 137-68.

2550 *Eine sehr klägliche Tragoedia von Tito Andronico.* In *Engelische Comedien und Tragedien.* N.p.: n.p., 1620. Repr. 1624; in vol. 1, *Deutsches Theater.* Ed. Ludwig Tieck. Berlin: Realschulbuchhandlung, 1817; in *Die Schauspiele der engelischen Komödianten.* Ed. Wilhelm M. A. Creizenach. Berlin: W. Spemann, [1889]; and in *Shakespeare in Germany.* Ed. Albert Cohn. London: Asher, 1865.

Commentary

See also The Tragedies (**3616-3734**) and The Roman Plays (after **3734**); **572, 733, 740, 742, 764, 768, 2886, 3106, 3329, 4407**, and **4457**.

2551 BOLTON, Joseph S. G. "*Tit:* Shakespeare at Thirty." *SP*, 30 (1933): 208-24.

2552 BRAEKMAN, W. *Shakespeare's* Tit: *Its Relationship to the German Play of 1620 and to Jan Vos's* Aran en Titus. Ghent: Blandijnberg, 1969.

2553 CUTTS, John P. "Shadow and Substance: Structural Unity in *Tit*." *CompD*, 2 (1968): 161-72.

2554 DESMONDE, William H. "The Ritual Origin of Shakespeare's *Tit*." *International Journal of Psycho-Analysis*, 36 (1955): 61-65.

2555 EBBS, John D. "A Note on Nashe and Shakespeare." *MLN*, 66 (1951): 480-81. [Date of *Tit*.]

2556 ETTIN, Andrew V. "Shakespeare's First Roman Tragedy." *ELH*, 37 (1970): 325-41.

2557 HAMILTON, Albert C. "*Tit:* The Form of Shakespearian Tragedy." *SQ*, 14 (1963): 201-13.

2558 HARRIS, Bernard. "A Portrait of a Moor." *ShS 11* (1958), pp. 89-97.

2559 HASTINGS, William T. "The Hardboiled Shakespere." *SAB*, 17 (1942): 114-25.

2560 HILL, R. F. "The Composition of *Tit*." *ShS 10* (1957), pp. 60-70.

2561 KELLER, Wolfgang. "*Tit*." *SJ*, 74 (1938): 137-62.

2562 LAW, Robert A. "The Roman Background of *Tit*." *SP*, 40 (1943): 145-53.

2563 McMANAWAY, James G. "Writing in Sand in *Tit* IV.i." *RES*, 9 (1958): 172-73.

2564 MAXWELL, James C. "Peele and Shakespeare: A Stylometric Test." *JEGP*, 49 (1950): 557-61. [Assigns *Tit* Act I to Peele.]

2565 OPPEL, Horst. *Tit: Studien zur dramengeschichtlichen Stellung von Shakespeares früher Tragödie.* Heidelberg: Quelle & Meyer, 1961.

2566 PARROTT, Thomas M. "Further Observations on *Tit*." *SQ*, 1 (1950): 22-29. [The "Henricus Peacham" drawing.]

2567 —. "*Tit*." *SAB*, 24 (1949): 117-23.

2568 PRICE, Hereward T. "The Authorship of *Tit*." *JEGP*, 42 (1943): 55-81.

2569 —. "The Language of *Tit*." *PMASAL,* 21 (1935): 501-7.

2570 SARGENT, Ralph M. "The Source of *Tit*." *SP*, 46 (1949): 167-83.

2571 SCHLÖSSER, Anselm. "*Tit*." *SJ* (East), 104 (1968): 75-84.

2572 SOMMERS, Alan. "Wilderness of Tigers: Structure and Symbolism in *Tit*." *EIC*, 10 (1960): 275-89.

2573 UNGERER, Gustav. "An Unrecorded Elizabethan Performance of *Tit*." *ShS 14* (1961), pp. 102-9.

2574 VOS, Jan. *Aran en Titus.* Amsterdam: Dominicus vander Stichel, 1641. Repr. many times before 1700; in Vos, *Alle de Gedichten.* Amsterdam: Jacob Lescaille, 1662-71.

2575 WAITH, Eugene M. "The Metamorphosis of Violence in *Tit*." *ShS 10* (1957), pp. 39-49.

2576 WILSON, J. Dover. "*Tit* on the Stage in 1595." *ShS 1* (1948), pp. 17-22.

TROILUS AND CRESSIDA

Editions

2577   HILLEBRAND, Harold N., ed. *Tro.* New Variorum. Philadelphia: Lippincott, 1953. [Completed by Thomas W. Baldwin.]

Textual Commentary

See also **684** and **713**.

2578   BULLOUGH, Geoffrey. "The Lost 'Troilus and Cressida.'" *E&S*, 17 (1964): 24-40. [Relation of Sh's play to an Admiral's play known from stage plot in British Museum Add. MS 10449.]

2579   DAWSON, Giles E. "A Bibliographical Problem in the First Folio of Shakespeare." *Library;* see **684**. [The printing of *Tro.*]

2580   FINKELPEARL, Philip J. "Henry Walley of the Stationers' Company and John Marston." *PBSA*, 56 (1962): 366-68. [Did Marston help Bonian and Walley secure MS of *Tro*?]

2581   GREG, Walter W. "The Printing of Shakespeare's *Tro* in the First Folio." *PBSA*, 45 (1951): 273-82.

2582   KIMBROUGH, Robert T. "The Origins of *Tro:* Stage, Quarto, and Folio." *PMLA*, 77 (1962): 194-99.

2583   SEWELL, Arthur. "Notes on the Integrity of *Tro.*" *RES*, 19 (1943): 120-27.

2584   TANNENBAUM, Samuel A. "A Critique of the Text of *Tro.*" *SAB*, 9 (1934): 55-74, 125-44, 198-214.

2585   WILLIAMS, Philip. "The 'Second Issue' of Shakespeare's *Tro*, 1609." *SB*, 2 (1949-50): 25-33.

2586   —. "Shakespeare's *Tro:* The Relationship of Quarto and Folio." *SB*, 3 (1950-51): 131-43.

Commentary

See also The Tragedies (**3616-3734**) and The Problem Plays (after **3734**); **151**, **297**, **721**, **733**, **2853**, **2870**, **2972**, **3082**, **3137**, **3230**, **3354**, **3383**, **3387**, **3394**, **3502**, **3694**, and **3736**.

2587   ALEXANDER, Peter. "*Tro*, 1609." *Library*, 9 (1928-29): 267-86.

2588   ARNOLD, Aerol. "The Hector-Andromache Scene in Shakespeare's *Tro.*" *MLQ*, 14 (1953): 335-40.

2589   BALDWIN, Thomas W. "Structural Analysis of *Tro.*" In *Shakespeare-Studien . . . für Heinrich Mutschmann,* **2778**.

2590   BERGER, Harry. "*Tro:* The Observer as Basilisk." *CompD*, 2 (1968): 122-36.

2591   BERNHARDT, William W. "Shakespeare's *Tro* and Dryden's *Truth Found Too Late.*" *SQ*, 20 (1969): 129-41.

2592   BOWDEN, William R. "The Human Shakespeare and *Tro.*" *SQ*, 8 (1957): 167-77.

2593   BRADBROOK, Muriel C. "What Shakespeare Did to Chaucer's *Troilus and Criseyde.*" *SQ*, 9 (1958): 311-19.

2594   BROOKE, C. F. Tucker. "Shakespeare's Study in Culture and Anarchy." *YR*, 17 (1927): 571-77. Repr. in *Essays on Shakespeare and Other Elizabethans*, 2888.

2595   CAMPBELL, Oscar J. *Comicall Satyre and Shakespeare's* Tro. San Marino, Calif.: Adcraft, 1938.

2596   COGHILL, Nevill. "Morte Hector: A Map of Honour." In *Shakespeare's Professional Skills*, 2927.

2596a   —. "A Prologue and an 'Epilogue.'" In *Shakespeare's Professional Skills*, 2927.

2597   DYER, Frederick B. "The Destruction of Pandare." In *Shakespeare Encomium*, 2802.

2598   ELTON, William R. "Shakespeare's Portrait of Ajax." *PMLA*, 63 (1948): 744-48.

2599   —. "Shakespeare's Ulysses and the Problem of Value." *ShakS 2 1966* (1967), pp. 95-111. Trans. as "Shakespeares Ulysses und die Frage des Wertes." *SJ* (East), 104 (1968): 49-74.

2600   FARNHAM, Willard E. "Troilus in Shapes of Infinite Desire." *SQ*, 15.2 (1964): 257-64. Also in *Shakespeare 400*, 2793.

2601   FOAKES, Reginald A. "*Tro* Reconsidered." *UTQ*, 32 (1963): 142-54.

2602   GAGEN, Jean. "Hector's Honor." *SQ*, 19 (1968): 129-37.

2603   HARGREAVES, H. A. "An Essentially Tragic *Tro.*" *HAB*, 18 (1967): 49-60.

2604   HARRIER, Richard C. "Troilus Divided." In *Studies in . . . Memory of Karl Julius Holzknecht*, 2762.

2605   HENDERSON, W. B. Drayton. "Shakespeare's *Tro.*" In *Essays . . . in Honor of T. M. Parrott*, 2771.

2606   HEUER, Hermann. "Troilus und Cressida in neuerer Sicht." *SJ*, 89 (1953): 106-27.

2607   KAUFMANN, Ralph J. "Ceremonies for Chaos: The Status of *Tro.*" *ELH*, 32 (1965): 139-59.

2608   KAULA, David. "Will and Reason in *Tro.*" *SQ*, 12 (1961): 271-83.

2609   KENDALL, Paul M. "Inaction and Ambivalence in *Tro.*" In *English Studies in Honor of James S. Wilson*, 2765.

2610   KERMODE, J. Frank. "Opinion, Truth, and Value." *EIC*, 5 (1955): 181-87.

2611   KIMBROUGH, Robert T. *Shakespeare's* Tro *and Its Setting.* Oxford U.P.; Harvard U.P., 1964.

2612   KNIGHTS, Lionel C. "*Tro* Again." *Scrutiny*, 18 (1951-52): 144-57.

2613   KNOWLAND, A. S. "*Tro*." *SQ*, 10 (1959): 353-65.

2614   LAWRENCE, William W. "Troilus, Cressida, and Thersites." *MLR*, 37 (1942): 422-37.

2615   LYONS, Charles. "Cressida, Achilles, and the Finite Deed." *EA*, 20 (1967): 233-42.

2616   McALINDON, Thomas. "Language, Style, and Meaning in *Tro*." *PMLA*, 84 (1969): 29-43.

2617   MAIN, William W. "Character Amalgams in Shakespeare's *Tro*." *SP*, 58 (1961): 170-78.

2618   MARSH, Derick R. C. "Interpretation and Misinterpretation: The Problem of *Tro*." *ShakS 1* (1965), pp. 182-98.

2619   MENDONÇA, Barbara H. C. de. "*Tro:* Romantic Love Revisited." *SQ*, 15 (1964): 327-32.

2620   MERTON, Stephen. "*Tmp* and *Tro*." *CE;* see **2462**.

2621   MORRIS, Brian. "The Tragic Structure of *Tro*." *SQ*, 10 (1959): 481-91.

2622   MUIR, Kenneth. "*Tro*." *ShS 8* (1955), pp. 28-39.

2623   NEWLIN, Jeanne T. "The Modernity of *Tro*." *Harvard Library Bulletin*, 17 (1969): 353-73.

2624   NOWOTTNY, Winifred M.T. " 'Opinion' and 'Value' in *Tro*." *EIC*, 4 (1954): 282-96.

2625   OATES, J. C. "The Ambiguity of *Tro*." *SQ*, 17 (1966): 141-53.

2626   POTTS, Abbie F. "*Cynthia's Revels, Poetaster,* and *Tro*." *SQ*, 5 (1954): 297-302.

2627   PRESSON, Robert K. *Shakespeare's* Tro *and the Legends of Troy.* U. of Wisconsin P., 1953.

2628   RABKIN, Norman. "*Tro:* The Uses of the Double Plot." *ShakS 1* (1965), pp. 265-82.

2629   REYNOLDS, George F. "*Tro* on the Elizabethan Stage." In *Adams Memorial Studies*, **2794**.

2630   RICHARDS, Ivor A. "*Tro* and Plato." *HudR*, 1 (1948): 362-76.

2631   RICKEY, Mary E. " 'Twixt the Dangerous Shores: *Tro* Again." *SQ*, 15.1 (1964): 3-13.

2632   SCHMIDT DI SIMONI, Karen. *Shakespeares* Tro: *Eine sprachlich-stilistische Untersuchung.* Heidelberg: Quelle & Meyer, 1960.

2633   SHALVI, Alice. " 'Honor' in *Tro*." *SEL*, 5 (1965): 283-302.

2634 SMITH, J. Oates. "Essence and Existence in Shakespeare's *Tro*." *PQ*, 46 (1967): 167-85.

2635 SOELLNER, Rolf. "Prudence and the Price of Helen: The Debate of the Trojans in *Tro*." *SQ*, 20 (1969): 255-63.

2636 SOUTHALL, Raymond. "*Tro* and the Spirit of Capitalism." In *Shakespeare in a Changing World,* **2792**.

2637 STAFFORD, Tony J. "Mercantile Imagery in *Tro*." In *Shakespeare in the Southwest,* **2817**.

2638 STAMM, Rudolf. "The Glass of Pandar's Praise: The Word-Scenery, Mirror Passages, and Reported Scenes in Shakespeare's *Tro*." *E&S*, 17 (1964): 55-77.

2639 STEIN, Arnold. "*Tro:* The Disjunctive Imagination." *ELH*, 36 (1969): 145-67.

2640 SWANSTON, Hamish F. G. "The Baroque Element in *Tro*." *DUJ*, 19 (1957): 14-23.

2641 TAYLOR, George C. "Shakespeare's Attitude towards Love and Honor in *Tro*." *PMLA*, 45 (1930): 781-86.

2642 THOMSON, Patricia. "Rant and Cant in *Tro*." *E&S,* 22 (1969): 33-56.

2643 TRAVERSI, Derek A. "*Tro*." *Scrutiny*, 7 (1938-39): 301-19.

TWELFTH NIGHT

Editions

See also **728**.

2644   FURNESS, Horace H., ed. *TN*. New Variorum. Philadelphia: Lippincott, 1901.
2645   WILSON, J. Dover, ed. *TN*. London: Faber & Gwyer, [1929]. [Facs. from Grenville copy of F1 in the British Museum.]

Commentary

See also The Comedies (**3444-3549**) and The Romances (after **3734**); **572, 740, 764, 1615, 2879, 3085, 3165, 3444, 3744, 3757, 3760, 4407**, and **4451**.

2646   BARNET, Sylvan. "Charles Lamb and the Tragic Malvolio." *PQ*, 33 (1954): 178-88.
2647   BRADLEY, Andrew C. "Feste the Jester." In *A Miscellany*, **2882**.
2648   BROWN, John R. "Directions for *TN*, or What You Will." *TDR*, 5 (1961): 77-88.
2649   CRANE, Milton. "*TN* and Shakespearean Comedy." *SQ*, 6 (1955): 1-8.
2650   DOWNER, Alan S. "Feste's Night." *CE*, 13 (1952): 258-65.
2651   EAGLETON, Terence. "Language and Reality in *TN*." *CQ*, 9 (1967): 217-28.
2652   FORBES, Lydia. "What You Will?" *SQ*, 13 (1962): 475-85.
2653   GREG, Walter W. "When Was Twelfth Night?" In *Elizabethan and Jacobean Studies Presented to F. P. Wilson*, **2772**.
2654   HARDY, Barbara. *TN*. Oxford: Blackwell, 1962.
2655   HOLLANDER, John. "Musica Mundana and *TN*." *EIE 1956* (1957), pp. 55-82.
2656   ——. "*TN* and the Morality of Indulgence." *SR*, 68 (1959): 220-38.
2657   HOTSON, Leslie. *The First Night of* TN. London: Hart-Davis, 1954.
2658   JENKINS, Harold. "Shakespeare's *TN*." *Rice Institute Pamphlet*, 45 (1959): 19-42.
2659   KAUFMAN, Helen A. "Nicolò Secchi as a Source of *TN*." *SQ*, 5 (1954): 271-80.
2660   KING, Walter N., ed. *Twentieth-Century Interpretations of* TN. Englewood Cliffs, N.J.: Prentice-Hall, 1968. [15 sel. from prev. pub. wks.]

2661   LEECH, Clifford. TN *and Shakespearean Comedy.* U. of Toronto P., 1968.

2662   LEWALSKI, Barbara K. "Thematic Patterns in *TN.*" *ShakS 1* (1965), pp. 168-81.

2663   MANHEIM, Leonard F. "The Mythical Joys of Shakespeare; or, What You *Will.*" In *Shakespeare Encomium,* **2802.**

2664   MARKELS, Julian. "Shakespeare's Confluence of Tragedy and Comedy: *TN* and *Lr.*" *SQ*; see **1594.**

2665   MELZI, Robert C. "From Lelia to Viola." *RenD*, 9 (1966): 67-81.

2666   MUESCHKE, Paul, and Jeannette Fleisher. "Jonsonian Elements in the Comic Underplot of *TN.*" *PMLA*, 48 (1933): 722-40.

2667   NAGARAJAN, S. " 'What You Will': A Suggestion." *SQ*, 10 (1959): 61-67.

2668   PALMER, D. J. "Art and Nature in *TN.*" *CQ*, 9 (1967): 201-12.

2669   PRUVOST, René. "*TGV, TN,* et Gl'Ingannati." *EA*, 13 (1960): 1-9.

2670   SALINGAR, L. G. "The Design of *TN.*" *SQ*, 9 (1958): 117-39.

2671   SCHWARTZ, Elias. "*TN* and the Meaning of Shakespearean Comedy." *CE*, 28 (1967): 508-19.

2672   SEIDEN, Melvin. "Malvolio Reconsidered." *UR*, 28 (1961): 105-14.

2673   SUMMERS, Joseph H. "The Masks of *TN.*" *UR*, 22 (1955): 25-32.

2674   THALER, Alwin. "The Original Malvolio?" *SAB*, 7 (1932): 57-71.

2675   TILLEY, Morris P. "The Organic Unity of *TN.*" *PMLA*, 29 (1914): 550-66.

2676   WEST, E. J. "Bradleyan Reprise: On the Fool in *TN.*" *SAB*, 24 (1949): 264-74.

2677   WILLIAMS, Porter. "Mistakes in *TN* and Their Resolution." *PMLA*, 76 (1961): 193-99.

2678   WRIGHT, Louis B. "A Conduct Book for Malvolio." *SP*, 31 (1934): 115-32.

THE TWO GENTLEMEN OF VERONA

Textual Commentary

See **191**.

Commentary

See also The Comedies (**3444-3549**); **742**, **768**, **3405**, **3465**, and **3760**.

2679   BROOKS, Harold F. "Two Clowns in a Comedy (to Say Nothing of the Dog): Speed, Launce (and Crab) in *TGV*." *E&S*, 16 (1963): 91-100.

2680   DANBY, John F. "Shakespeare Criticism and *TGV*." *CritQ*, 2 (1960): 309-21.

2681   GODSHALK, William L. "The Structural Unity of *TGV*." *SP*, 66 (1969): 168-81.

2682   KNORR, Friedrich. *Shakespeares* Die Beiden Veroneser. Coburg: Rosenwith, 1959.

2683   PARKS, George B. "The Development of *TGV*." *Huntington Library Bulletin,* 11 (1937): 1-11.

2684   PERRY, Thomas A. "Proteus, Wry-Transformed Traveller." *SQ*, 5 (1954): 33-40.

2685   PRICE, Hereward T. "Shakespeare as a Critic." *PQ*, 20 (1941): 390-99.

2686   PRUVOST, René. "*TGV, TN,* et Gl'Ingannati." *EA*; see **2669**.

2687   SARGENT, Ralph M. "Sir Thomas Elyot and the Integrity of *TGV*." *PMLA*, 65 (1950): 1166-80.

2688   SCOTT, William O. "Proteus in Spenser and Shakespeare: The Lover's Identity." *ShakS 1* (1965), pp. 283-93.

2689   SMALL, Samuel A. "The Ending of *TGV*." *PMLA*, 48 (1933): 767-76.

2690   WEIMANN, Robert. "Laughing with the Audience: *TGV* and the Popular Tradition of Comedy." In *ShS 22*, **3530**. Trans. as "Das Lachen mit dem Publikum: die beiden Veroneser und die Volkstümliche Komödientradition." *SJ* (East), 106 (1970): 85-99.

2691   WELLS, Stanley. "The Failure of *TGV*." *SJ*, 99 (1963): 161-73.

THE TWO NOBLE KINSMEN

Editions

2692   FARMER, John S., ed. *TNK, 1634*. Tudor Facs. Texts. Amersham: Farmer, 1913. Repr. New York: AMS.

2693   PROUDFOOT, C. Richard, ed. *TNK*. Regents Renaissance Drama. Nebraska U.P., 1970.

Textual Commentary

2694   WALLER, Frederick O. "Printer's Copy for *TNK*." *SB*, 11 (1958): 61-84.

Commentary

See also Canon (**570-605**), especially **589** and **596**; **2701** and **3063**.

2695   BERTRAM, Paul. *Shakespeare and* TNK. Rutgers U.P., 1965.

2696   BRADLEY, Andrew C. "Scene Endings in Shakespeare and *TNK*." In *A Miscellany*, **2882**.

2697   CUTTS, John P. "Shakespeare's Song and Masque Hand in *TNK*." *EM*, 18 (1967): 55-85.

2698   EDWARDS, Philip. "On the Design of *TNK*." *REL*, 5 (1964): 89-105.

2699   ELLIS-FERMOR, Una. "*TNK*." In *Shakespeare the Dramatist*, **2984**.

2700   HART, Alfred. "Shakespeare and the Vocabulary of *TNK*." *RES*, 10 (1934): 274-87.

2701   MINCOFF, Marco. "The Authorship of *TNK*." *ES*, 33 (1952): 97-115. [*Edw3, Per, TNK, Cardenio.*]

2702   MUIR, Kenneth. "Shakespeare's Hand in *TNK*." *ShS 11* (1958), pp. 50-59.

2703   SPENCER, Theodore. "*TNK*." *MP*, 36 (1938-39): 255-76.

VENUS AND ADONIS

Editions

See also Poems (**2153-62**).

2704   LEE, Sidney, ed. *Shakespeares* Ven, *Being a Reproduction in Facsimile of the First Edition 1593 from the Unique Copy in the Malone Collection in the Bodleian Library.* Oxford U.P., 1905.

2705   *Ven (1593).* Menston, Yorks., Eng.: Scolar, 1968. [Facs.]

Commentary

See also **559, 2358, 2871, 3048, 3247**, and **4452**.

2706   ALLEN, Don C. "On *Ven.*" In *Elizabethan and Jacobean Studies Presented to F. P. Wilson*, **2772**. Also in 2nd ed. of *Image and Meaning*, **3769**.

2707   ALLEN, Michael J. B. "The Chase: The Development of a Renaissance Theme." *CL*, 20 (1968): 301-12.

2708   BOWERS, Robert H. "Anagnorisis, or the Shock of Recognition in Shakespeare's *Ven.*" *RenP 1962* (1963), pp. 3-8.

2709   BRADBROOK, Muriel C. "Beasts and Gods: Greene's *Groatsworth of Witte* and the Social Purpose of *Ven.*" In *ShS 15*, **2161**.

2710   CANTELUPE, Eugene B. "An Iconographical Interpretation of *Ven*, Shakespeare's Ovidian Comedy." *SQ*, 14 (1963): 141-51.

2711   HATTO, A. T. "*Ven*—and the Boar." *MLR*, 41 (1946): 353-61.

2712   LEECH, Clifford. "Venus and Her Nun: Portraits of Women in Love by Shakespeare and Marlowe." *SEL*, 5 (1965): 247-68.

2713   LEVER, Julius W. "Venus and the Second Chance." In *ShS 15*, **2161**.

2714   MILLER, Robert P. "Venus, Adonis, and the Horses." *ELH*, 19 (1952): 249-64.

2715   MUIR, Kenneth. "*Ven*: Comedy or Tragedy?" In *Shakespearean Essays*, **2819**.

2716   PRICE, Hereward T. "Function of Imagery in *Ven.*" *PMASAL*, 31 (1945): 275-97.

2717   PUTNEY, Rufus. "Venus *Agonistes.*" *UCSLL*, 4 (1953): 52-66.

2718   ——. "*Ven:* Amour with Humor." *PQ*, 20 (1941): 533-48.

2719   RABKIN, Norman. "*Ven* and the Myth of Love." In *Pacific Coast Studies in Shakespeare*, **2796**.

THE WINTER'S TALE

Editions

2720   FURNESS, Horace H., ed. *WT*. New Variorum. Philadelphia: Lippincott, 1898.

2721   WILSON, J. Dover, ed. *WT*. London: Faber & Gwyer, 1929. [Facs. from Grenville copy of F1 in the British Museum.]

Textual Commentary

See also **191**.

2722   HOWARD-HILL, Trevor H. "Knight, Crane, and the Copy for the Folio *WT*." *N&Q*, 13 (1966): 139-40.

Commentary

See also The Comedies (**3444-3549**) and The Romances (after **3734**); **756, 757, 2834, 2887, 2971, 3108, 3177, 3293, 3382**, and **3951**.

2723   BARBER, Cesar L. "'Thou That Beget'st Him That Did Thee Beget': Transformation in *Per* and *WT*." In *ShS 22*, **3530**.

2724   BARBER, Charles L. "*WT* and Jacobean Society." In *Shakespeare in a Changing World*, **2792**.

2725   BETHELL, Samuel L. *WT: A Study*. London and New York: Staples, 1947.

2726   BIGGINS, Dennis. "'Exit Pursued by a Beare': A Problem in *WT*." *SQ*, 13 (1962): 3-13.

2727   BONJOUR, Adrien. "The Final Scene of *WT*." *ES*, 33 (1952): 193-208.

2728   ——. "Polixenes and the Winter of His Discontent." *ES*, 50 (1969): 206-12.

2729   BRYANT, Jerry H. "*WT*, and the Pastoral Tradition." *SQ*, 14 (1963): 387-98.

2730   BRYANT, Joseph A. "Shakespeare's Allegory: *WT*." *SR*, 63 (1955): 202-22.

2731   COX, Lee S. "The Role of Autolycus in *WT*." *SEL*, 9 (1969): 283-301.

2732   ELLIS, John. "Rooted Affection: The Genesis of Jealousy in *WT*." *CE*, 25 (1964): 545-47.

2733   EWBANK, Inga-Stina. "The Triumph of Time in *WT*." *REL*, 5 (1964): 83-100.

2734   FRYE, Northrop. "Recognition in *WT*." In *Essays . . . in Honor of Hardin Craig*, **2786**.

2735   GREENLAW, Edwin. "Shakespeare's Pastorals." *SP*, 13 (1916): 122-54.

2736   HARTWIG, Joan. "The Tragicomic Perspective of *WT*." *ELH*, 37 (1970): 12-36.

2737   HOENIGER, F. David. "The Meaning of *WT*." *UTQ*, 20 (1950-51): 11-26.

2738   HONIGMANN, Ernst A. J. "Secondary Sources of *WT*." *PQ*, 34 (1955): 27-38.

2739   HUGHES, Merritt Y. "A Classical vs. a Social Approach to Shakspere's Autolycus." *SAB*, 15 (1940): 219-26.

2740   KÜNSTLER, Ernst. "Julio Romano im *WT*." In *SJ*, 92, **793**.

2741   LAWLOR, John J. "*Pandosto* and the Nature of Dramatic Romance." *PQ*, 41 (1962): 96-113.

2742   LIVINGSTON, Mary L. "The Natural Art of *WT*." *MLQ*, 30 (1969): 340-55.

2743   MATCHETT, William H. "Some Dramatic Techniques in *WT*." In *ShS 22*, **3530**.

2744   MAVEETY, S. R. "What Shakespeare Did with *Pandosto:* An Interpretation of *WT*." In *Pacific Coast Studies in Shakespeare*, **2796**.

2745   MELDRUM, Ronald M. "Dramatic Intention in *WT*." *HAB*, 19.2 (1968): 52-60.

2746   MOWAT, Barbara A. "A Tale of Sprights and Goblins." *SQ*, 20 (1969): 37-46.

2747   MUIR, Kenneth. "The Conclusion of *WT*." In *The Morality of Art*, **2789**.

2748   ——, ed. *Shakespeare*–WT: *A Casebook*. London: Macmillan, 1968. [58 sel. from prev. pub. wks., 1611 to modern.]

2749   NATHAN, Norman. "Leontes' Provocation." *SQ*, 19 (1968): 19-24.

2750   NUTTALL, Anthony D. *Shakespeare: WT*. London: Arnold, 1966.

2751   PAFFORD, John H. P. "Music and the Songs in *WT*." *SQ*, 10 (1950): 161-75.

2752   PYLE, Fitzroy. *WT: A Commentary on the Structure*. London: Routledge & Kegan Paul; New York: Barnes & Noble, 1969.

2753   SCHANZER, Ernest. "The Structural Pattern of *WT*." *REL*, 5 (1964): 72-82.

2754   SIEGEL, Paul N. "Leontes a Jealous Tyrant." *RES*, 1 (1950): 302-7.

2755   SMITH, Jonathan. "The Language of Leontes." *SQ*, 19 (1968): 317-27.

2756   THORNE, William B. " 'Things Newborn': A Study of the Rebirth Motif in *WT*." *HAB*, 19.1 (1968): 34-43.

2757   TINKLER, F. C. "*WT*." *Scrutiny*, 5 (1936-37): 344-64.

2758   WILLIAMS, John A. *The Natural Work of Art: The Experience of Romance in Shakespeare's* WT. Harvard U.P.; Oxford U.P., 1967.

Commentary

COLLECTIONS OF ESSAYS

Includes collections of studies by more than one author.

2759   ALEXANDER, Peter, ed. *Studies in Shakespeare.* Oxford U.P., 1964. [OUP 81.] [10 British Academy lectures.]

2760   ALLEN, Don C., ed. *Studies in Honor of T. W. Baldwin.* U. of Illinois P., 1958.

2761   *Aspects of Shakespeare.* Ed. John W. Mackail. Oxford U.P., 1933. [9 slightly rev. British Academy lectures, 1923-31.]

2762   BENNETT, Josephine W., Oscar Cargill, and Vernon Hall, eds. *Studies in English Renaissance Drama in Memory of Karl Julius Holzknecht.* New York U.P., 1959.

2763   BLISTEIN, Elmer M., ed. *The Drama of the Renaissance: Essays for Leicester Bradner.* Brown U.P., 1970. [6 on Sh.]

2764   BLOOM, Edward A., ed. *Shakespeare, 1564-1964.* Brown U.P., 1964. [16 modern essays.]

2765   BOWERS, Fredson T., ed. *English Studies in Honor of James S. Wilson.* U. of Virginia Studies, 4. Charlottesville: U. of Virginia, 1951.

2766   BROWN, John R., and Bernard Harris, eds. *Early Shakespeare.* Stratford-upon-Avon Studies, 3. London: Arnold, 1961. Repr. New York: St. Martin's. [10 essays.]

2767   —, eds. *Later Shakespeare.* Stratford-upon-Avon Studies, 8. London: Arnold, 1966. Repr. New York: St. Martin's. [10 essays.]

2768   *Bulletin de la Faculté des Lettres de Strasbourg,* 63 (1965). [Entire issue: "Hommage à Shakespeare."]

2769   CALDERWOOD, James L., and Harold E. Toliver, eds. *Essays in Shakespearean Criticism.* Englewood Cliffs, N.J.: Prentice-Hall, 1970. [38 essays, most prev. pub.]

2770   CHAPMAN, Gerald W., ed. *Essays on Shakespeare.* Princeton U.P., 1965.

2771   CRAIG, Hardin, ed. *Essays in Dramatic Literature in Honor of T. M. Parrott.* Princeton U.P., 1935. Repr. New York: Russell & Russell. [7 essays on Sh.]

2772   DAVIS, Herbert, and Helen Gardner. *Elizabethan and Jacobean Studies Presented to F. P. Wilson.* Oxford U.P., 1959. [6 essays on Sh.]

2773   DEAN, Leonard F., ed. *Shakespeare: Modern Essays in Criticism*. Gloucester, Mass.: Peter Smith; New York: Oxford U.P., 1957. 2nd ed. rev., Oxford U.P., 1967. [GB OUP 46.] [1st ed.: 28 prev. pub. essays; 2nd ed.: 7 essays dropped, 9 added.]

2774   DOBRÉE, Bonamy, ed. *Shakespeare: The Writer and His Work*. London: Longmans, 1964. [Coll. of prev. pub. wks.]

2775   DUTHIE, George Ian, ed. *Papers Mainly Shakespearean*. Aberdeen U. Studies, 147. Edinburgh: Oliver & Boyd, 1964.

2776   *EA*, 17 (1964). *Shakespeare, 1564-1964*. [25 studies by different authors.]

2777   EASTMAN, Arthur M., and George B. Harrison, eds. *Shakespeare's Critics: From Jonson to Auden*. U. of Michigan P., 1964. [Short sel. from many wks. arranged by topic.]

2778   FISCHER, Walther, and Karl Wentersdorf, eds. *Shakespeare-Studien: Festschrift für Heinrich Mutschmann*. Marburg: Elwert, 1951.

2779   FORD, Boris, ed. *The Age of Shakespeare*. Vol. 2 of *A Guide to English Literature*. London: Cassell, 1955. 2nd ed. rev., 1961. [A291 Pelican.]

2780   GARRETT, John, ed. *More Talking of Shakespeare*. London: Longmans, Green, 1959. [Lectures, Sh Memorial Theatre summer schools, 1954-58.]

2781   —, ed. *Talking of Shakespeare*. London: Hodder & Stoughton, 1954. [Lectures, Sh Memorial Theatre summer schools, 1948-53.]

2782   GOLLANCZ, Israel, ed. *A Book of Homage to Shakespeare*. Oxford U.P., 1916. [About 150 items by different authors.]

2783   GRANVILLE-BARKER, Harley, and George B. Harrison, eds. *A Companion to Shakespeare Studies*. Cambridge U.P.; New York: Macmillan, 1934. [A191 Doubleday.] [Coll. of gen. introd. essays by different authors.]

2784   HARRISON, Thomas P., et al., eds. *Studies in Honor of DeWitt T. Starnes*. U. of Texas P., 1967.

2785   HENINGER, Simeon K., et al., eds. *RenP 1964* (1965). [Issue devoted to Sh.]

2786   HOSLEY, Richard, ed. *Essays on Shakespeare and Elizabethan Drama in Honor of Hardin Craig*. U. of Missouri P., 1962. [12 essays on Sh.]

2787   JACKSON, Berners W., ed. *Stratford Papers on Shakespeare, 1961–*. Toronto: Gage, 1962–. [Vol. 5: *Stratford Papers, 1965-67*, McMaster U. Library P.; Irish U.P., 1969.] [Papers from Sh seminars, Stratford, Ont.]

2788   Canceled.

2789   JEFFERSON, Douglas W., ed. *The Morality of Art: Essays Presented to G. Wilson Knight*. New York: Barnes & Noble; London: Routledge & Kegan Paul, 1969.

2790   KERMODE, J. Frank, ed. *Four Centuries of Shakespeare Criticism.*
        New York: Avon, 1965. [Avon Q52.] [More than 70 sel., poems,
        novels, critical essays.]

2791   KERNAN, Alvin B., ed. *Modern Shakespeare Criticism: Essays on
        Style, Dramaturgy, and the Major Plays.* New York: Harcourt,
        Brace & World, 1970. [26 prev. pub. essays.]

2792   KETTLE, Arnold, ed. *Shakespeare in a Changing World.*   Lon-
        don: Lawrence & Wishart, 1964. [NW Intl 46.]

2793   McMANAWAY, James G., ed. *Shakespeare 400.* New York: Holt,
        Rinehart & Winston, 1964. [Orig. pub. as *SQ*, 15.2 (1964).]

2794   —, Giles E. Dawson, and Edwin E. Willoughby, eds. *Joseph Quincy
        Adams Memorial Studies.* Washington, D.C.: Folger Shakespeare
        Library, 1948.

2795   McNEIR, Waldo F., ed. *Studies in English Renaissance Literature
        Dedicated to John Earle Uhler.* Louisiana State U.P., 1962.

2796   —, and Thelma N. Greenfield, eds. *Pacific Coast Studies in Shake-
        speare.* U. of Oregon P., 1966.

2797   MATTHEWS, Arthur D., and Clark M. Emery, eds. *Studies in
        Shakespeare.* U. of Miami P., 1953. Repr. New York: AMS. [12
        essays by different authors.]

2798   MATTHEWS, J. Brander, and Ashley H. Thorndike, eds. *Shak-
        sperian Studies.* Columbia U.P., 1916.

2799   MEHL, Dieter, ed. *Das englische Drama: Vom Mittelalter bis zur
        Gegenwart.* 2 vols. Düsseldorf: Bagel, 1970. [9 essays on Sh.]

2800   MUIR, Kenneth, and S. Schoenbaum, eds. *A New Companion to
        Shakespeare Studies.* Cambridge U.P., 1971. [18 essays by different
        authors.]

2801   ORNSTEIN, Robert T., ed. *Discussions of Shakespeare's Problem
        Comedies.* Boston: Heath, 1961. [18 sel. from prev. pub. wks.,
        Coleridge to modern.]

2802   PAOLUCCI, Anne, ed. *Shakespeare Encomium.* New York: City
        College, 1964. [13 essays, 2 poems by different authors.]

2803   PROUTY, Charles T., ed. *Shakespeare: Of an Age and for All Time.*
        Hamden, Conn.: Shoe String P., 1954. [Yale Sh Festival lectures: 6
        gen., *Mac, Ant.*]

2804   —, ed. *Studies in Honor of A. H. R. Fairchild.* U. of Missouri
        Studies, 21, No. 1. U. of Missouri, 1946.

2805   RABKIN, Norman, ed. *Approaches to Shakespeare.* New York:
        McGraw-Hill, 1964. [20 sel. from prev. pub. modern wks.]

2806   —, ed. *Reinterpretations of Elizabethan Drama.* Selected Papers
        from the English Institute. Columbia U.P., 1969. [4 essays on Sh.]

2807   RIDLER, Anne (Bradby), ed. *Shakespeare Criticism, 1919-35.* Ox-
        ford U.P., 1936. [WC 436.] [15 sel. from prev. pub. wks.]

2808 —, ed. *Shakespeare Criticism, 1935-1960.* Oxford U.P., 1963. [WC 590.] [18 sel. from prev. pub. wks.]

2809 SAMARIN, Roman, and Alexander Nikolyukin, eds. *Shakespeare in the Soviet Union: A Collection of Articles.* Moscow: Progress, 1966. [Wks. by poets, scholars, actors, producers.]

2810 SCHUELLER, Herbert M., ed. *The Persistence of Shakespeare Idolatry: Essays in Honor of Robert W. Babcock.* Wayne State U.P., 1964.

2811 SEN, Taraknath, ed. *Shakespeare Commemoration Volume.* Calcutta: Presidency College, 1966. [14 essays by different authors.]

2812 SIEGEL, Paul N., ed. *His Infinite Variety: Major Shakespeare Criticism since Johnson.* Philadelphia: Lippincott, 1964. [31 sel. from prev. pub. wks.]

2813 SMITH, D. Nichol, ed. *Eighteenth-Century Essays on Shakespeare.* Glasgow: MacLehose, 1903. Rev. ed., Oxford U.P., 1963.

2814 —, ed. *Shakespeare Criticism.* Oxford U.P., 1916. Repr. 1946. [WC 212.] [Sel. 1623-1840.]

2815 SMITH, Gordon R., ed. *Essays on Shakespeare.* Pennsylvania State U.P., 1965.

2816 SPENCER, Terence J. B., ed. *Shakespeare: A Celebration, 1564-1964.* Harmondsworth, Middlesex: Penguin, 1964. [A666 Penguin.] [8 essays by different authors.]

2817 STAFFORD, Tony J., ed. *Shakespeare in the Southwest: Some New Directions.* Texas Western U.P., 1969.

2818 SUTHERLAND, James, and Joel Hurstfield, eds. *Shakespeare's World: Centenary Essays.* New York: St. Martin's, 1964.

2819 THALER, Alwin, and Norman Sanders, eds. *Shakespearean Essays.* Tennessee U.P., 1964.

2820 WAIN, John, ed. *Interpretations.* London: Routledge & Kegan Paul, 1955.

2821 WEST, E. J., ed. *Elizabethan Studies and Other Essays in Honor of George F. Reynolds.* U. of Colorado, 1945.

2822 WILLIAMS, Arnold, ed. *A Tribute to George Coffin Taylor.* U. of North Carolina P., 1952.

2823 Wisconsin, University of. *Shakespeare Studies by Members of the Department of English.* U. of Wisconsin P., 1916.

2824 WOODS, Charles B., and Curt A. Zimansky, eds. *Studies in English Drama Presented to Baldwin Maxwell.* State U. of Iowa, 1962. [Issued also as *PQ*, 41.1 (1962).]

2825 WRIGHT, Louis B., ed. *Shakespeare Celebrated: Anniversary Lectures Delivered at the Folger Library.* Cornell U.P., 1966.

COMPREHENSIVE WORKS AND SINGLE STUDIES

See **128** for bibliography of foreign sources, **138** for bibliography of German dissertations, and **153** for bibliography of Shakespeare and the classical tradition. See also **437, 512, 1189, 4294,** and **4332.**

2826   ABERCROMBIE, Lascelles. *A Plea for the Liberty of Interpreting.* Oxford U.P., 1930. [*PBA 1930*, 16 (1931): 137-64.] Repr. in *Aspects of Shakespeare,* **2761**.

2827   ADAMS, Robert M. "Trompe-l'oeil in Shakespeare and Keats." *SR*, 61 (1953): 238-55.

2828   ADDISON, Joseph, and Richard Steele. *The Spectator.* London: S. Buckley, 1711-12, 1714. Repr., 4 vols., London: Dent and New York: Dutton, 1950 (ed. G. Gregory Smith); Oxford U.P., 1965 (ed. Donald F. Bond).   [Nos. 40, 45, 61, 141, 279, 370, 419, 540, 592.]

2829   —. *The Tatler.* London: J. Morphew, 1709-10. Repr., 4 vols. London: Duckworth, 1898-99 (ed. George A. Aitken).   [Nos. 8, 35, 41, 47, 68, 71, 90, 106, 111, 117, 167, 182.]

2830   ADES, John I. "Charles Lamb, Shakespeare, and Early Nineteenth-Century Theater." *PMLA*, 85 (1970): 514-26.

2831   ALDUS, Paul J. "Analogical Probability in Shakespeare's Plays." *SQ*, 6 (1955): 397-414.

2832   ALEXANDER, Peter. "'Under Which King, Bezonian?'" In *Elizabethan and Jacobean Studies Presented to F. P. Wilson,* **2772.** [Morality, esp. *Oth* and *Ham*.]

2833   ARMSTRONG, Edward A. *Shakespeare's Imagination: A Study of the Psychology of Association and Inspiration.* London: Lindsay Drummond, 1946. [BB 167.] Rev. ed., Gloucester, Mass.: Peter Smith, 1963. [Bison.]

2834   ARMSTRONG, John. *The Paradise Myth.* Oxford U.P., 1969. [*Ant, WT, Tmp.*]

2835   ARNOLD, Morris L. *The Soliloquies of Shakespeare: A Study in Technic.* Columbia U.P., 1911. Repr. New York: AMS.

2836   ARTHOS, John. *The Art of Shakespeare.* London: Bowes & Bowes; New York: Barnes & Noble, 1964.

2837   AUCHINCLOSS, Louis. *Motiveless Malignity.* Boston: Houghton Mifflin, 1969. [Esp. tragedies.]

2838   AUDEN, Wystan H. *The Dyer's Hand and Other Essays.* New York: Random House, 1962. [Sec. called "The Shakespearian City."]

2839   BABCOCK, Robert W. *The Genesis of Shakespeare Idolatry, 1766-1799.* U. of North Carolina P.; Oxford U.P., 1931.

2840   —. "Historical Criticism of Shakespeare." *MLQ*, 13 (1952): 6-20

2841 —. "William Richardson's Criticism of Shakespeare." *JEGP*, 28 (1929): 117-36.

2842 BAILEY, John C. *Shakespeare.* London and New York: Longmans, Green, 1929.

2843 BALDWIN, Thomas W. "Nature's Moulds." *SQ*, 3 (1952): 237-41.

2844 —. "On Atomizing Shakespeare." *SJ*, 91 (1955): 136-44.

2845 —. *On the Literary Genetics of Shakspere's Plays, 1592-1594.* U. of Illinois P., 1959.

2846 —. *Shakspere's Five-Act Structure.* U. of Illinois P., 1947.

2847 BARISH, Jonas A. "Shakespeare's Prose Style." In *Ben Jonson and the Language of Prose Comedy.* Harvard U.P., 1960.

2848 BARKER, George. "William Shakespeare and the Horse with Wings." *PR*, 20 (1953): 410-20.

2849 BARNET, Sylvan. "Coleridge on Puns: A Note to His Shakespeare Criticism." *JEGP*, 56 (1957): 602-9.

2850 —. "Some Limitations of a Christian Approach to Shakespeare." *ELH*, 22 (1955): 81-92.

2851 BARTON, Anne (Righter née Roesen). *Shakespeare and the Idea of the Play.* London: Chatto & Windus, 1962. [PSL1, Penguin.]

2852 BAYFIELD, Matthew A. *A Study of Shakespeare's Versification, with an Inquiry into the Trustworthiness of the Early Texts.* Cambridge U.P., 1920.

2853 BAYLEY, John. *The Characters of Love.* London: Constable, 1960. [*Tro, Oth.*]

2854 BEECHING, Henry C. *Shakespeare and the English Ideal.* Norwich: Public Library Committee, 1916.

2855 BENTLEY, Gerald E. "Shakespeare and the Blackfriars Theatre." *ShS 1* (1948), pp. 38-50.

2856 BERLIN, Normand. *The Base String: The Underworld in Elizabethan Drama.* Fairleigh Dickinson U.P., 1968. [Chap. on Sh.]

2857 BERMAN, Ronald S. "Power and Humility in Shakespeare." *SAQ*, 60 (1961): 410-19.

2858 BERRY, Francis. *Poets' Grammar: Person, Time, and Mood in Poetry.* London: Routledge & Kegan Paul, 1958. [Sec. on Sh, esp. *Son* and *Mac.*]

2859 —. *The Shakespearean Inset.* London: Routledge & Kegan Paul, 1965.

2860 BESTERMAN, Theodore. *Shakespeare and Voltaire.* New York: Pierpont Morgan Library, 1965.

2861 BETHELL, Samuel L. *Shakespeare and the Popular Dramatic Tradition.* London and New York: Staples, 1944.

2862   BEVINGTON, David M. "Shakespeare the Elizabethan Dramatist."
        In *A New Companion to Shakespeare Studies*, **2800**.

2863   BILTON, Peter. "Shakespeare Criticism and the 'Choric Character.'"
        ES, 50 (1969): 254-60.

2864   BLAND, D. S. "The Heroine and the Sea: An Aspect of Shake-
        speare's Last Plays." *EIC*, 3 (1953): 39-44.

2865   ——. "Shakespeare and the 'Ordinary' Word." *ShS 4* (1951), pp.
        49-55.

2866   BLOOM, Allan, and Harry V. Jaffa. *Shakespeare's Politics.* New
        York: Basic Books, 1964. [*Oth, MV, JC, Lr.*]

2867   BOAS, Frederick S. *Aspects of Classical Legend and History in
        Shakespeare.* Oxford U.P., 1943. [*PBA 1943*, 29 (1944): 107-
        32.]

2868   ——. *An Introduction to the Reading of Shakespeare.* Oxford U.P.,
        1927.

2869   ——. "The Play within the Play." In *A Series of Papers on Shake-
        speare and the Theatre*, **4133**.

2870   ——. "The Problem Plays." In *Shakspere and His Predecessors.*
        New York: Scribner's, 1896. [*AWW, MM, Tro, Ham.*]

2871   BONJOUR, Adrien. "From Shakespeare's Venus to Cleopatra's
        Cupids." In *ShS 15*, **2161**.

2872   BORINSKI, Ludwig. "Shakespeare's Comic Prose." *ShS 8* (1955),
        pp. 57-68.

2873   BOWERS, Fredson T. "Shakespeare's Art: The Point of View."
        In *Literary Views: Critical and Historical Essays.* Ed. Carroll C.
        Camden. U. of Chicago P., 1964.

2874   ——. "Shakespeare's Dramatic Vagueness." *VQR*, 39 (1963): 475-
        84.

2875   BOYCE, Benjamin. "The Stoic *Consolatio* and Shakespeare." *PMLA*,
        64 (1949): 771-80.

2876   BRADBROOK, Muriel C. "Fifty Years of the Criticism of Shake-
        speare's Style: A Retrospect." *ShS 7* (1954), pp. 1-11.

2877   ——. *Shakespeare and Elizabethan Poetry: A Study of His Earlier
        Work in Relation to the Poetry of the Time.* London: Chatto &
        Windus, 1951. Repr. 1964. [Penguin.]

2878   ——. "Shakespeare and the Use of Disguise in Elizabethan Drama."
        EIC, 2 (1952): 159-68.

2879   ——. *Shakespeare the Craftsman.* New York: Barnes & Noble;
        London: Chatto & Windus, 1969. [Chaps. on *TN, Wiv, JC, Ham, Tim.*]

2880   ——. "Shakespeare the Jacobean Dramatist." In *A New Companion
        to Shakespeare Studies*, **2800**.

2881   ——. *Shakespeare's Primitive Art.* Oxford U.P., 1965. [*PBA 1965*,
        51 (1966): 215-34.]

2882   BRADLEY, Andrew C. *A Miscellany*. London: Macmillan, 1929.

2883   —. *Oxford Lectures on Poetry*. London: Macmillan, 1904. Repr. New York: St. Martin's. [St. Martin's.]

2884   BRANDES, Georg M. C. *Shakespeare: A Critical Study*. Trans. William Archer et al. 2 vols. London: W. Heinemann, 1898.   Repr. New York: Ungar.

2885   BRIDGES, Robert S. *The Influence of the Audience: Considerations Preliminary to the Psychological Analysis of Shakespeare's Characters*. Garden City, N.Y.: Morison, 1926.

2886   BROCK, James H. E. *Iago and Some Shakespearean Villains*.   Cambridge: Heffer, 1937. [*Tit, Ado, Cym, Lr, Oth*.]

2887   BROCKBANK, J. P. "Shakespeare and the Fashion of These Times." *ShS 16* (1963), pp. 30-41. [Esp. *Ant, WT, MV*.]

2888   BROOKE, C. F. Tucker. *Essays on Shakespeare and Other Elizabethans*. Yale U.P., 1948. [Prev. pub. essays, 1913-45.]

2889   BROOKE, Nicholas. "The Characters of Drama." *CQ*, 6 (1964): 72-82.

2890   —. "Marlowe as Provocative Agent in Shakespeare's Early Plays." In *ShS 14*, **3917**.

2891   BROOKS, Harold F. "Marlowe and Early Shakespeare." In *Christopher Marlowe*. Ed. Brian Morris. London: Benn, 1968.

2892   BROWER, Reuben A. *Hero and Saint: Shakespeare and the Graeco-Roman Heroic Tradition*. Oxford U.P., 1970.

2893   BROWN, Arthur. "The Play within a Play: An Elizabethan Dramatic Device." *E&S*, 13 (1960): 36-48.

2894   BROWN, John R. "Mr. Beckett's Shakespeare." *CQ*, 5 (1963): 310-26.

2895   —. "Mr. Pinter's Shakespeare." *CQ*, 5 (1963): 251-65.

2896   —. "Theatre Research and the Criticism of Shakespeare and His Contemporaries." *SQ*, 13 (1962): 451-61.

2897   —. "The Theatrical Element of Shakespeare Criticism." In *Reinterpretations of Elizabethan Drama*, **2806**.

2898   BRYANT, Joseph A. *Hippolyta's View: Some Christian Aspects of Shakespeare's Plays*. U. of Kentucky P., 1961. Repr. New York: Barnes & Noble.

2899   BULLOUGH, Geoffrey. *Mirror of Minds*. London: Athlone, 1962.

2900   —. *Shakespeare the Elizabethan*. See **435**.

2901   BURCKHARDT, Sigurd. *Shakespearean Meanings*. Princeton U.P., 1968. [Coll. of wks., some prev. pub.]

2902   BURTON, Delores M. "Toward a Theoretical Description of Deviant Sequence." In *Proceedings of the Twenty-third National Conference of the Association for Computing Machinery.* Princeton U.P., 1968. Repr. as "Aspects of Word Order in Two Plays of Shakespeare." *CSHVB*, 3 (1970): 34-39. [*Ant, R2.*]

2903   BUSH, Douglas. "Classical Myth in Shakespeare's Plays." In *Elizabethan and Jacobean Studies Presented to F. P. Wilson,* **2772.**

2904   BUSH, Geoffrey. *Shakespeare and the Natural Condition.* Harvard U.P., 1956.

2905   BUTT, John E. *Pope's Taste in Shakespeare.* Shakespeare Association Lecture. Oxford U.P., 1936.

2906   CADOUX, Arthur T. *Shakespearian Selves: An Essay in Ethics.* London: Epworth, 1938.

2907   CAMPBELL, Oscar J. "Shakespeare and the 'New' Critics." In *Adams Memorial Studies,* **2794.**

2908   —. *Shakespeare's Satire.* Oxford U.P., 1943.

2909   CARLISLE, Carol J. "The Nineteenth-Century Actors *versus* the Closet Critics of Shakespeare." *SP,* 51 (1954): 599-615.

2910   CARVER, Patrick L. "The Influence of Maurice Morgann." *RES,* 6 (1930): 320-22. [Essay on Falstaff possibly known to Hazlitt and may have influenced Coleridge.]

2911   CHAMBERS, Edmund K. *The Disintegration of Shakespeare.* See **233.**

2912   —. *Shakespeare: A Survey.* London: Sidgwick & Jackson, 1925. [D14 Hill & Wang.]

2913   —. *Shakespearean Gleanings.* Oxford U.P., 1944.

2914   CHARLTON, Henry B. *Shakespeare, Politics, and Politicians.* Oxford U.P., 1929.

2915   —. *Shakespeare's Recoil from Romanticism.* Manchester U.P., 1931. [Also in *BJRL,* 15 (1931): 35-59.]

2916   CLARK, Cumberland. *Shakespeare and the Supernatural.* London: Williams & Norgate, 1931. [Pt. 1, Superstition; Pt. 2, Religion.]

2917   CLEMEN, Wolfgang. "Aims and Limitations of Shakespearian Studies." *Univ,* 6 (1964): 345-55.

2918   —. *Das Drama Shakespeares.* Göttingen: Vandenhoeck & Ruprecht, 1969. [Coll. of wks.]

2919   —. *Past and Future in Shakespeare's Drama.* Oxford U.P., 1966. [*PBA 1966,* 52 (1967): 231-52.]

2920   —. *Schein und Sein bei Shakespeare.* Munich: Bayerische Akademie der Wissenschaften, 1959.

2921   —. "Shakespeare and the Modern World." *ShS 16* (1963), pp. 57-62.

2922   —. *Shakespeares Bilder.* Bonn: Hanstein, 1936. Enl. Eng. ed.: *The Development of Shakespeare's Imagery.* London: Methuen, 1951. [D31 Hill & Wang.]

2923   —. *Shakespeare's Soliloquies.* Cambridge U.P., 1964. Enl. Ger. ed.: *Shakespeares Monologe.* Göttingen: Vandenhoeck & Ruprecht, 1964.

2924   —. *Wandlung des Botenberichts bei Shakespeare.* Munich: Bayerischen Akademie der Wissenschaften, 1952.

2925   —. "Wo stehen wir in der Shakespeare-Forschung?" *SJ*, 100 (1964): 135-50.

2926   COE, Charles N. *Shakespeare's Villains.* New York: Bookman, 1957. Rev. as *Demi-Devils: The Character of Shakespeare's Villains.* New York: Bookman, 1963.

2927   COGHILL, Nevill. *Shakespeare's Professional Skills.* Cambridge U.P., 1964.

2928   COHEN, Eileen Z. "The Visible Solemnity: Ceremony and Order in Shakespeare and Hooker." *TSLL*, 12 (1970): 181-95. [Esp. *R2*, *H4*, *H5*.]

2929   COLERIDGE, Samuel T. *Coleridge on Shakespeare: A Selection of the Essays, Notes, and Lectures.* Ed. Terence Hawkes. Harmondsworth: Penguin, 1969.

2930   —. *Seven Lectures on Shakespeare and Milton . . . : A List of All the Manuscript Emendations in Mr. Collier's Folio, 1632.* London: Chapman & Hall, 1856. Repr. New York: AMS. [From Collier's shorthand notes.]

2931   —. *Shakespearean Criticism.* Ed. Thomas M. Raysor. 2 vols. London: Constable, 1930. Repr. London: Dent, 1960, 1961-62.

2932   —. *Writings on Shakespeare: A Selection of the Essays, Notes, and Lectures.* Ed. Terence Hawkes. New York: Capricorn, 1959. [Cap. 11.]

2933   COLLIER, Jeremy. *A Short View of the Immorality and Profaneness of the English Stage.* London: S. Keble, R. Sare, & H. Hindmarsh, 1698. Repr. New York: Blom. [For the controversy that ensued, see Joseph Wood Krutch, *Comedy and Conscience after the Restoration* (Columbia U.P., [1949]), and Sister Rose Anthony, *The Jeremy Collier Controversy, 1698-1726* (Marquette U.P., 1937).]

2934   CRAIG, Hardin. "An Aspect of Shakespearean Study." *SAB*, 24 (1949): 247-57.

2935   —. *An Interpretation of Shakespeare.* New York: Dryden, 1948.

2936   —. "Man Successful." *SQ*, 15.2 (1964): 11-15. Also in *Shakespeare 400*, **2793**.

2937   —. "Motivation in Shakespeare's Choice of Materials." *ShS 4* (1951), pp. 26-34. [Tragedies and *MM*, *AWW*.]

2938   ——. "Shakespeare and Formal Logic." In *Studies in English Philology: A Miscellany in Honor of Frederick Klaeber.* Ed. Kemp Malone and Martin B. Ruud. U. of Minnesota P., 1929.

2939   ——. "Shakespeare and the All-Inclusive Law of Nature." In *Studies in Honor of DeWitt T. Starnes,* **2784.**

2940   ——. "Shakespeare and the Here and Now." *PMLA,* 67 (1952): 87-94.

2941   ——. "Shakespeare and the Trivium." In *Shakespeare, 1564-1964,* **2764.**

2942   ——. "Shakespeare's Bad Poetry." *ShS 1* (1948), pp. 51-56.

2943   ——. "Shakespeare's Depiction of Passions." *PQ,* 4 (1925): 289-301.

2944   ——. "Shakespeare's Development as a Dramatist." *SP,* 39 (1942): 226-38.

2945   ——. "Trend of Shakespeare Scholarship." *ShS 2* (1949), pp. 107-14.

2946   CRANE, Milton. *Shakespeare's Prose.* U. of Chicago P., 1951. [B127 Phoen.]

2947   CROCE, Benedetto. *Ariosto, Shakespeare, and Corneille.* Trans. Douglas Ainslie. New York: Holt, 1920. Repr. New York: Russell & Russell.

2948   CROSBY, Ernest H. "Shakespeare's Attitude toward the Working Classes." In *Tolstoy on Shakespeare,* **3386** .

2949   CROW, Charles R. "Chiding the Plays: Then till Now." *ShS 18* (1965), pp. 1-10.

2950   CRUTTWELL, M. J. Patrick. "Shakespeare Is Not Our Contemporary." *YR,* 59 (1969): 33-49.

2951   ——. *The Shakespearean Moment and Its Place in the Poetry of the Seventeenth Century.* London: Chatto & Windus, 1954. Repr. 1970. [V171 Vin.]

2952   CUMBERLAND, Richard. *The Observer.* 1785. 2nd ed., 5 vols., London: C. Dilly, 1786-90. Repr. as vols. 41-44 of *British Essayists* Ed. Alexander Chalmers. 45 vols. London: J. Johnson, 1802-3 Repr. many times. [Nos. 55, 56, 84, 86, 109 treat of *R3* and *Mac.,* Sh's exuberance, Falstaff, and Witches.]

2953   CURRY, Walter C. *Shakespeare's Philosophical Patterns.* Louisiana State U.P., 1937. 2nd ed., 1959; repr. Gloucester, Mass.: Peter Smith

2954   CUTTS, John P. *The Shattered Glass: A Dramatic Pattern in Shakespeare's Early Plays.* Wayne State U.P., 1968.

2955   DAICHES, David. "Guilt and Justice in Shakespeare." *Literary Essays.* Edinburgh and London: Oliver & Boyd, 1956. Corr. and repr., 1966.

2956 DANBY, John F. *Poets on Fortune's Hill: Studies in Sidney, Shakespeare, and Beaumont and Fletcher.* London: Faber & Faber, 1952. Repr. as *Elizabethan and Jacobean Poets,* 1964.

2957 DE NAGY, N. Christoph. "Die Funktionen der Gerichtsszene bei Shakespeare und in der Tradition des älteren englischen Dramas." *SJ 1967* (West), pp. 199-220.

2958 DENNIS, John *The Critical Works.* Ed. Edward N. Hooker. Johns Hopkins U.P., 1939. [Incl. *Grounds of Criticism in Poetry* and *Essay on the Genius and Writings of Shakespeare.*]

2959 DIXON, P. "Pope's Shakespeare." *JEGP,* 63 (1964): 191-203.

2960 DOBRÉE, Bonamy. "On (Not) Enjoying Shakespeare." *E&S,* 9 (1956): 39-55.

2961 DORAN, Madeleine. "Shakespeare as an Experimental Dramatist." In *Shakespeare Celebrated,* 2825.

2962 DOUCE, Francis. *Illustrations of Shakespeare.* 2 vols. London: Longman, 1807.

2963 DOWDEN, Edward. *Shakspere: A Critical Study of His Mind and Art.* 1875. New ed., New York and London: Harper & Bros., 1918.

2964 DOWNER, Alan S. "The Life of Our Design." *HudR,* 2 (1950): 242-63. ·

2965 DRAKE, Nathan. *Memorials of Shakespeare; or, Sketches of His Character and Genius by Various Writers, Now First Collected.* London: H. Colburn, 1828. Repr. New York: AMS; Franklin.

2966 DRAPER, John W. *The Humors and Shakespeare's Characters.* Duke U.P., 1945. Repr. New York: AMS.

2967 ——. "Political Themes in Shakespeare's Later Plays." *JEGP,* 35 (1936): 61-93. [Incl. some early plays.]

2968 ——. "Shakespeare's Ladies-in-Waiting." *Neophil,* 49 (1965): 255-61.

2969 ——. *Stratford to Dogberry: Studies in Shakespeare's Earlier Plays.* U. of Pittsburgh P., 1961. Repr. Freeport, N.Y.: Books for Libraries.

2970 ——. *The Tempo-Patterns of Shakespeare's Plays.* Heidelberg: Winter, 1957.

2971 DRIVER, Tom F. *The Sense of History in Greek and Shakespearean Drama.* Columbia U.P., 1960. [Columbia U.P. 76.] [Chaps. on *R3, Ham, Mac, WT.*]

2972 DRYDEN, John. *Essays.* Ed. William P. Ker. 2 vols. Oxford U.P., 1900. [3 essays and 3 prefaces relate to Sh, esp. *Ant* and *Tro.*]

2973 ——. *Of Dramatick Poesy: An Essay, 1668, ... Preceded by a Dialogue on Poetic Drama by T. S. Eliot.* London: F. Etchells and H. Macdonald, 1928.

2974 DUTHIE, George Ian. *Shakespeare.* London: Hutchinson, 1951.

2975   EAGLETON, Terence. *Shakespeare and Society: Critical Essays in Shakespearean Drama.* London: Chatto & Windus; New York: Schocken, 1967.

2976   EASTMAN, Arthur M. *A Short History of Shakespeare Criticism.* New York: Random House, 1968. [Random House X189.]

2977   EDWARDS, Philip. *Shakespeare and the Confines of Art.* London: Methuen; New York: Barnes & Noble, 1968.

2978   EIDSON, John O. "Dryden's Criticism of Shakespeare." *SP*, 33 (1936): 273-80.

2979   *EIE 1948* (1949). "Myth in the Later Plays of Shakespeare." [4 essays by different authors.]

2980   EKWALL, Eilert. *Shakespeare's Vocabulary.* Uppsala: The U.P., 1903. Repr. New York: AMS.

2981   ELLIS, Roger. "The Fool in Shakespeare: A Study in Alienation." *CQ*, 10 (1968): 245-68.

2982   ELLIS-FERMOR, Una. "English and American Shakespeare Studies, 1937-1952." *Anglia*; see **121**.

2983   —. "Shakespeare and the Dramatic Mode." *Neophil,* 37 (1953): 104-12. Repr. in *Shakespeare the Dramatist,* **2984**.

2984   —. *Shakespeare the Dramatist and Other Papers.* Ed. Kenneth Muir. London: Methuen; New York: Barnes & Noble, 1961.

2985   —. "Some Functions of Verbal Music in Drama." In *SJ*, 90, **3327**; repr. in *Shakespeare the Dramatist,* **2984**.

2986   —. *Some Recent Research in Shakespeare's Imagery.* Oxford U.P., 1937.

2987   —. *The Study of Shakespeare.* London: Methuen, 1948.

2988   ELTON, Oliver. *Style in Shakespeare.* Oxford U.P., 1936. [*PBA 1936*, 22 (1937): 69-95.]

2989   EMERSON, Ralph W. *Representative Men.* Vol. 4 of *Complete Works.* Centenary ed. Boston: Houghton, Mifflin, 1903-4.

2990   —. "Shakespeare." In *Essays.* Ed. Eugene D. Holmes, rev. Harold Y. Moffett. New York: Macmillan, 1905. Rev. ed., 1930.

2991   EMPSON, William. *Some Versions of Pastoral.* London: Chatto & Windus, 1950.

2992   —. *The Structure of Complex Words.* London: Chatto & Windus; New York: New Directions, 1951.

2993   EVANS, Benjamin I. *The Language of Shakespeare's Plays.* London: Methuen, 1952. [UP B&N 113.]

2994   EVANS, Bertrand. *Teaching Shakespeare in the High School.* New York: Macmillan, 1966.

2995   EVANS, G. Blakemore. "A Seventeenth-Century Reader of Shakespeare." *RES*, 21 (1945): 271-79. [Comments and quotations written after 18 April 1687 in Bodleian MS Eng. Misc. c. 34.]

2996   EWBANK, Inga-Stina. "Shakespeare's Poetry." In *A New Companion to Shakespeare Studies*, **2800**.

2997   FAIRCHILD, Arthur H. R. *Shakespeare and the Arts of Design—Architecture, Sculpture, and Painting*. U. of Missouri P., 1937.

2998   FALCONER, Alexander F. *Shakespeare and the Sea*. London: Constable, 1964.

2999   FARNAM, Henry W. *Shakespeare's Economics*. Yale U.P.; Oxford U.P., 1931.

3000   FERGUSSON, Francis. *The Human Image in Dramatic Literature*. Garden City, N.Y.: Doubleday, 1957. [Anchor A124.] [Sec. on Sh.]

3001   —. *Shakespeare: The Pattern in His Carpet*. New York: Delacorte, 1970. [Collected introds. Laurel Sh, & 5 gen. essays.]

3002   FINKENSTAEDT, Thomas. "Zur Methodik der Versuntersuchung bei Shakespeare." In *SJ*, 90, **3327**.

3003   FISCH, Harold. "Shakespeare and 'The Theatre of the World.'" In *The Morality of Art*, **2789**. [Esp. *Mac*, *Ham*.]

3004   FITCH, Robert E. *Shakespeare: The Perspective of Value*. Philadelphia: Westminster, 1969.

3005   FLATTER, Richard. "Shakespeare, der Schauspieler." *SJ*, 89 (1953): 35-50.

3006   —. *Triumph der Gnade: Shakespeare-Essays*. Vienna: Kurt Desch, 1956. [*Ham*, *MV*, *Oth*, *JC*, *MM*, *H4*.]

3007   FLUCHÈRE, Henri. *Shakespeare: Dramaturge Élisabéthain*. Toulouse: Cahiers du Sud, 1948. Repr. New York: Blom. Trans. Guy Hamilton as *Shakespeare*. London: Longmans, Green, 1953. Repr. as *Shakespeare and the Elizabethans*. New York: Hill & Wang. [D1 Hill & Wang.]

3008   —. "Les Tâches de la critique shakespearienne francaise de demain." In *EA*, 17, **2776**.

3009   FOAKES, Reginald A. "Contrasts and Connections: Some Notes on Style in Shakespeare's Comedies and Tragedies." In *SJ*, 90, **3327**.

3010   —. "The Profession of Playwright." In *Early Shakespeare*, **2766**.

3011   —. "Suggestions for a New Approach to Shakespeare's Imagery." *ShS 5* (1952), pp. 81-92.

3012   FRANZ, Wilhelm. *Die Sprache Shakespeares in Vers und Prosa, unter Berücksichtigung des amerikanischen Entwicklungsgeschichtlich dargestellt*. Halle/Salle: Niemeyer, 1939.

3013   FRICKER, Robert. *Kontrast und Polarität in den Charakterbilden Shakespeares*. Bern: Francke, 1951.

3014   —. "Shakespeare und das Drama des Absurden." *SJ 1966* (West); see **1557**.

3015   FRIESNER, Donald N. "William Shakespeare, Conservative." *SQ*, 20 (1969): 165-78.

3016   FROST, David L. *The School of Shakespeare: The Influence of Shakespeare on English Drama, 1600-1642.* New York: Cambridge U.P., 1968.

3017   FRYE, Dean. "Reading Shakespeare Backwards." *SQ*, 17 (1966): 19-24.

3018   FRYE, Northrop. "Nature and Nothing." In *Essays on Shakespeare*, **2770**.

3019   FRYE, Roland M. *Shakespeare and Christian Doctrine.* Princeton U.P., 1963. [Princeton U.P. 4.]

3020   —. *Shakespeare: The Art of the Dramatist.* Boston: Houghton Mifflin, 1970.

3021   GARDNER, Helen. *The Business of Criticism.* Oxford U.P., 1959.

3022   GARROD, Heathcote W. "Milton's Lines on Shakespeare." *E&S*, 12 (1926): 7-23.

3023   GERSTNER-HIRZEL, Arthur. *The Economy of Action and Word in Shakespeare's Plays.* Bern: Francke, 1957. Repr. New York: AMS.

3024   GILBERT, Allan H. *The Principles and Practice of Criticism: Oth, Wiv, Ham.* Wayne State U.P., 1959.

3025   GITTINGS, Robert, ed. *The Living Shakespeare.* London: Heinemann, 1960. Repr. New York: Barnes & Noble, 1967. [16 gen. essays by different authors.]

3026   GODDARD, Harold C. *The Meaning of Shakespeare.* 2 vols. U of Chicago P., 1951. [U. Chic. P50 and P51.]

3027   GOETHE, Johann W. *Goethe on Shakespeare, Being Selections from Carlyle's Translation of Wilhelm Meister.* London: De La Mare, 1904.

3028   —. *On the Theater: Selections from the Conversations with Eckerman.* Ed. William W. Lawrence. New York: Dramatic Museum of Columbia U., 1919. [Sel. from *Conversations*, trans. John Oxenford rev. ed. (London: Bell, 1913).]

3029   —. *Wilhelm Meister's Apprenticeship.* Trans. R. Dillon Boylan, 1855. Repr. London: Bell, 1875. [First German ed., 1795-96.]

3030   GOLDSMITH, Robert H. *Wise Fools in Shakespeare.* Michigan State U.P., 1955.

3031   GORDON, George S. *Shakespearian Comedy, and Other Studies.* Ed. Edmund K. Chambers. Oxford U.P., 1944.

3032   GOVE, Philip B. "Shakespeare's Language in Today's Dictionary." *TSLL*, 7 (1965): 127-36.

3033   GRACE, William J. *Approaching Shakespeare.* New York: Basic Books, 1964.

3034   GRANVILLE-BARKER, Harley. *From* H5 *to* Ham. Oxford U.P., 1925. [*PBA 1924-25*, 11 (1926): 283-309.] Repr. in *Aspects of Shakespeare*, **2761**, and *Studies in Shakespeare*, **2759**.

3035   —. *Prefaces to Shakespeare.* 6 vols. London: Sidgwick & Jackson, 1927-48. 5 series: 1st, *LLL, JC, Lr*, 1928; 2nd, *Rom, MV, Ant, Cym*, 1930; 3rd, *Ham*, 1936; 4th, *Oth*, 1945; 5th, *Cor*, 1948. Repr., 4 vols., Princeton U.P., 1965. [Princeton U.P.]

3036   GRAY, Henry D. "The Evolution of Shakespeare's Heroine." *JEGP*, 12 (1913): 122-37.

3037   GREEN, Henry. *Shakespeare and the Emblem Writers.* London: Trübner, 1870. Repr. New York: Franklin.

3038   GREENFIELD, Thelma N. "Nonvocal Music: Added Dimension in Five Shakespeare Plays." In *Pacific Coast Studies in Shakespeare*, **2796**. [*R2, MV, Cor, Ham, Mac.*]

3039   GREYERTZ, Georg von. *The Reported Scenes in Shakespeare's Plays.* Berne: Pochon-Jent, 1965.

3040   GRIFFITH, Elizabeth. *The Morality of Shakespeare's Drama.* London: T. Cadell, 1775. Repr. New York: AMS.

3041   GRILLO, Ernesto N. G. *Shakespeare and Italy.* Glasgow: Maclehose, 1949. [Mostly in Italian.]

3042   GRIVELET, Michel. "Shakespeare as 'Corrupter of Words.'" *ShS 16* (1963), pp. 70-76.

3043   HABICHT, Werner. "'With an Auspicious and a Dropping Eye': Antithetische Mimik in Shakespeares Dramen." *Anglia*, 87 (1969): 147-66.

3044   HALLIDAY, Frank E. *The Cult of Shakespeare.* London: Duckworth, 1957.

3045   —. *The Enjoyment of Shakespeare.* London: Duckworth, 1952.

3046   —. *The Poetry of Shakespeare's Plays.* London: Duckworth; New York: Barnes & Noble, 1954. [UP B&N 51.]

3047   —. *Shakespeare and His Critics.* London: Duckworth, 1950. 2nd ed. rev., 1958. [Schocken 41.]

3048   HAMILTON, Albert C. *The Early Shakespeare.* San Marino, Calif.: Huntington Library, 1967. [Coll. of essays: 9 early plays, *Ven, Luc.*]

3049   HANFORD, James H. "Suicide in the Plays of Shakespeare." *PMLA*, 27 (1912): 380-97.

3050   HANKINS, John E. *Shakespeare's Derived Imagery.* U. of Kansas P., 1953. Repr. New York: Octagon.

3051   HAPGOOD, Robert. "Shakespeare and the Included Spectator." In *Reinterpretations of Elizabethan Drama*, **2806**.

3052   —. "Shakespeare and the Ritualists." *ShS 15* (1962), pp. 111-24.

3053   —. "Shakespeare's Delayed Reactions." *EIC*, 13 (1963): 9-16. [*R2, 2H4, JC.*]

3054   HARBAGE, Alfred. *As They Liked It: An Essay on Shakespeare and Morality.* New York: Macmillan, 1947. [TS 1035.]

3055   ——. *Conceptions of Shakespeare.* Harvard U.P.; Oxford U.P., 1966.

3056   ——. "Shakespeare and the Myth of Perfection." *SQ*, 15.2 (1964): 1-10. Also in *Shakespeare 400*, **2793**.

3057   ——. *Shakespeare and the Professions.* George Washington U., 1965.

3058   ——. *Shakespeare and the Rival Traditions.* New York: Macmillan, 1952.

3059   ——. *Shakespeare without Words.* Oxford U.P., 1970. [*PBA 1969*, 55 (1971): 129-44.]

3060   ——. "Shakespeare's Ideal Man." In *Adams Memorial Studies*, **2794**.

3061   HARRISON, George B. *Introducing Shakespeare.* New York: New American Library, 1939. Rev. and enl. 3rd ed., 1948; repr. Harmondsworth: Penguin, 1968. [Pelican A43; Mentor M14.]

3062   ——. *Shakespeare at Work, 1592-1603.* London: Routledge, 1933. [AA U. of Mich. Pr. 16.] Pub. as *Shakespeare under Elizabeth.* New York: Holt, 1933.

3063   HART, Alfred. *Shakespeare and the Homilies.* Melbourne U.P., 1934. Repr. New York: AMS. [Chaps. on *2H4, TNK.*]

3064   HAVENS, George R. *Voltaire and the English Critics of Shakespeare.* New York: American Society of the French Legion of Honor, 1944.

3065   HAWKES, Terence. *Shakespeare and the Reason: A Study of the Tragedies and the Problem Plays.* London: Routledge & Kegan Paul, 1964.

3066   HAZLITT, William. *Characters of Shakespear's Plays.* London: C. H. Reynell, 1817. Repr. as *Roundtable* [and] *Characters of Shakespear's Plays.* London: Dent; 1936, 1957.

3067   ——. *Complete Works.* Centenary ed. Ed. P. P. Howe after Alfred R. Waller and Arnold Glover. 21 vols. London and Toronto: Dent, 1930-34. [Vol. 4, *Characters of Shakespear's Plays*; vol. 5, *Lectures on the English Poets; A View of the English Stage*; vol. 6, *Lectures on the English Comic Writers; Lectures on the Dramatic Literature of the Age of Elizabeth.*]

3068   ——. *Lectures on the English Poets.* 2nd ed. London: Taylor & Hessey, 1819. 3rd ed., London: Templeman, 1841 (ed. William Hazlitt, Jr.). Repr. London: Russell & Russell.

3069   HEARN, Lafcadio. *Lectures on Shakespeare.* Tokyo: Hokuseido, 1928.

3070   HEILMAN, Robert B. "The Role We Give Shakespeare." In *Essays on Shakespeare*, **2770**.

3071   HERBERT, T. Walter. "Shakespeare Announces a Ghost." *SQ*, 1 (1950): 247-54.

3072   HERFORD, Charles H. "Shakespeare and the Arts." *BJRL*, 11 (1927): 273-85.

3073 —. "Shakespeare's Treatment of Love and Marriage." *Edda*, 6 (1916): 92-111. Repr. in *Shakespeare's Treatment of Love and Marriage and Other Essays*. London: Unwin, 1921.

3074 —. *A Sketch of Recent Shakespearean Investigation*. London: Blackie, 1923.

3075 HOFFMANN, Gerhard. "Wandlungen des Gebets im Elisabethanischen Drama." *SJ 1966* (West), pp. 173-210.

3076 HOLLAND, Norman N. *Psychoanalysis and Shakespeare*. New York: McGraw-Hill, 1966.

3077 —. *Shakespearean Imagination: A Critical Introduction*. New York: Macmillan, 1964. [114MB Ind U Pr.]

3078 HOLLOWAY, John. "Dramatic Irony in Shakespeare." In *The Charted Mirror: Literary and Critical Essays*. London: Routledge & Kegan Paul, 1960.

3079 HOLZKNECHT, Karl J. *The Background of Shakespeare's Plays*. New York: American Book, 1950.

3080 HOMAN, Sidney R. "The Uses of Silence: The Elizabethan Dumb Show and the Silent Cinema." *CompD*, 2 (1968): 213-28.

3081 HOME, Henry (Lord Kames). *Elements of Criticism*. 2nd ed., rev. and enl. 3 vols. Edinburgh: A. Millar, 1763.

3082 HOROWITZ, David. *Shakespeare: An Existentialist View*. New York: Hill & Wang, 1965. [*Ado, Ant, Lr, Tmp, Tro, MV*.]

3083 HOSLEY, Richard. "The Formal Influence of Plautus and Terence." In *Elizabethan Theatre*, **3794**.

3084 HOWARTH, Herbert. "Shakespeare's Gentleness." In *ShS 14*, **3917**; repr. in *The Tiger's Heart*, **3085**.

3085 —. *The Tiger's Heart*. New York: Oxford U.P., 1970. [*MV, Ham, AYL, TN, MM, H8*, world-picture.]

3086 HOWSE, Ernest M. *Spiritual Values in Shakespeare*. New York: Abdingdon P., 1955. Repr. 1965.

3087 HOY, Cyrus. *The Hyacinth Room: An Investigation into the Nature of Comedy, Tragedy, and Tragicomedy*. New York: Knopf, 1964.

3088 —. "Renaissance and Restoration Dramatic Plotting." *RenD*, 9 (1966): 247-64. [Sh passim, *Edw3*.]

3089 HUBBELL, Lindley W. *Lectures on Shakespeare*. Tokyo: Nan'undo, 1959. Repr. New York: AMS.

3090 HUBLER, Edward L. "Three Shakespeare Myths: Mutability, Plenitude, and Reputation." In *EIE 1948*, **2979**.

3091 HUGHES, Arthur E. *Shakespeare and His Welsh Characters*. Devizes: Simpson, 1918.

3092 HULME, Hilda M. *Explorations in Shakespeare's Language*. London: Longmans, Green, 1962; New York: Barnes & Noble, 1963.

3093   HUNTER, Edwin R. *Shakespeare and Common Sense.* Boston: Christopher, 1954.

3094   HUXLEY, Aldous. "Shakespeare and Religion." In *Aldous Huxley: A Memorial Volume, 1894-1964.* Ed. Julian Huxley. New York: Harper, 1965.

3095   HYDE, Mary C. *Playwrighting for Elizabethans 1600-1605.* Columbia U.P., 1949.

3096   JAMES, David G. *Scepticism and Poetry.* London: Allen & Unwin, 1937.

3097   JAMESON, Anna B. *Characteristics of Women, Moral, Political, and Historical.* 2 vols. 1832. 2nd ed., London: Saunders & Otley, 1833. Repr. as *Shakespeare's Heroines.* London: Bell,1879; New York: AMS.

3098   JESPERSEN, Otto. "Shakespeare and the Language of Poetry." In *The Growth and Structure of the English Language.* Leipzig: Trübner, 1905. 2nd ed. rev., 1912. 9th ed. rev., 1938; repr. Oxford: Blackwell, 1943.

3099   JOHNSON, Charles F. *Shakespeare and His Critics.* Boston and New York: Houghton Mifflin, 1909. Repr. New York: AMS.

3100   JOHNSON, Francis R. "Shakespeare's Imagery and Senecan Imitation." In *Adams Memorial Studies,* **2794.**

3100a   JOHNSON, Samuel. *Johnson on Shakespeare.* Ed. Walter A. Raleigh. Oxford U.P., 1908. Repr. many times. Rev. ed., 1925; repr. many times.

3101   —. *Johnson on Shakespeare.* Ed. Arthur Sherbo. Vols 7, 8 of *Works of Samuel Johnson.* Yale U.P., 1968.

3102   —. *Mr. Johnson's Preface to His Edition of Shakespear's Plays.* London: J. & R. Tonson, 1765. Repr. Yale U.P.; Oxford U.P., 1937 (ed. Allen T. Hazen).

3103   —. *Notes to Shakespeare.* Ed. Arthur Sherbo. Augustan Reprint Society, nos. 59-60, 65-66, 71. Los Angeles: William Andrews Clark Library, 1956-58. [Vol. 1, Comedies; vol. 2, Histories; vol. 3, Tragedies.]

3104   —. *Samuel Johnson on Shakespeare.* Ed. William K. Wimsatt. New York: Hill & Wang, 1960. [D22.]

3105   JORGENSEN, Paul A. *Redeeming Shakespeare's Words.* U. of California P., 1962.

3106   —. "Shakespeare's Dark Vocabulary." In *The Drama of the Renaissance,* **2763.** [*Tit, Ham, Mac.*]

3107   —. *Shakespeare's Military World.* U. of California P., 1956.

3108   JOSEPHS, Lois. "Shakespeare and a Coleridgean Synthesis." *SQ,* 18 (1967): 17-21. [Cleopatra, Leontes, and Falstaff.]

3109   JUSSERAND, Jean A. A. J. "Ben Jonson's Views on Shakespeare's Art." In *The School for Ambassadors and Other Essays.* London: Unwin, 1924.

3110   —. *What to Expect of Shakespeare.* New York: Oxford U.P., 1911. [*PBA 1911-12*, 5 (1913): 223-44.] Repr. in *The School for Ambassadors and Other Essays*, **3109**.

3111   KAISER, Walter. *Praisers of Folly.* Harvard U.P., 1963. [Erasmus, Rabelais, Sh.]

3112   KANZER, Mark. "The Central Theme in Shakespeare's Works." *PsyR*, 38 (1951): 1-16.

3113   KAUFMANN, Ralph J. "The Senecan Perspective and the Shakespearean Poetic." *CompD*, 1 (1967): 182-98.

3114   KEETON, George W. *Shakespeare's Legal and Political Background.* London: Pitman, 1967; New York: Barnes & Noble, 1968.

3115   KENNEDY, Milton B. *The Oration in Shakespeare.* U. of North Carolina P., 1942.

3116   KETTLE, Arnold. "Some Tendencies in Shakespeare Criticism." *SJ* (East), 102 (1966): 23-36.

3117   KIERNAN, V. G. "Human Relationships in Shakespeare." In *Shakespeare in a Changing World,* **2792**.

3118   KILBY, Clyde S. "Horace Walpole on Shakespeare." *SP*, 38 (1941): 480-93.

3119   KIROV, Todor T. "The First Step of a Giant." *SJ* (East), 104 (1968): 109-40. [Early imagery.]

3120   KIRSCH, Arthur C. "An Essay on *Dramatick Poetry* (1681)." *HLQ*, 28 (1964-65): 89-91. [Anonymous tribute to Sh for his style and consistency of characterization.]

3121   —, ed. *Literary Criticism of John Dryden.* Regents Critics. U. of Nebraska P., 1966. [Includes "Heads of an Answer to Rymer."] [BB 408.]

3122   KIRSCHBAUM, Leo. *Character and Characterization in Shakespeare.* Wayne State U.P., 1962. [Wayne St UP WB4.]

3123   KITTREDGE, George L. *Shakspere: An Address.* Harvard U.P., 1916. Repr. New York: AMS.

3124   KNIGHT, G. Wilson. *Byron and Shakespeare.* London: Routledge & Kegan Paul, 1966.

3125   —. *Myth and Miracle: An Essay on the Mystic Symbolism of Shakespeare.* London: Burrow, 1929. Repr. in *The Crown of Life*, **3500**.

3126   —. *The Olive and the Sword: A Study of England's Shakespeare.* Oxford U.P., 1944.

3127   —. *Shakespeare and Religion.* London: Routledge & Kegan Paul; New York: Barnes & Noble, 1967. [Essays 1927-66.]

3128   —. "Shakespeare and Theology: A Private Protest." *EIC*, 15 (1965): 95-104.

3129   —. *The Shakespearian Tempest.* Oxford U.P., 1932. Repr. London: Methuen; 1953, 1960.

3130   —. *The Sovereign Flower.* London: Methuen, 1958. [Sh as poet of royalty, *A WW*, indexes to earlier vols.]

3131   KNIGHTS, Lionel C. *Explorations.* London: Chatto & Windus, 1946.

3132   —. *Further Explorations.* London: Chatto & Windus, 1965. [5 essays on Sh.]

3133   —. *How Many Children Had Lady Macbeth? An Essay in the Theory and Practice of Shakespeare Criticism.* Cambridge: Minority Press, 1933. Repr. in *Explorations*, 3131.

3134   —. "On Historical Scholarship and the Interpretation of Shakespeare." *SR*, 63 (1955): 223-40. Repr. in *Further Explorations*, 3132.

3135   —. "The Question of Character in Shakespeare." In *Further Explorations*, 3132.

3136   —. *Shakespeare's Politics.* Oxford U.P., 1958. [*PBA 1957*, 43 (1958): 115-32.] Repr. in *Further Explorations, 3132.*

3137   —. *Some Shakespearean Themes.* London: Chatto & Windus, 1959. Repr. in *Some Shakespearean Themes; An Approach to* Ham. Stanford U.P., 1966. [SP 23.] [*Son, 2H4, Tro, Lr, Mac, Ant, Cor.*]

3138   KNOWLTON, Edgar C. "Nature and Shakespeare." *PMLA*, 51 (1936): 719-44.

3139   KÖKERITZ, Helge. *Shakespeare's Pronunciation.* Yale U.P., 1948. [Illustrative record accompanies text.]

3140   KOLBE, Frederick C. *Shakespeare's Way: A Psychological Study.* London: Sheed & Ward, 1930. [Iterative imagery.]

3141   KOTT, Jan. *Szkice o Szekspirze.* Warsaw: Państwowy Instytut Wydawniczy, 1961. Trans. Boleslaw Taborski as *Shakespeare Our Contemporary.* Garden City, N.Y.: Doubleday, 1964. [Anch 499.]

3142   KOZINTSEV, Grigori. *Shakespeare: Time and Conscience.* Trans. Joyce Vining. New York: Hill & Wang, 1966. [Orig. pub. in Russ. as *Our Contemporary: William Shakespeare.* Incl. theater, *Lr, Ham, H4.*]

3143   KREIDER, Paul V. *Repetition in Shakespeare's Plays.* Princeton U.P., 1941.

3144   KUCKHOFF, Armin-Gerd. "Zufall und Notwendigkeit im Drama William Shakespeares." *SJ* (East), 105 (1969): 121-39.

3145   LANGBAUM, Robert. "Character versus Action in Shakespeare." *SQ*, 8 (1957): 57-69.

3146   LANIER, Sidney. *Shakspere and His Forerunners: Studies in Elizabethan Poetry and Its Development from Early English.* New York: Doubleday, Page, 1902. Repr. New York: AMS.

3147   LAWLOR, John J. "Continuity and Innovation in Shakespeare's Dramatic Career." *REL*, 5 (1964): 11-23.

3148 —. "Mind and Hand: Some Reflections on the Study of Shakespeare's Imagery." *SQ*, 8 (1957): 179-93.

3149 —. "On Historical Scholarship and the Interpretation of Shakespeare: A Reply to L. C. Knights." *SR*, 64 (1956): 186-206.

3150 LAWRENSON, Thomas E. "Voltaire and Shakespeare. Ordeal by Translation." In *Papers Mainly Shakespearean*, **2775.**

3151 LEAVIS, Frank R. *The Common Pursuit.* London: Chatto & Windus, 1952. [Essays coll. from *Scrutiny*.]

3152 LECOCQ, Louis. *La Satire en Angleterre de 1588 à 1603.* Paris: Didier, 1969.

3153 LEE, Sidney. *The Impersonal Aspect of Shakespeare's Art.* Oxford U.P., 1909.

3154 LEECH, Clifford. "The 'Capability' of Shakespeare." *SQ*, 11 (1960): 123-36.

3155 —. "Shakespeare and the Idea of the Future." *UTQ*, 35 (1965-66): 213-28.

3156 —. "Shakespeare, Elizabethan and Jacobean." *QQ*, 72 (1965): 5-25.

3157 —. "Shakespeare's Prologues and Epilogues." In *Studies in Honor of T. W. Baldwin*, **2760.**

3158 —. "Venus and Her Nun: Portraits of Women in Love by Shakespeare and Marlowe." *SEL*; see **2712.**

3159 LEGOUIS, Émile H. *The Bacchic Element in Shakespeare's Plays.* Oxford U.P., 1926. [*PBA 1926*, 12 (1927): 115-32.] Repr. in *Aspects of Shakespeare,* **2761.**

3160 LEVIN, Harry. "Shakespeare's Nomenclature." In *Essays on Shakespeare*, **2770.**

3161 LEWIS, Anthony J. "The Dog, Lion, and Wolf in Shakespeare's Descriptions of Night." *MLR*, 66 (1971): 1-10.

3162 LEWIS, Wyndham. *The Lion and the Fox: The Rôle of the Hero in the Plays of Shakespeare.* New York and London: Harper, 1927. Repr. New York: Barnes & Noble; London: Methuen, 1966. [UP B&N 68.]

3163 LINDHEIM, Bogislav von. "Syntaktische Funktionsverschiebung als Mittel des barocken Stils bei Shakespeare." In *SJ*, 90, **3327.**

3164 LOUNSBURY, Thomas R. *Shakespeare as a Dramatic Artist, with an Account of His Reputation at Various Periods.* New York: Scribner's, 1901. Repr. New York: Ungar.

3165 LUDOWYK, Evelyn F. C. *Understanding Shakespeare.* Cambridge U.P., 1962. [CUP 242.] [*MV, H5, JC, TN, Mac.*]

3166 LÜTHI, Max. "Die Macht des Nichtwirklichen in Shakespeares Spielen." *SJ*, 97 (1961): 13-33.

3167   —. *Shakespeares Dramen.* Berlin: de Gruyter, 1957. 2nd ed. rev., 1966.

3168   MACARDLE, Dorothy. *Shakespeare.* London: Faber & Faber, 1961.

3169   MACK, Maynard. "Engagement and Detachment in Shakespeare's Plays." In *Essays . . . in Honor of Hardin Craig,* 2786.

3170   MACKAIL, John W. *The Approach to Shakespeare.* Oxford U.P., 1930.

3171   —. *Shakespeare after Three Hundred Years.* Oxford U.P., 1916. [*PBA 1915-16,* 7 (1917): 319-38.]

3172   MACKENZIE, Henry. *The Lounger.* Edinburgh: W. Creech, 1785-86. Repr. as vols. 38-40 of *British Essayists.* Ed. Alexander Chalmers. 45 vols. London: J. Johnson, 1802-3. Repr. many times. [Nos. 68, 69 on Falstaff.]

3173   —. *The Mirror.* Edinburgh: W. Creech, 1779-80. Repr. as vols. 35-37 of *British Essayists.* Ed. Alexander Chalmers. 45 vols. London: J. Johnson, 1802-3. Repr. many times. [Nos. 66, 99, 100 on *R3, Ham,* and *Lr.*]

3174   McMANAWAY, James G. *Studies in Shakespeare, Bibliography, and Theater.* New York: Shakespeare Association of America, 1969.

3175   McPEEK, James A. S. *The Black Book of Knaves and Unthrifts in Shakespeare and Other Renaissance Authors.* U. of Connecticut P., 1969.

3176   MAHOOD, Molly M. "Love's Confined Doom." In *ShS 15,* 2374.

3177   —. *Shakespeare's Wordplay.* London: Methuen; New York: Barnes & Noble, 1965. [UP B&N 242.] [*Ant, Rom, R2, Son, Ham, Mac, WT.*]

3178   MARDER, Louis. *His Exits and His Entrances: The Story of Shakespeare's Reputation.* Philadelphia: Lippincott, 1963; London: Murray, 1964.

3179   MARRIOTT, John A. R. "Shakespeare and Politics." *Cornhill,* 63 (1927): 678-90.

3180   MARTIN, Helena S. (Faucit). *On Some of Shakespeare's Female Characters.* Edinburgh and London: W. Blackwood, 1885. Repr. New York: AMS.

3181   MASEFIELD, John E. *Shakespeare and Spiritual Life.* Oxford U.P., 1924. Repr. in Masefield, *Recent Prose.* Rev. ed., London: Heinemann, 1932.

3182   —. *William Shakespeare.* London: Williams & Norgate; New York: Holt, 1911. Rev. ed., London: Heinemann, 1954. Repr. New York: Barnes & Noble. [Premier R238.]

3183   MATTHEWS, Honor M. V. *Character and Symbol in Shakespeare's Plays.* Cambridge U.P., 1962.

3184   MATTHEWS, J. Brander. *Shakspere as a Playwright.* New York: Scribner's, 1913. Repr. New York: AMS.

3185   MATTHEWS, John, ed. *Shaw's Dramatic Criticism (1895-98).* New York: Hill & Wang, 1959. [D 17.]

3186   MAUNTZ, Alfred von. *Heraldik in Diensten der Shakespeare-Forschung.* Berlin: Mayer & Muller, 1903. Repr. Detroit, Mich.: Gale.

3187   MAXWELL, James C. "The Ghost from the Grave: A Note on Shakespeare's Apparitions." *DUJ*, 17 (1956): 55-59.

3188   MAYHALL, Jane. "Shakespeare and Spenser: A Commentary on Differences." *MLQ*, 10 (1949): 356-63.

3189   MEHL, Dieter. "Emblems in English Renaissance Drama." *RenD*, 2 (1969): 39-57.

3190   MEISSNER, Paul. *Shakespeare.* Berlin: de Gruyter, 1954.

3191   MENDL, Robert W. S. *Revelation in Shakespeare.* London: Calder, 1964. [Humanities.]

3192   MĒNŌN, C. Nārāyana. *Shakespeare Criticism.* Oxford U.P., 1938.

3193   MERCHANT, W. Moelwyn. "Shakespeare's Theology." *REL*, 5 (1964): 72-86.

3194   —. "Visual Elements in Shakespeare Studies." In *SJ*, 92, **793.**

3195   MERES, Francis. *Palladis Tamia, Wits Treasury.* London: C. Burbie, 1598. Repr. in facs. (with suppressed leaves), New York: Scholars' Facsimiles & Reprints, 1938 (ed. Don C. Allen); New York: AMS. [See also **4288.**]

3196   MILES, L. Wardlaw. "Shakespeare's Old Men." *ELH*, 7 (1940): 286-99.

3197   MILLER, George M. *The Historical Point of View in English Literary Criticism from 1570-1770.* Heidelberg: C. Winter, 1913. Repr. New York: Franklin.

3198   MONK, Samuel H. "Dryden and the Beginnings of Shakespeare Criticism in the Augustan Age." In *Essays in Honor of Robert W. Babcock*, **2810.**

3199   MONTAGU, Elizabeth. *An Essay on the Writings and Genius of Shakespear, Compared with the Greek and French Dramatic Poets, with Some Remarks upon the Misrepresentations of Mons. de Voltaire.* London: J. Dodsley, 1769. Repr. of 6th ed., corr., 1810, New York: AMS.

3200   MOORMAN, Frederic W. "Shakespeare's Ghosts." *MLR*, 1 (1906): 192-201.

3201   MOROZOV, Mikhail M. "The Individualization of Shakespeare's Characters through Imagery." *ShS* 2 (1949), pp. 83-106. [*Oth, Mac, Ham.*]

3202   —. "On the Dynamism of Shakespeare's Characters." In *Shakespeare in the Soviet Union*, **2809**.

3203   MOULTON, Richard G. *The Moral System of Shakespeare: A Popular Illustration of Fiction as the Experimental Side of Philosophy.* New York and London: Macmillan, 1903. Repr. as *Shakespeare as a Dramatic Thinker.* New York: Macmillan, 1907; 1916.

3204   —. *Shakespeare as a Dramatic Artist.* 1885. 3rd ed., rev. and enl., Oxford U.P., 1906. [Dover.]

3205   MUIR, Kenneth. "Fifty Years of Shakespearian Criticism: 1900-1950." *ShS 4* (1951), pp. 1-25.

3206   —. "Shakespeare and Politics." In *Shakespeare in a Changing World*, **2792**.

3207   —. "Shakespeare and Rhetoric." In *SJ*, 90, **3327**.

3208   —. *Shakespeare as Collaborator.* See **596**.

3209   —. "Shakespeare's Imagery—Then and Now." *ShS 18* (1965), pp. 46-57.

3210   —. "Some Freudian Interpretations of Shakespeare." *PLPLS-LHS*, 7 (1952): 43-52.

3211   —. "The Uncomic Pun." *CamJ*, 3 (1950): 472-85.

3212   —, and Sean O'Loughlin. *The Voyage to Illyria: A New Study of Shakespeare.* London: Methuen, 1937. Repr. 1970.

3213   MULHOLLAND, Joan. "'Thou' and 'You' in Shakespeare: A Study in the Second Person Pronoun." *ES*, 48 (1967): 34-43.

3214   MURRAY, Patrick J. *The Shakespearian Scene.* New York: Barnes & Noble, 1969.

3215   MURRY, John Middleton. *Countries of the Mind.* New York: Dutton, 1922. Rev. and enl. ed., Oxford U.P., 1931. [Incl. "Shakespeare and Love."]

3216   —. *Countries of the Mind, Second Series.* Oxford U.P., 1931. [Incl. "Shakespeare's Dedication."]

3217   —. *Discoveries.* London: Collins, 1924.

3218   —. *John Clare and Other Studies.* London and New York: Nevill, 1950. [Incl. "Shakespeare's Dedication," "Shakespeare and Love."]

3219   —. *The Problem of Style.* Oxford U.P., 1921. [OUP 11.]

3220   —. *Shakespeare.* London: Cape, 1936. Repr. 1955. [Humanities.]

3221   MUSGROVE, Sydney. *Shakespeare and Jonson.* Auckland U. College, 1957. Repr. New York: AMS.

3222   NAIK, M. K. "Humanitarianism in Shakespeare." *SQ*, 19 (1968): 139-47.

3223   NEILSON, William A., and Ashley H. Thorndike. *Facts about Shakespeare.* New York: Macmillan, 1931. Rev. ed., 1962. [Mac 38619.]

3224 NESS, Frederic W. *The Use of Rhyme in Shakespeare's Plays.* Yale U.P.; Oxford U.P., 1941.

3225 NEWMANN, Joshua A. "Shakespearean Criticism in *The Tatler* and *Spectator.*" *PMLA*, 39 (1924): 612-23.

3226 NICOLL, Allardyce. *Co-operation in Shakespearian Scholarship.* Oxford U.P., 1953. [*PBA 1952*, 38 (1953): 71-88.]

3227 ——. *Shakespeare.* London: Methuen, 1952.

3228 ——. "Tragical-Comical-Historical-Pastoral." *BJRL*, 43 (1960): 70-87.

3229 NOBLE, Richmond S. H. *Shakespeare's Biblical Knowledge and the Use of the Book of Common Prayer, As Exemplified in the Plays of the First Folio.* London: Society for Promoting Christian Knowledge, 1935.

3230 NOSWORTHY, James M. *Shakespeare's Occasional Plays: Their Origin and Transmission.* London: Arnold, 1965. [*Mac, Tro, Wiv, Ham.*]

3231 OPPEL, Horst. "Kontrast und Kontrapunkt im Shakespeare-Drama." *SJ*, 97 (1961): 153-82.

3232 ——. "Shakespeare und das Leid." *SJ*, 93 (1957): 38-81.

3233 ——. *Shakespeares Tragödien und Romanzen: Kontinuität oder Umbruch?* Wiesbaden: Akademie der Wissenschaften und der Literatur in Mainz, 1954.

3234 ——. *Der Späte Shakespeare.* Hamburg: Ellermann, 1949.

3235 ORNSTEIN, Robert T. "Character and Reality in Shakespeare." In *Shakespeare, 1564-1964,* **2764.**

3236 OVERHOLSER, Winfred. "Shakespeare's Psychiatry—And After." *SQ*, 10 (1959): 335-52.

3237 PALMER, John L. *Political and Comic Characters of Shakespeare.* London: Macmillan, 1962. Repr. New York: St. Martin's. [2 ser. of essays, orig. pub. separately.]

3238 ——. *Political Characters of Shakespeare.* London: Macmillan, 1945. Repr. in *Political and Comic Characters,* **3237.** [*JC, R3, R2, H5, Cor.*]

3239 PARIS, Jean. *Shakespeare.* New York: Grove, 1960. [Evergreen Profile 10.]

3240 PARKER, Marion D. H. *The Slave of Life: A Study of Shakespeare and the Idea of Justice.* London: Chatto & Windus, 1955.

3241 PARROTT, Thomas M. *Shakespearean Comedy.* See **3518.** [Incl. all plays.]

3242 PARTRIDGE, Astley C. *Orthography in Shakespeare and Elizabethan Drama: A Study of Colloquial Contractions, Elision, Prosody, and Punctuation.* U. of Nebraska P., 1964.

3243 PARTRIDGE, Eric H. *Shakespeare's Bawdy: A Literary and Psychological Essay and a Comprehensive Glossary.* London: Routledge, 1947. Repr. London: Routledge & Kegan Paul, 1955. Rev. and enl. ed., 1968. [Dutton D55.]

3244 PATER, Walter. *Appreciations, with an Essay on Style.* London: Macmillan, 1918. [Pp. 161-204 on Sh.]

3245 PEARN, B. R. "Dumb-Show in Elizabethan Drama." *RES,* 11(1935): 385-405.

3246 PEYRE, Henri. "Shakespeare and Modern French Criticism." In *Essays in Honor of Robert W. Babcock,* **2810.**

3247 PHILLIPS, Gerald W. *Lord Burghley in Shakespeare: Falstaff, Sly, and Others.* London: Butterworth, 1936. [*1H4, 2H4, Wiv, Shr, MND, MV, Ham, Ven, Luc.*]

3248 POTTS, Abbie F. *Shakespeare and* The Faerie Queene. Cornell U.P., 1958. [*Ham, MM.*]

3249 PRAZ, Mario. "Shakespeare's Italy." *ShS* 7 (1954), pp. 95-106.

3250 PRESSON, Robert K. "Some Traditional Instances of Setting in Shakespeare's Plays." *MLR,* 61 (1966): 12-22.

3251 PRICE, Hereward T. *Construction in Shakespeare.* U. of Michigan P., 1951.

3252 —. "Mirror Scenes in Shakespeare." In *Adams Memorial Studies,* **2794.**

3253 PROUDFOOT, C. Richard. "Shakespeare and the New Dramatists of the King's Men, 1606-1613." In *Later Shakespeare,* **2767.**

3254 QUILLER-COUCH, Arthur T. *Notes on Shakespeare's Workmanship.* New York: Holt, 1917. Pub. as *Shakespeare's Workmanship.* Cambridge U.P., 1918; repr. 1931.

3255 —. *Paternity in Shakespeare.* Oxford U.P., 1932. [*PBA 1932,* 18 (1933): 93-110.]

3256 QUINONES, Ricardo J. "Views of Time in Shakespeare." *JHI,* 26 (1965): 327-52.

3257 QUIRK, Randolph. "Shakespeare and the English Language." In *A New Companion to Shakespeare Studies,* **2800.**

3258 RABKIN, Norman. *Shakespeare and the Common Understanding.* New York: Free P., 1967. [92565 Free P.]

3259 Canceled.

3260 RALEIGH, Walter A. *Shakespeare.* London and New York: Macmillan, 1907. Repr. 1950; New York: St. Martin's; AMS.

3261 —. *Shakespeare and England.* Oxford U.P., 1918. [*PBA 1917-18,* 8 (1918): 403-18.]

3262 RALLI, Augustus. *A History of Shakespearian Criticism.* 2 vols. Oxford U.P., 1932.

3263   ——. *Later Critiques.* London: Longmans, 1933. Repr. Freeport, N.Y.: Books for Libraries. [3 essays on Sh.]

3264   RANSOM, Harry. "Some Legal Elements in Elizabethan Plays." *TxSE*, No. 16 (1936): pp. 53-76.

3265   RANSOM, John C. "On Shakespeare's Language." *SR*, 55 (1947): 181-98.

3266   RAYSOR, Thomas M. "The Study of Shakespeare's Characters in the Eighteenth Century." *MLN*, 42 (1927): 495-500.

3267   REESE, Max M. *Shakespeare: His World and His Work.* London: Arnold, 1953. Repr. New York: St. Martin's.

3268   REYHER, Paul. *Essai sur les idées dans l'oeuvre de Shakespeare.* Paris: Didier, 1947.

3269   RIBNER, Irving. "Marlowe and Shakespeare." *SQ*, 15.2 (1964): 41-53. Also in *Shakespeare 400,* **2793**.

3270   ——. "Shakespeare Criticism, 1900-1964." In *Shakespeare, 1564-1964,* **2764**.

3271   ——. "Shakespeare's Christianity and the Problem of Belief." *CentR*, 8 (1964): 99-108.

3272   RICHARDSON, William. *Cursory Remarks on Tragedy, on Shakespear.* London: W. Owen, 1774. Repr. New York: AMS.

3273   ——. *A Philosophical Analysis and Illustration of Some of Shakespeare's Remarkable Characters.* Edinburgh: W. Creech & J. Murray, 1774. Pub. as *Essays on Shakespeare's Dramatic Characters of Macbeth, Hamlet, Jaques, and Imogen.* London: J. Murray, 1785; repr. New York: AMS.

3274   RICHMOND, Hugh M. *Shakespeare's Political Plays.* New York: Random House, 1967. [SLL12 Random.] [Histories, *JC, Cor.*]

3275   RIDLEY, Maurice R. *On Reading Shakespeare.* Oxford U.P., 1940. [*PBA 1940*, 26 (1941): 197-225.]

3276   ——. *Shakespeare's Plays: A Commentary.* London: Dent, 1937.

3277   ROBERTSON, John M. *Croce as Shakespearean Critic.* London: Routledge, 1922.

3278   ——. *The State of Shakespeare Study: A Critical Conspectus.* London: Routledge, 1931.

3279   ROBINSON, Herbert S. *English Shakespearian Criticism in the Eighteenth Century.* New York: Wilson, 1932. Repr. New York: Gordian.

3280   RÖHRMAN, H. *The Way of Life—Marlowe and Shakespeare: A Thematic Exposition of Some of Their Plays.* Arnhem: von Loghum Slaterus, 1952. Repr. New York: AMS.

3281   ROOT, Robert K. *Classical Mythology in Shakespeare.* New York: Holt, 1903.

3282   ROSS, Lawrence J. "The Meaning of Strawberries in Shakespeare."
       SRen, 7 (1960): 225-40.

3283   —. *Wingless Victory: Michelangelo, Shakespeare, and the "Old
       Man."* Literary Monographs, 2. U. of Wisconsin P., 1969.

3284   ROSSITER, Arthur P. *Angel with Horns.* Ed. Graham Storey.
       London: Longmans, Green, 1961. [Coll. of essays. *R2, R3, Lr, Ham,
       Mac*, histories.]

3285   RUDOLPH, Johanna. "Karl Marx und Shakespeare." *SJ* (East),
       105 (1969): 25-53.

3286   RYLANDS, George H. W. *Shakespeare's Poetic Energy.* Oxford
       U.P., 1951. [*PBA 1951*, 37 (1952): 99-119.]

3287   —. *Words and Poetry.* London: Woolf, 1928. Repr. New York:
       AMS.

3288   SAINTSBURY, George E. B. *Shakespeare.* New York: Macmillan;
       Cambridge U.P., 1934. [2 chaps. on Sh from *Cam. Hist. Eng. Lit.*,
       18a.]

3289   —. "Shakespeare and the Grand Style." *E&S*, 1 (1910): 113-35.

3290   SANDERS, Wilbur. *The Dramatist and the Received Idea: Studies
       in the Plays of Marlowe and Shakespeare.* Cambridge U.P., 1968.
       [*R3, R2, Mac.*]

3291   SCHANZER, Ernest. "Atavism and Anticipation in Shakespeare's
       Style." *EIC*, 7 (1957): 242-56.

3292   —. "Heywood's *Ages* and Shakespeare." *RES*, 11 (1960): 18-28.

3293   —. "Plot-Echoes in Shakespeare's Plays." *SJ 1969* (West), pp.
       103-21. [*1, 2 H4, Lr, Ant, Tim, Cor, WT.*]

3294   —. *The Problem Plays of Shakespeare.* London: Routledge &
       Kegan Paul, 1963. [*MM, JC, Ant.*]

3295   SCHELL, J. Stewart. "Shakspere's Gulls." *SAB*, 15 (1940): 23-33.

3296   SCHELLING, Felix E. *Shakespeare and "Demi-Science": Papers on
       Elizabethan Topics.* U. of Pennsylvania P., 1927. Repr. New York:
       AMS.

3297   SCHIRMER, Walter F. "Shakespeare und die Rhetorik." *SJ*, 71
       (1935): 11-31.

3298   SCHLÖSSER, Anselm. "Zur Bedeutung der Anachronismen bei
       Shakespeare." *SJ* (East), 105 (1969): 7-24.

3299   SCHLÜTER, Kurt. "Die Erzählung der Vorgeschichte in Shake-
       speares Dramen." In *SJ*, 90, **3327**.

3300   SCHNEIDER, Reinhold. "Das Bild der Herrschaft in Shakespeares
       Drama." *SJ*, 93 (1957): 9-37.

3301   SCHOPF, Alfred. "Leitmotivische Thematik in Shakespeares Dra-
       men." In *SJ*, 90, **3327**.

3302   SCHÜCKING, Levin L. *Die Charakterprobleme bei Shakespeare.* Leipzig: Tauchnitz, 1919. Trans. as *Character Problems in Shakespeare's Plays.* London: Harrap, 1922.

3303   SCOTT, William I. D. *Shakespeare's Melancholics.* London: Mills & Boon, 1962.

3304   SCRIMGEOUR, Gary J. "The Messenger as a Dramatic Device in Shakespeare." *SQ*, 19 (1968): 41-54.

3305   SEDGEWICK, Garnett G. *Of Irony, Especially in Drama.* 1935. 2nd ed., U. of Toronto P., 1948.

3306   SEHRT, Ernst T. *Vergebung und Gnade bei Shakespeare.* Stuttgart: Koehler, 1952.

3307   SEN, Sailendra K. "A Neglected Critic of Shakespeare: Walter Whiter." *SQ*, 13 (1962): 173-85.

3308   SEN GUPTA, Subodh C. *The Whirligig of Time: The Problem of Duration in Shakespeare's Plays.* Bombay: Orient Longmans, 1961.

3309   SEVERS, Kenneth. "Imagery and Drama." *DUJ*, 41(1948): 24-33.

3310   SEWELL, William A. *Character and Society in Shakespeare.* Oxford U.P., 1951.

3311   SHAABER, Matthias A. "Shakespeare Criticism: Dryden to Bradley." In *A New Companion to Shakespeare Studies*, **2800.**

3312   SHACKFORD, Martha H. *Shakespeare, Sophocles: Dramatic Themes and Modes.* New York: Bookman, 1960. [L8. Coll. & UP.]

3313   "Shakespeare Scholars at Work: An Age of Discovery and Advance [1837-1937]." *TLS*, 1 May 1937, pp. 334-35.

3314   SHARPE, Robert B. *Irony in the Drama: An Essay on Impersonation, Shock, and Catharsis.* U. of North Carolina P., 1959. [Chap. on Sh.]

3315   SHAW, George B. *Shaw on Shakespeare.* See **3430.**

3316   —. *Shaw's Dramatic Criticism (1895-98).* See **3185.**

3317   SIEGEL, Paul N. *Shakespeare in His Time and Ours.* U. of Notre Dame P., 1969. [NDP 90.] [9 essays, some prev. pub.; *Rom, Lr,* comedies, *Ado, MND, MV.*]

3318   SIMPSON, Lucie. *The Secondary Heroes of Shakespeare, and Other Essays.* London: Kingswood, 1951.

3319   SIMPSON, Percy. "Shakespeare's Use of Latin Authors." In *Studies in Elizabethan Drama*, **3321.**

3320   —. "Shakespeare's Versification." In *Studies in Elizabethan Drama*, **3321.**

3321   —. *Studies in Elizabethan Drama.* Oxford U.P., 1955.

3322   SIMPSON, Robert R. *Shakespeare and Medicine.* Edinburgh: Livingstone, 1959.

3323   SIMS, James H. *Dramatic Uses of Biblical Allusions in Marlowe and Shakespeare.* U. of Florida P., 1966.

3324 SINGLETON, Esther. *The Shakespeare Garden.* New York: Century, 1922. Repr. New York: AMS.

3325 SIPE, Dorothy L. *Shakespeare's Metrics.* Yale U.P., 1968.

3326 SITWELL, Edith. *A Notebook on William Shakespeare.* London: Macmillan, 1948. Repr. 1962. [BP118 Beacon.] [*Lr, Mac, Oth, Ant, Cym.*]

3327 *SJ*, 90 (1954). [Issue devoted chiefly to Shakespeare's style.]

3328 SMART, John S. *Shakespeare: Truth and Tradition.* See **493**.

3329 SMIRNOV, Aleksandr A. *Shakespeare: A Marxist Interpretation.* Trans. Sonia Volochova et al. New York: Critics Group, 1936.

3330 SMITH, Charles G. *Shakespeare's Proverb Lore.* Harvard U.P., 1963.

3331 SMITH, D. Nichol, ed. *Dryden's Essay of Dramatic Poesy.* Glasgow: Blackie, 1900.

3332 —. *Shakespeare in the Eighteenth Century.* Oxford U.P., 1928. Repr. 1967.

3333 SMITH, Logan P. *On Reading Shakespeare.* New York: Harcourt, Brace, 1933.

3334 SMITH, Marion B. *Dualities in Shakespeare.* U. of Toronto P., 1966.

3335 —. "Shakespeare and the Polarity of Love." *HAB*, 16 (1965): 7-18.

3336 SNUGGS, Henry L. *Shakespeare and Five Acts: Studies in a Dramatic Convention.* New York: Vantage, 1960.

3337 SOELLNER, Rolf. "Shakespeare, Aristotle, Plato, and the Soul." *SJ 1968* (West), pp. 56-71.

3338 SPALDING, Kenneth J. *The Philosophy of Shakespeare.* New York: Philosophical Library, 1953.

3339 SPALDING, Thomas A. *Elizabethan Demonology.* London: Chatto & Windus, 1880.

3340 SPEAIGHT, Robert. *Shakespeare and Politics.* London: Marshall, 1946.

3341 SPENCER, Terence J. B. "The Great Rival: Shakespeare and the Classical Dramatists." In *Shakespeare, 1564-1964,* **2764**.

3342 —. "Shakespeare and the Noble Woman." *SJ 1966* (West), pp. 49-62.

3343 —. "The Sophistry of Shakespeare." *English Studies Today,* 4 (1966): 169-85.

3344 —. *The Tyranny of Shakespeare.* Oxford U.P., 1960. [*PBA 1959,* 45 (1960): 153-71.] Repr. in *Studies in Shakespeare,* **2759**.

3345 SPENCER, Theodore. *Shakespeare and the Nature of Man.* New York: Macmillan, 1943. 2nd ed., 1961. [05400 Collier.]

3346 SPIVACK, Bernard. *Shakespeare and the Allegory of Evil.* Columbia U.P., 1958.

3347   SPRAGUE, Arthur C. "Shakespeare and Melodrama." *E&S*, 18 (1965): 1-12.

3348   SPURGEON, Caroline F. E. *Shakespeare's Imagery and What It Tells Us.* Cambridge U.P., 1935; New York: Macmillan, 1936. Repr. Cambridge U.P., 1965. [CUP 258.]

3349   —. *Shakespeare's Iterative Imagery.* Oxford U.P., 1931. [*PBA 1931,* 17 (1932): 147-78.] Repr. in *Aspects of Shakespeare,* **2761**.

3350   SQUIRE, John C. *Shakespeare as a Dramatist.* London: Cassell, 1935.

3351   STACK, Richard. "An Examination of an Essay on the Dramatic Character of Sir John Falstaff." *Trans. Royal Irish Academy*, 2 (1788): 3-37. [A rebuttal of Morgann, **1243**.]

3352   STAHL, Hannelore. "Schöpferische Wortbildung bei Shakespeare?" In *SJ*, 90, **3327**.

3353   STAMM, Rudolf. *Shakespeare's Word-Scenery, with Some Remarks on Stage-History and the Interpretation of His Plays.* Zurich and St. Gallen: Polygraphischer Verlag, 1954. Repr. in *The Shaping Powers at Work,* **3354**.

3354   —. *The Shaping Powers at Work.* Heidelberg: Winter, 1967. [Essays written 1936-65, some prev. pub. *Ant, Cym, Tro, Ham, Mac.*]

3355   —. "Wer war Shakespeare?" *SJ 1965* (West), pp. 80-102.

3356   STAUFFER, Donald A. *Shakespeare's World of Images: The Development of His Moral Ideas.* New York: Norton, 1949. [U Ind MB 87.]

3357   STAVISKY, Aron Y. *Shakespeare and the Victorians: Roots of Modern Criticism.* U. of Oklahoma P., 1969.

3358   STEVENSON, Robert. *Shakespeare's Religious Frontier.* The Hague: Nijhoff, 1958. [Humanities.]

3359   STEWART, John I. M. *Character and Motive in Shakespeare.* London and New York: Longmans, Green, 1949. Repr. 1959; New York: Barnes & Noble.

3360   STIRLING, Brents. *The Populace in Shakespeare.* Columbia U.P.; Oxford U.P., 1949. Repr. New York: AMS.

3361   STOCKELBACH, Lavonia. *The Birds of Shakespeare.* London: Batsford, 1954.

3362   STOLL, Elmer E. "Anachronism in Shakespeare Criticism." *MP*, 7 (1910): 557-75.

3363   —. *Art and Artifice in Shakespeare.* Cambridge U.P., 1933. Repr. London: Methuen, 1963.

3364   —. *From Shakespeare to Joyce.* Garden City, N.Y.: Doubleday, Doran, 1944. Repr. New York: Ungar.

3365   —. "Intentions and Instinct." *MLQ,* 14 (1953): 375-412.

3366   —. *Poets and Playwrights.* U. of Minnesota P., 1930. Repr. New York: Russell & Russell. [MP 1.] [Sh, Jonson, Spenser, Milton.]

3367   ——. *Shakespeare and Other Masters.* Harvard U.P.; Oxford U.P., 1940. [10 essays on Sh.]

3368   ——. *Shakespeare Studies: Historical and Comparative in Method.* New York: Macmillan, 1927.

3369   ——. *Shakespeare's Young Lovers.* Oxford U.P., 1937. Repr. New York: AMS.

3370   STRATHMANN, Ernest A. "The Devil Can Cite Scripture." *SQ,* 15.2 (1964): 17-23. Also in *Shakespeare 400, 2793.* [*Oth, Lr, Ham.*]

3371   STRINDBERG, August. *Open Letters to the Intimate Theater.* Trans. and ed. Walter Johnson. Washington U.P., 1966.

3372   STROUT, Alan L. "John Wilson (Christopher North) as a Shakespeare Critic: A Study of Shakespeare in the English Romantic Movement." *SJ,* 72 (1936): 93-123.

3373   SUTHERLAND, William O. S. "Polonius, Hamlet, and Lear in Aaron Hill's *Prompter.*" *SP,* 49 (1952): 605-18.

3374   SWINBURNE, Algernon C. *A Study of Shakespeare.* London: Chatto & Windus, 1880. 3rd ed. rev., 1895. Repr. New York: AMS.

3375   TERRY, Ellen A. *Four Lectures on Shakespeare.* London: Hopkinson, 1932. Repr. New York: Blom.

3376   THALER, Alwin. *Shakespeare and Our World.* U. of Tennessee P., 1966.

3377   ——. "Shakespeare on Style, Imagination, and Poetry." *PMLA,* 53 (1938): 1019-36.

3378   ——. *Shakspere's Silences.* Harvard U.P., 1929. [Sh, Sh and Milton.]

3379   THIRLWALL, Connop. "On the Irony of Sophocles." *Philological Museum,* 2 (1833): 483-537. [Early discussion of dramatic irony.]

3380   THOMSON, James A. K. *Shakespeare and the Classics.* London: Allen & Unwin, 1952. Repr. New York: Barnes & Noble.

3381   THORNDIKE, Ashley H. *The Influence of Beaumont and Fletcher on Shakespeare.* Worcester, Mass.: Wood, 1901. Repr. New York: Russell & Russell; AMS.

3382   TILLYARD, Eustace M. W. *Essays Literary and Educational.* London: Chatto & Windus, 1962. [Coll. prev. pub. essays, 5 on Sh.]

3382a   ——. "Reality and Fantasy in Elizabethan Literature." In *Essays Literary and Educational, 3382.* [*AYL, WT.*]

3383   ——. *Shakespeare's Problem Plays.* London: Chatto & Windus, 1950. Repr. 1964. [U of Toronto P.] [*Ham, Tro, AWW, MM.*]

3384   TOLIVER, Harold E. "Shakespeare and the Abyss of Time." *JEGP,* 64 (1965): 234-54.

3385   ——. "Shakespeare's Kingship: Institution and Dramatic Form." In *Essays in Shakespearean Criticism, 2769.*

3386 TOLSTOY, Leo. *Tolstoy on Shakespeare.* Trans. V. Tchertkoff and I. F. M. New York and London: Funk & Wagnalls, 1906.

3387 TOOLE, William B. *Shakespeare's Problem Plays: Studies in Form and Meaning.* The Hague: Mouton; New York: Humanities P., 1966. [*Ham, AWW, MM, Tro.*]

3388 TRAVERSI, Derek A. *Approach to Shakespeare.* London; Sands, 1938. Rev., 1957. 3rd rev. & enl. ed., 2 vols., London: Hollis & Carter, 1968. [Anch 74.]

3389 TREE, H. Beerbohm. *Thoughts and After-Thoughts.* London and New York: Cassell, 1913. [Essays, chiefly Sh.]

3390 TUPPER, Frederick. "The Shakespearean Mob." *PMLA*, 27 (1912): 486-523.

3391 TURNER, Frederick. *Shakespeare and the Nature of Time: Moral and Philosophical Themes in Some Plays and Poems by William Shakespeare.* Oxford U.P., 1970.

3392 TYRWHITT, Thomas. *Observations and Conjectures upon Some Passages in Shakespeare.* Oxford U.P., 1766. Repr. New York: AMS. [First use of Meres's *Palladis Tamia* in study of the canon.]

3393 UPTON, John. *Critical Observations on Shakespeare.* London: G. Hawkins, 1746. Rev. ed., 1748; repr. New York: AMS.

3394 URE, Peter. *William Shakespeare: The Problem Plays.* London: Longmans, Green, 1961. [*Tro, AWW, MM, Tim.*]

3395 VANDIVER, Edward P. "The Elizabethan Dramatic Parasite." *SP*, 32 (1935): 411-27.

3396 VAN DOREN, Carl. "Shakspere on His Art." In *Shaksperian Studies,* **2798.**

3397 VAN DOREN, Mark. *Shakespeare.* New York: Holt, 1939. Repr. London: Allen, 1941. [All Anch.]

3398 VAN LAAN, Thomas F. *The Idiom of Drama.* Cornell U.P., 1970.

3399 VELZ, John W. "Mr. Hales of Eton and the Two Lords Falkland." *SQ*, 14 (1963): 476-77.

3400 VICKERS, Brian. *The Artistry of Shakespeare's Prose.* London: Methuen; New York: Barnes & Noble, 1968.

3401 ——. "Shakespeare's Use of Rhetoric." In *A New Companion to Shakespeare Studies,* **2800.**

3402 VIËTOR, Wilhelm. *Shakespeare's Pronunciation: A Shakespeare Phonology; A Shakespeare Reader in the Old Spelling and with a Phonetic Transcription.* 2 vols. Marburg: Elwert; New York: Lemcke & Buechner (2nd vol. only), 1906. Repr. New York: AMS (2nd vol.); Ungar (2 vols.).

3403 VISWANATHAN, S. "'Illeism with a Difference' in Certain Middle Plays of Shakespeare." *SQ*, 20 (1969): 407-15.

3404 VYVYAN, John. *Shakespeare and Platonic Beauty.* London: Chatto & Windus; New York: Barnes & Noble, 1961. Repr. 1970.

3405   —. *Shakespeare and the Rose of Love: A Study of the Early Plays in Relation to the Medieval Philosophy of Love.* London: Chatto & Windus, 1960. Repr. New York: Barnes & Noble. [*LLL, TGV, Rom.*]

3406   —. *The Shakespearean Ethic.* London: Chatto & Windus, 1959. Repr. New York: Barnes & Noble.

3407   WAGNER, Bernard M., ed. *The Appreciation of Shakespeare: A Collection of Criticism—Philosophic, Literary, and Esthetic—by Great Writers and Scholar-Critics of the Eighteenth, Nineteenth, and Twentieth Centuries.* Georgetown U.P., 1949.

3408   WAIN, John. *The Living World of Shakespeare: A Playgoer's Guide.* London: Macmillan, 1964. Repr. New York: St. Martin's. [Pelican A824.]

3409   WALDER, Ernest. *Shaksperian Criticism, Textual and Literary, from Dryden to the End of the Eighteenth Century.* Bradford: T. Brear, 1895. Repr. New York: AMS.

3410   WALKER, Roy O. "The Celestial Plane in Shakespeare." *ShS 8* (1955), pp. 109-117.

3411   WARNER, Beverley E., ed. *Famous Introductions to Shakespeare's Plays by the Notable Editors of the Eighteenth Century.* New York: Mead, 1906. Repr. New York: Franklin; New York: AMS.

3412   WARTON, Joseph. *The Adventurer.* Ed. John Hawkesworth. London: J. Payne, 1752-54. Repr. as vols. 23-25 of *British Essayists.* Ed. Alexander Chalmers. 45 vols. London: J. Johnson, 1802-3. Repr. many times. [Nos. 93, 97, 113, 116, and 122 treat of *Tmp* and *Lr.*]

3413   WASSERMAN, Earl R. "Shakespeare and the English Romantic Movement." In *Essays in Honor of Robert W. Babcock,* **2810.**

3414   WATKINS, Walter B. C. *Shakespeare and Spenser.* Princeton U.P., 1950. [Princeton U P 60.]

3415   WEBSTER, Margaret. *Shakespeare Today.* London: Dent, 1957.

3416   WEILGART, Wolfgang. *Shakespeare's Psychognostic: Character Evolution and Transformation.* Tokyo: Hokuseido, 1952. Repr. New York: AMS.

3417   WEIMANN, Robert. "The Soul of the Age: Towards a Historical Approach to Shakespeare." In *Shakespeare in a Changing World,* **2792.**

3418   WELLS, Stanley. "Happy Endings in Shakespeare." *SJ 1966* (West), pp. 103-23.

3419   —. "Shakespeare Criticism since Bradley." In *A New Companion to Shakespeare Studies,* **2800.**

3420   WEST, Robert H. *Shakespeare and the Outer Mystery.* U. of Kentucky P., 1968. [*Mac, Ham, Oth, Lr, Tmp.*]

3421   WESTFALL, Alfred V. *American Shakespearean Criticism, 1607-1865.* New York: Wilson, 1939. Repr. New York: Blom.

3422   WHITAKER, Virgil K. *Shakespeare's Use of Learning.* San Marino, Calif.: Huntington Library, 1953.

3423   WHITEHOUSE, John H. *The Boys of Shakespeare.* Birmingham, Eng.: Cornish, 1953.

3424   WHITER, Walter. *A Specimen of a Commentary on Shakespeare.* London: T. Cadell, 1794. Repr. London: Methuen; New York: Barnes & Noble; AMS. Rev. ed., *A Specimen of a Commentary, Being the Text of the First (1794) Edition Revised by the Author and Never Previously Published.* Ed. Alan Over, completed by Mary Bell. London: Methuen, 1967. [Notes on *AYL.* First study of imagery.]

3425   Canceled.

3426   WILLCOCK, Gladys D. *Language and Poetry in Shakespeare's Early Plays.* Oxford U.P., 1954. [*PBA 1954,* 40 (1955): 103-17.]

3427   —. "Shakespeare and Elizabethan English." *ShS* 7 (1954), pp. 12-24.

3428   —. *Shakespeare as a Critic of Language.* Oxford U.P., 1934.

3429   WILLIAMS, Charles. "The Cycle of Shakespeare." In *The English Poetic Mind.* Oxford U.P., 1932.

3430   WILSON, Edwin, ed. *Shaw on Shakespeare.* New York: Dutton, 1961.

3431   WILSON, Frank P. *Marlowe and the Early Shakespeare.* Oxford U.P., 1953.

3432   —. *The Proverbial Wisdom of Shakespeare.* Presidential Address, 1961. Cambridge: Modern Humanities Research Association, 1961.

3433   —. *Shakespeare and the Diction of Common Life.* Oxford U.P., 1941. [*PBA 1941,* 27 (1942): 167-97.]

3434   WILSON, J. Dover. *The Elizabethan Shakespeare.* Oxford U.P., 1929. [*PBA 1929,* 15 (1930):101-25.]

3435   —. *The Essential Shakespeare.* Cambridge U.P., 1932. [CUP 110.]

3436   WITHINGTON, Robert. "Shakespeare and Race Prejudice." In *Elizabethan Studies . . . in Honor of George F. Reynolds,* 2821. [*MV, Oth.*]

3437   WRIGHT, James. *Country Conversations.* London: H. Bonwicke, 1694. [Modern comedy, poets, and poetry.]

3438   WRIGHT, Louis B. *Shakespeare for Everyman.* New York: Washington Square, 1964. [W1081 WSP.]

3439   YEATS, William B. "At Stratford-on-Avon." In *Essays and Introductions.* New York: Macmillan, 1961. Repr. 1968 [Collier 05561.]

3440   YODER, Audrey. *Animal Analogy in Shakespeare's Character Portrayal.* New York: King's Crown; Oxford U.P., 1948.

3441   YOUNG, George M. *Shakespeare and the Termers.* Oxford U.P. 1947. [*PBA 1947,* 33 (1948): 81-99.]

3442   YOUNG, Karl. "Samuel Johnson on Shakespeare: One Aspect." In *Studies by Members of the Department of English, Series No. 3.* U of Wisconsin Studies in Language and Literature, No. 18.   Madison 1923.

3443   ZACHRISSON, Robert E. *The English Pronunciation at Shakespeare's Time As Taught by William Bullokar.* Uppsala: Almquist & Widsell, 1927.   Repr. New York: AMS.

THE COMEDIES

See also **3067** and **4403**.

3444   AUDEN, Wystan H. "Notes on the Comic." In *The Dyer's Hand*, **2838**. [*TN, 1H4, MND.*]

3445   BARBER, Cesar L. *Shakespeare's Festive Comedy.* Princeton U.P., 1959. [*LLL, MND, MV, H4, AYL, TN.*]

3446   BAXTER, John S. "Present Mirth: Shakespeare's Romantic Comedies." *QQ*, 72 (1965): 52-77.

3447   BERMAN, Ronald S. "Shakespearean Comedy and the Uses of Reason." *SAQ*, 63 (1964): 1-9.

3448   BERRY, Francis. "Word and Picture in the Final Plays." In *Later Shakespeare*, **2767**.

3449   BLISTEIN, Elmer M. *Comedy in Action.* Duke U.P., 1964.

3450   BONAZZA, Blaze O. *Shakespeare's Early Comedies: A Structural Analysis*. The Hague: Mouton, 1966.

3451   BORINSKI, Ludwig. "Shakespeare's Comic Prose." *ShS 8* (1955), pp. 57-68.

3452   BOUGHNER, Daniel C. *The Braggart in Renaissance Comedy.* U. of Minnesota P., 1954.

3453   BRADBROOK, Muriel C. *The Growth and Structure of Elizabethan Comedy.* London: Chatto & Windus, 1955. [Peregrine Y30.]

3454   —. *Shakespeare's Primitive Art.* See **2881**.

3455   BROOKS, Charles. "Shakespeare's Romantic Shrews." *SQ*, 11 (1960): 351-56.

3456   BROWN, Arthur. "Shakespeare's Treatment of Comedy." In *Shakespeare's World*, **2818**.

3457   BROWN, John R. "The Interpretation of Shakespeare's Comedies, 1900-1953." *ShS 8* (1955), pp. 1-13.

3458   —. "Laughter in the Last Plays." In *Later Shakespeare*, **2767**.

3459   —. *Shakespeare and His Comedies.* London: Methuen, 1957. 2nd ed. enl., 1962. [UP239 B&N.]

3460   CAZAMIAN, Louis F. *The Development of English Humour.* Duke U.P., 1952. [3 chaps. on Sh.]

3461   —. *L'Humour de Shakespeare.* Paris: Aubier, 1945.

3462   CECIL, David. "Shakespearean Comedy." In *The Fine Art of Reading and Other Literary Studies.* London: Constable; New York: Bobbs-Merrill, 1957.

3463   CHAMPION, Larry S. *The Evolution of Shakespeare's Comedy: A Study in Dramatic Perspective.* Harvard U.P., 1970.

3464   CHARLTON, Henry B. *Shakespearian Comedy.* London: Methuen, 1938. [B&N UP156.]

3465   CODY, Richard. *The Landscape of the Mind.* Oxford U.P., 1969. [Sh's early comedies and Italian tragedies, *TGV, LLL, MND.*]

3466   COGHILL, Nevill. "The Basis of Shakespearian Comedy." *E&S,* 3 (1950): 1-28.

3467   CONN, Naomi. "The Promise of Arcadia: Nature and the Natural Man in Shakespeare's Comedies." In *Shakespeare Encomium,* **2802.**

3468   CRANE, Milton. "Shakespeare's Comedies and the Critics." *SQ,* 15.2 (1964): 67-73. Also in *Shakespeare 400,* **2793.**

3469   CURRY, John V. *Deception in Elizabethan Comedy.* Loyola U.P., 1955.

3470   CUTTS, John P. *Rich and Strange: A Study of Shakespeare's Last Plays.* Washington State U.P., 1968.

3471   DANBY, John F. "Sidney and the Late-Shakespearean Romance." In *Poets on Fortune's Hill,* **2956.**

3472   DESAI, Chiatamoni N. *Shakespearean Comedy.* Indore City: Agra U.P., 1952. Repr. New York: AMS.

3473   DRAPER, John W. "Mistaken Identity in Shakespeare's Comedies." *Revue Anglo-Americaine,* 11 (1933-34): 289-97.

3474   EDWARDS, Philip. "Shakespeare's Romances: 1900-1957." *ShS 11* (1958), pp. 1-18.

3475   EVANS, Bertrand. *Shakespeare's Comedies.* Oxford U.P., 1960. [OUP 128.]

3476   EVANS, Hugh C. "Comic Constables—Fictional and Historical." *SQ,* 20 (1969): 427-33. [*LLL, MM, Ado.*]

3477   FARNHAM, Willard E. "The Mediaeval Comic Spirit in the English Renaissance." In *Adams Memorial Studies,* **2794.**

3478   FELVER, Charles S. "The *Commedia dell'Arte* and English Drama in the Sixteenth and Early Seventeenth Centuries." *RenD,* 6 (1963): 24-34.

3479   FISCHER, Walther. "Shakespeares späte Romanzen." *SJ,* 91 (1955): 7-24.

3480   FRYE, Northrop. "The Argument of Comedy." In *EIE 1948,* **2979.**

3481   —. "Characterization in Shakespearian Comedy." *SQ,* 4 (1953): 271-77.

3482   —. *A Natural Perspective: The Development of Shakespearean Comedy and Romance.* Columbia U.P., 1965.

3483   —. "Old and New Comedy." In *ShS 22,* **3530.**

3484   GORDON, George S. *Shakespearian Comedy, and Other Studies.* See **3031.**

3485   GREENLAW, Edwin. "Shakespeare's Pastorals." *SP*; see **2735.**

3486   GRENE, David. *Reality and the Heroic Pattern: Last Plays of Ibsen, Shakespeare, and Sophocles.* Chicago U.P., 1967.

3487   GRIVELET, Michel. "Shakespeare, Molière, and the Comedy of Ambiguity." In *ShS 22*, **3530**. [Esp. *Err.*]

3488   HAWKINS, Sherman. "The Two Worlds of Shakespearean Comedy." *ShakS 3 1967* (1968), pp. 62-80.

3489   HAZLITT, William. *Lectures on the English Comic Writers.* London: Taylor & Hessey, 1819. Repr. London: Dent, 1963. [Doubleday Dolphin.]

3490   HERBERT, T. Walter. "The Villain and the Happy End of Shakespeare Comedy." *RenP 1966* (1967), pp. 69-74.

3491   HERRICK, Marvin T. *Comic Theory in the Sixteenth Century.* U. of Illinois P., 1950.

3492   HUBLER, Edward L. "The Range of Shakespeare's Comedy." *SQ*, 15.2 (1964): 55-66. Also in *Shakespeare 400*, **2793**.

3493   HUNTER, George K. *Shakespeare: The Late Comedies.* London: Longmans, Green, 1962.

3494   HUNTER, Robert G. *Shakespeare and the Comedy of Forgiveness.* Columbia U.P., 1965. [*Ado, AWW, Cym, WT.*]

3495   INGRAM, R. W. "Musical Pauses and the Vision Scenes in Shakespeare's Last Plays." In *Pacific Coast Studies in Shakespeare*, **2796**.

3496   JAMES, David G. "The Failure of the Ballad Makers." In *Scepticism and Poetry*, **3096**. [Last plays.]

3497   KANTAK, V. Y. "An Approach to Shakespearian Comedy." In *ShS 22*, **3530**.

3498   KAUL, A. N. *The Action of English Comedy: Studies in the Encounter of Abstraction and Experience from Shakespeare to Shaw.* Yale U.P., 1970.

3499   KERMODE, J. Frank. *Shakespeare: The Final Plays.* London: Longmans, Green, 1963.

3500   KNIGHT, G. Wilson. *The Crown of Life: Essays in Interpretations of Shakespeare's Final Plays.* London: Methuen, 1947. Repr. New York: Barnes & Noble. [UP B&N 57.]

3501   LASCELLES, Mary M. *Shakespeare's Comic Insight.* Oxford U.P., 1962. [*PBA 1962*, 48 (1963): 171-86.]

3502   LAWRENCE, William W. *Shakespeare's Problem Comedies.* New York: Macmillan, 1931. 2nd ed., New York: Ungar, 1960. [Penguin.] [*AWW, MM, Tro, Cym.*]

3503   LEAVIS, Frank R. "The Criticism of Shakespeare's Late Plays." In *The Common Pursuit*, **3151**.

3504   LEECH, Clifford. "Shakespeare's Comic Dukes." *REL*, 5 (1964): 101-14.

3505   ——. "The Structure of the Last Plays." In *ShS 11*, **3529**.

3506   ——. TN *and Shakespearean Comedy.* See **2661**.

3507   LERNER, Laurence, ed. *Shakespeare's Comedies: An Anthology of Modern Criticism.* Middlesex, Eng.: Penguin, 1967. [PSL2 Penguin.] [35 sel. from prev. pub. wks.]

3508   MARSH, Derick R. C.   *The Recurring Miracle: A Study of* Cym *and the Last Plays.* See **985**.

3509   MARTZ, William J. *Shakespeare's Universe of Comedy.* London: Methuen, 1970. [*Shr, MND, AYL, Ado, TN.*]

3510   MEADER, William G. *Courtship in Shakespeare: Its Relation to the Tradition of Courtly Love.* Columbia U.P., 1954.

3511   MINCOFF, Marco. "Shakespeare and Lyly." In *ShS 14,* **3917**.

3512   —. "Shakespeare's Comedies and the Five-Act Structure." *BFLS*, 63 (1965): 131-46.

3513   MUIR, Kenneth. *Last Periods of Shakespeare, Ibsen, Racine.* Wayne State U.P., 1961.

3514   —, ed. *Shakespeare, the Comedies: A Collection of Critical Essays.* Englewood Cliffs, N.J.: Prentice-Hall, 1965. [STC47 Spec P-H.] [12 sel. from prev. pub. wks.]

3515   OLSON, Elder. *The Theory of Comedy.* Indiana U.P., 1968.

3516   ORNSTEIN, Robert T. "Shakespearian and Jonsonian Comedy." In *ShS 22,* **3530**.

3517   PALMER, John L. *Comic Characters of Shakespeare.* London: Macmillan, 1946. Repr. in *Political and Comic Characters of Shakespeare,* **3237**. [Berowne, Touchstone, Shylock, Bottom, Beatrice, Benedick.]

3518   PARROTT, Thomas M. *Shakespearean Comedy.* Oxford U.P., 1949.

3519   PETTET, Ernest C. *Shakespeare and the Romance Tradition.* London: Staples, 1949. Repr. London: Methuen, 1970.

3520   PHIALAS, Peter G. "Comic Truth in Shakespeare and Jonson." *SAQ*, 62 (1963): 78-91.

3521   —. *Shakespeare's Romantic Comedies.* U. of North Carolina P., 1966.

3522   PRIESTLEY, John B. *The English Comic Characters.* London: Lane, 1925. [Bottom, Touchstone, the Illyrians, Falstaff.]

3523   QUILLER-COUCH, Arthur T. "Shakespeare's Comedies." In *Studies in Literature, Third Series.* Cambridge U.P., 1929.

3524   SALINGAR, L. G. "Time and Art in Shakespeare's Romances." *RenD*, 9 (1966): 3-35.

3525   SANDERS, Norman. "The Comedy of Greene and Shakespeare." In *Early Shakespeare,* **2766**.

3526   SEHRT, Ernst T. *Wandlungen der Shakespeareschen Komödie.* Göttingen: Vandenhoeck & Reprecht, 1961.

3527   SEN GUPTA, Subodh C. *Shakespearian Comedy.* Calcutta, New York, London: Oxford U.P., 1950. Repr. 1968.

3528 SHAABER, Matthias A. "The Comic View of Life in Shakespeare's Comedies." In *The Drama of the Renaissance,* **2763**.

3529 *ShS 11* (1958). [7 essays on last plays.]

3530 *ShS 22* (1969). [11 essays on comedies.]

3531 SPENCER, Theodore. "Appearance and Reality in Shakespeare's Last Plays." *MP*, 39 (1942): 265-74.

3532 SPRAGUE, Arthur C. "The Moments of Seriousness in Shakespearian Comedy." *SJ 1965* (West), pp. 240-47.

3533 STERNFELD, Frederick W. "Le Symbolisme dans quelques pièces de Shakespeare presentées à la cour d'Angleterre." In *Les Fêtes de la Renaissance.* Ed. Jean Jacquot. 2 vols. Paris: Centre National de la Recherche Scientifique, 1956-60.

3534 STEVENSON, David L. *The Love-Game Comedy.* Columbia U.P., 1946. Repr. New York: AMS. [3 chaps. on Sh.]

3535 STRACHEY, G. Lytton. "Shakespeare's Final Period." In *Books and Characters.* New York: Harcourt, Brace, 1922.

3536 STYAN, John L. *The Dark Comedy.* Cambridge U.P., 1962.

3537 TAVE, Stuart M. "Corbyn Morris: Falstaff, Humor, and Comic Theory in the Eighteenth Century." *MP*, 50 (1952-53): 102-15.

3538 THOMPSON, Karl F. "Shakespeare's Romantic Comedies." *PMLA* , 67 (1952): 1079-93.

3539 TILLYARD, Eustace M. W. *The Nature of Comedy and Shakespeare.* Oxford U.P., 1958. Repr. in *Essays Literary and Educational,* **3382** .

3540 ——. *Shakespeare's Early Comedies.* New York: Barnes & Noble, 1965.

3541 ——. *Shakespeare's Last Plays.* London: Chatto & Windus, 1938. Repr. 1951; New York: Barnes & Noble.

3542 TRAVERSI, Derek A. *Shakespeare: The Last Phase.* London: Hollis & Carter, 1954.

3543 ——. *William Shakespeare: The Early Comedies.* London: Longmans, Green, 1960. 2nd ed. rev., 1964.

3544 VYVYAN, John. *Shakespeare and Platonic Beauty.* See **3404**.

3545 WELLS, Stanley. "Shakespeare and Romance." In *Later Shakespeare,* **2767**.

3546 WILSON, J. Dover. *Shakespeare's Happy Comedies.* London: Faber & Faber, 1962.

3547 WIMSATT, William K., ed. *English Stage Comedy. EIE 1954* (1955). [Incl. essays on *H4* and *Tmp.*]

3548 WINCOR, Richard. "Shakespeare's Festival Plays." *SQ*, 1 (1950): 219-40.

3549 WINSLOW, Ola E. *Low Comedy as a Structural Element in English Drama from the Beginnings to 1642.* Chicago U.P., 1926.

THE HISTORY PLAYS

See also **3274, 3284, 3671, 3738, 3747,** and **3755.**

3550 ALLEN, John W. *A History of Political Thought in the Sixteenth Century*. London: Methuen, 1928. 2nd ed., 1941.

3551 ARMSTRONG, William A. "The Elizabethan Conception of the Tyrant." *RES*, 22 (1946): 161-81.

3552 ——. "The Influence of Seneca and Machiavelli on the Elizabethan Tyrant." *RES*, 24 (1948): 19-35.

3553 BERMAN, Ronald S. "Shakespeare's Conscious Histories." *DR*, 41 (1962): 485-95.

3554 BETHELL, Samuel L. "The Comic Element in Shakespeare's Histories." *Anglia*, 71 (1952): 82-101.

3555 BORINSKI, Ludwig. "Shakespeare's Conception of History." *BFLS*, 63 (1965): 47-66.

3556 BRUNNER, Karl. "Middle-Class Attitudes in Shakespeare's Histories." *ShS 6* (1953), pp. 36-38.

3557 BULLOUGH, Geoffrey. "The Uses of History." In *Shakespeare's World*, **2818.**

3558 CAMPBELL, Lily B. *Shakespeare's "Histories," Mirrors of Elizabethan Policy*. San Marino, Calif.: Huntington Library, 1947. Repr. London: Methuen, 1964.

3559 CANNING, Albert S. G. *Thoughts on Shakespeare's Historical Plays*. London: Allen, 1884.

3560 CHAPMAN, Raymond. "The Wheel of Fortune in Shakespeare's Historical Plays." *RES*, 1 (1950): 1-7.

3561 CLEMEN, Wolfgang. "Anticipation and Foreboding in Shakespeare's Early Histories." *ShS 6* (1953), pp. 25-35.

3562 ——. "Shakespeare und das Königtum." *SJ*, 68 (1932): 56-79.

3563 CRAIG, Hardin. "Shakespeare and the History Play." In *Adams Memorial Studies*, **2794.**

3564 DAVID, Richard. "Shakespeare's History Plays: Epic or Drama?" *ShS 6* (1953), pp. 129-39.

3565 DEAN, Leonard F. "*R2* to *H5:* A Closer View." In *Studies in Honor of DeWitt T. Starnes*, **2784.**

3566 DORIUS, Raymond J., ed. *Discussions of Shakespeare's Histories: R2 to H5*. Boston: Heath, 1964. [14 prev. pub. essays, 18th-20th century.]

3567 ——. "A Little More Than a Little: Prudence and Excess in *R2* and the Histories." *SQ*, 11 (1960): 13-26. [Esp. *H4, H5.*]

3568 FORKER, Charles R. "Shakespeare's Chronicle Plays as Historical-Pastoral." *ShakS 1* (1965), pp. 85-104.

3569   FREEMAN, Leslie. "Shakespeare's Kings and Machiavelli's Prince." In *Shakespeare Encomium,* **2802.**

3570   HAPGOOD, Robert. "Shakespeare's Thematic Modes of Speech: *R2* to *H5.*" *ShS 20* (1967), pp. 41-49.

3571   HENNEKE, Agnes. "Shakespeares Englische Könige." *SJ,* 66 (1930): 79-144.

3572   HUMPHREYS, Arthur R. "Shakespeare and the Tudor Perception of History." In *Stratford Papers on Shakespeare, 1964,* **2787.** Repr. in *Shakespeare Celebrated,* **2825.**

3573   —. *Shakespeare's Histories and "The Emotion of Multitude."* Oxford U.P., 1968. [*PBA 1968,* 54 (1970): 265-87.]

3574   HUNTER, George K. "Shakespeare's Politics and the Rejection of Falstaff." *CritQ;* see **1234.**

3575   JENKINS, Harold. "Shakespeare's History Plays: 1900-1951." *ShS 6* (1953), pp. 1-15.

3576   KELLER, Wolfgang. "Shakespeares Königsdramen." *SJ,* 63 (1927): 35-53.

3577   KELLY, Henry A. *Divine Providence in the England of Shakespeare's Histories.* Cambridge U.P., 1970.

3578   KERNAN, Alvin B. "The Henriad: Shakespeare's Major History Plays." *YR,* 59 (1969): 3-32.

3579   KINGSFORD, Charles L. *English Historical Literature in the Fifteenth Century.* Oxford U.P., 1913. Repr. New York: Franklin. [Sh passim.]

3580   KNIGHTS, Lionel C. *Shakespeare: The Histories.* London: Longmans, Green, 1962. [*R3, Jn, R2, H5.*]

3581   LA GUARDIA, Eric. "Ceremony and History: The Problem of Symbol from *R2* to *H5.*" In *Pacific Coast Studies in Shakespeare,* **2796.**

3582   LAW, Robert A. "Links between Shakespeare's History Plays." *SP,* 50 (1953): 168-87.

3583   LEECH, Clifford. *Shakespeare: The Chronicles.* London: Longmans, Green, 1962. [*H6, H4, Wiv, H8.*]

3584   MACLEAN, Hugh. "Time and Horsemanship in Shakespeare's Histories." *UTQ,* 35 (1965-66): 229-45.

3585   MANHEIM, Michael. "The Weak King History Play of the Early 1590's." *RenD,* 2 (1969): 71-80. [*Jn; 1, 2, 3 H6; R2.*]

3586   MESSIAEN, Pierre. "Drames historiques de Shakespeare: Style oratoirs, style lyrique, style dramatique." *Revue Universitaire,* 48 (1939): 23-31.

3587   MICHEL, Laurence A., and Cecil C. Seronsy. "Shakespeare's History Plays and Daniel." *SP,* 52 (1955): 549-77.

3588   MOORMAN, Frederic W. "Shakespeare's History-Plays and Daniel's *Civile Wars.*" *SJ*, 40 (1904): 69-83.

3589   MORTON, A. L. "Shakespeare's Historical Outlook." *SJ* (East), 100/101 (1965): 208-26.

3590   MROZ, Mary B. *Divine Vengeance: A Study in the Philosophical Backgrounds of the Revenge Motif As It Appears in Shakespeare's Chronicle History Plays.* Catholic U.P., 1941.

3591   MUIR, Kenneth. "Source Problems in the Histories." *SJ*, 96 (1960): 47-63. [Esp. *R2.*]

3592   PEARCE, Josephine A. "Constituent Elements in Shakespeare's English History Plays." In *Studies in Shakespeare*, 2797.

3593   QUINN, Michael. "Providence in Shakespeare's Yorkist Plays." *SQ*, 10 (1959): 45-52.

3594   REESE, Max M. *The Cease of Majesty.* London: Arnold, 1961.

3595   RIBNER, Irving. *The English History Play in the Age of Shakespeare.* Princeton U.P., 1957. Rev. and enl. ed., New York: Barnes & Noble; London: Methuen, 1965. [Bibliog.]

3596   ——. "Shakespeare's History Plays Revisited." *BFLS*, 63 (1965): 67-74.

3597   RICHARDSON, Arleigh D. "The Early Historical Plays." In *Shakespeare: Of an Age and for All Time*, 2803.

3598   ROGERS, William N. *Shakespeare and English History.* Totowa, N.J.: Littlefield, Adams, 1966. [Littlefield 31.]

3599   SCHELLING, Felix E. *The English Chronicle Play: A Study in the Popular Historical Literature Environing Shakespeare.* New York: Macmillan, 1902. Repr. New York: Franklin; AMS.

3600   SCOTT-GILES, Charles W. *Shakespeare's Heraldry.* London: Dent, 1950.

3601   SEN GUPTA, Subodh C. *Shakespeare's Historical Plays.* Oxford U.P., 1964.

3602   SPRAGUE, Arthur C. *Shakespeare's Histories: Plays for the Stage.* London: Society for Theatre Research, 1964.

3603   STRIBRNÝ, Zdeněk. *Shakespeare's History Plays.* Prague: Czechoslovak Academy of Sciences, 1959. Repr. New York: AMS.

3604   SZENCZI, Miklos. "The Nature of Shakespeare's Realism." *SJ* (East), 102 (1966): 37-59.

3605   TALBERT, Ernest W. *The Problem of Order.* U. North Carolina P., 1962.

3606   THAYER, C. G. "Shakespeare's Second Tetralogy: An Underground Report." *OUR*, 9 (1967): 5-15.

3607   TILLYARD, Eustace M. W. "Shakespeare's Historical Cycle: Organism or Compilation?" *SP*, 51 (1954): 34-39.

3608   ——. *Shakespeare's History Plays.* London: Chatto & Windus, 1944. Repr. 1964. [Collier 01286.] [Incl. *Mac.*]

3609   TRAVERSI, Derek A. *Shakespeare from R2 to H5.* Stanford U.P., 1957. Repr. 1968.

3610   TURNER, Robert Y. "Characterization in Shakespeare's Early History Plays." *ELH*, 31 (1964): 241-58.

3611   ——. "Shakespeare and the Public Confrontation Scene in Early History Plays." *MP*, 62 (1964): 1-12.

3612   WAITH, Eugene M., ed. *Shakespeare: The Histories.* Englewood Cliffs, N.J.: Prentice-Hall, 1965. [Introd. and 11 sel. from prev. pub. modern wks.]

3613   WEBBER, Joan. "The Renewal of the King's Symbolic Role: From *R2* to *H5*." *TSLL*, 4 (1962-63): 530-38.

3614   WINNY, James. *The Player King: A Study of Shakespeare's Later History Plays.* New York: Barnes & Noble, 1968.

3615   ZEEVELD, W. Gordon. "The Influence of Hall on Shakespeare's English Historical Plays." *ELH*, 3 (1936): 317-53.

THE TRAGEDIES

See also **1624, 1767, 2937, 3065, 3817, 3897, 3941, 4236, 4419,** and **4422.**

3616   ADAMS, Robert P. "Shakespeare's Tragic Vision." In *Pacific Coast Studies in Shakespeare*, **2796.**

3617   BAKER, Howard. *Induction to Tragedy*. Louisiana State U.P., 1939. Repr. New York: Russell & Russell. [*Tit.*]

3618   BARROLL, J. Leeds. "Ethical Premises in Shakespearean Criticism." *SRO*, 2 (1966): 24-37.

3619   ——. "Shakespeare and Roman History." *MLR*, 53 (1958): 327-43 . [*Ant, Cor, JC.*]

3620   BATTENHOUSE, Roy W. *Shakespearean Tragedy: Its Art and Its Christian Premises*. Indiana U.P., 1969.

3621   BLACK, Matthew W. "Aristotle's 'Mythos' and the Tragedies of Shakespeare." *SJ 1968* (West), pp. 43-55.

3622   ——. "*Hamartia* in Shakespeare." *LC*, 30 (1964): 100-116.

3623   BOWERS, Fredson T. "Death in Victory." *SoAB*, 30 (1965): 1-7. Expanded version in *Studies in Honor of DeWitt T. Starnes*, **2784.** [Esp. *Ham, Ant.*]

3624   BOYER, Clarence V. *The Villain as Hero in Elizabethan Tragedy*. London: Routledge; New York: Dutton, 1914.

3625   BRADBROOK, Muriel C. *Themes and Conventions in Elizabethan Tragedy*. Cambridge U.P., 1935. [CUP.]

3626   BRADLEY, Andrew C. *Shakespearean Tragedy: Lectures on* Ham, Oth, Lr, Mac. London: Macmillan, 1904. Repr. New York: St. Martin's. [Premier M263; St. Martin's.]

3627   BRERETON, Geoffrey. *Principles of Tragedy: A Rational Examination of the Tragic Concept in Life and Literature*. U. of Miami Press, 1969. [*Mac* and *Ham.*]

3628   BROOKE, Nicholas. *Shakespeare's Early Tragedies*. London: Methuen, 1968.

3629   ——. "The Tragic Spectacle in *Tit* and *Rom.*" In *Shakespeare: The Tragedies*, **3686.**

3630   BROWN, Huntington. "Enter the Shakespearean Tragic Hero." *EIC,* 3 (1953): 285-302.

3631   CALARCO, Joseph N. *Tragic Being: Apollo and Dionysus in Western Drama*. U. of Minnesota P., 1969. [Esp. *Lr,* Sh passim.]

3632   CAMPBELL, Lewis. *Tragic Drama in Aeschylus, Sophocles, and Shakespeare*. London: Smith, Elder, 1904. Repr. New York: Russell & Russell.

3633   CAMPBELL, Lily B. *Shakespeare's Tragic Heroes: Slaves of Passion*. Cambridge U.P., 1930. [B&N 433.]

3634 CHARLTON, Henry B. *Shakespearian Tragedy.* Cambridge U.P., 1948.

3635 CHARNEY, Maurice, ed. *Discussions of Shakespeare's Roman Plays.* Boston: Heath, 1964. [14 prev. pub. essays.]

3636 ——. "The Persuasiveness of Violence in Elizabethan Plays." *RenD*, 2 (1969): 59-70. [Incl. *Lr* and *Mac.*]

3637 ——. *Shakespeare's Roman Plays.* Harvard U.P., 1961.

3638 ——. "Shakespeare's Style in *JC* and *Ant.*" *ELH*, 26 (1959): 355-67.

3639 CLEMEN, Wolfgang. *Die Tragödie vor Shakespeare.* Heidelberg: Quelle & Meyer, 1955. Trans.Theodor S. Dorsch as *English Tragedy before Shakespeare.* London: Methuen, 1961. [B&N 205.]

3640 COX, Roger L. *Between Earth and Heaven: Shakespeare, Dostoevsky, and the Meaning of Christian Tragedy.* New York: Holt, Rinehart, and Winston, 1969. [*Ham, Lr, Mac.*]

3641 CUNLIFFE, John W. *The Influence of Seneca on Elizabethan Tragedy.* New York: Macmillan, 1893. Repr. Stechert, 1907; Shoe String P.

3642 CUNNINGHAM, James V. *Woe or Wonder: The Emotional Effect of Shakespearean Tragedy.* U. of Denver P., 1951. Repr. Denver: Swallow, 1964.

3643 DICKEY, Franklin M. *Not Wisely but Too Well: Shakespeare's Love Tragedies.* San Marino, Calif.: Huntington Library, 1957.

3644 DRAPER, John W. "The Humours: Some Psychological Aspects of Shakespeare's Tragedies." *Journal of the American Medical Association*, 188 (1964): 259-62.

3645 ——. "'Hybris' in Shakespeare's Tragic Heroes." *EA*, 18 (1965): 228-34.

3646 ——. "The Realism of Shakespeare's Roman Plays." *SP*, 30 (1933): 225-42.

3647 DYSON, Henry V. D. *The Emergence of Shakespeare's Tragedy.* Oxford U.P., 1953. [*PBA 1950*, 36 (1951): 69-93.]

3648 ELIOT, Thomas S. "Shakespeare and the Stoicism of Seneca." In *Elizabethan Essays,* 3817. Also in *Selected Essays.* London: Faber & Faber, 1934.

3649 EVANS, Gareth L. "Shakespeare, Seneca, and the Kingdom of Violence." In *Roman Drama.* Ed. Thomas A. Dorey and Donald R. Dudley. London: Routledge & Kegan Paul, 1965.

3650 FAIRCHILD, Arthur H. R. *Shakespeare and the Tragic Theme.* U. of Missouri P., 1944.

3651 FARNHAM, Willard E. *The Medieval Heritage of Elizabethan Tragedy.* U. of California P.; Oxford: Blackwell, 1956. Repr. New York: Barnes & Noble.

3652 —. *Shakespeare's Tragic Frontier.* U. of California P., 1950. [85 U of Cal Pr.] [*Tim, Mac, Ant, Cor.*]

3653 FOAKES, Reginald A. "Shakespeare's Later Tragedies." In *Shakespeare, 1564-1964,* **2764.**

3654 FRYE, Northrop. *Fools of Time: Studies in Shakespearean Tragedy.* U. of Toronto P., 1967.

3655 GARDNER, Helen. "Milton's 'Satan' and the Theme of Damnation in Elizabethan Tragedy." *E&S,* 1 (1948): 46-66. [*Mac.*]

3656 GILBERT, Allan H. "Seneca and Criticism of Elizabethan Tragedy." *PQ,* 13 (1934): 370-81.

3657 HADOW, William H. *The Use of the Comic Episode in Tragedy.* English Association Pamphlet, 31. Oxford U.P., 1915. Repr. in Hadow, *Collected Essays.* Oxford U.P., 1928. [Sh passim.]

3658 HAPGOOD, Robert. "Shakespeare's Maimed Rites: The Early Tragedies." *CentR,* 9 (1965): 494-508.

3659 HARBAGE, Alfred, ed. *Shakespeare: The Tragedies, a Collection of Critical Essays.* Englewood Cliffs, N.J.: Prentice-Hall, 1964. [19 sel. from prev. pub. wks.]

3660 HARDISON, Osborne B. "Three Types of Renaissance Catharsis." *RenD,* 2 (1969): 3-22. [Esp. *Ham.*]

3661 HARRISON, George B. *Shakespeare's Tragedies.* London: Routledge & Kegan Paul, 1951. Repr. Oxford U.P., 1969. [Galaxy 267.]

3662 HATHORN, Richmond Y. *Tragedy, Myth, and Mystery.* Indiana U.P., 1962.

3663 HEILMAN, Robert B. "'From Mine Own Knowledge': A Theme in the Late Tragedies." *CentR,* 8 (1964): 17-38.

3664 —. "Manliness in the Tragedies." In *Shakespeare, 1564-1964,* **2764.**

3665 —. "To Know Himself: An Aspect of Tragic Structure." *REL,* 5 (1964): 36-57.

3666 —. *Tragedy and Melodrama: Versions of Experience.* Washington U.P., 1969. [Sh passim.]

3667 —. "'Twere Best Not Know Myself': Othello, Lear, Macbeth." *SQ,* 15.2 (1964): 89-98. Also in *Shakespeare 400,* **2793.**

3668 HENN, Thomas R. "Towards a Shakespearian Synthesis." In *The Harvest of Tragedy.* London: Methuen, 1956. [UP 70.]

3669 HERNDL, George C. *The High Design: English Renaissance Tragedy and the Natural Law.* U.P. of Kentucky, 1970.

3670 HERRICK, Marvin T. *Italian Tragedy in the Renaissance.* Illinois U.P., 1966.

3671 HILL, R. F. "Shakespeare's Early Tragic Mode." *SQ,* 9 (1958): 455-69. [Histories and tragedies.]

3672   HOLLAND, Norman N. "Shakespearean Tragedy and the Three Ways of Psychoanalytic Criticism." *HudR*, 15 (1962): 217-27. Repr. in *Psychoanalysis and Shakespeare,* **3076.**

3673   HOLLOWAY, John. *The Story of the Night.* London: Routledge & Kegan Paul, 1961. [U Neb Pr Bison 172.]

3674   HUNTER, George K. "The Last Tragic Heroes." In *Later Shakespeare,* **2767.**

3675   JAMES, David G. *The Dream of Learning.* Oxford U.P., 1951. [*Ham* and *Lr.*]

3676   JENKINS, Harold. *The Catastrophe in Shakespearean Tragedy.* Edinburgh U.P., 1969.

3677   ——. "The Tragedy of Revenge in Shakespeare and Webster." In *ShS 14,* **3917.**

3678   KETTLE, Arnold. "From *Ham* to *Lr.*" In *Shakespeare in a Changing World,* **2792.**

3679   KIRSCH, James. *Shakespeare's Royal Self.* New York: Putnam, 1966. [*Ham, Lr, Mac.*]

3680   KIRSCHBAUM, Leo. "Shakespeare's Stage Blood." *PMLA,* 64 (1949): 517-29. [*JC* and *Cor.*]

3681   KNIGHT, G. Wilson. *The Imperial Theme: Further Interpretations of Shakespeare's Tragedies.* Oxford U.P., 1931. [UP 58.]

3682   ——. *The Wheel of Fire: Essays in Interpretation of Shakespeare's Sombre Tragedies.* Oxford U.P., 1930. 4th rev. ed., London: Methuen, 1949, repr. 1962. [M 43; UP 12.]

3683   KNIGHTS, Lionel C. "Shakespeare's Tragedies and the Question of Moral Judgment." *Shenandoah,* 19 (1968): 29-45.

3684   KROOK, Dorothea. *Elements of Tragedy.* Yale U.P., 1969. [*Ant.*]

3685   LAWLOR, John J. *The Tragic Sense in Shakespeare.* London: Chatto & Windus, 1960.

3686   LEECH, Clifford, ed. *Shakespeare: The Tragedies, a Collection of Critical Essays.* U. of Chicago P., 1965. [PLC 2.]

3687   ——. *Shakespeare's Tragedies and Other Studies in Seventeenth-Century Drama.* London: Chatto & Windus, 1950.

3688   LENGELER, Rainer. *Tragische Wirklichkeit als groteske Verfremdung bei Shakespeare.* Cologne: Böhlau, 1964.

3689   LERNER, Laurence, ed. *Shakespeare's Tragedies: An Anthology of Modern Criticism.* Harmondsworth: Penguin Books, 1964. [Pelican A645.]

3690   LUCAS, Frank L. *Seneca and Elizabethan Tragedy.* Cambridge U.P., 1922.

3691   McDONALD, Charles O. *The Rhetoric of Tragedy: Form in Stuart Drama.* Massachusetts U.P., 1966. [Sh passim, chap. on *Ham.*]

3692   McFARLAND, Thomas. *Tragic Meanings in Shakespeare.* New York: Random House, 1966. [SLL 1.]

3693   MACK, Maynard. "The Jacobean Shakespeare: Some Observations on the Construction of the Tragedies." In *Jacobean Theatre,* **3795.**

3694   MacLURE, Millar. "Shakespeare and the Lonely Dragon." *UTQ,* 24 (1955): 109-20. [*Tro, Cor, Ant.*]

3695   McNEAL, Thomas H. "Shakespeare's Cruel Queens." *HLQ,* 22 (1958-59): 41-50. [*Lr, Mac, Ado.*]

3696   MARGESON, John M. R. *The Origins of English Tragedy.* Oxford U.P., 1967. [Sh passim.]

3697   MASON, Harold A. *Shakespeare's Tragedies of Love.* London: Chatto & Windus, 1970. [*Rom, Oth, Lr, Ant.*]

3698   MAXWELL, James C. "Shakespeare's Roman Plays, 1900-1956." *ShS 10* (1957), pp. 1-11.

3699   MICHEL, Laurence A. "Yardsticks for Tragedy." *EIC,* 5 (1955): 81-88.

3700   MINCOFF, Marco. "Shakespeare, Fletcher, and Baroque Tragedy." *ShS 20* (1967), pp. 1-15.

3701   ——. "The Structural Pattern of Shakespeare's Tragedies." *ShS 3* (1950), pp. 58-65.

3702   MUIR, Kenneth. *Shakespeare and the Tragic Pattern.* Oxford U.P., 1958. [*PBA 1958,* 44 (1959): 145-62.]

3703   ——. *William Shakespeare: The Great Tragedies.* London: Longmans, Green, 1961.

3704   MULLER, Herbert J. *The Spirit of Tragedy.* New York: Knopf, 1956. [30 pp. on Sh.]

3705   NICOLL, Allardyce. *Studies in Shakespeare.* London: Woolf, 1927.

3706   NOWOTTNY, Winifred M. T. "Shakespeare's Tragedies." In *Shakespeare's World,* **2818.**

3707   PHILLIPS, James E. *The State in Shakespeare's Greek and Roman Plays.* Columbia U.P., 1940.

3708   PRIOR, Moody E. *The Language of Tragedy.* Columbia U.P., 1947. Repr. Gloucester, Mass.: Peter Smith, 1964. [Sh passim, esp. *Rom* and *Lr.*]

3709   PROSER, Matthew N. *The Heroic Image in Five Shakespearean Tragedies.* Princeton U.P., 1965. [*JC, Mac, Oth, Cor, Ant.*]

3710   RIBNER, Irving. *Patterns in Shakespearian Tragedy.* London: Methuen; New York: Barnes & Noble, 1960.

3711   ROSEN, William. *Shakespeare and the Craft of Tragedy.* Harvard U.P., 1960. [*Lr, Mac, Ant, Cor.*]

3712   SCHÜCKING, Levin L. *The Baroque Character of the Elizabethan Tragic Hero.* Oxford U.P., 1938.

3713   ——. *Shakespeare und der Tragödienstil seiner Zeit.* Bern: Funke, 1947.

3714 SCHWARTZ, Elias. "The Idea of the Person in Shakespearean Tragedy." *SQ*, 16 (1965): 39-47.

3715 SEWALL, Richard B. "Ahab's Quenchless Feud: The Tragic Vision in Shakespeare and Melville." *CompD*, 1 (1967): 207-18.

3716 SIEGEL, Paul N. *Shakespearean Tragedy and the Elizabethan Compromise.* New York U.P., 1957.

3717 SISSON, Charles J. *Shakespeare's Tragic Justice.* London: Methuen, 1962.

3718 SOMERVILLE, Henry. *Madness in Shakespearian Tragedy.* London: Richards P., 1929.

3719 SPEAIGHT, Robert. *Nature in Shakespearian Tragedy.* London: Hollis & Carter, 1955. [Collier 01274.] [Incl. *Tmp.*]

3720 SPENCER, Terence J. B. "Shakespeare and the Elizabethan Romans." *ShS 10* (1957), pp. 27-38.

3721 ——. *Shakespeare: The Roman Plays.* London: Longmans, Green, 1963.

3722 SPENCER, Theodore. *Death and Elizabethan Tragedy.* Harvard U.P., 1936.

3723 SPEVACK, Marvin. "Hero and Villain in Shakespeare: On Dualism and Tragedy." *TSL*, 12 (1967): 1-11.

3724 STIRLING, Brents. *Unity in Shakespearian Tragedy.* Columbia U.P., 1956.

3725 TRAVERSI, Derek A. *Shakespeare: The Roman Plays.* Stanford U.P., 1963.

3726 URE, Peter. *Shakespeare and the Inward Self of the Tragic Hero.* U. of Durham P., 1961.

3727 WAITH, Eugene M. *The Herculean Hero in Marlowe, Chapman, Shakespeare, and Dryden.* Columbia U.P., 1962. [*Ant, Cor.*]

3728 WALKER, Roy O. "The Northern Star: An Essay on the Roman Plays." *SQ*, 2 (1951): 287-93. [Incl. *Cym.*]

3729 WATSON, Curtis B. "T. S. Eliot and the Interpretation of Shakespearean Tragedy in Our Time." In *EA*, 17, **2776.**

3730 WEIDHORN, Manfred. "The Relation of Title and Name to Identity in Shakespearean Tragedy." *SEL*, 9 (1969): 303-19.

3731 WEISINGER, Herbert. "The Study of Shakespearean Tragedy since Bradley." *SQ*, 6 (1955): 387-96.

3732 WHITAKER, Virgil K. *The Mirror Up to Nature: The Technique of Shakespeare's Tragedies.* San Marino, Calif.: Huntington Library, 1965.

3733 WILSON, Harold S. *On the Design of Shakespearian Tragedy.* U. of Toronto P., 1957. Repr. 1968. [Canadian U. Paperbacks 76.]

3734 WOOD, Frederick T. "Shakespeare and the Plebs." *E&S*, 18 (1933): 53-73. [*JC, Cor.*]

THE PROBLEM PLAYS

There is no general agreement about what plays to include in this classification. *AWW*, *Ant*, *Ham*, *JC*, *MM*, *Tim*, and *Tro* have been proposed. For valuable discussions, see **2801**, **2870**, **3065**, **3294**, **3383**, **3387**, **3394**, **3494**, **3502**, **3518**, and **3536**.

THE ROMAN PLAYS

The plays usually treated under this heading are *Ant*, *Cor*, *JC*, *Tit*, and sometimes *Cym*. See **153**, **2556**, **3619**, **3623**, **3628**, **3629**, **3635**, **3637**, **3638**, **3641**, **3645**, **3646**, **3658**, **3663**, **3671**, **3674**, **3680**, **3681**, **3694**, **3698**, **3707**, **3709**, **3720**, **3721**, **3725**, **3727**, **3728**, **3734**, **3758**, **3759**, and **3761**.

THE ROMANCES

Strictly speaking, these are *Cym*, *Per*, *Tmp*, and *WT*; but *H8* is sometimes considered, and there are romance elements in the romantic comedies. See **2439**, **2864**, **2979**, **3458**, **3459**, **3463**, **3464**, **3466**, **3467**, **3470**, **3471**, **3472**, **3474**, **3475**, **3479**, **3480**, **3482**, **3485**, **3486**, **3493**, **3494**, **3495**, **3496**, **3499**, **3500**, **3503**, **3505**, **3508**, **3513**, **3518**, **3519**, **3524**, **3527**, **3529**, **3530**, **3531**, **3535**, **3541**, **3542**, **3545**, **3735**, **3743**, **3831**, **4390**, **4403**, and **4412**.

Special Topics

SOURCES

See **128** for bibliography of foreign sources.

3735 ADAMS, Martha L. "The Greek Romance and William Shakespeare." *SEL,* 8 (1967): 43-52. [*Rom, Ant, AWW, Ado, MM.*]

3736 BALDWIN, Thomas W. "Perseus Purloins Pegasus." *PQ,* 20 (1941): 361-70. [Use of Ovid, esp. *H5, Tro.*]

3737 BORINSKI, Ludwig. "The Origin of the Euphuistic Novel and Its Significance for Shakespeare." In *Studies in Honor of T. W. Baldwin,* **2760.**

3738 BOSWELL-STONE, Walter G., ed. *Shakespeare's Holinshed: The Chronicle and the Plays Compared.* London and New York: Longmans, Green, 1896. 2nd ed., London: Chatto & Windus; New York: Duffield, 1907. [Dover.]

3739 BULLOUGH, Geoffrey, ed. *Narrative and Dramatic Sources of Shakespeare.* London: Routledge & Kegan Paul; Columbia U.P., 1957–. [6 vols., vol. 7 in progress.]

3740 CHWALEWIK, Witold, ed. *Anglo-Polish Renaissance Texts for the Use of Shakespeare Students.* Warsaw: Polish Scientific Publishers, 1968. [Sel. in facs. from Goslicius, Belleforest, Botero, Munday, Cromer, Beard, Ossolinski.]

3741 COGHILL, Nevill. "Shakespeare's Reading in Chaucer." In *Elizabethan and Jacobean Studies Presented to F. P. Wilson,* **2772.**

3742 COULTER, Cornelia C. "The Plautine Tradition in Shakespeare." *JEGP,* 19 (1920): 66-83.

3743 GESNER, Carol. *Shakespeare and the Greek Romance.* U.P. of Kentucky, 1970.

3744 GRIFFIN, Alice S. (Venezky), ed. *The Sources of Ten Shakespearean Plays.* New York: Crowell, 1966. [*Rom, Shr, 1, 2 H4, H5, JC, TN, Oth, Mac, Ant.*]

3745 HODGEN, Margaret T. "Montaigne and Shakespeare Again." *HLQ,* 16 (1952-53): 23-42.

HOLINSHED, Raphael. See **3738, 3747, 3755.**

3746 HONIGMANN, Ernst A. J. "Shakespeare's Plutarch." *SQ,* 10 (1959): 25-33.

3747 HOSLEY, Richard, ed. *Shakespeare's Holinshed.* New York: Putnam, 1968.

3748　　HUNTER, George K. "Shakespeare's Reading." In *A New Companion to Shakespeare Studies,* **2800.**

3749　　KLOSE, Dietrich. "Shakespeare und Ovid." *SJ 1968* (West), pp. 72-93.

3750　　LENNOX, Charlotte. *Shakespear Illustrated; or, The Novels and Histories on Which the Plays . . . Are Founded.*　3 vols.　London: A. Millar, 1753-54.　Repr. New York: AMS.

3751　　MacNALTY, Arthur S. "Shakespeare and Sir Thomas More." *E&S,* 12 (1959): 36-57.　[Infl. of More's writings.]

3752　　MESSIAEN, Pierre. "Shakespeare et l'Histoire romaine."　*Culture,* 2 (1939): 351-57.

3753　　MUIR, Kenneth, ed. *Shakespeare's Sources.*　London: Methuen; New York: Hillary House, 1957.　Repr. New York: Barnes & Noble. [Comedies and tragedies.]

3754　　MURRY, John Middleton. "North's Plutarch." In *Countries of the Mind, Second Series,* **3216.**

3755　　NICOLL, Allardyce, and Josephine Calina, eds.　*Holinshed's Chronicle As Used in Shakespeare's Plays.*　London: Dent, 1927.

　　　　OVID.　See **3756.**

　　　　PLUTARCH.　See **3759, 3761.**

3756　　ROUSE, William H. D., ed. *Shakespeare's Ovid: The Metamorphoses.*　Trans. Arthur Golding.　London: De la More, 1904.　Repr. Southern Illinois U.P., 1961.　[N336 Norton.]

3757　　SATIN, Joseph, ed. *Shakespeare and His Sources.*　Boston: Houghton Mifflin, 1966.　[HM 3-49805.]　[*R3, R2, MV, 1, 2 H4, H5, JC, TN, Ham, Oth, Lr, Mac, Ant.*]

3758　　SCHANZER, Ernest, ed. *Shakespeare's Appian.*　Liverpool U.P., 1956.

3759　　SHACKFORD, Martha H. *Plutarch in Renaissance England.*　N.p.: n.p., 1929.

3760　　SPENCER, Terence J. B., ed. *Elizabethan Love Stories.*　Harmondsworth: Penguin, 1968.　[Penguin SL3.]　[Sources: *AWW, Rom, TN, MM, TGV, Cym, MV, Oth.*]

3761　　—, ed. *Shakespeare's Plutarch.*　Harmondsworth: Penguin, 1964. [Peregrine Books Y43.]

3762　　STAMM, Rudolf. "Elizabethan Stage-Practice and the Transmutation of Source Material by the Dramatists." In *ShS 12,* **4139.**

3763　　TAYLOR, George C. "Montaigne-Shakespeare and the Deadly Parallel." *PQ,* 22 (1943): 330-37.

3764　　THALER, Alwin. *Shakespeare and Sir Philip Sidney: The Influence of* The Defense of Poesy.　Harvard U.P., 1947.

3765　　THORNDIKE, Ashley H. "Shakspere as a Debtor." In *Shaksperian Studies,* **2798.**

3766 TYNAN, Joseph L. "The Influence of Greene on Shakspere's Early Romance." *PMLA,* 27 (1912): 246-64.

3767 WILSON, Frank P. "Shakespeare's Reading." *ShS 3* (1950), pp. 14-21.

3768 WRIGHT, Herbert G. *Boccaccio in England.* London: Athlone, 1957.

BACKGROUND

See also **1048, 2783, 2800, 3079,** and **3114.**

3769   ALLEN, Don C. *Image and Meaning: Metaphoric Traditions in Renaissance Poetry.* Johns Hopkins U.P., 1960. 2nd ed. enl., 1968. [4 new essays, incl. Sh.]

3770   —. *The Star-Crossed Renaissance: The Quarrel about Astrology and Its Influence in England.* Duke U.P., 1941.

3771   ANDERSON, Ruth L. *Elizabethan Psychology and Shakespeare's Plays.* U. of Iowa, 1927. Repr. New York: Russell & Russell.

3772   ARMSTRONG, William A. "The Elizabethan Conception of the Tyrant." *RES;* see **3551.** [*Mac.*]

3773   —. "The Influence of Seneca and Machiavelli on the Elizabethan Tyrant." *RES;* see **3552.** [*Mac.*]

3774   BABB, Lawrence. *The Elizabethan Malady: A Study of Melancholia in English Literature from 1580 to 1642.* Michigan State College P., 1951.

3775   —. "On the Nature of Elizabethan Psychological Literature." In *Adams Memorial Studies,* **2794.**

3776   BARBER, Charles L. *The Idea of Honour in the English Drama, 1591-1700.* Göteborg: Elanders, 1957.

3777   BASKERVILL, Charles R. *The Elizabethan Jig and Related Song Drama.* Chicago U.P., 1929. Repr. New York: Dover.

3778   BEVINGTON, David M. *From* Mankind *to* Marlowe: Growth of Structure in the Popular Drama of Tudor England.* Harvard U.P., 1962.

3779   —. *Tudor Drama and Politics: A Critical Approach to Topical Meaning.* Harvard U.P., 1968.

3780   BIRCH, Thomas. *The Court and Times of James the First.* 2 vols. London: H. Colburn, 1849. Repr. New York: AMS.

3781   —. *Memoirs of the Reign of Queen Elizabeth.* 2 vols. London: A. Millar, 1734. Repr. New York: AMS.

3782   BOAS, Frederick S. *An Introduction to Stuart Drama.* Oxford U.P., 1946.

3783   —. *An Introduction to Tudor Drama.* Oxford U.P., 1933.

3784   —. *Queen Elizabeth in Drama and Related Studies.* London: Allen & Unwin, 1950.

3785   BOWDEN, William R. "The Bed Trick, 1603-1642: Its Mechanics, Ethics, and Effects." *ShakS 5 1969* (1970), pp. 112-23.

3786   —. *English Dramatic Lyric, 1603-42.* Yale U.P., 1951.

3787   BOWERS, Fredson T. *Elizabethan Revenge Tragedy, 1587-1642.* Princeton U.P., 1940. Repr. Gloucester, Mass.: Peter Smith, 1959. [Princeton U Pr 30.]

3788   BRADBROOK, Muriel C. *English Dramatic Form: A History of Its Development.* London: Chatto & Windus, 1965.

3789   BRIGGS, Katharine M. "The Folds of Folklore." In *ShS 17,* **3918.**

3790   ——. *Pale Hecate's Team: An Examination of the Beliefs on Witchcraft and Magic among Shakespeare's Contemporaries and His Immediate Successors.* London: Routledge & Kegan Paul, 1962.

3791   BROTANEK, Rudolf. *Die englischen Maskenspiele.* Vienna and Leipzig: Braumüller, 1902.

3792   BROWN, Arthur. "The Printing of Books." In *ShS 17,* **3918.**

3793   ——. "Studies in Elizabethan and Jacobean Drama since 1900." *ShS 14* (1961), pp. 1-14.

3794   BROWN, John R., and Bernard Harris, eds. *Elizabethan Theatre.* Stratford-upon-Avon Studies, 9. London: Arnold, 1966. [10 essays, none specifically Sh.]

3795   ——, eds. *Jacobean Theatre.* Stratford-upon-Avon Studies, 1. London: Arnold, 1960. [Capricorn 279.] [8 essays, 2 on Sh.]

3796   BUNDY, Murray W. "Shakespeare and Elizabethan Psychology." *JEGP,* 23 (1924): 516-49.

3797   BUSH, Douglas. *Mythology and the Renaissance Tradition in English Poetry.* U. of Minnesota P., 1932.

3798   ——. *Prefaces to Renaissance Literature.* Harvard U.P., 1965.

3799   BUXTON, John. *Elizabethan Taste.* London: Macmillan, 1963.

3800   BYRNE, M. St. Clare. *Elizabethan Life in Town and Country.* London: Methuen, 1925. 7th ed. rev., 1954.

3801   ——. "The Foundations of Elizabethan Language." In *ShS 17,* **3918.**

3802   CAMDEN, Carroll C. *The Elizabethan Woman.* Houston, Texas: Elsevier, 1952.

3803   CHAMBERS, Raymond W. "The Elizabethan and Jacobean Shakespeare." In *Man's Unconquerable Mind.* London: Cape, 1939. Repr. 1952.

3804   CHARLTON, Kenneth. *Education in Renaissance England.* London: Routledge & Kegan Paul, 1965.

3805   CHEW, Samuel C. *The Pilgrimage of Life.* Yale U.P., 1962.

3806   CLARKSON, Paul S., and Clyde T. Warren. *The Law of Property in Shakespeare and the Elizabethan Drama.* Johns Hopkins U.P., 1942. Repr. New York: Gordian.

3807   COLIE, Rosalie. *Paradoxia Epidemica: The Renaissance Tradition of Paradox.* Princeton U.P., 1966. [Chaps. on *Lr, Ham.*]

3808   CORMICAN, L. A. "Medieval Idiom in Shakespeare: (1) Shakespeare and the Liturgy; (2) Shakespeare and the Medieval Ethic." *Scrutiny,* 17 (1950-51): 186-202, 298-317.

3809   CRAIG, Hardin. *The Enchanted Glass: The Elizabethan Mind in Literature.* New York: Oxford U.P., 1936. Repr. 1950.

3810   —. "Morality Plays and Elizabethan Drama." *SQ*, 1 (1950): 64-72.

3811   CREIZENACH, Wilhelm M. A. *The English Drama in the Age of Shakespeare.* London: Sidgwick & Jackson, 1916. Repr. New York: Haskell House. [Trans. Cécile Hugon, rev. Alfred F. Schuster, of part of vol. 4 of *Geschichte des neueren Dramas:Das englische Drama im Zeitalter Shakespeares.* Halle: Niemeyer, 1909.]

3812   CURTIS, M. H. "Education and Apprenticeship." In *ShS 17,* **3918.**

3813   DAVIES, David W. *Dutch Influences on English Culture, 1558-1625.* Cornell U.P. for the Folger Shakespeare Library, 1964.

3814   DOBB, Clifford. "London's Prisons." In *ShS 17,* **3918.**

3815   DORAN, Madeleine. *Endeavors of Art: A Study of Form in Elizabethan Drama.* U. of Wisconsin P., 1954. [W37 U Wisc.]

3816   DYER, T. F. Thiselton. *Folk-Lore of Shakespeare.* London: Griffith & Farran, *ca.* 1883. [Dover T 1614.]

3817   ELIOT, Thomas S. *Elizabethan Essays.* London: Faber & Faber, 1934. [2 on Sh: tragedies, *Ham.*]

3818   ELLIS-FERMOR, Una. *The Frontiers of Drama.* London: Methuen, 1945.

3819   —. *The Jacobean Drama.* London: Methuen, 1936. 3rd ed. rev., 1953. [UP; Vin Random V261.]

3820   ELTON, William R. "Shakespeare and the Thought of His Age." In *A New Companion to Shakespeare Studies,* **2800.**

3821   ENGSTROM, John E. *Coins in Shakespeare: A Numismatic Guide.* Hanover, N.H.: Dartmouth College Museum, 1964.

3822   EYLER, Ellen C. *Early English Gardens and Garden Books.* Cornell U.P. for the Folger Shakespeare Library, 1963. Repr. U.P. of Virginia.

3823   FANSLER, Harriott E. *The Evolution of Technic in Elizabethan Tragedy.* Chicago: Row, Peterson, 1914.

3824   FORD, Boris, ed. *The Age of Shakespeare.* Vol. 2 of *A Guide to English Literature.* London: Cassell, 1961.

3825   FOWLER, Elaine W. *English Sea Power in the Early Tudor Period, 1485-1558.* Cornell U.P. for The Folger Shakespeare Library, 1965.

3826   FOX, Levi. *The Borough Town of Stratford-upon-Avon.* Stratford-upon-Avon Corp., 1953.

3827   —. *Shakespeare's Town and Country.* [Stratford-upon-Avon]: Cotman House, 1964. [Illus.]

3828   FREEBURG, Victor O. *Disguise Plots in Elizabethan Drama: A Study in Stage Tradition.* Columbia U.P., 1915. Repr. New York: Blom.

3829   GREEN, A. Wigfall. *The Inns of Court and Early English Drama.* Yale U.P., 1931. Repr. New York: Blom.

3830 GREENFIELD, Thelma N. *The Induction in Elizabethan Drama.* Oregon U.P., 1969.

3831 GREG, Walter W. *Pastoral Poetry and Pastoral Drama.* London: Sidgwick & Jackson, 1906.

3832 HABICHT, Werner. *Studien zur Dramenform vor Shakespeare: Moralität, Interlude, romaneskes Drama.* Heidelberg: Winter, 1968.

3833 HALE, John R. *The Art of War and Renaissance England.* Washington, D.C.: Folger Shakespeare Library, 1961. Repr. U.P. of Virginia.

3834 HALL, Marie B. "Scientific Thought." In *ShS 17,* **3918.**

3835 HALLAR, Marianne. *The English Court-Masque and Its Influence upon Shakespearean Dramaturgy.* Copenhagen: University Fund, 1968.

3836 HALLER, William. *Elizabeth I and the Puritans.* Cornell U.P. for The Folger Shakespeare Library, 1964. Repr. U.P. of Virginia.

3837 HALLIDAY, Frank E. *Shakespeare in His Age.* London: Duckworth, 1956.

3838 HARDISON, Osborne B. *Christian Rite and Christian Drama in the Middle Ages.* Johns Hopkins U.P., 1965.

3839 ——. *The Enduring Monument: A Study of the Idea of Praise in Renaissance Literary Theory and Practice.* U. of North Carolina P., 1962.

3840 HARRIS, Bernard. "Dissent and Satire." In *ShS 17,* **3918.**

3841 HARRISON, George B. *An Elizabethan Journal . . . 1591-94.* London: Constable, 1928. This vol., *A Second Elizabethan Journal,* **3845,** and *A Last Elizabethan Journal,* **3844,** were repr. as *The Elizabethan Journals.* London: Routledge, 1938. Repr., U. of Michigan P., 1955; Gloucester, Mass.: Peter Smith (2 vols.). [Anch.]

3842 ——. *England in Shakespeare's Day.* London: Methuen, 1928.

3843 ——. *A Jacobean Journal . . . 1603-1606.* London: Routledge, 1941.

3844 ——. *A Last Elizabethan Journal . . . 1599-1603.* London: Constable, 1933. Repr. as part of *The Elizabethan Journals,* see **3841.**

3845 ——. *A Second Elizabethan Journal . . . 1595-98.* London: Constable, 1931. Repr. as part of *The Elizabethan Journals,* see **3841.**

3846 ——. *The Story of Elizabethan Drama.* Cambridge U.P., 1924.

3847 HERRICK, Marvin T. *Italian Comedy in the Renaissance.* U. of Illinois P., 1960.

3848 HOENIGER, F. David, and Judith F. M. Hoeniger. *The Development of Natural History in Tudor England.* U.P. of Virginia for the Folger Shakespeare Library, 1969.

3849 ——. *The Growth of Natural History in Stuart England: From Gerard to the Royal Society.* U.P. of Virginia for The Folger Shakespeare Library, 1969.

3850 HOLMES, Elizabeth. *Aspects of Elizabethan Imagery.* Oxford: Blackwell, 1929. Repr. New York: Russell & Russell. [Chap. on Sh.]

3851 HOLMES, Martin. *Elizabethan London.* New York: Praeger, 1969.

3852 *Horizon Book of the Elizabethan World.* Ed. Norman Kotker; text, Lacey B. Smith. New York: American Heritage, 1967.

3853 HOSKINS, W. G. "Provincial Life." In *ShS 17,* **3918.**

3854 HUNTER, George K. "Elizabethans and Foreigners." In *ShS 17,* **3918.**

3855 HURSTFIELD, Joel. "The Historical and Social Background." In *A New Companion to Shakespeare Studies,* **2800.**

3856 ING, Catherine. *Elizabethan Lyrics.* London: Chatto & Windus, 1951.

3857 IVES, E. W. "The Law and the Lawyers." In *ShS 17,* **3918.**

3858 IYENGAR, K. R. S. *Shakespeare: His World and His Art.* London: Asia, 1965.

3859. JACQUOT, Jean, ed. *Les Tragédies de Sénéque et le théatre de la Renaissance.* Paris: Centre National de la Recherche Scientifique, 1964.

3860 JOHNSON, Francis R. *Astronomical Thought in Renaissance England.* Johns Hopkins U.P., 1937.

3861 JONES, Eldred D. *The Elizabethan Image of Africa.* U.P. of Virginia for The Folger Shakespeare Library, 1971.

3862 JONES, Marion. "The Court and the Dramatists." In *Elizabethan Theatre,* **4009.**

3863 KAUFMAN, Helen A. "The Influence of Italian Drama on Pre-Restoration English Comedy." *Italica,* 31 (1954): 9-23.

3864 KELLY, Faye C. *Prayer in Sixteenth-Century England.* U. of Florida, 1966.

3865 KELSO, Ruth. *Doctrine for the Lady of the Renaissance.* U. of Illinois P., 1956.

3866 —. *Doctrine of the English Gentleman.* U. of Illinois P., 1929.

3867 KNIGHT, G. Wilson. *The Christian Renaissance, with Interpretations of Dante, Shakespeare, and Goethe.* Toronto: Macmillan of Canada, 1933.

3868 KNIGHTS, Lionel C. *Drama and Society in the Age of Jonson.* London: Chatto & Windus, 1937. Repr. New York: Barnes & Noble. [Norton Lib.]

3869 —. *Explorations: Essays in Criticism Mainly on the Literature of the Seventeenth Century.* London: Chatto & Windus, 1946. [NYU P.]

3870 KOCHER, Paul H. *Science and Religion in Elizabethan England.* San Marino, Calif.: Huntington Library, 1953.

3871 KORNINGER, Siegfried. "Die Geisterszene im Elisabethanischen Drama." *SJ 1966* (West), pp. 124-45.

3872   LaMAR, Virginia A. *English Dress in the Age of Shakespeare.* Washington, D.C.: Folger Shakespeare Library, 1958. Repr. U.P. of Virginia, and in *Life and Letters,* 3958.

3873   ——. *Travel and Roads in England.* Washington, D.C.: Folger Shakespeare Library, 1960.

3874   LATHAM, Minor W. *The Elizabethan Fairies: The Fairies of Folklore and the Fairies of Shakespeare.* Columbia U.P., 1930.

3875   LATHROP, Henry B. *Translations from the Classics into English from Caxton to Chapman.* U. of Wisconsin Studies, 35. Madison, 1933.

3876   LEA, Kathleen M. *Italian Popular Comedy.* 2 vols. Oxford U.P., 1934. [Pt. 3 on relation to Eng. drama.]

3877   LEE, Sidney. *Elizabethan and Other Essays.* Ed. Frederick S. Boas. Oxford U.P., 1929. Repr. Freeport, N.Y.: Books for Libraries.

3878   ——. *The French Renaissance in England: An Account of the Literary Relations of England and France in the Sixteenth Century.* Oxford U.P., 1910.

3879   ——. *Shakespeare and the Italian Renaissance.* Oxford U.P., 1915. [*PBA 1915-16,* 7 (1917): 121-43.]

3880   ——, and Charles T. Onions, eds. *Shakespeare's England: An Account of the Life and Manners of His Age.* 2 vols. Oxford U.P., 1916. [30 essays by different authors.]

3881   LIEVSAY, John L. *The Elizabethan Image of Italy.* Cornell U.P. for The Folger Shakespeare Library, 1964.

3882   LOVEJOY, Arthur O. *The Great Chain of Being: A Study of the History of an Idea.* Harvard U.P., 1953.

3883   MASON, Dorothy E. *Music in Elizabethan England.* Washington, D.C.: Folger Shakespeare Library, 1958. Repr. U.P. of Virginia, and in *Life and Letters,* 3958.

3884   MASON, Eudo C. "Satire on Women and Sex in Elizabethan Tragedy." *ES,* 31 (1950): 1-10.

3885   MATTINGLY, Garrett. *The "Invincible" Armada and Elizabethan England.* Cornell U.P. for The Folger Shakespeare Library, 1963.

3886   MEHL, Dieter. "Forms and Functions of the Play within a Play." *RenD,* 8 (1965): 41-62.

3887   ——. *Die Pantomime im Drama der Shakespearezeit.* Heidelberg: Quelle & Meyer, 1964. Trans. as *The Elizabethan Dumb Show.* London: Methuen, 1965.

3888   MILLER, Edwin H. *The Professional Writer in Elizabethan England: A Study of Nondramatic Literature.* Harvard U.P., 1959.

3889   MUIR, Kenneth. *Introduction to Elizabethan Literature.* New York: Random House, 1967. [Random House X635.]

3890   MURRAY, Patrick J. *The Shakespearean Scene.* New York: Barnes & Noble; London: Longmans, Green, 1969.

3890a   NEALE, John E. *England's Elizabeth.* Washington, D.C.: Folger Shakespeare Library, 1958. Repr. in *Life and Letters,* **3958.**

3891   NICHOLS, John, ed. *The Progresses, and Public Processions, of Queen Elizabeth.* 3 vols. London: the Editor, 1788-1805. Repr. New York: AMS; Franklin.

3892   —, ed. *The Progresses, Processions, and Magnificent Festivities of King James the First.* 4 vols. London: J. B. Nichols, 1828. Repr. New York: AMS; Franklin.

3893   NICOLL, Allardyce. *The Elizabethans.* Cambridge U.P., 1957. [Illus.]

3894   NICOLSON, Marjorie H. "The 'New Astronomy' and English Literary Imagination." *SP,* 32 (1935): 428-62.

3895   ORAS, Ants. "Lyrical Instrumentation in Marlowe: A Step towards Shakespeare." In *Studies in Shakespeare,* **2797.**

3896   ORDISH, Thomas F. *Shakespeare's London.* 1897. New, enl. ed., London: Dent, 1904. Repr. of 1897 ed., New York: AMS.

3897   ORNSTEIN, Robert T. *The Moral Vision of Jacobean Tragedy.* U. of Wisconsin P., 1960. [W44.]

3898   PARKES, H. B. "Nature's Diverse Laws: The Double Vision of the Elizabethans." *SR,* 58 (1950): 402-18.

3899   PELLEGRINI, G. "Symbols and Significances." In *ShS 17,* **3918.**

3899a   PENROSE, Boies. *Tudor and Early Stuart Voyaging.* Cornell U.P. for The Folger Shakespeare Library, 1962. Repr. U.P. of Virginia.

3899b   POYNTER, F. N. L. "Medicine and Public Health." In *ShS 17,* **3918.**

3900   PRAZ, Mario. "The English Emblem Literature." *ES,* 16 (1934): 129-40.

3901   —. *Machiavelli and the Elizabethans.* Oxford U.P., 1928.

3902   QUINN, David B. "Sailors and the Sea." In *ShS 17,* **3918.**

3903   RAE, Thomas I. *Scotland in the Time of Shakespeare.* Cornell U.P. for The Folger Shakespeare Library, 1965.

3904   READ, Conyers. *The Government of England under Elizabeth.* Washington, D.C.: Folger Shakespeare Library, 1960. Repr. U.P. of Virginia, and in *Life and Letters,* **3958.**

3905   REDDAWAY, T. F. "London and the Court." In *ShS 17,* **3918.**

3906   REED, Robert R. *The Occult on the Tudor and Stuart Stage.* London: Christopher, 1965.

3907   REYHER, Paul. *Les Masques anglais: Étude sur les ballets et la vie de cour en Angleterre (1512-1640).* Paris: Hachette, 1909. Repr. New York: Blom.

3908 RIBNER, Irving. *Jacobean Tragedy: The Quest for Moral Order.* London: Methuen, 1962.

3909 RINGLER, William A. "The First Phase of the Elizabethan Attack on the Stage, 1558-1579." *HLQ*, 5 (1941-42): 391-418.

3910 RITSON, Joseph. *Fairy Tales, Now First Collected.* London: Payne & Foss, 1831. Repr., with addition, of 1875 ed., New York: AMS.

3911 ROBBINS, Rossell H. *The Encyclopedia of Witchcraft and Demonology.* New York: Crown, 1959.

3912 ROSSITER, Arthur P. *English Drama from Early Times to the Elizabethans.* London: Hutchinson, 1950.

3913 SCHELLING, Felix E. *Foreign Influences in Elizabethan Plays.* New York: Harper, 1923. Repr. New York: AMS.

3914 SCHMIDT, Albert J. *The Yeoman in Tudor and Stuart England.* Washington, D.C.: Folger Shakespeare Library, 1961. Repr. U.P. of Virginia.

3915 SCOT, Reginald. *The Discovery of Witchcraft.* London: Brome, 1584. Repr. London: E. Stock, 1886 (ed. Brinsley Nicholson); London: Rodker, 1930 (ed. Montague Summers).

3916 SHEAVYN, Phoebe. *The Literary Profession in the Elizabethan Age.* Manchester U.P., 1909. 2nd ed. rev., New York: Barnes & Noble; Manchester U.P., 1967 (ed. John W. Saunders).

3917 *ShS 14* (1961). [7 essays on Shakespeare and his contemporaries.]

3918 *ShS 17* (1964). [17 essays on Shakespeare's background.]

3919 SIBLY, John. "The Duty of Revenge in Tudor and Stuart Drama." *REL*, 8 (1967): 46-54.

3920 SIMMONS, Judith. "Publications of 1623." *Library*, 21 (1966): 206-22. [Life and times—reading matter.]

3921 SIMON, Joan. *Education and Society in Tudor England.* Cambridge U.P., 1966.

3922 SISSON, Charles J. "Marks as Signatures." *Library*, 9 (1928-29): 1-37, 7 plates.

3923 SOELLNER, Rolf. "Baroque Passion in Shakespeare and His Contemporaries." *ShakS 1* (1965), pp. 294-302.

3924 SPENCER, Terence J. B. "Shakespeare v. the Rest." In *ShS 14,* **3917.**

3925 STEPHENSON, Henry T. *Shakespeare's London.* New York: Holt, 1905. Repr. New York: AMS.

3926 STONE, Lilly C. *English Sports and Recreations.* Washington, D.C.: Folger Shakespeare Library, 1960. Repr. U.P. of Virginia, and in *Life and Letters,* **3958.**

3927 STOW, John. *A Survey of London.* Ed. Charles L. Kingsford. 2 vols. Oxford U.P., 1908.

3928 STUBBES, Philip. *Anatomy of the Abuses in Shakespeare's Youth, A.D. 1583.* Ed. Frederick J. Furnivall. 2 vols. London: Trübner, 1877-82. Repr. Nendeln, Liechtenstein: Kraus-Thomson.

3929 STYLES, Philip. "Borough of Stratford-upon-Avon." In *Victoria History of the County of Warwick,* 3, 221-82. Oxford U.P. for The U. of London Institute of Historical Research, 1945.

3930 ——. "The Commonwealth." In *ShS 17,* **3918.**

3931 SULLIVAN, Mary I. *Court Masques of James I: Their Influence on Shakespeare.* New York and London: Putnam's, 1913.

3932 SWINBURNE, Algernon C. *The Age of Shakespeare.* London: Chatto & Windus, 1908. Repr. New York: AMS.

3933 TALBERT, Ernest W. *Elizabethan Drama and Shakespeare's Early Plays.* U. of North Carolina P., 1963.

3934 ——. *The Problem of Order.* U. of North Carolina P., 1962.

3935 THOMPSON, Craig R. *The Bible in English, 1525-1611.* Washington, D.C.: Folger Shakespeare Library, 1958. Repr. U.P. of Virginia, and in *Life and Letters,* **3958.**

3936 ——. *The English Church in the Sixteenth Century.* Washington, D.C.: Folger Shakespeare Library, 1958. Repr. U.P. of Virginia, and in *Life and Letters,* **3958.**

3937 ——. *Schools in Tudor England.* Washington, D.C.: Folger Shakespeare Library, 1959. Repr. U.P. of Virginia, and in *Life and Letters,* **3958.**

3938 ——. *Universities in Tudor England.* Washington, D.C.: Folger Shakespeare Library, 1959. Repr. U.P. of Virginia, and in *Life and Letters,* **3958.**

3939 THOMPSON, Elbert N. S. *The Controversy between the Puritans and the Stage.* New York: Holt, 1903. Repr. New York: AMS.

3940 TILLYARD, Eustace M. W. *The Elizabethan World Picture.* London: Chatto & Windus, 1943. [V162 Random.]

3941 TOMLINSON, Thomas B. *A Study of Elizabethan and Jacobean Tragedy.* Cambridge U.P., 1964.

3942 TUVE, Rosemond. *Elizabethan and Metaphysical Imagery.* U. of Chicago P., 1947. [U Chic P68.]

3943 UNGERER, Gustav. *Anglo-Spanish Relations in Tudor Literature.* Bern: Francke, 1956. Repr. New York: AMS. [Chap. on Sh.]

3944 URE, Peter. "Shakespeare and the Drama of His Time." In *A New Companion to Shakespeare Studies,* **2800.**

3945 WAGGONER, George R. "An Elizabethan Attitude toward Peace and War." *PQ,* 33 (1954): 20-33.

3946 WATSON, Curtis B. *Shakespeare and the Renaissance Concept of Honour.* Princeton U.P., 1960.

3947 WELSFORD, Enid. *The Court Masque.* Cambridge U.P., 1927. Repr. New York: Russell & Russell.

3948 —. *The Fool: His Social and Literary History.* London: Faber & Faber, 1935. Repr. Gloucester, Mass.: Peter Smith, 1962. [Anch.]

3949 WEST, Robert H. "Elizabethan Belief in Spirits and Witchcraft." In *Studies in Shakespeare,* **2797.**

3950 —. *The Invisible World: A Study of Pneumatology in Elizabethan Drama.* U. of Georgia P., 1939. Repr. New York: Octagon.

3951 WICKHAM, Glynne. *Shakespeare's Dramatic Heritage.* New York: Barnes & Noble, 1968. [*R2, MND, Ham, Mac, Cor, WT.*]

3952 WILLEFORD, William. *The Fool and His Scepter: A Study in Clowns and Jesters and Their Audience.* Northwestern U.P., 1969.

3953 WILLEY, Basil. *The Seventeenth-Century Background.* London: Chatto & Windus, 1934. Repr. Columbia U.P., 1942. [Anch.]

3954 WILSON, Frank P. *Elizabethan and Jacobean.* Oxford U.P., 1945.

3955 —. *The Plague in Shakespeare's London.* Oxford U.P., 1927. Rev. ed., 1963. [OUP 65.]

3956 WILSON, J. Dover, ed. *Life in Shakespeare's England.* Cambridge U.P., 1911. 2nd ed., 1913; repr. 1920, 1964; New York: Barnes & Noble.

3957 WRIGHT, Louis B. *Middle-Class Culture in Elizabethan England.* U. of North Carolina P., 1966.

3958 —, and Virginia A. LaMar, eds. *Life and Letters in Tudor and Stuart England.* Cornell U.P., 1962. [Coll. of first 12 Folger booklets.]

3959 ZITNER, Sheldon P. "Gosson, Ovid, and the Elizabethan Audience." *SQ,* 9 (1958): 206-8.

PLAYHOUSES, STAGES, STAGING, ACTORS TO 1660

See also **2, 4, 13, 20, 24, 47, 48, 49, 50, 64, 68, 76, 79, 95, 96, 97, 98, 101,** and **104** .

3960   ADAMS, John C. *The Globe Playhouse.* Harvard U.P.; Oxford U.P., 1943. Repr. New York: Barnes & Noble.

3961   —. "'That Virtuous Fabrick.'" *SQ*, 2 (1951): 3-11.

3962   ADAMS, Joseph Q. "The Conventual Buildings of Blackfriars, London, and the Playhouses Constructed Therein." *SP*, 14 (1917): 64-87. Repr. New York: AMS.

3963   —. "The Housekeepers of the Globe." *MP*, 17 (1919-20): 1-8.

3964   —. *Shakespearean Playhouses.* Boston and New York: Houghton Mifflin, 1917. Repr. London: Constable, 1920.

3965   ALBRIGHT, Victor E. "Two of Percy's Plays as Proof of the Elizabethan Stage." *MP*, 11 (1913-14): 237-46.

3966   ARMSTRONG, William A. "Actors and Theatres." In *ShS 17,* **3918.**

3967   —. *The Elizabethan Private Theatres: Facts and Problems.* London: Society for Theatre Research, 1958.

3968   —. "The Enigmatic Elizabethan Stage." *English,* 13 (1961): 216-20. [Booths or tents.]

3969   BALD, R. Cecil. "The Entrance to the Elizabethan Theater." *SQ,* 3 (1952): 17-20.

3970   BALDWIN, Thomas W. *The Organization and Personnel of the Shakespearean Company.* Princeton U.P.; Oxford U.P., 1927.

3971   —. "Posting Henslowe's Accounts." *JEGP*, 26 (1927): 42-91.

3972   —. "The Revels Books of 1604-5, and 1611-12." *Library,* 10 (1929-30): 327-38. [Not forged.]

3973   BASKERVILL, Charles R. "The Custom of Sitting on the Elizabethan Stage." *MP*, 8 (1910-11): 581-89.

3974   BECKERMAN, Bernard. *Shakespeare at the Globe, 1599-1609.* New York: Macmillan, 1962. [01206 Collier.]

3975   BENTLEY, Gerald E., ed. *The Seventeenth-Century Stage.* U. of Chicago P., 1968. [PLC6 U Chicago.] [9 sel. from prev. pub. wks. by different authors, 1609-1964.]

3976   —. *Shakespeare and His Theatre.* U. of Nebraska P., 1964. [U of Nebr P 179.]

3977   BERNHEIMER, Richard M. "Another Globe Theatre." *SQ,* 9 (1958): 19-29, 2 illus. [Robert Fludd's "theatre."]

3978   BERRY, Herbert. "Dr. Fludd's Engravings and Their Beholders." *ShakS 3 1967* (1968), pp. 11-21.

3979   ——. "The Playhouse in the Boar's Head Inn, Whitechapel." In *Elizabethan Theatre,* **4009**.

3980   ——. "The Stage and Boxes at Blackfriars." *SP,* 63 (1966): 163-86.

3981   BETHELL, Samuel L. "Shakespeare's Actors." *RES,* 1 (1950): 193-205.

3982   BRADBROOK, Muriel C. *Elizabethan Stage Conditions: A Study of Their Place in the Interpretation of Shakespeare's Plays.* Cambridge U.P., 1932. Repr. 1968. [CUP 539.]

3983   ——. *The Rise of the Common Player: A Study of Actor and Society in Shakespeare's England.* London: Chatto & Windus, 1962.

3984   BROOKS, Charles. "Shakespeare's Heroine-Actresses." *SJ,* 96 (1960): 134-44.

3985   BROWN, John R. "The Theatrical Element of Shakespeare." In *Reinterpretations of Elizabethan Drama,* **2806**.

3986   ——, and Bernard Harris, eds. *Elizabethan Theatre.* See **3794**.

3987   ——, eds. *Jacobean Theatre.* See **3795**.

3988   CAMPBELL, Lily B. *Scenes and Machines on the English Stage during the Renaissance, a Classical Revival.* Cambridge U.P., 1923. Repr. New York: Barnes & Noble.

3989   CHAMBERS, Edmund K. "The Stage of the Globe." In *Shakespearean Gleanings,* **2913**.

3990   CHILD, Harold H. "The Elizabethan Theatre." Chap. 10, vol. 4 of *Cam. Hist. Eng. Lit.,* **18a**.

3991   COLLINS, Fletcher. "The Relation of Tudor Halls to Elizabethan Public Theatres." *PQ,* 10 (1931): 313-16.

3992   COWLING, George H. "Shakespeare and the Elizabethan Stage." In *A Series of Papers on Shakespeare and the Theatre,* **4133**.

3993   DAVID, Richard. *Shakespeare and the Players.* Oxford U.P., 1961. [*PBA 1961,* 47 (1962): 139-59.] Repr. in *Studies in Shakespeare,* **2759**.

3994   DAVIES, Thomas. *Dramatic Miscellanies . . . Critical Observations on Several Plays of Shakspeare.* 3 vols. London: the author, [1783-84.] Repr. New York: AMS.

3995   DAVIES, William R. *Shakespeare's Boy Actors.* London: Dent, 1939.

3996   DAWSON, Giles E. "London's Bull-Baiting and Bear-Baiting Arena in 1562." *SQ,* 15.1 (1964): 97-101, 2 plates.

3997   DE BANKE, Cécile. *Shakespearean Stage Production Then and Now.* New York: McGraw-Hill, 1953.

3998   DOWNER, Alan S. "Prolegomenon to a Study of Elizabethan Acting." *MuK,* 10 (1964): 625-36.

3999   ——. "The Tudor Actor: A Taste of His Quality." *TN,* 5 (1951): 76-81.

4000   ECCLES, Mark. "Martin Peerson and the Blackfriars." *ShS 11* (1958), pp. 100-106.

4001   EVANS, M. Blakemore. "'An Early Type of Stage.'" *MP*, 9 (1911-12): 421-26, 1 plate.

4002   FISHER, Sidney. *The Theatre, the Curtain, and the Globe.* McGill U. Library, 1964.

4003   FLATTER, Richard. *Shakespeare's Producing Hand.* London: Heinemann, 1948.

4004   FOAKES, Reginald A. "Henslowe and the Theatre of the 1590's." *RenD*, 6 (1963): 4-6.

4005   ——. "The Player's Passion, Some Notes on Elizabethan Psychology and Acting." *E&S*, 7 (1954): 62-77.

4006   ——. "The Profession of Playwright." In *Early Shakespeare,* **2766.**

4007   ——. "Tragedy at the Children's Theatres after 1600: A Challenge to the Adult Stage." In *Elizabethan Theatre II,* **4010.**

4008   ——, and R. T. Rickert. "An Elizabethan Stage Drawing?" *ShS 13* (1960), pp. 111-12.

4009   GALLOWAY, David, ed. *The Elizabethan Theatre.* Toronto: Macmillan of Canada, 1969. [Papers given at the Int. Conf. on Eliz. Theatre, U. of Waterloo, Ontario, 1968.]

4010   ——, ed. *The Elizabethan Theatre II.* Hamden, Conn.: Archon, 1970. [Papers Int. Conf. on Eliz. Theatre, U. of Waterloo, Ontario, 1969. Esp. dramatic companies and personnel.]

4011   GAW, Allison. "John Sincklo as One of Shakespeare's Actors." *Anglia*, 49 (1926): 289-303.

4012   GOLDSTEIN, Leonard. "On the Transition from Formal to Naturalistic Acting in the Elizabethan and Post-Elizabethan Theater." *BNYPL,* 62 (1958): 330-49.

4013   GRANVILLE-BARKER, Harley. "A Note upon Chapters XX and XXI of *The Elizabethan Stage.*" *RES*, 1 (1925): 60-71. [Elizabethan staging.]

4014   GRAVES, Thornton S. "The 'Act Time' in Elizabethan Theatres." *SP,* 12 (1915): 101-34.

4015   ——. "Notes on Elizabethan Theatres." *SP*, 13 (1916): 110-21. [See also *SP*, 17 (1920): 170-82.]

4016   ——. "'Playeng in the Dark' during the Elizabethan Period." *SP*, 14 (1917): 88-116.

4017   ——. "Some Aspects of Extemporal Acting." *SP*, 19 (1922): 429-56.

4018   ——. "Women on the Pre-Restoration Stage." *SP*, 22 (1925): 184-97.

4019   GREG, Walter W. "Act-Divisions in Shakespeare." *RES*, 4 (1928): 152-58. [Analysis of plays, 1591-1610, for adult and children's companies; also promptbooks.]

4020   —. "Edward Alleyn." In *A Series of Papers on Shakespeare and the Theatre*, **4133**.

4021   —. "The Evidence of Theatrical Plots for the History of the Elizabethan Stage." *RES*, 1 (1925): 257-74.   See also **39**.

4022   GRIFFIN, Alice S. (Venezky). *Pageantry on the Elizabethan Stage.* New York: Twayne, 1951.

4023   GURR, Andrew. *The Shakespearean Stage, 1571-1642.* Cambridge U.P., 1970.

4024   HAINES, Charles M. "The Development of Shakespeare's Stagecraft." In *A Series of Papers on Shakespeare and the Theatre*, **4133**.

4025   —. "The 'Law of Re-entry' in Shakespeare." *RES*, 1 (1925): 449-51.

4026   HARBAGE, Alfred. "Elizabethan Acting." *PMLA*, 54 (1939): 685-708.

4027   HARRISON, George B. *Elizabethan Plays and Players.* London: Routledge, 1940. [AA U of Mich P 2.]

4028   —. "Shakespeare's Actors." In *A Series of Papers on Shakespeare and the Theatre*, **4133**.

4029   HART, Alfred. "The Time Allotted for Representation of Elizabethan and Jacobean Plays." *RES*, 8 (1932): 395-413.

4030   HEYWOOD, Thomas. *An Apology for Actors (1612). A Refutation of the Apology for Actors (1615) by I. G.* [J. Green(e)?]. Ed. Richard H. Perkinson. New York: Scholars' Facsimiles and Reprints, 1941.

4031   HODGES, C. Walter. "The Globe Playhouse: Some Notes on a New Reconstruction." *TN*, 1 (1947): 108-11, 2 plates.

4032   —. *The Globe Restored.* London: Benn, 1953. Rev. and enl. ed., Oxford U.P., 1968.

4033   —. "The Lantern of Taste." In *ShS 12*, **4139**.

4034   —. *Shakespeare and the Players.* London: Benn, 1948.

4035   —. "Unworthy Scaffolds: A Theory for the Reconstruction of Elizabethan Playhouses." *ShS 3* (1950), pp. 83-94.

4036   HOLMES, Martin. "A New Theory about the Swan Drawing." *TN*, 10 (1956): 80-83, 1 plate. [Shows a rehearsal.]

4037   HOLZKNECHT, Karl J. "Theatrical Billposting in the Age of Elizabeth." *PQ*, 2 (1923): 267-81.

4038   HOOK, Lucyle. "The Curtain." *SQ*, 13 (1962): 499-504. [Location.]

4039   HOSLEY, Richard. "An Approach to the Elizabethan Stage." *RenD*, 6 (1963): 72-78.

4040   —. "The Discovery-Space in Shakespeare's Globe." In *ShS 12*, **4139**.

4041   —. "An Elizabethan Tiring-House Façade." *SQ*, 9 (1958): 588, 1 plate.

4042   —. "The Gallery over the Stage, in the Public Playhouse." *SQ*, 8 (1957): 15-31.

4043   —. "The Origins of the Shakespearian Playhouse." *SQ*, 15.2 (1964): 29-39, 2 plates, 5 figures. Also in *Shakespeare 400*, **2793**.

4044   —. "The Origins of the So-called Elizabethan Multiple Stage." *TDR*, 12 (1968): 28-50.

4045   —. "The Playhouses and the Stage." In *A New Companion to Shakespeare Studies*, **2800**.

4046   —. "Reconstitution du Théatre du Swan." In *Le Lieu théâtral a la Renaissance*, **4056**.

4047   —. "A Reconstruction of the Second Blackfriars." In *Elizabethan Theatre*, **4009**.

4048   —. "Shakespeare's Use of a Gallery over the Stage." *ShS 10* (1957), pp. 77-89.

4049   —. "Was There a Music-Room in Shakespeare's Globe?" *ShS 13* (1960), pp. 113-23.

4050   HOTSON, Leslie. *The Commonwealth and Restoration Stage.* Harvard U.P., 1928.

4051   —. *Shakespeare's Motley.* London: Hart-Davis, 1952.

4052   —. *Shakespeare's Wooden O.* London: Hart-Davis, 1959.

4053   ISAACS, Jacob. *Production and Stage Management at the Blackfriars Theatre.* Oxford U.P., 1933.

4054   —. "Shakespeare as Man of the Theatre." In *A Series of Papers on Shakespeare and the Theatre*, **4133**.

4055   JACQUOT, Jean, ed. *Dramaturgie et société: Rapports entre l'oeuvre théâtrale, son interprétation et son public aux xvie et xviie siècles: Nancy 14-21 avril 1967.* 2 vols. Paris: Editions du Centre National de la Recherche Scientifique, 1968.

4056   —, ed. *Le Lieu théâtral a la Renaissance.* Paris: Editions du Centre National de la Recherche Scientifique, 1964.

4057   —, and André Veinstein, eds. *La Mise en scène des oeuvres du Passé.* Paris: Centre National de la Recherche Scientifique, 1957. [See "Les Etudes shakespeariennes, problèmes et methodes: L'Exemple de *Mac*," pp. 176-209.]

4058   JENSEN, Ejner. "The Style of Boy Actors." *CompD*, 2 (1968): 100-114.

4059   JONAS, Maurice. *Shakespeare and the Stage, with a Complete List of Theatrical Terms Used by Shakespeare in His Plays and Poems.* London: Davis & Orioli, 1918.

4060   JOSEPH, Bertram L. *Acting Shakespeare.* London: Routledge & Kegan Paul, 1960.

4061 —. *Elizabethan Acting.* Oxford U.P., 1951. 2nd ed. enl., 1964.

4062 —. "The Elizabethan Stage and the Art of Elizabethan Drama." *SJ*, 91 (1955): 145-60.

4063 —. *The Tragic Actor.* London: Routledge & Kegan Paul, 1959.

4064 KELLY, Francis M. *Shakespearian Costume for Stage and Screen.* London: Black, 1938. Rev. ed., 1970 (ed. Alan Mansfield).

4065 KERNODLE, George R. *From Art to Theatre: Form and Convention in the Renaissance.* U. of Chicago P., 1944.

4066 —. "The Open Stage: Elizabethan or Existentialist?" In *ShS 12*, **4139**.

4067 KING, T. J. "Staging of Plays at the Phoenix in Drury Lane, 1617-42." *TN*, 19 (1965): 146-66.

4068 KLEIN, David. "Elizabethan Acting." *PMLA*, 71 (1956): 280-82.

4069 —. "Time Allotted for an Elizabethan Performance." *SQ*, 18 (1967): 434-38.

4070 LAMBORN, Edmund A. G., and George B. Harrison. *Shakespeare: The Man and His Stage.* Oxford U.P., 1923.

4071 LANGHANS, Edward. "A Picture of the Salisbury Court Theatre." *TN*, 19 (1965): 100-101.

4072 LAWRENCE, William J. "Bells on the Elizabethan Stage." *Fortnightly Review*, July 1924, pp. 59-70.

4073 —. *The Elizabethan Playhouse and Other Studies.* 2 series. Stratford-upon-Avon: Shakespeare Head P., 1912-13.

4074 —. *Old Theatre Days and Ways.* London: Harrap, 1935.

4075 —. *The Physical Conditions of the Elizabethan Playhouse.* Harvard U.P.; Oxford U.P., 1927. Repr. New York: Cooper Square.

4076 —. *Pre-Restoration Stage Studies.* Harvard U.P.; Oxford U.P., 1927. Repr. New York: Blom.

4077 —. *Shakespeare's Workshop.* Oxford: Blackwell, 1928.

4078 —. *Speeding Up Shakespeare.* London: Argonaut, 1937. Repr. New York: Blom.

4079 —. *Those Nut-Cracking Elizabethans: Studies of the Early Theatre and Drama.* London: Argonaut, 1933.

4080 LEECH, Clifford. "The Function of Locality in the Plays of Shakespeare and His Contemporaries." In *Elizabethan Theatre*, **4009**.

4081 LENNAM, Trevor N. S. "The Children of Paul's, 1551-1582." In *Elizabethan Theatre II*, **4010**.

4082 LINTHICUM, Marie C. *Costume in the Drama of Shakespeare and His Contemporaries.* Oxford U.P., 1936.

4083 McDOWELL, John H. "Conventions of Medieval Art in Shakespearian Staging." *JEGP*, 47 (1948): 215-29, 7 plates.

4084   ——. "Tudor Court Staging: A Study in Perspective." *JEGP*, 44 (1945): 194-207.

4085   McMANAWAY, James G. "A New Shakespeare Document." *SQ*, 2 (1951): 119-22, 2 plates. [Bill for plays at Court, 1630.]

4086   ——. "Notes on Two Pre-Restoration Stage Curtains." In *Studies . . . Presented to Baldwin Maxwell*, **2824.**

4087   MARKER, Lise-Lone. "Nature and Decorum in the Theory of Elizabethan Acting." In *Elizabethan Theatre II*, **4010.**

4088   MILLER, William E. "*Periaktoi* in the Old Blackfriars." *MLN*, 74 (1959): 1-3. [See also Miller's "*Periaktoi:* Around Again." *SQ*, 15.1 (1964): 61-65.]

4089   MITCHELL, Lee. "The Advent of Scenic Design in England." *QJS*, 23 (1937): 189-97.

4090   NAGLER, Alois M. *Shakespeare's Stage*. Trans. Ralph Manheim. Yale U.P., 1958. [Y108 Yale UP.]

4091   ——. "Sixteenth-Century Continental Stages." *SQ*, 5 (1954): 359-70.

4092   NICOLL, Allardyce. "Passing over the Stage." In *ShS 12*, **4139.**

4093   ——. *Stuart Masques and the Renaissance Stage*. London: Harrap, 1938. Repr. New York: Blom.

4094   ——. "Studies in the Elizabethan Stage since 1900." *ShS 1* (1948), pp. 1-16.

4095   NOBLE, Richmond S. H. "Shakespeare's Songs and Stage." In *A Series of Papers on Shakespeare and the Theatre*, **4133.**

4096   "A Note on the Swan Theatre Drawing." *ShS 1* (1948), pp. 23-24.

4097   PAFFORD, John H. P. "Simon Forman's 'Bocke of Plaies.'" *RES*, 10 (1959): 289-91. [Joseph Hunter stated in 1845 that Dr. Bliss called Forman's notes to his attention in Oxford in 1832.]

4098   PATERSON, Morton. "The Stagecraft of the Revels Office during the Reign of Elizabeth." In *Studies in the Elizabethan Theatre*, **4102.**

4099   PINCISS, G. M. "The Queen's Men, 1583-1592." *ThS*, 11 (1970): 50-65.

4100   PRANGE, Gerda. "Shakespeares Äusserungen über die Tänze seiner Zeit." *SJ*, 89 (1953): 132-61.

4101   PROUTY, Charles T. "An Early Elizabethan Playhouse." *ShS 6* (1953), pp. 64-74.

4102   ——, ed. *Studies in the Elizabethan Theatre*. Hamden, Conn.: Shoe String P., 1961.

4103   PURDOM, Charles B. *Producing Shakespeare*. London: Pitman, 1950.

4104   RANNIE, David W. *Scenery in Shakespeare's Plays*. Oxford: Blackwell, 1926. Repr. 1931.

4105   REYES, Consuelo M. de. *On the Acting of Shakespeare's Plays.* London and Glasgow: Blackie, 1928.

4106   REYNOLDS, George F. "Another Principle of Elizabethan Staging." In *The Manly Anniversary Studies in Language and Literature.* U. of Chicago P., 1923.

4107   ——. "'Lines' of Parts in Shakespeare's Plays." *SAB*, 5 (1930): 102-3.

4108   ——. *On Shakespeare's Stage.* Ed. Richard K. Knaub. U. of Colorado P., 1967.

4109   ——. "Performances in the Elizabethan Manner." *SAB*, 6 (1931): 145-47.

4110   ——. "The Return of the Open Stage." In *Essays . . . in Honor of Hardin Craig,* **2786.**

4111   ——. *Some Principles of Elizabethan Staging.* Chicago U.P., 1905. Repr. New York: AMS. [Repr. from *MP*, 2 (1904-5): 581-614; 3 (1905-6): 69-97.]

4112   ——. "Staging Elizabethan Plays." *SAB*, 24 (1949): 258-63.

4113   ——. *The Staging of Elizabethan Plays at the Red Bull Theater, 1605-25.* New York: Modern Language Association; Oxford U.P., 1940.

4114   ——. "Two Conventions of the Open Stage (As Illustrated in *Lr*)." In *Studies . . . Presented to Baldwin Maxwell,* **2824.**

4115   ——. "Was There a 'Tarras' in Shakespeare's Globe?" *ShS 4* (1951), pp. 97-100.

4116   ——. "What a Theatre for Shakespeare Should Be." *SQ*, 1 (1950): 12-17.

4117   ——. "William Percy and His Plays, with a Summary of the Customs of Elizabethan Staging." *MP*, 12 (1914-15): 241-60.

4118   RHODES, R. Crompton. *The Stagery of Shakespeare.* Birmingham: Cornish, 1922.

4119   RICHTER, Bodo L. "Recent Studies in Renaissance Scenography." *RenQ*, 19 (1966): 344-58.

4120   ROSENBERG, Marvin. "Elizabethan Actors: Men or Marionettes?" *PMLA*, 69 (1954): 915-27.

4121   ——. "Public Night Performances in Shakespeare's Time." *TN*, 8 (1954): 44-45.

4122   ROSS, Lawrence J. "The Use of a 'Fit-Up' Booth in *Oth*." *SQ*, 12 (1961): 359-70.

4123   ROTHWELL, W. F. "Was There a Typical Elizabethan Stage?" In *ShS 12,* **4139.**

4124   ROWAN, Donald F. "The Cockpit-in-Court." In *Elizabethan Theatre,* **4009.**

4125   ——. "A Neglected Jones/Webb Theatre Project, Part 2: A Theatrical Missing Link." In *Elizabethan Theatre II,* **4010.**

4126   RULFS, Donald J. "Reception of the Elizabethan Playwrights on the London Stage, 1776-1833." *SP,* 46 (1949): 54-69.

4127   SARLOS, Robert K. "Development and Operation of the First Blackfriars Theatre." In *Studies in the Elizabethan Theatre,* **4102.**

4128   SAUNDERS, John W. "Staging at the Globe, 1595-1613." *SQ,* 11 (1960): 401-25, 5 diagrams.

4129   SCHANZER, Ernest. "Hercules and His Load." *RES,* 19 (1968): 51-53. [William Oldys (1696-1761) is the earliest authority for the Globe's motto.]

4130   SELTZER, Daniel. "The Actors and the Staging." In *A New Companion to Shakespeare Studies,* **2800.**

4131   ——. "Shakespeare's Texts and Modern Productions." In *Reinterpretations of Elizabethan Drama,* **2806.**

4132   ——. "The Staging of the Last Plays." In *Later Shakespeare,* **2767.**

4133   Shakespeare Association. *A Series of Papers on Shakespeare and the Theatre . . . by Members of the Shakespeare Association.* Oxford U.P., 1927.

4134   SHAPIRO, I. A. "The Bankside Theatres: Early Engravings." *ShS 1* (1948), pp. 25-37.

4135   ——. "An Original Drawing of the Globe Theatre." *ShS 2* (1949), pp. 21-23.

4136   ——. "Robert Fludd's Stage-Illustration." *ShakS 2 1966* (1967), pp. 192-209.

4137   SHARPE, Robert B. *The Real War of the Theatres: Shakespeare's Fellows in Rivalry with the Admiral's Men, 1594-1603.* Boston: Heath, 1935. Repr. New York: Kraus.

4138   SHIRLEY, Frances A. *Shakespeare's Use of Off-Stage Sounds.* U. of Nebraska P., 1963.

4139   *ShS 12* (1959). [9 essays on Elizabethan theater.]

4140   SMITH, Irwin. " 'Gates' on Shakespeare's Stage." *SQ,* 7 (1956): 159-76.

4141   ——. "Notes on the Construction of the Globe Model." *SQ,* 2 (1951): 13-18.

4142   ——. *Shakespeare's Blackfriars Playhouse.* New York U.P., 1964.

4143   ——. *Shakespeare's Globe Playhouse.* New York: Scribner, 1956.

4144   ——. "Theatre into Globe." *SQ,* 3 (1952): 113-20.

4145   ——. "Their Exits and Re-entrances." *SQ,* 18 (1967): 7-16.

4146   SMITH, Warren D. "The Elizabethan Stage and Shakespeare's Entrance Announcements." *SQ,* 4 (1953): 405-10.

4147   —. "Evidence of Scaffolding on Shakespeare's Stage." *RES*, 2 (1951): 22-29.

4148   —. "New Light on Stage Directions in Shakespeare." *SP*, 47 (1950): 173-81.

4149   —. "Stage Business in Shakespeare's Dialogue." *SQ*, 4 (1953): 311-16.

4150   —. "Stage Settings in Shakespeare's Dialogue." *MP*, 50 (1952): 32-35.

4151   SORELL, Walter. "Shakespeare and the Dance." *SQ*, 8 (1957): 367-84.

4152   SOUTHERN, Richard. "The Contribution of the Interludes to Elizabethan Staging." In *Essays . . . in Honor of Hardin Craig*, **2786**.

4153   —. "On Reconstructing a Practicable Elizabethan Public Playhouse." In *ShS 12*, **4139**.

4154   —. *The Open Stage*. New York: Theatre Arts Books, 1959.

4155   —. *The Seven Ages of the Theatre*. New York: Hill & Wang, 1961.

4156   —. "A 17th-Century Indoor Stage." *TN*, 9 (1954): 5-11, 1 plate. [Interpretation of an illustration in Adriaen van de Venne's *Tafereel van de b'elacchende werelt . . . aengevvesen . . . op de Haegsche Kermis* (The Hague: 1635), p. 69.]

4157   —, and C. Walter Hodges. "Colour in the Elizabethan Theatre." *TN*, 6 (1952): 57-60. [Van Buchel's drawing of the Swan. Marbled classic columns. A seventeenth-century Heaven.]

4158   SPENCER, Hazelton. "How Shakespeare Staged His Plays." *Johns Hopkins Alumni Magazine*, 20 (1932): 205-21.

4159   SPENCER, Terence J. B. "Shakespeare: The Elizabethan Theatre-Poet." In *Elizabethan Theatre*, **4009**.

4160   STAMM, Rudolf. "Elizabethan Stage-Practice and the Transmutation of Source Material by the Dramatists." In *ShS 12*, **4139**.

4161   STINSON, James. "Reconstructions of Elizabethan Public Playhouses." In *Studies in the Elizabethan Theatre*, **4102**.

4162   STYAN, John L. "The Actor at the Foot of Shakespeare's Platform." In *ShS 12*, **4139**.

4163   —. *Shakespeare's Stagecraft*. Cambridge U.P., 1967. [CUP 435.]

4164   THALER, Alwin. "Minor Actors and Employees in the Elizabethan Theatre." *MP*, 20 (1922): 49-60.

4165   —. "Playwrights' Benefits and 'Interior Gathering' in the Elizabethan Theatre." *SP*, 16 (1919): 187-96.

4166   —. "The Travelling Players in Shakespeare's England." *MP*, 17 (1919-20): 489-514.

4167   THORNDIKE, Ashley H. *Shakespeare's Theatre*. New York: Macmillan, 1916. [MP 26.]

4168   WALLACE, Charles W. *The Children of the Chapel at Blackfriars, 1597-1603.* U. of Nebraska, 1908. Repr. New York: AMS.

4169   ——. *The First London Theatre: Materials for a History.* University Studies, 13, nos. 1, 2, 3. U. of Nebraska, 1913.

4170   ——. *Three London Theatres of Shakespeare's Time.* U. of Nebraska, 1909.

4171   WATKINS, Ronald. *On Producing Shakespeare.* London: Michael Joseph, 1950. Repr. New York and London: Blom.

4172   WEIMANN, Robert. *Shakespeare und die Tradition des Volkstheaters: Soziologie, Dramaturgie, Gestaltung.* Berlin: Henschelverlag, 1967.

4173   WEINER, Albert B. "Elizabethan Interior and Aloft Scenes: A Speculative Essay." *ThS*, 2 (1961): 15-34.

4174   WHALLEY, Joyce I. "The Swan Theatre in the 16th Century." *TN*, 20 (1965-66): 73, plates 3, 4.

4175   WICKHAM, Glynne. "Emblème et image: Quelques remarques sur la manière de figurer et de représenter le lieu sur la scène anglaise au xvie siècle." In *Le Lieu théâtral a la Renaissance,* **4056.**

4176   WILSON, Frank P. "The Elizabethan Theatre." *Neophil*, 39 (1955): 40-58.

4177   WOOD, D. T. B. "The Suspected Revels Books." *RES*, 1 (1925): 166-72. [See also Wood, "The Revels Books," pp. 72-74.]

4178   WRIGHT, James. *Historia Histrionica: An Historical Account of the English-Stage.* London: W. Haws, 1699. Repr. London: Tuckett, 1872 (Occasional Fac-Simile Reprints, no. 30, ed. Edmund W. Ashbee); London: Nimmo, 1889 (in *An Apology for the Life of Mr. Colley Cibber,* ed. Robert W. Lowe, 2 vols.: 1, xix-li); New York: AMS.

4179   WRIGHT, Louis B. "Animal Actors on the English Stage before 1642." *PMLA*, 42 (1927): 656-69.

4180   ——. "Madmen as Vaudeville Performers on the Elizabethan Stage." *JEGP*, 30 (1931): 48-54.

4181   ——. *Shakespeare's Theatre and the Dramatic Tradition.* Washington, D.C.: Folger Shakespeare Library, 1958. Repr. U.P. of Virginia, and in *Life and Letters,* **3958.**

4182   ——. "Stage Duelling in the Elizabethan Theatre." *MLR*, 22 (1927): 265-75.

4183   ——. "Variety Entertainment by Elizabethan Strolling Players." *JEGP*, 26 (1927): 294-303.

4184   ——. "Vaudeville Dancing and Acrobatics on the Elizabethan Stage." *EStn*, 63 (1928): 59-76.

4185   YATES, Frances A. *The Art of Memory.* London: Routledge & Kegan Paul, 1966. [Fludd's theater.]

4186   ——. "New Light on the Globe Theater." *New York Review of Books*, 6 (26 May 1966): 16-22.

4187   ——. *Theatre of the World.* London: Routledge & Kegan Paul, 1969.

4188   YOUNG, Karl. "An Elizabethan Defence of the Stage." In *Shakespeare Studies*, 2823.

STAGE HISTORY AFTER 1660

See also Reputation and Influence (**4284-4376**); **21, 27, 31, 51, 70, 74,** and **110**.

4189   AGATE, James. *Brief Chronicles: A Survey of the Plays of Shakespeare and the Elizabethans in Actual Performance.* London: Cape, 1945. Repr. New York: Blom. [Reviews from *Sunday Times*, 1923-42.]

4190   —, ed. *The English Dramatic Critics: An Anthology.* New York: Hill & Wang. [D 15.]

4191   ARCHER, William, and Robert W. Lowe, eds. *Hazlitt on Theatre.* New York: Hill & Wang, 1957. [Drama.] [Sel. from *View of the English Stage* and *Criticisms and Dramatic Essays.*]

4192   ARMSTRONG, William A. "Actors and Theatres." In *ShS 17,* **3918.**

4193   —. "The Art of Shakespearean Production in the Twentieth Century." *E&S*, 15 (1962): 74-87.

4194   AVERY, Emmett L. "The Shakespeare Ladies' Club." *SQ*, 7 (1956): 153-58.

4195   BALL, Robert H. "The Shakespeare Film as Record: Sir Herbert Beerbohm Tree." *SQ*, 3 (1952): 227-36.

4196   —. *Shakespeare on Silent Film.* London: Allen & Unwin, 1968.

4197   BROOK, Donald. *A Pageant of English Actors.* New York: Macmillan; London: Rockliff, 1950.

4198   BROWN, Ivor. *Shakespeare and the Actors.* London: Bodley Head, 1970.

4199   BROWN, John R. "English Criticism of Shakespeare Performances Today." *SJ 1967* (West), pp. 163-74.

4200   —. "On the Acting of Shakespeare's Plays." *QJS*, 39 (1953): 477-84.

4201   —. *Shakespeare's Plays in Performance.* London: Arnold, 1966. Repr. New York: St. Martin's. [Coll. of prev. pub. essays, some rev.]

4202   —. "The Study and Practice of Shakespeare Production." *ShS 18* (1965), pp. 58-69.

4203   —. "Theater Research and the Criticism of Shakespeare and His Contemporaries." *SQ*, 13 (1962): 451-62.

4204   BRUSTEIN, Robert. "No More Masterpieces: Towards a Creative Treatment of the Past." *MQR*, 6 (1967): 185-92. [Sh et al.]

4205   BURNIM, Kalman A. "The Significance of Garrick's Letters to Hayman." *SQ*, 9 (1958): 149-52. [Garrick's staging of *Lr* and *Oth*.]

4206   BYRNE, M. St. Clare. "Fifty Years of Shakespearian Production: 1898-1948." *ShS 2* (1949), pp. 1-20.

4207 CARLISLE, Carol J. *Shakespeare from the Greenroom: Actors' Criticisms of Four Major Tragedies.* U. of North Carolina P., 1970. [*Ham, Lr, Mac, Oth.*]

4208 CHILD, Harold H. *The Shakespearian Productions of John Philip Kemble.* Oxford U.P., 1935.

4209 CLARK, Cumberland. *Shakespeare and Costume.* London: Mitre, 1937.

4210 CLARK, William S. "Restoration Prompt Notes and Stage Practices." *MLN*, 51 (1936): 226-30.

4211 COGHILL, Nevill. "University Contributions to Shakespeare Production in England." *SJ*, 93 (1957): 175-85.

4212 COHEN, Nathan. "Stratford after Fifteen Years." *QQ*, 75 (1968): 35-61. [Ontario.]

4213 DAVID, Richard. "Actors and Scholars: A View of Shakespeare in the Modern Theatre." *ShS 12* (1959), pp. 76-87.

4214 ——. "Shakespeare's Comedies and the Modern Stage." *ShS 4* (1951), pp. 129-38.

4215 DAY, Muriel C., and John C. Trewin. *The Shakespeare Memorial Theatre.* London and Toronto: Dent, 1932.

4216 DEELMAN, Christian. *The Great Shakespeare Jubilee.* London: Michael Joseph, 1964.

4217 DONOHUE, Joseph W. *Dramatic Character in the English Romantic Age.* Princeton U.P., 1970. [Pt. 3 on Sh.]

4218 DOWNER, Alan S. "For Jesus' Sake Forbear: Shakespeare vs. the Modern Theater." *SQ*, 13 (1962): 219-30.

4219 ——. "Mr. Dangle's Defense: Acting and Stage History." *EIE 1946* (1947), pp. 159-90.

4220 ——. "Shakespeare in the Contemporary American Theater." *SJ*, 93 (1957): 154-69.

4221 ELLIS, Ruth. *The Shakespeare Memorial Theatre.* London: Winchester, 1948.

4222 ENGLAND, Martha W. *Garrick's Jubilee.* Ohio State U.P., 1964.

4223 FARJEON, Herbert. *The Shakespearean Scene: Dramatic Criticisms.* London and New York: Hutchinson, 1949.

4224 GIELGUD, John. "Tradition, Style, and the Theatre To-day." *ShS 4* (1951), pp. 101-8.

4225 GLICK, Claris. "William Poel: His Theories and Influence." *SQ*, 15.1 (1964): 15-25.

4226 GRANVILLE-BARKER, Harley. *Associating with Shakespeare.* Oxford U.P., 1932.

4227 GRIFFIN, Alice S. (Venezky). "Shakespeare through the Camera's Eye." *SQ*, 4 (1953): 331-36; 6 (1955): 63-66; 7 (1956): 235-40; 17 (1966): 383-87.

4228 HARBAGE, Alfred. *Theatre for Shakespeare.* U. of Toronto P., 1955.

4229 HAWKES, Terence. "Postscript: Theatre against Shakespeare?" In *Elizabethan Theatre,* **4009.**

4230 HUNT, Hugh. *Old Vic Prefaces: Shakespeare and the Producer.* London: Routledge & Kegan Paul, 1954.

4231 HUNT, Leigh. *Dramatic Criticism.* Oxford U.P., 1950.

4232 KEMP, Thomas C. "Acting Shakespeare: Modern Tendencies in Playing and Production." *ShS 7* (1954), pp. 121-27.

4233 —, and John C. Trewin. *The Stratford Festival.* Birmingham: Cornish, 1953.

4234 KITCHIN, Laurence. "Shakespeare on the Screen." *ShS 18* (1965), pp. 70-74.

4235 —. "Shakespeare: The Actor's Problem." *E&S,* 17 (1964): 88-97.

4236 KNIGHT, G. Wilson. *Principles of Shakespearean Production.* London and New York: Macmillan, 1936. 2nd ed. rev. and enl., Harmondsworth: Penguin, 1949. 3rd ed. rev., London: Routledge & Kegan Paul, 1968. [Esp. tragedies and *Tmp, MV, H8.*]

4237 LEECH, Clifford. "The Acting of Marlowe and Shakespeare." *ColQ,* 13 (1964): 25-42.

4238 McAFEE, Helen, ed. *Pepys on the Restoration Stage.* Yale U.P.; Oxford U.P., 1916. Repr. New York: Blom.

4239 MATTHEWS, J. Brander. "Shaksperian Stage Traditions." In *Shaksperian Studies,* **2798.**

4240 MELCHINGER, Siegfried. "Shakespeare heute." *SJ 1965* (West), pp. 59-79.

4241 MERCHANT, W. Moelwyn. "Classical Costume in Shakespearian Productions." *ShS 10* (1957), pp. 71-76.

4242 MONCK, Nugent. "The Maddermarket Theatre and the Playing of Shakespeare." *ShS 12* (1959), pp. 71-75.

4243 NICOLL, Allardyce. *The World of Harlequin.* Cambridge U.P., 1963.

4244 ODELL, George C. D. *Annals of the New York Stage.* 15 vols. Columbia U.P., 1927-49.

4245 —. *Shakespeare from Betterton to Irving.* 2 vols. New York: Scribner's, 1920; London: Constable, 1921. Repr. New York: Blom (with new introd. by Robert H. Ball). [Dover.]

4246 POEL, William. *Shakespeare in the Theatre.* London and Toronto: Sidgwick & Jackson, 1913. Repr. New York: Blom.

4247 RICHMOND, Evelyn B. "Historical Costuming: A Footnote." *SQ,* 11 (1960): 233-34, 2 plates. [Planché's *Jn* at Covent Garden, 24 Nov. 1823.]

4248 SCOUTEN, Arthur H. "The Increase in Popularity of Shakespeare's Plays in the Eighteenth Century: A Caveat for Interpreters of Stage History." *SQ*, 7 (1956): 189-202. [See also Scouten, "Shakespeare's Plays in the Theatrical Repertory When Garrick Came to London." *TxSE* (1944): pp. 257-68.]

4249 SPEAIGHT, Robert. *William Poel and the Elizabethan Revival.* London: Society for Theatre Research and William Heinemann, 1954.

4250 SPRAGUE, Arthur C. *Shakespeare and the Actors: The Stage Business in His Plays, 1660-1905.* Harvard U.P., 1944. Repr. Oxford U.P., 1948; New York: Russell & Russell.

4251 ——. "Shakespeare's Plays on the English Stage." In *A New Companion to Shakespeare Studies,* **2800**.

4252 ——. *Shakespearian Players and Performances.* Harvard U.P., 1953; London: Black, 1954. Repr. New York: Greenwood.

4253 ——. *The Stage Business in Shakespeare's Plays: A Postscript.* London: Society for Theatre Research, 1954.

4254 STEVENSON, Allan H. "The Case of the Decapitated Cast." *SQ*, 6 (1955): 275-96. [Actors and promptbooks of the Smock Alley Theatre, Dublin.]

4255 STOCHHOLM, Johanne M. *Garrick's Folly: The Shakespeare Jubilee of 1769 at Stratford and Drury Lane.* London: Methuen, 1964.

4255a STONE, George W. "David Garrick's Significance in the History of Shakespearean Criticism." *PMLA*, 65 (1950): 183-97.

4256 TAYLOR, John R. "Shakespeare in Film, Radio, and Television." In *Shakespeare: A Celebration,* **2816**.

4257 THALER, Alwin. *Shakespeare to Sheridan.* Harvard U.P., 1922.

4258 THORP, Margaret F. "Shakespeare and the Movies." *SQ*, 9 (1958): 357-66.

4259 TREWIN, John C. *Shakespeare on the English Stage, 1900-1964: A Survey of Productions.* London: Barrie & Rockliff, 1964.

4260 VAN LENNEP, William. "The Smock Alley Players of Dublin." *ELH;* see **761**.

4261 WEBSTER, Margaret. *Shakespeare Today.* London: Dent, 1957.

4262 ——. *Shakespeare without Tears.* Cleveland: World, 1942. Repr. 1955. Rev. ed., Greenwich, Conn.: Fawcett, 1964. [Premier R223.]

4263 WEST, E. J. "George Bernard Shaw on Shakespearean Production." *SP*, 45 (1948): 216-35.

4264 WINTER, William. *Shakespeare on the Stage.* 3 series. New York: Moffat, Yard, 1911, 1915, 1916. Repr. New York: Blom.

AUDIENCE

4265   ARMSTRONG, William A. "The Audience of the Elizabethan Private Theatres." *RES*, 10 (1959): 234-49.

4266   BENNETT, H. Stanley. *Shakespeare's Audience*. Oxford U.P., 1944. [*PBA 1944*, 30 (1945): 73-86.]   Repr. in *Studies in Shakespeare*, **2759.**

4267   ——. "Shakespeare's Stage and Audience." *Neophil*, 33 (1949): 40-51.

4268   BRADLEY, Andrew C. "Shakespeare's Theatre and Audience." In *Oxford Lectures on Poetry*, **2883.**

4269   BRIDGES, Robert S. *The Influence of the Audience on Shakespeare's Drama*. Oxford U.P., 1927.

4270   BYRNE, M. St. Clare. "Shakespeare's Audience." In *A Series of Papers on Shakespeare and the Theatre*, **4133.**

4271   HARBAGE, Alfred B. *Shakespeare and the Rival Traditions*. New York: Macmillan, 1952. Repr. New York: Barnes & Noble.

4272   ——. *Shakespeare's Audience*. Columbia U.P.; Oxford U.P., 1941.

4273   HOLMES, Martin. *Shakespeare's Public*. London: Murray, 1960.

4274   PRIOR, Moody E. "The Elizabethan Audience and the Plays of Shakespeare." *MP*, 49 (1951): 101-23.

4275   SISSON, Charles J. *Le Goût public et le théâtre élisabéthain jusqu'à la mort de Shakespeare*. Dijon: Darantière, 1922.

4276   SPRAGUE, Arthur C. *Shakespeare and the Audience: A Study in the Technique of Exposition*.   Harvard U.P.; Oxford U.P., 1935. Repr. New York: Russell & Russell.

ALLUSIONS

See also **4288** and **4292**.

4277   BALD, R. Cecil. "The *Locrine* and *George-a-Greene* Title-Page Inscriptions." *Library*, 15 (1934-35): 295-305, 4 plates. [Genuine.]

4278   BLACK, Alfred B., and Robert M. Smith. *Shakespeare Allusions and Parallels.* Lehigh U.P., 1931. Repr. New York: AMS.

4279   GREG, Walter W. "Three Manuscript Notes by Sir George Buc." *Library*, 12 (1931-32): 307-21, 9 plates. [One names Shakespeare, p. 308.]

4280   HOENIGER, F. David. "New Harvey Marginalia on *Ham* and *R3*." *SQ*, 17 (1966): 151-55, 1 illus.

4281   INGLEBY, Clement M., Lucy T. Smith, and Frederick J. Furnivall, eds. *The Shakspere Allusion-Book... from 1591 to 1700.* 2 vols. Reedited John Munro. 2 vols. London: Chatto & Windus; New York: Duffield, 1909. Repr. with Preface by Edmund K. Chambers, Oxford U.P., 1932.

4282   MUNRO, John. "More Shakspere Allusions." *MP*, 13 (1915-16): 497-544.

4283   THORN-DRURY, George. *Some Seventeenth Century Allusions to Shakespeare and His Works Not Hitherto Collected.* London: P. J. & A. E. Dobell, 1920. [See also Thorn-Drury, *More Seventeenth Century Allusions to Shakespeare and His Works Not Hitherto Collected* (London: Dobell, 1924).]

REPUTATION AND INFLUENCE

See also Translations (**762-94**); **127**, **1041**, **2809**, **2860**, **2890**, and **3931**.

4284   ABEND, Murray. "Shakespeare's Influences in Beaumont and Fletcher." *N&Q*, 197 (1952): 272-74, 360-63.

4285   ADAMS, Joseph Q. "William Heminge and Shakespeare." *MP*, 12 (1914-15): 51-64. [The younger Heminge.]

4286   ALBERT, Gábor. "Selected Bibliography of Shakespeare's Works Published in Hungarian." *NHQ*, 5 (1964): 112-18.

4287   ALEXANDER, Edward. "Shakespeare's Plays in Armenia." *SQ*, 9 (1958): 387-94.

4288   ALLEN, Don C., ed. *Francis Meres's Treatise* Poetrie: *A Critical Edition*. U. of Illinois P., 1933. See also **3195**.

4289   AND, Metin. "Shakespeare in Turkey." *ThR*, 6 (1964): 75-84.

4290   ANDERSON, Donald K. "*R2* and *Perkin Warbeck*." *SQ*, 13 (1962): 260-63.

4291   BAKER, D. S. "Shakespeare in Ghana." *ShS 16* (1963), pp. 77-82.

4292   BENTLEY, Gerald E. *Shakespeare and Jonson: Their Reputations in the Seventeenth Century Compared*. 2 vols. U. of Chicago P.; Cambridge U.P., 1945. [See also Walter W. Greg, "Shakespeare and Jonson." *RES*, 22 (1946): 58, and David L. Frost, "Shakespeare in the Seventeenth Century." *SQ*, 16 (1965): 81-89.]

4293   BERKELMAN, Robert. "Lincoln's Interest in Shakespeare." *SQ*, 2 (1951): 303-12.

4294   BESTERMAN, Theodore, ed. *Voltaire on Shakespeare*. Vol. 54 of *Studies on Voltaire and the Eighteenth Century*. Geneva: Institut et Musée Voltaire, 1967.

4295   BEZA, Marcu. *Shakespeare in Roumania*. London: Dent, 1931.

4296   BRANDL, Alois. *Shakespeare and Germany*. Oxford U.P., 1913. [*PBA 1913-14*, 6 (1914): 249-60.]

4297   CALGARI, Guido. "Fortuna di Shakespeare in Italia e in Francia." *Hesperia*, 3 (1952): 191-99.

4298   CALINA, Josephine (Nicoll). *Shakespeare in Poland*. Oxford U.P., 1923.

4299   DAVIDSON, Levette J. "Shakespeare in the Rockies." *SQ*, 4 (1953): 39-49.

4300   DAVRIL, Robert. "Shakespeare and Ford." *SJ*, 94 (1958): 121-31.

4301   DE GRUYTER, D., and Wayne Hayward. "Shakespeare on the Flemish Stage of Belgium, 1876-1951." *ShS 5* (1952), pp. 106-10.

4302   DUNN, C. J. "Shakespeare Production in Japan." *East-West Review* (Kyoto), 2 (1965): 1-16.

4303   DUNN, Esther C. *Shakespeare in America*. New York: Macmillan, 1939. Repr. New York: Blom.

4304 DUŢU, Alexandru. "Recent Shakespeare Performances in Romania." *ShS 20* (1967), pp. 125-31.

4305 —. *Shakespeare in Rumania: A Bibliographical Essay*. Bucharest: Meridiane, 1964.

4306 FALK, Robert. "Shakespeare in America: A Survey to 1900." *ShS 18* (1965), pp. 102-18.

4307 FERRANDO, Guido. "Shakespeare in Italy." *SAB*, 5 (1930): 157-68.

4308 FLUCHÈRE, Henri. "Shakespeare in France: 1900-1948." *ShS 2* (1949), pp. 115-25.

4309 GEORGE, Louise W. "Shakespeare in La Ceiba." *SQ*, 3 (1952): 359-65.

4310 GIBIAN, George. "Shakespeare in Soviet Russia." *Russian Review*, 11 (1952): 24-34.

4311 GYULAI, Ágost. *Shakespeare in Hungary*. London: Gale & Polden, 1908.

4312 HAHN, Wiktor. *Shakespeare w Polsce: Bibliografia*. Wrocław: Zakład Narodowy im Ossolińskich, 1958.

4313 HAINES, Charles M. *Shakespeare in France: Criticism, Voltaire to Victor Hugo*. Oxford U.P., 1925.

4314 HARBAGE, Alfred. "Shakespeare as Culture Hero." *HLQ*, 27 (1963-64): 211-27.

4315 HARRIES, Frederick J. *Shakespeare and the Scots*. Edinburgh: Henderson, 1932.

4316 —. *Shakespeare and the Welsh*. London: Unwin, 1919.

4317 HAVENS, George R. "The Abbé Prévost and Shakespeare." *MP*, 17 (1919-20): 177-98.

4318 HENRIQUES, Alf. "Shakespeare and Denmark, 1900-1949." *ShS 3* (1950), pp. 107-15.

4319 HORN-MONVAL, Madeleine. *Les Traductions françaises de Shakespeare, à l'occasion du quatrième centenaire de sa naissance, 1564-1964*. Paris: Centre National de la Recherche Scientifique, 1963.

4320 JACQUOT, Jean. *Shakespeare en France: Mises en scène d'hier et d'aujourd'hui*. Paris: Le Temps, 1964.

4321 JENSEN, Niels L. "Shakespeare in Denmark." *DUJ*, 25 (1964): 91-98.

4322 JONES, Henry A. *Shakespeare and Germany*. London: Whittingham, 1916.

4323 JOVANOVIC, Slobodan. "Shakespeare en Yougoslavie." *ThR*, 7 (1966): 159-62.

4324 KAIEDA, Susuma. "Shakespeare in Japan, 1925-1945." *Area and Culture Studies* (Tokyo Foreign Languages U.), no. 13, pp. 115-30.

4325   KAWATAKE, Toshio. "Shakespeare in the Japanese Theatre." *ThR*, 2 (1960): 82-87.

4326   KLAJN, Hugo. "Shakespeare in Yugoslavia." *SQ*, 5 (1954): 41-45.

4327   KOHT, Halvdan. "Shakespeare and Ibsen." *JEGP*, 44 (1945): 79-86.

4328   LANCASTER, Henry C. "The Alleged First Foreign Estimate of Shakespeare." *MLN*, 63 (1948): 509-12. [1717.]

4329   [LEVIDOVA, Inna M., ed.] *Shekspir; Bibliografiya Russkikh Perevodov I Kriticheskoi Literatury na Russkom Yakyke, 1748-1962.* Moscow: Kniga, 1964. [Continuation for 1963-64 in 1969.]

4330   LE WINTER, Oswald, ed. *Shakespeare in Europe.* Cleveland: World, 1963. [M156 Meridan.] [Sel. from 25 European critics, esp. 19th cent.]

4331   LIRONDELLE, André. *Shakespeare en Russie, 1748-1840.* Paris: Hachette, 1912.

4332   LOUNSBURY, Thomas R. *Shakespeare and Voltaire.* New York: Scribner's, 1902. Repr. New York: Blom; AMS.

4333   McKEITHAN, Daniel M. *The Debt to Shakespeare in the Beaumont and Fletcher Plays.* Austin, Tex.: Privately printed, distrib. by Texas Book Store, 1938. Repr. New York: AMS.

4334   McMANAWAY, James G. "Shakespeare in the United States." *PMLA*, 79 (1964): 513-18. Repr. in *Studies in Shakespeare, Bibliography, and Theater,* **3174**.

4335   MENDONÇA, Barbara H. C. de (Almeida). "Shakespeare in Brazil." *ShS 20* (1967), pp. 121-24.

4336   MOORE, John R. "Defoe and Shakespeare." *SQ*, 19 (1968): 71-80.

4337   MOREIRA GOMES, Celuta, and Thereza da Silva Aguiar. *William Shakespeare no Brasil.* Rio de Janeiro: Biblioteca nacional, 1965.

4338   MORLEY, Christopher D. *Shakespeare and Hawaii.* Garden City, N.Y.: Doubleday, Doran, 1933.

4339   MOROZOV, Mikhail M. *Shakespeare on the Soviet Stage.* Trans. David Magarshack. Introd. J. Dover Wilson. London: Soviet News, 1947.

4340   NOCK, Francis J. "E. T. A. Hoffmann and Shakespeare." *JEGP*, 53 (1954): 369-82.

4341   PAR, Alfonso. *Contribución a la Bibliografía Española de Shakespeare.* Barcelona: Instituto del Teatro Nacional, 1930.

4342   —. *Representaciones Shakespearianas en España.* Madrid: Suárez, 1936.

4343   PASCAL, Roy, ed. *Shakespeare in Germany, 1740-1815.* Cambridge U.P., 1937.

4344   POPOVIĆ, Vladeta. "Shakespeare in Post-War Yugoslavia." *ShS 4* (1951), pp. 117-22.

4345   —. *Shakespeare in Serbia.* Oxford U.P., 1928.

4346   PRICE, Lawrence M. "Shakespeare in Germany." In *English Literature in Germany.* U. of California Studies in Modern Philology, 71. U. of California P., 1953.

4347   *La Revue d'Histoire du Théâtre,* 16 (1965). [Devoted to Shakespeare on the foreign stage—France, Russia, Hungary, Italy.]

4348   RICHTER, Kurt A. *Beiträge zum Bekanntwerder Shakespeares in Deutschland.* 3 vols. Breslau: Grass, Barth, 1909-12.

4348a   ROBERTSON, J. G. "Shakespeare on the Continent." Chap. 12, vol. 5 of *Cam. Hist. Eng. Lit., 18a.*

4349   RUUD, Martin B. *An Essay towards a History of Shakespeare in Denmark.* U. of Minnesota P., 1920.

4350   ŠEŠPLAUKIS, Alfonsas. "Shakespeare in Litauen." *SJ 1968* (West), pp. 193-206.

4351   *Die Shakspeare-Literatur in Deutschland: Vollständiger Catalog sämmtlicher in Deutschland erschienen Uebersetzungen W. Shakspeares..., aller bezüglichen Erläuterungs- und Ergänzungsschriften... von 1762 bis Ende 1851.* Kassel: E. Balde, 1852.

4352   SIDERIS, Joannis. "Shakespeare in Greece." *ThR,* 6 (1964): 85-99.

4353   ŠIMKO, Ján. "Shakespeare in Slovakia." *ShS 4* (1951), pp. 109-16.

4354   SIMON, Henry W. *The Reading of Shakespeare in American Schools and Colleges: An Historical Survey.* New York: Simon & Schuster, 1932. Repr. New York: AMS.

4355   SISSON, Charles J. *Shakespeare in India.* Oxford U.P., 1926.

4356   SPURGEON, Caroline F. E. *Keats's Shakespeare: A Descriptive Study Based on New Material.* Oxford U.P., 1928. Repr. 1966.

4357   STAHL, Ernst L. *Shakespeare und das deutsche Theater.* Stuttgart: Kohlhammer, 1947.

4358   STAIGER, Emil. "Shakespeare in Deutschland." *Hesperia,* 3 (1952): 173-82.

4359   STEIN, Jess M. "Horace Walpole and Shakespeare." *SP,* 31 (1934): 51-68.

4360   STOVALL, Floyd. "Whitman, Shakespeare, and Democracy." *JEGP,* 51 (1952): 457-72.

4361   —. "Whitman's Knowledge of Shakespeare." *SP,* 49 (1952): 643-69.

4362   STŘÍBRNÝ, Zdeněk. "Shakespeare in Czechoslovakia." In *Shakespeare Celebrated,* 2825.

4363   THOMAS, Henry. *Shakespeare in Spain.* Oxford U.P., 1950. [*PBA 1949,* 35 (1950): 87-108.]

4364   THORNDIKE, Ashley H. *Shakespeare in America.* Oxford U.P., 1927. [*PBA 1927,* 13 (1928): 153-72.]

4365   TOYODA, Minoru. *Shakespeare in Japan: An Historical Survey.* Tokyo: Iwani Shoten for the Shakespeare Association of Japan, 1940.

4366   VIOLI, Unicio J. "Shakespeare and the Americans Today." *Literary Half-Yearly,* 8 (1967): 50-56.

4367   VOČADLO, Otakar. "Shakespeare and Bohemia." *ShS 9* (1956), pp. 101-10.

4368   WAHR, Fred B. "Goethe's Shakespeare." *PQ,* 11 (1932): 344-58.

4369   WEIGAND, Hermann J. "Shakespeare in German Criticism." In *Essays in Honor of Robert W. Babcock,* **2810.**

4370   WHITTAKER, Herbert. "Shakespeare in Canada before 1953." In *Stratford Papers on Shakespeare, 1964,* **2787.**

4371   WILLOUGHBY, Edwin E. "The Reading of Shakespeare in Colonial America." *PBSA,* 31 (1937): 45-96.

4372   WITTE, William. "Deus Absconditus: Shakespeare in Eighteenth-Century Germany." In *Papers Mainly Shakespearean,* **2775.**

4373   WOLFF, Max J. "Antonio Conti in seinem Verhältnis zu Shakespeare." *JEGP,* 37 (1938): 555-58. [The earliest Continental admirer?]

4374   WRIGHT, Louis B., ed. *Shakespeare in School and College.* Champaign, Ill.: National Council of Teachers of English, 1964. [Essays 1st appeared as articles in *CE* and *EJ.*]

4375   ZBIERSKI, Henryk. "Shakespeare in Poland." *ThR,* 2 (1960): 136-40.

4376   ZELAK, Dominik. *Tieck und Shakespeare: Ein Beitrag zur Geschichte der Shakespeareomanie in Deutschland.* Ternopol: Podolische, 1900.

MUSIC

See also **1171, 1721, 1754, 2088, 2209, 3038,** and **3883.**

4377 ARKWRIGHT, G. E. P. "Elizabethan Choirboy Plays and Their Music." International Musicological Society, *Sammelbände,* 40 (1913-14): 117-38.

4378 AUDEN, Wystan H. "Music in Shakespeare." In *The Dyer's Hand and Other Essays,* **2838.**

4379 BAYLISS, Stanley A. "Music for Shakespeare." *Music and Letters,* 15 (1934): 61-65.

4380 BRIDGE, J. Frederick. *Shakespearean Music in the Plays and Early Operas.* London and Toronto: Dent; New York: Dutton, 1923.

4381 —. *Songs from Shakespeare: The Earliest Known Settings.* London: Novello, *ca.* 1894.

4382 CAULFIELD, John, ed. *Collection of the Vocal Music in Shakespeare's Plays.* 2 vols. London: Caulfield, 1864.

4383 CHAPPELL, William. *Popular Music of the Olden Time.* 2 vols. London: Chappell, 1855-59. Repr. Gloucester, Mass.: Peter Smith. Rev. as *Old English Popular Music.* Ed. Harry E. Wooldridge. London: Chappell; New York: Novello & Ewer, 1893.

4384 COWLING, George H. *Music on the Shakespearian Stage.* Cambridge U.P., 1913.

4385 CUDWORTH, Charles. "Song and Part-Song Settings of Shakespeare's Lyrics, 1660-1960." In *Shakespeare in Music,* **4397.**

4386 CUTTS, John P. *La Musique de scène de la troupe de Shakespeare: The King's Men sous le règne de Jacques Ier.* Paris: Centre National de la Recherche Scientifique, 1959.

4387 DEAN, Winton. "Shakespeare and Opera." In *Shakespeare in Music,* **4397.**

4388 —. "Shakespeare in the Opera House." *ShS 18* (1965), pp. 75-93. [A list of operas based on the plays.]

4389 DENT, Edward. "Musical Interpretations of Shakespeare on the Modern Stage." *Musical Quarterly,* 2 (1916): 523-37.

4390 DUNN, Catherine M. "The Functions of Music in Shakespeare's Romances." *SQ,* 20 (1969): 391-405.

4391 EDWARDS, Edward. *A Book of Shakespeare's Songs, with Musical Settings by Various Composers.* New York: Shirmer, 1903.

4392 ELSON, Louis C. *Shakespeare in Music: A Collation of the Chief Musical Allusions in the Plays of Shakespeare.* London: David Nutt, 1901. Repr. New York: AMS.

4393 FISKE, Roger. "Shakespeare in the Concert Hall." In *Shakespeare in Music,* **4397.**

4394 Canceled.

4395 GALPIN, Francis W. *Old English Instruments of Music.* London: Methuen, 1910. Repr. 1932.

4396 GREENHILL, James, William A. Harrison, and Frederick J. Furnivall, eds. *A List of All the Songs and Passages in Shakspere Which Have Been Set to Music.* Rev. ed., New Shakspere Society Publications, ser. 8, Miscellanies 3. London: N. Trübner, 1884.

4397 HARTNOLL, Phyllis, ed. *Shakespeare in Music: A Collection of Essays.* London: Macmillan, 1964. Repr. New York: St. Martin's. [Incl. catalogue of musical works based on plays and poetry of Sh.]

4398 ISTEL, Edgar. "Verdi und Shakespeare." *SJ,* 53 (1917): 69-124.

4399 LAMSON, Roy. "Musical Settings for the Poems." In *Poems,* **2155.**

4400 LAWRENCE, William J. "Music in the Elizabethan Theatre." *SJ,* 44 (1908): 36-50.

4401 LONG, John H., ed. *Music in English Renaissance Drama.* U. of Kentucky P., 1968. [7 essays, none on Sh.]

4402 —. *Shakespeare's Use of Music: A Study of the Music and Its Performance in the Original Productions of Seven Comedies.* U. of Florida P., 1955.

4403 —. *Shakespeare's Use of Music: The Final Comedies.* U. of Florida P., 1961.

4404 MANIFOLD, John S. *The Music in English Drama: From Shakespeare to Purcell.* London: Rockliff, 1956.

4405 MOORE, John R. "The Function of the Songs in Shakespeare's Plays." In *Shakespeare Studies,* **2823.**

4406 —. "The Songs of the Public Theater in the Time of Shakespeare." *JEGP,* 28 (1929): 166-202.

4407 *Music for the Theatre: Shakespeare.* New York: Guglietto-Black, 1970. [Rental music available in mono, stereo, score, and tape: *AWW, AYL, Err, Ham, 1H4, H8, JC, Jn, Lr, Mac, MM, MV, Wiv, MND, Oth, R3, Rom, Tmp, Tit, TN.*]

4408 NAYLOR, Edward W. *The Poets and Music.* London and Toronto: Dent, 1928. [Chap. on Sh.]

4409 —. *Shakespeare and Music.* London: Dent, 1896. Repr. New York: AMS. Rev. ed., London: Dent, 1931; repr. New York: Da Capo & Blom.

4410 —, ed. *Shakespeare Music.* London: Curwen, 1913.

4411 NOBLE, Richmond S. H. *Shakespeare's Use of Song with the Text of the Principal Songs.* Oxford U.P., 1923. Rev. ed., London: Dent; New York: Dutton, 1931; repr. New York: De Capo; Blom.

4412 NOSWORTHY, James M. "Music and Its Function in the Romances of Shakespeare." In *ShS 11,* **3529.**

4413   PATTISON, Bruce. *Music and Poetry of the English Renaissance.* London: Methuen, 1948.

4414   ROBERTS, William W. "Music in Shakespeare." *BJRL,* 7 (1923): 480-93.

4415   RUPPEL, K. H. "Verdi und Shakespeare." In *SJ,* 92, **793**.

4416   SCHOLES, Percy. "The Purpose behind Shakespeare's Use of Music." *Proceedings of the Royal Musical Association,* 43 (1916-17): 1-15.

4417   SENG, Peter J. *The Vocal Songs in the Plays of Shakespeare: A Critical History.* Harvard U.P.; Oxford U.P., 1967.

4417a   *ShS 15* (1962). [2 essays on songs and music.]

4418   STERNFELD, Frederick W. "Music and Ballads." In *ShS 17,* **3918**.

4419   ——. *Music in Shakespearean Tragedy.* London: Routledge & Kegan Paul, 1963. [Incl. comedy.]

4420   ——. "Shakespeare and Music." In *A New Companion to Shakespeare Studies,* **2800**.

4421   ——. "Shakespeare's Use of Popular Song." In *Elizabethan and Jacobean Studies Presented to F. P. Wilson,* **2772**.

4422   ——. *Songs from Shakespeare's Tragedies: A Collection of Songs for Concert or Dramatic Use, Edited from Contemporary Sources.* Oxford U.P., 1963.

4423   ——. "Twentieth-Century Studies in Shakespeare's Songs and Music." In *ShS 15,* **4417a**.

4424   STEVENS, John. "Shakespeare and the Music of the Elizabethan Stage." In *Shakespeare in Music,* **4397**.

4425   WILSON, Christopher. *Shakespeare and Music.* London: "The Stage" Office, 1922.

4426   WOODFILL, Walter L. *Musicians in English Society from Elizabeth to Charles I.* Princeton U.P., 1953.

4427   WRIGHT, Louis B. "Extraneous Song in Elizabethan Drama after the Advent of Shakespeare." *SP,* 24 (1927): 261-74.

RECORDINGS

4428   *Ages of Man.* Gielgud [sel. from 12 plays & *Son*], Col. OL-5390.

4429   *Cym.* Folio Theatre Players, Sp. Arts 889.

4430   *Elizabethan Life, Shakespeare's London, Shakespeare's Theatre, Shakespeare's Life, Shakespeare's Stage Production.* Lex. 76937.

4431   *Great Actors.* Gry. 900.

4432   *Ham.* Gielgud, 2-Vic. LM-6007. Baylor Theatre, 3-Word 6002-3. Burton, Broadway Cast, 4-Col. DOS-702. Kinski Ensemble [German excerpts], 2-Amadeo 1030/1. Olivier [excerpts, also *H5*], Vic. LM 1924.

4433   *Homage.* Evans, Gielgud, Leighton, Col. OS-2520.

4434   *Homage to Shakespeare.* Argo ZNF-4. [Speeches from later plays, and tributes.]

4435   *John Barrymore.* 2-Audio Rarities 2280/1.

4436   *JC.* Mercury Theatre, Welles, 2-Lex. 7570/75.

4437   *Lr.* Dublin Gate Theatre, 4-Sp. Word A9.

4438   *Mac.* Old Vic, 2-Vic. LM-6010. Dublin Gate Theatre, Sp. Arts 782.

4439   Marlowe Society. Argo. [36 plays, Poems and *Son; PhT* with *Tmp.*]

4440   Marlowe Society. *Scenes from the Comedies, Histories, and Tragedies.* Argo DA 1/4.

4441   *Men and Women.* Gielgud, Worth, Vic. VDS-115.

4442   *MV.* Sparer, Marchant, Lex 7540. [Abridged.]

4443   *MND.* Old Vic, 2-Vic LM 6115.

4444   *Ado.* British National Theatre, 3-Vic. VDS-104.

4445   *Oth.* Robeson, Ferrer, 3-Col. CSL-153. Dublin Gate Theatre, Sp. Arts 783. Marshall, Robinson, Claire, Donegan, 2-Folk 9618. Olivier, 4-Vic. VDS-100.

4446   *Rom.* Bloom, Badel, 2-Vic. LM 6110. Kinski Ensemble [German excerpts], 2-Amadeo 1028/9.

4447   Shakespeare Recording Society. Caed. [30 plays, *Ven, Luc, Son.*]

4448   *Son.* Speaight, Nos. 1-51, 3-Sp. Arts 947/9.

4449   *Shr.* Shakespeare Students Co., 2-Folk 9621. Watkinson, Casson, Sp. Arts 884.

4450   *Tmp.* Carrol, Casson, Sp. Arts 886.

4451   *TN.* Folio Theatre, Sp. Arts 887.

4452   *Ven,* Poems, *Luc.* Speaight, Audley, Sp. Arts 942-3.

ILLUSTRATIONS

See also **1137.**

4453 BOYDELL, John. *A Catalogue of the Pictures, &c. in the Shakspeare Gallery, Pall-Mall.* 1789. London: The Proprietors, 1802.

4454 BOYDELL, Josiah, and John Boydell. *Collection of Prints from Pictures Painted for the Purpose of Illustrating the Dramatic Works of Shakespeare by the Artists of Great Britain.* 2 vols. London: J. and J. Boydell, 1803.

4455 BRERETON, Austin. *Shakespearean Scenes and Characters, with Descriptive Notes on the Plays, and the Principal Shakespearean Players, from Betterton to Irving.* London and New York: Cassell, 1886.

4456 BURNIM, Kalman A. "Eighteenth-Century Theatrical Illustrations in the Light of Contemporary Documents." *TN*, 14 (1960): 45-55.

4457 CHAMBERS, Edmund K. "The First Illustration to 'Shakespeare.'" *Library*, 5 (1924-25): 326-30, 1 plate. [*Tit.*]

4458 DOWDEN, Edward, ed. *Shakespeare Scenes and Characters ... Designed by Adams, Hofmann, Makart, Schwoerer, and Spiess.* London: Macmillan, 1876.

4459 HARD, Frederick. *The Sculptured Scenes from Shakespeare: A Description of John Gregory's Marble Reliefs.* Washington, D.C.: Folger Shakespeare Library, 1959.

4460 MERCHANT, W. Moelwyn. "Francis Hayman's Illustrations of Shakespeare." *SQ*, 9 (1958): 141-47, 8 plates.

4461 —. *Shakespeare and the Artist.* Oxford U.P., 1959.

4462 SALAMAN, Malcolm C. *Shakespeare in Pictorial Art.* Ed. Charles Holme. London: "The Studio," 1916. Repr. New York: Blom.

4463 *Shakespeare in Art: Paintings, Drawings, and Engravings Devoted to Shakespearean Subjects.* London: Arts Council, 1964.

4464 *The Shakspere Gallery, Being a Collection of Forty-five Steel Engravings after Pictures by Eminent Artists.* London: Virtue, 1879.

4465 TAYLOR, Charles, ed. *The Picturesque Beauties of Shakespeare, Being a Selection of Scenes from the Works of That ... Author.* London: C. Taylor, 1783-87. [Engravings after Robert Smirke and Thomas Stothard.]

AUTHORSHIP

4466   ALLEN, Percy. *The Case for Edward de Vere, 17th Earl of Oxford, as William Shakespeare.* London: Palmer, 1930.

4467   AMPHLETT, H. *Who Was Shakespeare? A New Enquiry.* London: Heinemann, 1955. [Oxford.]

4468   ARENSBERG, Walter C. *The Magic Ring of Francis Bacon.* Pittsburgh, Pa.: n.p., 1930.

4469   BACON, Delia S. *The Philosophy of the Plays of Shakespeare Unfolded.* Boston: Ticknor & Fields, 1857. [Bacon.]

4470   BAXTER, James T. *The Greatest of Literary Problems: The Authorship of the Shakespeare Works.* Boston: Houghton Mifflin, 1915. Repr. New York: AMS. [Bacon.]

4471   BROOKS, Alden. *Will Shakespere and the Dyer's Hand.* New York: Scribners, 1943. [Dyer.]

4472   CHURCHILL, Reginald C. *Shakespeare and His Betters: A History and a Criticism of the Attempts . . . to Prove That Shakespeare's Works Were Written by Others.* London: Reinhardt, 1958. [Orthodox.]

4473   CLARK, Eva T. *The Man Who Was Shakespeare.* New York: Smith, 1937. Repr. New York: AMS. [Oxford.]

4474   DAVIS, Latham. *Shake-speare: England's Ulysses.* Seaford, Del.: Willey, 1905. [Essex.]

4475   DEMBLON, Célestin. *Lord Rutland est Shakespeare.* Paris: Ferdinando, 1912.

4476   DONNELLY, Ignatius. *The Great Cryptogram: Francis Bacon's Cipher in the So-called Shakespeare Plays.* Chicago: Peale, 1888. Repr. New York: AMS.

4477   DURNING-LAWRENCE, Edwin G. *Bacon Is Shakespeare.* London and New York: Gay & Hancock, 1910. Repr. New York: Greenwood.

4478   EVANS, Alfred J. *Shakespeare's Magic Circle.* London: Barker, 1956. [Group led by William Stanley, Earl of Derby.]

4479   FEIL, John P. "Bacon-Shakespeare: The Tobie Matthew Postscript." *SQ*, 18 (1967): 73-76. [Not Francis Bacon but Thomas Bacon, alias Southwell.]

4480   FRIEDMAN, William F., and Elizebeth S. Friedman. *The Shakespearean Ciphers Examined.* Cambridge U.P., 1957.

4481   GALLUP, Elizabeth W. *The Bi-Literal Cypher of Sir Francis Bacon Discovered in His Works and Deciphered.* Detroit: Howard, 1899. Repr. New York: AMS.

4482   GIBSON, Harry N. *The Shakespeare Claimants.* New York: Barnes & Noble; London: Methuen, 1962. [Bacon, Oxford, Derby, Marlowe.]

4483 GREG, Walter W. "Derby His Hand—and Soul." *Library*, 7 (1926-27): 39-45, 4 plates. [Pp. 41-45 confute A. Lefranc's *Sous le masque de "William Shakespeare."*]

4484 GREGORY, Tappan, ed. *Shakespeare Cross-Examination.* Chicago: Cuneo P. for American Bar Association Journal, 1961. [10 articles, also correspondence, 1st pub. in the ABA *Journal.*]

4485 HARMAN, Edward G. *The "Impersonality" of Shakespeare.* London: Palmer, 1925. [Bacon.]

4486 HART, Joseph C. *The Romance of Yachting.* New York: Harper, 1848. [Pp. 208-42 advocate theory of group composition.]

4487 HOFFMAN, Calvin. *The Man Who Was Shakespeare.* London: Parrish, 1955. [Marlowe.]

4488 HOLMES, Nathaniel. *The Authorship of Shakespeare.* New York: Hurd & Houghton, 1866. [Bacon.]

4489 HUTCHESON, William J. F. *Shakespeare's Other Anne.* Glasgow: Maclellan, 1950. [Anne Whateley.]

4490 JAMIESON, Robert. "Who Wrote Shakespeare?" *Chambers's Edinburgh Journal*, no. 449 (Aug. 7, 1852), pp. 87-89.

4491 JOHNSON, Edward D. *The Shakespeare Illusion.* London: Mitre, 1947. 3rd ed. rev. and enl., 1965. [Bacon.]

4492 KENT, William, et al. *Edward de Vere 17th Earl of Oxford: The Real Shakespeare.* London: The Shakespeare Fellowship, 1957.

4493 LANG, Andrew. *Shakespeare, Bacon, and the Great Unknown.* London: Longmans, Green, 1912. Repr. New York: AMS.

4494 LEE, Sidney. "More Doubts about Shakespeare." *QR*, 232 (1919): 194-206. [Anti-Derby.]

4495 LEFRANC, Abel. *Sous le masque de "William Shakespeare."* 2 vols. Paris: Payot, 1918-19. [Derby.]

4496 LOONEY, John T. *"Shakespeare" Identified.* London: Palmer, 1920. Repr. New York: Duell, Sloan & Pearce, 1949. [Oxford.]

4497 McMANAWAY, James G. *The Authorship of Shakespeare.* Washington, D.C.: The Folger Shakespeare Library, 1962. Repr. U.P. of Virginia; in *Studies in Shakespeare, Bibliography, and Theater*, 3174; and *Life and Letters*, 3958. [Orthodox.]

4498 McMICHAEL, George, and Edgar Glenn, eds. *Shakespeare and His Rivals: A Casebook on the Authorship Controversy.* New York: Odyssey, 1962. [Odyssey P.]

4499 MAXWELL, John M. *The Man behind the Mask: Robert Cecil, First Earl of Salisbury, the Only True Author of William Shakespeare's Plays.* Indianapolis: Harrington & Folger, 1916.

4499a MOORMAN, Frederic W. "Plays of Uncertain Authorship Attributed to Shakespeare." Chap. 10, vol. 5 of *Cam. Hist. Eng. Lit.*, 18a.

4500 NICOL, James C. *The Real Shakespeare.* London: Nicol, 1905. [Southampton.]

4501   OGBURN, Dorothy, and Charlton Ogburn. *Shake-Speare: The Man behind the Name.* New York: Morrow, 1962. [Apollo A74.] [Oxford.]

4502   —. *This Star of England.* New York: Coward-McCann, 1952. [Oxford.]

4503   PEMBERTON, Henry. *Shakspere and Sir Walter Raleigh.* Philadelphia and London: Lippincott, 1914.

4504   POTT, Constance M. *Francis Bacon and His Secret Society.* Chicago: Schulte; London: Low, Marston, 1891. Rev. ed., London: Banks, 1911.

4505   SLATER, Gilbert. *Seven Shakespeares.* London: Palmer, 1931. [Bacon, Derby, Oxford, Countess of Pembroke, Marlowe, Rutland, Raleigh.]

4506   SMITH, William H. *Bacon and Shakespeare: An Inquiry Touching Players, Playhouses, and Play-Writers in the Days of Elizabeth.* London: Smith, 1856.

4507   SPURGEON, Caroline F. E. "The Use of Imagery by Shakespeare and Bacon." *RES,* 9 (1933): 385-96.

4508   SURTEES, Scott F. *William Shakespere of Stratford-on-Avon.* London: Gray, 1888. [Shirley.]

4509   SWEET, George E. *Shake-speare: The Mystery.* Stanford U.P., 1956. [Elizabeth I.]

4510   SYKES, Claud W. *Alias William Shakespeare.* London: Aldor, 1947. [Rutland.]

4511   TITHERLEY, Arthur W. *Shakespeare's Identity: William Stanley, Sixth Earl of Derby.* Winchester, Eng.: Warren, 1952.

4512   TOWNSEND, George H. *William Shakespeare Not an Imposter.* London and New York: Routledge, 1857.

4513   WADSWORTH, Frank W. *The Poacher from Stratford.* U. of California P., 1958. [Digest of cases for claimants.]

4514   WESTFALL, Alfred V. "It Started with a Bullfight." In *Studies in Honor of A. H. R. Fairchild,* **2804.** [Rejects attribution to Bacon.]

4515   WILLIAMS, David R. *Shakespeare, Thy Name Is Marlowe.* New York: Philosophical Library, 1966.

4516   WINDLE, Catherine F. *Address to the New Shakspere Society of London: Discovery of Lord Verulam's Undoubted Authorship of the "Shakspere" Works.* San Francisco: Winterburn, 1881. [Bacon.]

4517   WRIGHT, Louis B. "The Anti-Shakespeare Industry and the Growth of Cults." *VQR,* 35 (1959): 289-303.

4518   WYMAN, William H. *Bibliography of the Bacon-Shakespeare Controversy, with Notes and Extracts.* Cincinnati: P. G. Thomson, 1884.

4519   ZEIGLER, Wilbur G. *It Was Marlowe: A Story of the Secret of Three Centuries.* Chicago: Donohue, Henneberry, 1895. [Novel.]

Index

Index of Authors, Editors, and Translators

Numbers refer to entries, not pages.

Abbott, Edwin A., 1
Abend, Murray, 4284
Abercrombie, Lascelles, 2826
Adamowski, T. H., 2026
Adams, Barry B., 2274
Adams, Herbert M., 403
Adams, John C., 1522, 2275, 2276,
    2422, 2543, 3960, 3961
Adams, John F., 795
Adams, Joseph Q., 2, 3, 4, 5, 6, 7, 184,
    421, 522, 627, 1010, 1496, 1684,
    2114, 2542, 3962, 3963, 3964,
    4285
Adams, Martha L., 3735
Adams, Robert M., 2827
Adams, Robert P., 3616
Adams, W. Davenport, 748
Addison, Joseph, 2828, 2829
Ades, John I., 2830
Agate, James, 4189, 4190
Agnew, Gates K., 1652
Ainslie, Douglas, 2947
Aitken, George A., 2829
Akrigg, George P. V., 554
Albert, Gábor, 4286
Albright, Evelyn M., 8
Albright, Victor E., 3965
Alden, John, 404
Alden, Raymond M., 422, 2157, 2316
Aldus, Paul J., 2831
Alekseev, Konstantin S. [Stanislavsky],
    2097
Alekseev, Mikhail P., 781
Alexander, Edward, 4287
Alexander, Peter, 185, 186, 187, 424,
    425, 426, 613, 1019, 1038, 1340,
    1383, 2381, 2382, 2393, 2587,
    2759, 2832
Allen, Don C., 2165, 2423, 2706, 2760,
    3195, 3769, 3770, 4288

Allen, John A., 1946
Allen, John W., 3550
Allen, Michael J. B., 2707
Allen, Ned B., 2027, 2028
Allen, Percy, 4466
Almeida, see Mendonça
Alpers, Paul J., 1523, 2157a
Altick, Richard D., 1039, 2177
Alvarez, A., 2140
Amnéus, Daniel A., 1687, 1688
Amphlett, H., 4467
Amyot, Thomas, 2383
And, Metin, 4289
Andersen, Peter S., 1436
Anderson, Donald K., 4290
Anderson, M. J., 1112
Anderson, Ruth L., 1702, 2505, 3771
Andrews, Mark E., 1858
Anshutz, H. L., 1524
Anson, John S., 1437
Anthony, see Rose Anthony
Arber, Edward, 9, 10
Archer, William, 432, 2884, 4191
Arensberg, Walter C., 4468
Arkwright, G. E. P., 4377
Armstrong, Edward A., 2833
Armstrong, John, 2834
Armstrong, Ray L., 574
Armstrong, William A., 3551, 3552, 3772,
    3773, 3966, 3967, 3968, 4192,
    4193, 4265
Arnold, Aerol, 2245, 2588
Arnold, Morris L., 2835
Arnott, James F., 110
Arthos, John, 796, 907, 1703, 2029,
    2123, 2836
Ash, D. F., 1408
Ashbee, Edmund W., 4178
Ashley, Leonard R. N., 570
Ashton, Florence H., 2384

73